# Union Jacks

Michael J. Bennett

CIVIL WAR AMERICA

Gary W. Gallagher, editor

Union

Yankee Sailors in the Civil War

# Jacks

The University of
North Carolina Press
Chapel Hill & London

© 2004
The University of
North Carolina Press
All rights reserved
Designed by
Richard Hendel
Set in Melior and
Poplar types by
Tseng Information Systems
Manufactured in the
United States of America

The paper in this book meets the guidelines for
permanence and durability of the Committee on
Production Guidelines for Book Longevity of the
Council on Library Resources.

Library of Congress Cataloging-in-Publication Data
Bennett, Michael J.
Union Jacks : Yankee sailors in the Civil War / by
Michael J. Bennett.
p. cm. — (Civil War America)
Includes bibliographical references (p. ) and index.
ISBN 0-8078-2870-x (alk. paper)
1. United States. Navy—History—Civil War, 1861–1865.
2. United States. Navy—Sea life—History—19th
century. 3. Sailors—United States—History—19th
century. 4. Sailors—United States—Social
conditions—19th century. 5. United States—History—
Civil War, 1861–1865—Naval operations. 6. United
States—History—Civil War, 1861–1865—Social
aspects. I. Title. II. Series.
E591.B46 2004
973.7'58'0922—dc22        2003024974

08   07   06   05   04      5   4   3   2   1

Portions of this book were previously published as
"Frictions: Shipboard Relations between White and
Contraband Sailors," *Civil War History* 47 (June
2001): 118–45; and "Saving Jack: Union Sailors,
Religion, and Benevolent Organizations," in *Union
Soldiers and the Northern Home Front: Wartime
Experiences, Postwar Adjustments*, ed. Paul A.
Cimbala and Randall M. Miller (New York: Fordham
University Press, 2002). Used with permission.

TO DAD

# Contents

List of Tables and Illustrations  viii

Preface  ix

1  Dissenters from the American Mood:
   *Why Men Joined the United States Navy
   during the Civil War*  1

2  Any Man Can Become a Soldier:
   *The Making of Union Sailors*  28

3  Ships of Fools:
   *The Sailor's Experience on the Union Blockade*  54

4  The Devil's Own Purgatory:
   *The Experience of Gunboatmen in the
   Mississippi Squadron*  77

5  All Hands Drunk and Rioting:
   *The Maritime Culture of Union Sailors*  99

6  Saving Jack:
   *Religion, Union Sailors, and the United States
   Christian Commission*  126

7  Frictions:
   *Shipboard Relations between White and
   Contraband Union Sailors*  155

8  My Youthfull Emagination of Hell:
   *The Face of Battle for Union Sailors*  182

Epilogue  209

Notes  211

Selected Bibliography  307

Index  327

# Tables & Illustrations

TABLES

Occupations of Union Sailors and Soldiers  7

Places of Birth of Union Sailors and Soldiers  10


ILLUSTRATIONS

An 1863 recruiting broadside for the navy  16

A navy recruiting broadside listing pay scale for sailors  18

"Holystoning the Deck"  46

"All Hands Up Anchor"  48

"Small Arms Drill"  49

At battle stations aboard the USS *Kearsarge*  50

"The Eleven Inch Gun"  51

"Drilling at the Mortar"  52

"All Hands Scrub Clothes"  71

The crew of the USS *Cairo*  78

"Six Bells in the Dogwatch"  102

The sailors' band aboard the USS *Wabash*  103

"Splicing the Main Brace"  104

A besotted "liberty man"  107

"Skylarking"  117

Sunday morning inspection  137

"Sunday Morning—Reading the Articles of War"  138

Sailors and officers at divine service  139

"Morning Prayer"  141

White and contraband sailors on the USS *Hunchback*  175

The sailors of the USS *Miami*  178

"In Action"  195

An ordinary seaman's courage  200

The sinking of the USS *Tecumseh*  203

# Preface

During the Vicksburg campaign, sailors from the *Manitou* of the Mississippi Squadron found themselves grounded on battery emplacements constructed by General William T. Sherman's soldiers. Off the boat for the first time in months, the sailors followed their normal routine. Working with instinctual determination, they re-created their ship on shore. They quickly constructed a wooden plank floor similar to the deck of a ship. Over this, they raised a tent and slung their hammocks. Every morning, to the continuing amazement of onlooking soldiers, they pulled a stone attached to ropes back and forth across their miniature wooden deck until it was declared shipshape. After cleaning, the sailors sat down in their mess groups and ate from nautical mess tables using knives.[1] Amused soldiers who saw this odd re-creation knew they were witnessing a service and brand of men entirely different from their own.

Reactions like these replayed themselves throughout the war. As soon as sailors sailed into port or made landfall, curious civilians, watchful policemen, and mindful Northern soldiers dropped whatever they were doing and gawked.[2] "We are a great curiosity to them," wrote landsman Joseph Fry from Pensacola, Florida, "and they make the most original remarks you ever heard."[3] The *Cincinnati Daily Commercial* reported that residents of Cairo, Illinois, proved instantly intrigued by the sailors landing in their town. Even though they had witnessed thousands of soldiers pour through their rumpled village, the newspaper reported that the sailors' black-ribboned hats, short blue jackets, and voluminous breeches drew the rapt attention of Cairo's citizens.[4] As one onlooker wrote as he gazed upon a group of sailors working and playing aboard a blockade vessel: "There are characters enough among them to furnish material for a volume."[5]

Yet no volume exists.[6] Even though sailors proved instrumental in the North's victory by manning the blockade and helping subdue the Mississippi River, the Civil War was and continues to be a soldiers' war. During hostilities, politicians, newspapers, and citizens ignored the contributions made by sailors. After the war, sailors enjoyed little of the hallowed glow enjoyed by soldiers. In 1894, a still angry Cornelius

Cronin, a gunner on the *Brooklyn*, grumbled, "The sailors were first in the war, and last out of it; and *last* 'In the hearts of their countrymen.'"[7]

Without question, the attention to soldiers has been rightly justified. Common Union soldiers did most of the fighting, suffering, and dying during the war. Part of the reason for the neglect was the nature of the naval war. Since the Confederates possessed a small navy, there were, save the *Monitor* and the *Merrimac*, no epic battles to memorialize and no myths to mount. Moreover, Union sailors served on the fringes of the war, severed from land, severed from home, and severed from the persistent gaze of war correspondents and politicians. As a result, soldiers garnered the lion's share of attention, and Union sailors languished on the conflict's periphery as oddities, sidelights, or sources of amusement.

More important, common Union sailors—known as "bluejackets" or "Jacks"—never fully registered in the nation's consciousness for two reasons. First, their numbers paled in comparison to the over two million men who served as Northern soldiers; only 118,044 men enlisted as sailors during the war. Second, Union sailors bore little resemblance to the mythical and historical portrait of the war's poster boys, common Yankee soldiers. Sailors tended to come from different segments of society and enlisted for different reasons. They came from the poor and working classes of Northern cities rather than rural towns and farms. Many sailors were foreigners fleeing hunger and economic turmoil and slaves running to freedom.

On a deeper level, the men who enlisted as sailors also possessed a markedly different set of values and ideas. The typical Union sailor was a hard, pragmatic, and cynical man who bore little patience for patriotism, reform, and religion. He drank too much, fought too much, and prayed too little. He preferred adventure to stability and went for quick and lucrative jobs rather than steady and slow employ under the tightening strictures of the new market economy. He was rough, dirty, and profane. Out of date before his time, he was aggressively masculine in a Northern society bent on gentling men.

Overall, Union sailors proved less committed to emerging Northern values and were less ideological than soldiers for whom the broader issues of freedom, market success, and constitutional government proved constant touchstones during the war. Sailors possessed weaker support for the war. Most did not join the navy to save the Union, free the slaves, or prove their courage. Instead, the decisions by sailors to join the war proved more dependent on the practical factors of economic need, ethnic tendencies, class outlook, and race. In short, huge numbers of immigrants, former slaves, and working-class men enlisted as sailors and did so based on individual rather than collective reasons.

Yankee sailors also fought a different type of Civil War. Although they participated in traditional naval campaigns, their wartime experiences were marked by a number of personal battles—with training, with monotony, with officers, and with religion. Many struggled with the bottle. Others violently contested the presence of former slaves who shipped as new sailors. In the process, Union sailors carved out a war, shipboard lives, and a maritime culture that was uniquely their own and unquestionably different.

This book attempts to perform four tasks. First, it examines the everyday moments of sailors' lives in order to illuminate how common sailors—from old salts to new fishes—lived and fought in ships during the war. The book shows how Union bluejackets trained, fought, and interacted for months at a time in wooden and metal worlds removed from the familiar text of land, society, and the war. Second, it uncovers, for the first time, the social origins of the men who became Union sailors. To that end, it analyzes why they enlisted, where they came from, and how their origins shaped their service and informed their lives.

Third, the book attempts to re-create what it may have been like for a landlubber to amble up to a rendezvous, make his mark, and then land onto a ship. The problem of going to sea had particular resonance for Union sailors since most had never been on a ship until they enlisted. I admit that I have given myself more than a few nightmares, waking up in the middle of the night dreaming I was in a hammock, on a blockader, and surrounded by unsavory souls as the ship creaked back and forth.

The book's fourth and final task—and perhaps its most slippery— is to use the wartime service of sailors as a kind of social and cultural laboratory for investigating the major issues of the war that historians have rarely found a systematic way to study. Consequently, *Union Jacks* explores both the broader problems faced by men when they go to sea, such as isolation and monotony, as well as the seminal issues of the war, including the relation between race and class, the role of religion and reform in wartime, and the significance of class and ethnicity in deciding to participate in the war.[8] The composite portrait that emerges places Union sailors not only within the context of men and the sea but also firmly within the experiences and the problems of the war. The hope is that historians and students of the war will be better informed about who these Union Jacks were and will gain a more nuanced understanding of what the war and going to war at sea was all about.

In general, part of the problem of studying sailors of the past has been that they tended to be peripatetic. They wrote less, moved around more, and left fewer reminders of their presence except for the wonderful lore and stories. This source problem has largely held true for Union seamen except for a couple of critical and fortunate differences. First, the majority of Union sailors were not sailors before the war and as a result possessed sufficiently more education than the typical nineteenth-century sailor. This meant that Union sailors, although they wrote little, probably wrote more than the average sailor. Second, owing to the years many of them spent floating on ships with no respite, many men, who may not have been inclined to write had they had something else better to do, did write because they had the time.

Nevertheless, in order to write a social history of the bluejackets, a historian must rely on the words and thoughts of the men themselves or otherwise risk presenting a homogenized and softer picture of who they were. Thus *Union Jacks* draws primarily on the published and unpublished diaries, letters, and journals of 169 common sailors who served during the war, many of them previously unknown to historians. The quoted material preserves the sailors' misspellings and grammatical mistakes.

The work's conclusions are grounded on a sample of 4,570 common sailors who enlisted in the navy at naval rendezvous between April 1861 and April 1865.[9] The sample was obtained by taking every twenty-fifth name from every rendezvous report from every rendezvous opened during the war. It provides a statistical catalog of demographic information about the men who shipped as Union sailors. By comparing the comments of the men with the demographic statistics of age, place of birth, and occupation, a vivid and controversial picture of Union sailors emerges, one which, at times, does not fit neatly into the history books.

The book focuses on the naval war from the perspective of the common swabbie, from the young apprentices and raw recruits the navy took in to teach the trade to hardened seamen who had spent their lives aboard ship. Although certain elements of the black sailors' perspective will surface, the book tells the story from the perspective of white sailors.[10] The sailors come from all significant squadrons deployed during the war. The bulk of them are from the blockade squadrons since these fleets were where most sailors served. However, there is also strong representation from the navy's inland fleet, the Mississippi Squadron, and even a few sailors from the Cruisers, which prowled the oceans in search of Confederate privateers, and from the Pacific Squadron, which guarded the shipments of gold from California.

Although the book cites the observations of petty and commissioned officers, it does so skeptically. Naval officers tended to view all sailors —even Union sailors—through a stereotypical lens that colored their words and thoughts. In many instances, officers treated Union sailors like the Jacky of naval folklore, who was seen as drunk, reckless, and aimless. On a ship the officers lived in a world of their own; because their social and cultural interactions with sailors proved rare to non-existent, they could easily hold to their prejudices.

Sailors helped perpetuate the stereotypes by living up to them, as can be seen in the observations of certain valuable "intermediaries" aboard ship, men in service who were neither officers nor sailors. They possessed no formal rank but had constant contact with sailors owing to their official duties. Often they had never previously met or seen sailors. Many were civilians before the war and were not steeped in naval culture and prejudice. They tended to marvel at what they saw and drank deep of the odd and fascinating world of the common Union sailor. The most formidable of these intermediaries were surgeons, chaplains, and paymasters, who took care of sailors when they were ill, heartsick, and broke. Their observations, while harsh, were honest since they dealt with sailors at first hand and without the blurring quality of rank.

The collective result is a portrait of Union sailors that is frank as well as unfiltered. Some of it is shocking, some old, some familiar, and some plain fodder for chin scratching. It is not so much intended as an end as it is a beginning. It is offered as a study of a different set of men who fought the war on different terms. It is also proffered as an encouraging nudge for Civil War historians to examine the war from alternate perspectives. There may be too many anecdotes for some tastes. For this, I accept full responsibility. It is a result of a belief that the men with whom I have spent the better part of the last seven years would not have suffered a poorly told tale. This much they have taught me.

A project such as this has been helped by many hands. Like my subjects, money moved me along. The Saint Louis University Graduate School and History Department provided travel funds and a yearlong fellowship that enabled me to do research full time and nationwide. Critical funding was also provided by the Huntington Library in San Marino, California, and the Illinois State Historical Society in Springfield, Illinois. My thanks go to Robert C. Ritchie, director of research at the Huntington Library, and Thomas F. Schwartz, Illinois State Historian and director of the Illinois State Historical Library, for granting me fellowships at both institutions.

My friend and colleague Stu Cordell allowed me the opportunity to practice law at Warren and Young in Ashtabula, Ohio, in order to keep the lights on while I spent three years writing. Thanks to him and to William E. Riedel and Carl F. Muller for allowing a mumbling academic to wander their halls and get paid. I express a special debt of gratitude to Kimberley Fenton who helped turn a jumble of statistics from the rendezvous reports into a workable database.

Archivists and librarians nationwide helped me sort out the sources and, more importantly, find coffee in the area. I extend special thanks to Cheryl Schnirring, curator of manuscripts at the Illinois State Historical Library, for being so helpful and for locating the original of the George Yost Diary. Donald Fraser and Megan Hahn tolerated me for almost three solid months at the New-York Historical Society. Rebecca A. Livingston and Richard Peuser at the National Archives were helpful, understanding, and informative in helping me wade through the rendezvous reports and the Navy Subject File. Jim Lee, curator of the Naval Historical Foundation Collection at the Washington Navy Yard provided critical river sailor documentation. Kym Cook, former head of the library at the Ashtabula campus of Kent State University and a fellow St. Louis refugee, kindly granted me full borrowing privileges when I had none.

Members of my dissertation committee—Professor Thomas F. Curran of Saint Louis University, Professor Louis S. Gerteis of the University of Missouri, St. Louis, and Professor Mark E. Neely Jr. of Pennsylvania State University—offered sound and well-reasoned comments that made the work more thoughtful and relevant. Paul Cimbala and Randall Miller of Fordham University Press contributed mightily to the chapter on sailors and religion. Joseph P. Reidy of Howard University, who is performing groundbreaking research on black sailors, provided needed comments to the chapter on race relations.

I was told about midway through this endeavor, by a wise young sage, that writing a book can be one of the loneliest endeavors imaginable. He was almost right. My college roommate, Patrick A. Day, rented me his Central Park West couch for nine months. His friendship and expertise in finding stumbling-distance watering holes made my research time almost enjoyable and memorable. My mother and sister helped me keep my wits at various times. My niece, Mia, saved the whole project one muggy August afternoon with a simple entreaty not to worry about sailors anymore and instead focus on eating ice cream.

My weightiest debt, however, is owed to the woman who very nearly kept me together body and soul. Gina M. Radio listened to all my woes and all my frustrations with love and understanding. She kept the faith when I did not. Most importantly, she read my chapters and told me they were perfect, and then handed me proofed copies highlighting all of their flaws. I could not have done this without her, or as well.

How I got to this place is primarily my father's fault. He loved history and particularly the Civil War. I can still remember sitting at his knee listening to him preach about the daring of the American Revolution, the brilliance of the Constitution, and the awful importance of the Civil War. At times, I was the most historically steeled third-grader at Saint Catherine's School. Dad told me stories of Great Grandfather John Jefferis's service with the 78th Ohio in the Army of the Cumberland during the war. I took from these stories a lifelong curiosity about this country that prods me to this day. Whether he knew it or not, he made me a Civil War historian.

# Union Jacks

# 1

## Dissenters from the American Mood
### Why Men Joined the United States Navy during the Civil War

To understand who joined the United States Navy during the Civil War and why they did so requires a break from prevailing treatments of Yankee soldiers. The current interpretation holds that the average Union soldier was a virtuous farmer or craftsmen, lived in a small town or on a farm, and went off to war, with patriotic send-offs from friends and family, to fight for commonly held goals.[1] While this model helps us understand how Union regiments were filled, it packs little explanatory power for the navy's crews. Apart from age, sailors shared few characteristics with soldiers. Union sailors tended to be Eastern and urban rather than rural. The majority emanated from the working class. They were foreign and poor. Many were former slaves. Sailors did not join the navy to uphold the predominant values and ideals attributed to soldiers. They did not enlist to preserve the Union, end slavery, or prove their courage. Instead, practical circumstances formed within the realities of class, ethnicity, and race played a larger role in pushing men out to sea and shaped their motivations for entering the war.[2]

When the war broke out, there were only 7,600 sailors in the navy. By 1863, that number had grown to 38,000. In 1865, 51,500 sailors were serving in ships engaged in the blockade of the Confederacy, in gunboats up and down the Western rivers, and in squadrons around the globe. While these figures paled in comparison to the 2.2 million men who enlisted in the Northern armies, the buildup represented a more than 500 percent increase in sailor enlistment.[3] Moreover, the navy had never sought so many sailors at once, and it knew that the process of attracting sailors would be different both in terms of approach and location than for soldiers.

Nothing trumpeted this sharp divergence like the enlistment process. Generally, when a man enlisted as a sailor, there were no torchlit parades to the village square, no patriotic speeches, and little of the pomp and circumstance that attended early soldier enlistment waves.[4] Men who enlisted as sailors often did so alone, with little fanfare, and under less-than-romantic conditions.[5]

While newspaper advertisements and recruiting broadsides plastered on post office walls, rail stations, and the sides of buildings proved helpful in attracting sailors, naval recruiting stations called "rendezvous" functioned as the traditional conduits into the navy.[6] Located near the water's edge in large Eastern cities such as New York, Boston, and Philadelphia and small coastal and river towns, rendezvous operated in shadowy storefronts and in sections of cities where polite citizens usually feared to tread.

The locations of the rendezvous were not haphazard. The navy planted them near places where sailors frequented when on land: boardinghouses for transients, restaurants, and saloons. Recruiting officers kept a keen eye on the window in the event a curious type stopped to linger. Officers, knowing that the power of a uniform swayed young men, sometimes clad recent enlistees in smart blue suits and paraded them in front of the rendezvous hoping to attract onlookers.[7] If one did, they bombarded the loiterer with tales of prize money, daily grog, and three square meals a day.

In order to intensify recruiting efforts, rendezvous hired civilian agents called "runners." Runners scoured sailors' haunts and working-class neighborhoods looking for recruits to bring back to the rendezvous. They received three dollars for each recruit they secured who could pass the navy physical.[8] Women running boardinghouses proved especially proficient as runners.[9]

Rendezvous were not romantic and contained more than a whiff of coercion. General La Fayette C. Baker of the Bureau of the Secret Service, who investigated both army and navy recruiting practices, called the fraud at the New York City rendezvous "stupendous." "Out of seven of these naval recruiting rendezvous," Baker reported, "but three could be entered without first passing through a public drinking saloon of the lowest and vilest character."[10]

Innocent pedestrians often walked by rendezvous at their own peril. Irate businessmen described in a letter of protest to Rear Admiral H. Paulding, the atmosphere around the 156 South Street Rendezvous, located on the lower east side of Manhattan: "The citizen as he passes, is wantonly insulted, often dragged into the Rendezvous, and when they cannot overawe him to enlist, they commence to beat him without mercy. There is hardly a day that passes, that the most corrupt and outrageous means are used by these said runners to decoy the citizens into the U.S. Navy, and when expostulated with, they are very insulting."[11]

There was a good deal of rough treatment and fraud among recruiters and runners at naval rendezvous. Runners proved adept at coercing, tricking, or forcing unwilling recruits into the navy. Some employed the time-tested tactics of the notorious "crimping" gangs who once roamed English and American seaports.[12] Naval officials, desperate for men, often looked the other way or tacitly participated in such frauds. Navy recruiters constructed elaborate subterfuges through which passersby, naval yard artisans, and the curious would be lured onto a ship with promises of money, information, or a tour.[13]

Tactics ranged from simple lying about the terms of naval service to the infamous practice of "shanghaiing," whereby agents plied men full of liquor, drugged, or beat them into the service.[14] British and Canadian recruits complained that they were often "punched out or knocked out with whiskey." In Niagara Falls, it was alleged that recruiters from the Buffalo Rendezvous drugged Canadian boys and then transported them across the border for induction. Once in the United States, runners handed the groggy recruits to naval officials who slapped them on ships. By the time they awoke, the boys found themselves on the decks of the *Michigan* in the middle of Lake Erie.[15]

In part, recruiters could employ these methods for trapping sailors because, in the parts of town where rendezvous operated, coercive behavior drew less attention and the practice of dragging sailors back to ships from liberty was not uncommon. Recruiters employed such tactics because throughout the war not enough men joined the navy.[16] The reasons for such recruiting shortfalls proved numerous. First and foremost, states, counties, municipalities, and the federal government offered army recruits cash bounties that ranged from $75 to $300.[17] The navy did not offer bounties until near the end of the war.[18] John D. Harty, the recruiting officer of the Chicago Rendezvous, complained to Rear Admiral David Dixon Porter that army bounties "retarded enlistments" into the navy.[19]

Second, Union armies organized their units by states, within cities and local communities under the auspices of civic, business, or political leaders. These leaders often secured officer commissions based solely on the ability to deliver recruits. This method of organizing army regiments under the local control of a town leader created an intense esprit de corps that the navy, owing to its national organization and federal control, could not duplicate.[20] Moreover, the navy refused to exchange commissions for recruits. Some men did offer the navy large numbers of recruits in exchange for an officer's commission, only to find their offers refused. The navy saw itself as a professional service that depended on the experience and skill of its officers and enlisted men. The navy simply could not afford, in the words of Commander J. A. Winslow, to fill its ships with "useless officers" in order to obtain enlisted men.[21]

Third, the offering of bounties and the intensely local nature of the army's organization also served to underscore the reality that the fielding of large armies absorbed the primary attention and priority of the United States government and the Northern public. For the most part, the Lincoln administration and the general public concentrated their energies and pinned their hopes in the Civil War on Northern armies.[22] It was on the fields of battle, many believed, that the outcome of the war would be won or lost. This mind-set was also reflected in governmental policies regarding manpower allocations during the war.[23] Conscription and volunteer systems ignored naval needs. Until July 1864, men who joined the navy were not granted draft exemptions, received no credit toward recruiting quotas for their home districts, and could be drafted into the army literally off the decks of ships.[24]

Fourth, the government's priority on manning armies also reflected the public's perceptions of how the Civil War was to be fought and who should do the fighting. At the war's outset, many Northerners viewed the Civil War as a test of courage for white American male citizens. In this courage-conscious environment, the ultimate and proper testing ground for proving a patriot's mettle lay not on the decks of a ship but on the field of battle, charging headlong into the enemy's lines under the hail of bullets.[25] The collective nature of naval warfare clashed with the public's romanticized, ill-informed notions concerning the army's capacity for individual heroism. The vocation for a man who was interested in proving his courage and saving the republic was soldiering and not sailoring.

Men who ultimately enlisted in the navy did so at the risk of shame. Dodging shots and shells under the cover of a ship, sheathed with plates of iron, did not resemble fighting in "man fashion."[26] Northerners often accused sailors of being "cowards."[27] Throughout the war, sailors proved extremely sensitive to the accusations that they were not doing their part.[28] Families and friends often chided those men who opted for naval service. "Some of my neighbors think I am in an easy place," commented Seaman William Bock in a pained letter to his mother back in Springfield, Illinois. "You have a chance to see much of the world," wrote Ann Preston to her son Fowler, but "not much chance of fighting." Mary Osborne hinted to her brother Joseph, serving on the *Vandalia*, that the family considered it a disgrace for him to serve in the navy rather than the army. Joseph retorted heatedly, "It is no disgrace for any man to be in the service of the country." [29]

Last, sailors labored under many negative stereotypes. More than a few Northerners viewed sailors as a hapless and godless set of men whose poor state of affairs had either sprung from wretched beginnings or resulted from lives made miserable by excessive drinking, careless spending, and whore mongering. Catchphrases such as "drank like a sailor" or "swore like a sailor" carried with them potent social and moral judgments in pre–Civil War America about the suspect character of sailors' lives. At best, prevailing prewar stereotypes cast sailors as adventure-seeking boys possessed by wanderlust. At worst, popular perceptions equated sailors with drunks, thieves, drifters, and murderers. [30] The combination of all of these negative characteristics registered sailors as "the lowest class of humanity" in the American spectrum by 1861. Sailors were not the stuff of which patriots were made. [31]

The widespread belief of both contemporaries and historians has been that the Northern army and navy were competing for the same pool of men. In some respects, this was true since the nation had a finite number of men of legal military age. Many potential recruits, even those who had seafaring experience, examined both branches of service, weighed the financial and social repercussions of joining one or the other, and then chose the army. However, this analysis not only oversimplifies the process but also obscures the fact that, despite the factors pushing men into the army, 118,044 men voluntarily chose the navy over the army between 1861 and 1865. [32]

Who, then, became sailors? First, the average sailor recruit tended to be on average twenty-six years old. [33] Second, Easterners rather than Westerners tended to become sailors. More than 78 percent of Union sailors came from the Atlantic coast. Eastern states and cities produced more sailors, largely owing to the maritime trade in states like New York and Massachusetts. This heritage, coupled with the presence of rendezvous in cities like New York, Philadelphia, and Boston, helped to instill an imbalance of Easterners. New York State and New York City provided the bulk of the nation's sailors (35,164), followed by Massachusetts (19,983), and Pennsylvania (14,037). Of the 118,044 men who enlisted, only approximately 12,375 came from the Western states. Ohio and its river port of Cincinnati yielded 3,274 sailors, the most of any Western state.[34]

Third, sailors were city dwellers. Based on the personal statistics contained in a sample of 4,570 Union sailors who enlisted at all naval rendezvous—East and West—between April 1861 and April 1865 ("Rendezvous Sample"), only 3 percent of recruits made their living on a farm before the war. The ones who did primarily came from the Western states. Farmers constituted 23 percent of Western sailor recruits. This statistic stands in stunning contrast to the rural backgrounds of most soldiers. According to samples done by the United States Sanitary Commission, Bell I. Wiley, and James McPherson, nearly half of all soldiers worked on a farm before the war.[35]

Union sailors evoked those sections of America from which they came and where the navy recruited—the poor and working-class neighborhoods of large Eastern cities. In fact, based on the letters, journals, and logs of sailors as well as the results of the Rendezvous Sample, three dominant groups sought out the navy during the war—the working class, the foreign born, and former slaves.

The occupations that Union sailors gave when they enlisted at rendezvous indicate that a majority of them emanated from the working class.[36] As used here, the term "working class" encompassed a broad social group determined by the type of work a man did. Occupation was critical to membership in this group. Men who possessed a mechanical skill—such as a blacksmith, carpenter, or baker—would fall in the working class. In addition, those men who depended on strength to earn a living, such as common laborers—unless they were farmers— would have been considered part of the working class. The working class also consisted of the unskilled, the unemployed, and the idle. The working class did not include professionals such as doctors and lawyers or white-collar or commercial occupations such as salesman or clerk.[37]

The largest segment of working-class men who enlisted as sailors were from the skilled trades, such as butchers, bakers, and coopers. The Rendezvous Sample indicates that over one-half (53.5 percent) listed occupations in which they made a living with skilled hands. Carpenters, firemen, blacksmiths, shoemakers, and machinists constituted the largest occupational blocs. Common laborers, men without mechanical skills or not in skilled trades, and those who worked from physical job to physical job constituted over 7 percent of sailor recruits.[38] These findings contrast sharply with the percentages of skilled tradesmen among

**Table 1.** *Occupations of Union Sailors and Soldiers*

| Occupational Categories | Union Sailors | Union Soldiers | All Males |
|---|---|---|---|
| Farmers and farm laborers | 3.10% | 47.50% | 42.9% |
| Skilled laborers | 53.50 | 25.10 | 24.90 |
| Unskilled laborers | 7.48 | 15.90 | 16.7 |
| White-collar and commercial | 2.01 | 5.10 | 10.00 |
| Professional | 0.53 | 3.20 | 3.50 |
| None/unemployed | 33.38 | 3.20 | 2.00 |

Source: The percentages for sailors are drawn from the Rendezvous Sample of 4,570 men. The percentages for Union soldiers are from the numbers collected by the U.S. Sanitary Commission. See B. A. Gould, *Sanitary Memoirs of the War of the Rebellion: Investigations in the Military and Anthropological Statistics of American Soldiers* (Cambridge, Mass.: Riverside Press, 1869), 208–11. The percentages for the general population are from the 1860 Census as tabulated by James M. McPherson and Patricia McPherson. See U.S. Government, *Population of the United States in 1860* (Washington, D.C.: Government Printing Office, 1864), 656–80; and James M. McPherson, *Battle Cry of Freedom: The Civil War Era* (New York: Oxford University Press, 1988), 608.

soldiers. According to James McPherson, only 25 percent of soldiers came from the skilled trades.[39]

Ironically, a large number of men from the working class enlisted unemployed.[40] In fact, when sailor recruits were asked by recruiting officers what their occupation was at the time of enlistment, "none" represented the single most common response among nonskilled men. Between 1861 and 1865, almost 34 percent of sailor enlistees cited nothing under the heading "Occupation" on enlistment records, meaning that they lacked any form of employment or skill at the time of enlistment.[41] None of the studies done by the Sanitary Commission, Bell Wiley, or James McPherson uncovered such an incidence of unemployment among soldiers.[42]

Generally, the men showing up at naval rendezvous with no job and no skills were from a segment of the working class that reformers in the nineteenth century had referred to as the "urban idle."[43] Many were not likely idle but were men who lived from day to day on the streets or in rough boardinghouses taking odd jobs and looking for work. Some were young men still finding their way; others joined the navy hoping to learn a skill.[44] Some had fallen on hard times. "They are not able to earn a living ashore," Coal Heaver William Wainwright wrote concerning his shipmates, "and are compelled to go aboard of a man of war to get their living."[45] Seaman William Van Cleaf admitted to his mother that "I could do better than I could do on land."[46] One sailor remarked that many men on the blockade joined not out of patriotism but the inducements of "loaves and fishes."[47]

The lure of food and shelter to men down on their luck proved so pervasive that by 1864 some naval recruiting posters dropped all pretenses of appealing to higher motives. Instead, navy broadsides and advertisements promised merely regular meals and a guaranteed place to sleep rather than prize money or glory. "On board the Gunboats," one recruiting poster on the Ohio River offered, "you have your meals regularly and in fact are always at home."[48]

Although the notion of thousands of unemployed Northerners enlisting out of economic duress runs counter to the traditional picture of the citizen leaving his steady job to fight for the Union, the idea of the working poor escaping poverty through sea service was not new. Since the seventeenth century and throughout the Anglo-American maritime world, economic hardship was a powerful motivation pushing men to sea.[49] Before the war, the uneducated, the unemployed, and the poor living in cities utilized the navy as an economic outlet. In the 1840s and 1850s, a surplus of labor in Eastern cities had created a sizable class of urban unemployed.[50] The war did not buoy the outlook for workers. A depression plagued the North during the first few months of the war, and bouts of high unemployment occurred periodically until 1863.[51]

Although many skilled workers likely enlisted because the navy offered the opportunity to put their vocations to work aboard ship, they too may have been driven to sea out of economic worries. Skilled tradesmen faced a crisis in the 1860s owing to two generations of falling wages and a lack of proper training with the advent of machine technology. Many apprentices and journeymen faced the prospect of never owning their own shop or, worse, the risk of obsolescence in an increasingly deskilling world. Skilled workers feared that despite all of their training and hard work, they could spend the rest of their lives being "machine tenders" at less than subsistence wages.[52]

Another explanation for the high degree of unemployment among Eastern sailors was that many were recent immigrants. The Rendezvous Sample reveals that over 41 percent of Irish recruits were unemployed at the time of enlistment.[53] The lack of skills placed many immigrants in dire straits. "Being without any trade," Irish Seaman Patrick Meade recorded in his journal, "I had to work at anything that came up." He added, "I soon found out there was nothing to be had by such occupation but hard knocks and abuse."[54] William Burton, in *Melting Pot Soldiers*, states that it was not uncommon to see throngs of immigrants, particularly the Irish, poring over recruiting posters promising bare offers of beer and sausage. One New Yorker recalled, "I saw poor, famished Irishmen devour these posters with their eyes."[55]

To foreigners, the lure of becoming a sailor proved so strong that, despite an 1813 statute formally barring unnaturalized citizens from enlisting, immigrants in large numbers joined the navy.[56] According to the Rendezvous Sample, sailors born in foreign countries constituted a whopping 45 percent of total naval recruits.[57] Although it is difficult to tell how many of these foreign-born sailors were naturalized citizens, the high percentage of foreign births among sailors was significant for two reasons. First, the percentage of men of foreign birth and military age living in states loyal to the Union during the war was 27 percent. This meant that foreign-born men of military age were overrepresented in the navy since they joined in greater numbers than their presence in the general population. Second, while the strong contributions of immigrants to the army have been much trumpeted, the actual percentage of immigrant soldiers only hovered around 25 percent, meaning that foreign-born men were actually underrepresented in the army.[58]

One reason why so many foreigners became sailors was the fact that nativist sentiment ran strong in the army. The crews on American merchant and naval vessels had a long tradition of national diversity.[59] Many immigrants probably felt that they would have an easier time assimilating into a multinational crew on a U.S. ship rather than integrating into an army regiment from New York or Ohio. The association of "sailor" with "foreigner" became so pervasive that many army officers utilized navy transfer requests to "weed" their commands of foreign soldiers. A soldier in the 4th Illinois Cavalry wrote that the men who were transferred from his unit to the navy were not native born. "They were mostly Norwegians and Germans that could barely speak English."[60]

The Irish made up the largest contingent of foreign-born sailors, providing 20 percent of the navy's manpower. They enlisted in great numbers even though they were the butt of many jokes about every conceivable failing—such as their purported mental thickness, chronic laziness, and penchant for drunkenness.[61] Recruiting officers often showed intense disdain for the Irish and called them "potato diggers" and "stupid turf-lumps."[62] Navy prejudices toward Irish Jacks did not limit themselves to insults and often affected the way they were treated

**Table 2.** *Places of Birth of Union Sailors and Soldiers*

| Place of Birth | Union Sailors | Union Soldiers | All Males of Military Age (18–45) |
|---|---|---|---|
| United States | 54.66% | 75.30% | 72.86% |
| Canada | 4.70 | 2.65 | 1.70 |
| England | 10.26 | 2.25 | 3.90 |
| Germany | 4.01 | 8.76 | 8.50 |
| Ireland | 20.04 | 7.14 | 10.60 |
| Norway | 1.13 | 0.32 | 0.30 |
| Sweden | 1.00 | 1.30 | 0.12 |
| France | 0.74 | 0.48 | 0.62 |
| Other countries | 3.46 | 1.80 | 1.40 |

Source: The percentages of sailors are drawn from the Rendezvous Sample of 4,570 sailors. The percentages for Union soldiers are based on figures compiled by Benjamin Gould and Ella Lonn. Gould concluded that the total number of different (non-reenlistees and non–bounty jumpers) white soldier enlistees during the war was 2,018,200 and the number of foreign-born in that total was 494,933, counting men of British American (Canadian), English, Irish, German, and miscellaneous origins. See B. A. Gould, *Sanitary Memoirs of the War of the Rebellion: Investigations in the Military and Anthropological Statistics of American Soldiers*, 27. The figures for Norwegians and Swedes in column 2 are from estimates cited in Lonn, *Foreigners in the Union Army and Navy* (Baton Rouge: Louisiana State University Press, 1951), 579–80. The percentage of French soldiers is an estimate roughly corresponding to census records. The percentages in column 2 were tabulated by dividing the number of soldiers from a given place over the total number of soldiers.

The total number of white males eligible by age for military service in states loyal to the Union was 5,149,227. See U.S. Census Office, *Population of the United States in 1860*, xvii. The numbers of military age men for each ethnic group living in loyal states are based on the 1860 census figures plus immigration accretions for each group during the war tabulated by Gould. See Gould, *Sanitary Memoirs of the War of the Rebellion*, 3.

The total number of men eligible for service among ethnic groups was determined by taking the total number of foreign-born living in the loyal states from the 1860 census multiplied by .30. Gould concluded that 30 percent of foreigners living in the loyal states in 1860 were white men of military age (18–45). See U.S. Census Office, *Population of the United States in 1860*, xxix, and Gould, *Sanitary Memoirs of the War of the Rebellion*, 3. Gould estimated that 229,532 men of military age came to the United States during the war, but he did not calculate the numbers for each individual place of birth. I tabulated the 1861–65 additions to each group by multiplying 229,532 by the percentage of immigrants living in the United States in 1860. See Gould, *Sanitary Memoirs of the War of the Rebellion*, 3.

aboard ship. Seaman John Swift complained, "If a man is discovered to be an Irishman he immediately loses caste."[63]

English sailors constituted over 10 percent of recruits, followed by Canadians (4.70 percent), both peoples with a strong history of seafaring. Germans—who formed the largest single bloc of foreign-born recruits in the army—represented only 4 percent of sailor recruits.[64] The last groups of significance were Swedes (1.0 percent) and Norwegians (1.13 percent).[65] The percentages of foreign-born sailors did not vary significantly between East and West, except that more Germans enlisted in the West.[66]

The foreign flavor of most crews jarred native-born sailors. George Geer, a fireman on the *Monitor*, wrote that "on a crew of 40 there is only 8 of us American born." "I chum with them in place of these dand foreigners."[67] Charles Poole, a coal heaver on the *Kearsarge*, marveled at the diversity of his mates. "We only want one or two or more to make all Nations," Poole jotted in his log. "Some can hardly speak English. . . . We have got Americans, English, Irish, Scotsh, Welsh, Portugese, Italian, Russian, Dutch and Belgian."[68]

Confederates circulated rumors that recruiters often marched immigrants directly from ports of entry to recruiting stations, but, according to one Irish sailor, immigrants were not forced into service.[69] Writing to his brothers back in Dublin, Seaman William E. Hinch admitted that he had heard such rumors but assured his relatives that they had little truth. In Hinch's experience, the naval service of foreigners was "optional" and "voluntary." According to Hinch, foreigners were not subject to the draft unless they declared their intention of becoming citizens.[70] The navy facilitated immigrant preferences by offering one-year, rather than three-year, terms of enlistment during times of critical manpower needs. Foreign-born sailors preferred these one-year terms because they offered a recruit a chance to try out the navy, make some money, and ease the assimilation into his new country, all without making a long-term commitment.[71]

The Irish may have had an emotional reason for joining the navy. In 1847, Congress authorized two naval warships, the *Jamestown* and the *Macedonian*, to carry famine relief from the United States to Ireland. The memory of American warships and sailors unloading vital supplies and foodstuffs in Cork to ease their suffering likely remained strong among many Irishmen. The large percentage of Irish recruits perhaps indicates an unspoken affection for the service.[72]

Former slaves were the third group who enlisted as sailors. Although a predominately white institution, the navy had permitted, unlike the army, limited numbers of free blacks to enlist before the war. Standing naval regulations allowed free blacks to join as long as they made up no more than 5 percent of monthly and weekly enlistments.[73] However, as blockade vessels and river gunboats penetrated the inlets and inner waterways of the Confederacy, slaves gradually worked their way onto Union ships. The navy's history of permitting blacks to serve in white crews, coupled with severe recruiting shortfalls of white sailors, eventually compelled the unlimited shipping of free blacks and former slaves.[74] As early as July 1861, former slaves, called "contrabands," began filling the manpower requirements of ships, almost one full year before the army allowed the formation of black regiments.[75]

Historians have been unable to agree on the exact number of African American sailors who served in the navy. Herbert Aptheker in his 1947 article "The Negro in the Union Navy" concluded that 20 percent of total enlistees in the navy were black.[76] David Valuska challenged these findings in *The African American in the Union Navy* (1993). In examining the rendezvous reports for Union sailors during the war, Valuska determined that only 8 percent of navy recruits were black.[77]

Part of the problem in ascertaining an accurate figure lies in the fact that most contraband sailors did not enlist at naval rendezvous and, instead, joined a ship's crew in the South. Many times, these informal inductions escaped formal reporting to rendezvous. To remedy this problem, Professor Joseph Reidy of Howard University is currently amassing data from every ship muster roll with the intention of determining an accurate figure for black service in the navy. To date, Reidy's work reveals that an estimated 18,000 African Americans served in the navy during the Civil War. This number represents over 15 percent of the total number of Union sailor recruits.[78]

Although the identification of high percentages of recruits among certain groups lends a better understanding of who became sailors, this, by itself, lacks the power of language. Personal motivations, evidenced in the written record, explain the decisions to enlist. Personal motivations answer different questions than social factors do. Social factors are broad and are limited to the extent that they only help historians identify individuals sharing a common characteristic or tendency. They are instructive in that they enable scholars to provide a framework for understanding different human behavior by flagging certain potential consistencies in behavior among classes, races, and ethnic groups.

Once it is determined, with a degree of reliability, that certain types of people form a group, the historian can then investigate the personal motivations within that group to determine whether the personal motivations are consistent with the social factors.

When the two mesh, as they do here, they can provide powerful statements about the realities of the past. The reality for Union sailors was that they shared few of the motivations that guided soldiers into service. Although some men joined the navy for many of the reasons that prompted others to become soldiers, most did not enlist out of patriotism, political bias, ambition, or love of adventure.[79] They did not view the war as a chance to preserve or extend their ideological or religious beliefs.[80] Moreover, men did not ship to free the slaves or prove their courage.[81] In fact, given the limited space Yankee seamen devoted to such subjects in their letters and diaries, they evidently expressed little interest in ideology, patriotism, or duty.[82] After examining the motives compelling men to enlist in the Civil War, one can conclude that Union Jacks seemed every bit "the dissenters from the American mood."[83]

Overall, a mixed assortment of practical motivations influenced sailors to go into service. The easiest motivations to understand were those of contraband sailors. They joined the navy seeking freedom and protection. The motivations of white sailors featured a network of interlocking considerations and interests. For example, a craftsman might enlist in the navy because he was unemployed, could put his skills to work aboard ship, and could join a service with strong ties to the working class. As sailor Joseph McDonald explained, "I wanted to be where there was machinery."[84] A foreigner might have joined the navy because he felt more comfortable in the navy than in the army and was unemployed or unskilled. Drunks, hard types, and young urban toughs might enlist to free themselves from societal constraints while being paid and provided a regular ration of whiskey. Nevertheless, across all groups, the two most recurring motivations expressed by sailors for enlisting were "getting clean" and making money.

"Getting clean" meant joining the war but avoiding the hardship and risk associated with being a soldier. Repelled by stories of long marches, poor rations, and the haphazard nature of camp life, some Northerners chose the navy in order to join what many considered to be an easier, more comfortable means of service.[85] For these men, becoming a sailor represented a compromise of sorts. They were not the ideological, religious, or patriotic types that truly desired to place their lives completely on the line. Many clearly felt some pressure to do something to serve the Union cause but at limited exposure to personal hardship and death. Peer and community pressure, as well as the sight of friends and acquaintances leaving home for the army, exerted a powerful compulsive influence—not strong enough, however, to prod them into the army.

This process—whereby a man enlisted in the navy out of a sense of shame, communal pressure, or a fear of the army—became commonplace.[86] "I saw everyone else leaving home," Coal Heaver Charles Poole wrote, "and I thought I must do the same."[87] James Henneberry enlisted as a sailor, over the objections of his mother, because "a chum" was going.[88] Poole and Henneberry were not alone in their sentiments. Seaman William E. Hinch neatly encapsulated the subtle—yet persuasive—effect that watching other men go to war played on him. "I have seen many of my comrades going to the war," Hinch wrote. "They went untill I was almost alone."[89]

Becoming sailors proved the answer to their dilemmas. Men could put on a uniform without the daily hardships endured by soldiers. The most significant hardships these men wanted to avoid were the traditional gripes of all soldiers—marching, sleeping on the ground, and eating cold rations. Charles Poole believed that being a sailor would be "better than Army marching under a hot sun in Virginia."[90] Joseph Osborne confidently wrote to his sister Mary that in the navy "no long marches lay before me."[91] Believing the navy offered "all the comforts of home," Samuel J. Bartlett used glowing terms to defend the wisdom of his choice. "It is much more easy, nicer, and better than in the army," Bartlett wrote home to his brother. Bartlett liked the fact that sailors had "comfortable sleeping apartments and in fact all the comforts of home except dear friends."[92]

Others liked the security and stability that a ship promised. Charles Poole cited the idea of a "dry hammock" and being "sure of his Food such as it is."[93] Rowland Stafford True, a landsman serving on the *Silver Lake*, admitted that he liked being a sailor because his bed was in a "dry place" and his "provisions safely stored." One of the best features of the navy, True wrote, was that "we know where everything is."[94]

Other men trying to get clean enlisted because they believed the navy offered little chance of being killed. Many knew the Confederates possessed no large, formidable navy so there stood little chance of traditional naval battles where ships pulled alongside and poured shot and shell onto each other at close range. The blockade would require nothing more than sitting on a ship watching for lightly armed blockade runners more interested in running than fighting. "You need not be frightened when you read this," Seaman John Swift boldly wrote to his mother, "as there is no danger *in the service I am going on* except from dysentery & I am not afraid of that."[95] Joseph Osborne penned to his sister that there was "no danger in going under fire if there is a fight."[96] Clearly, these men did not want to die for their country. "I am always looking out for No. 1," wrote Fireman George Geer to his wife, "and am not going to get killed or Drowned in this War."[97]

Although some of these comments may have been made to assuage the fears of a nervous mother, sister, or wife, they did not represent the sort of sentiments usually associated with fighting in the Civil War. Motivations such as safety, comfort, and personal security were not acceptable reasons compelling American men to go to war in 1861. In the eyes of many, they were certainly not the sort of attributes that would win that war.

The notion of the navy as a softer branch of service proved so prevalent that soldiers, when granted the opportunity, often used the navy to escape the army. The navy had originally sought soldier-transfers when rivermen failed to enlist in the Mississippi Squadron.[98] Bored by the monotony of camp life, hating marches in hot weather and cold mud, and now fearing combat, many soldiers naively jumped at the opportunity to transfer to the navy.[99] As in the case of nonsoldier recruits, personal safety played a key role in the decision to transfer. "I consider myself as safe in her as in a fort," stated relieved soldier-turned-sailor William Van Cleaf to friends and family back in New Jersey.[100] Later in the war, with manning quotas falling woefully short, thousands of seamen who had originally joined the army received the opportunity to transfer to the navy. After what they had been through in the army, they took it. At war's end, the army had authorized the transfer of an estimated 10,000 to 12,000 soldiers to the navy.[101]

Entering the army through the draft carried with it a social stigma. With the advent of military conscription and the realities of Antietam and Fredericksburg sinking into the Northern consciousness, after 1862 men unabashedly joined the navy—not owing to community pressure—but to avoid combat and the stigma of conscription. By 1863, military victories were few and romantic tales of military combat even fewer. As C. G. Leland uncovered in an article for *Continental Monthly*, the reality of war had been exposed to civilians all across the North in the lame and crippled soldiers returning home. "The poor souls," wrote Leland, "ragged and sun-burnt, may be seen at every corner. . . . They

## Men wanted

### FOR

## THE NAVY!

**All able bodied men and boys**

Will be enlisted into the NAVAL SERVICE

upon application at the Naval Rendezvous.

Come forward and serve your Country

## WITHOUT CONSCRIPTION!

Roanoke Island, Dec. 8th, 1863.

*An 1863 recruiting broadside for the navy. It invites men to become
sailors willingly and avoid the social stigma of conscription.
Courtesy of the National Archives.*

sit in the parks with unhealed wounds, they hobble along the streets,
many of them weary and worn."[102]

The use of the navy as a means to escape forced service was uncomfortably accepted as fact by Secretary of the Navy Gideon Welles. Welles
commented in his diary that a "desire to enter the Navy to avoid the
draft is extensive." Although Welles believed that the use of the navy to

avoid the conscription system was a "perversion," the service did not turn away recruits who used the navy to dodge the army.[103] Welles later explained why in his diary: "Our recruiting rendezvous are, for the time being overrun."[104] Assistant Secretary of the Navy Gustavus Vasa Fox was a little more enthusiastic about the situation. "The draft helps us," Fox wrote, "by driving sailors into our arms."[105]

Local recruiters, however, had no philosophical problem about making navy enlistments, in the words of Gideon Welles, "a primary object of the draft."[106] Walter S. Thomas, the recruiting officer in Troy, Ohio, was convinced that many recruits only joined the navy out of fear of the army. "I am certain of getting quite a number of recruits," Thomas wrote to Rear Admiral David Dixon Porter, "who will not ship unless strong fear of being drafted into the Army."[107] With war weariness setting in, local recruiters began to tout the popular perception, negative at the war's outset, that being a sailor was a safer form of service. Navy broadsides beckoned men with such unpatriotic calls as "Serve Your Country without Conscription," "The Conscript Bill! How To Avoid It!!" and "Avoid Conscription!" The inferences of such posters were left to the reader, although "Join the Navy and Live!" could have functioned as the new recruiting slogan at many rendezvous after 1862.[108]

Sailors who enlisted after 1862 often freely admitted that they had enlisted to avoid the draft.[109] Seaman Joseph Osborne, who had served in the army before he joined the navy, wrote to his sister that he had reenlisted in 1865 purposefully to avoid the draft and the army. He justified his decision in that there were "no long marches before me, through the dust and heat." "In the Army," Osborne wrote, "I used to hate a march worse than a fight."[110] William Wainwright was absolutely convinced that many of the new recruits he encountered in 1864 had shipped to avoid the draft. He believed they were the sort of men who would desert "at 1st opportunity."[111]

Besides getting clean, the second most commonly stated motivation for becoming a Union sailor was money. At first blush, it does "seem preposterous" that a man would enlist for $14 a month, the pay of seamen during most of the war. However, as many recruits noted, steady and certain work proved difficult throughout the war.[112] More importantly, the navy offered two types of money that the army did not—big money and ready money.

Big money for sailors was prize money. Prize money—a share of the cash value of blockade runners seized by their ships—dangled as a sort of lottery scheme for sailors.[113] The navy heavily touted prize

THE CONSCRIPT BILL!
HOW TO AVOID IT!!
U. S. NAVY.
1,000 MEN WANTED, FOR 12 MONTHS!

Seamen's Pay, - - - - - - $18.00 per month.
Ordinary Seamen's Pay, : : : 14.00 " "
Landsmen's Pay, . . . . . 12.00 " "
$1.50 extra per month to all, Greg Money.

$50,000,000 PRIZES!

Already captured, a large share of which is awarded to Ships Crews. The laws for the distributing of Prize money carefully protects the rights of all the captors.

PETTY OFFICERS.—PROMOTION.—Seamen have a chance for promotion to the offices of Master at Arms, Boatswain's Mates, Quarter Gunners, Captain of Tops, Forecastle, Holds, After-Guard, &c.
Landsmen may be advanced to Armorers, Armorers' Mates, Carpenter's Mates, Sailmakers' Mates, Painters, Coopers, &c.
PAY OF PETTY OFFICERS.—From $20.00 to $45.00 per month.
CHANCES FOR WARRANTS, BOUNTIES AND MEDALS OF HONOR.—All those who distinguish themselves in battle or by extraordinary heroism, may be promoted to forward Warrant Officers or Acting Masters' Mates,—and upon their promotion receive a guaranty of $100, with a medal of honor from their country.
All who wish may leave HALF PAY with their families, to commence from date of enlistment.
Minors must have a written consent, sworn to before a Justice of the Peace.

For further information apply to U. S. NAVAL RENDEZVOUS,
E. Y. BUTLER, U. S. N. Recruiting Officer,
No. 14 FRONT STREET, SALEM, MASS.

FROM WRIGHT & POTTER'S BOSTON PRINTING ESTABLISHMENT, No. 4 SPRING LANE, CORNER OF DEVONSHIRE STREET.

*A navy recruiting broadside listing pay scale for sailors and promoting the allure of prize money. Courtesy of the National Archives.*

money in its recruiting campaign. Broadsides posted in working-class and poor neighborhoods promised staggering amounts of prize money, often as much as $50 million to potential sailors. Many starry-eyed recruits who gazed at recruiting posters gaudily trumpeting such figures likely thought the navy offered a quick way out of financial distress and into riches.[114] As Seaman Tim Finn noted in 1861, "Boys were thinking they had lots of prize money coming to them." William Anderson summarized the thoughts of many as he entered the navy: "As I looked upon the trim, clean model of my ship, visions of unlimited prize money rose before me."[115]

The ready money that attracted potential sailors came in the form of salary advances. Throughout the war, the navy adopted the practice of advancing seamen, experienced sailors, three months' salary. Landsmen, recruits with absolutely no ship experience, received two-month advances.[116] The navy had adopted this practice because the recruits showing up at rendezvous often conditioned their enlistment on the payment of an advance. Bounties, which the army usually paid to soldiers in installments or upon their discharge, were of little use to these men.[117] They needed ready money to pay outstanding bills with boardinghouses and saloons.[118]

Immigrants and the unemployed proved in particular need of ready money.[119] In September 1861, Andrew H. Foote, the first commander of the Western Flotilla, complained to Secretary of the Navy Gideon Welles, "I find it also very difficult to get men to enter this service without giving them some advance to pay their board bills, etc."[120] The necessity of granting advances to debt-laden recruits continued throughout the war. John D. Harty, chief recruiting officer at the Chicago Rendezvous, concluded in 1864 that "a few dollars down is the greatest inducement I can offer the men."[121]

The presence of these self-serving motivations also highlighted the fact that Union sailors were a unique set of men.[122] Their stated motivations revealed a number of things about themselves: they needed money; they did not want to die or suffer for their country if they could avoid it; and they were honest, brutally honest. Officers and sailors themselves often struggled to figure out why Union sailors were unique. They marveled at the odd personality quirks and behavior of "Jack," the generic, faceless term that officers, outsiders, and civilians affixed to the ordinary Union sailor.[123] Charles Post, a landsman on the *Florida*, recalled his first impressions of the sailors he met on the blockade in 1863. After spending his first few days watching them work and live Post exclaimed, "Sailors are queer cattle!"[124]

Surely the uniform helped. Sailors wore hip-hugging, bell-bottomed blue pants, a dark blue wool flat cap, and a bloused blue wool frock adorned by jumper flaps—called a "sailor's collar"—on front and back. A black handkerchief was often tied snugly round the neck. Lastly, the uniform was set off by a dark blue, double-breasted shell jacket, with wide lapels and two rows of nine navy buttons, from which sailors earned one more of their more popular nicknames, "bluejackets."[125]

There were also physical differences. Sailors proved to be shorter, stockier, and scarier-looking than the average enlistee. According to statistics compiled by Benjamin A. Gould, an actuary for the United States Sanitary Commission, the mean height of sailors was less than that of soldiers by 1.14 inches. Sailors also had longer legs and thicker necks. Their feet were the same dimensions, but the thickness of sailors' feet was greater. Sailors' arms and hands were smaller than those of soldiers.[126] Moreover, according to the descriptive remarks contained in Rendezvous Reports, sailor recruits sported pronounced facial scars, bulging veins, and twitching eyelids and were covered with tattooed crosses, sinister daggers, and provocative dancing girls. Fireman George Geer wrote to his wife that sailors were "regular Picture Books. They have India Ink pricked all over ther body."[127]

Leaving aside outward appearances, the working-class origins of most sailors shaped their essence.[128] In fact, Yankee tars exhibited many of the same attributes ascribed by historians to the working class of the 1850s and 1860s.[129] Their prewar jobs were as tough as they were, and their personal behavior and values paralleled working-class ideals. Sailors were cocky, arrogant, and abundantly self-assured. Aggressively masculine, they focused on honor codes, wanderlust, and playful violence. Union sailors were manly men first, and they believed that men should fight, drink, and swear without curbs imposed by churches, women, or employers. To their contemporaries, Union sailors were rough, mean, and undisciplined.[130]

In many respects, their values and behavior offered a stunning contrast to the reform-minded, domesticated, striving Northern gentleman of the 1860s and his wartime culmination—the Union soldier boy. Michael Barton, in *Goodmen: The Character of Civil War Soldiers*, after analyzing the letters and diaries of 400 soldiers, from the North and the South, concludes that Northern soldiers were, for the most part, "goodmen," whose hallmarks were submission, law and order, piety, and self-control. The social manifestation of the goodman was the "gentleman" and entailed what the term stated—a man of kind heart, gentle behavior, and polite manners. A gentleman worked six days a week at a steady, albeit unexciting position, soundly provided for his wife and children, and stood sober on Saturday night and in church on Sunday.[131]

Union sailors in word, thought, and deed bore little resemblance to these "goodmen." They were a coarse and sometimes brutal lot; so rough—so different—that, in striking contrast to the title "goodmen" affixed to soldiers, many Union sailors earned the label "bad men."[132] Officers, chaplains, paymasters, and sailors themselves routinely marveled at how rough sailors were and complained that many possessed a "bad character."[133]

Officers found sailor behavior and beliefs so offensive that they used the most damning terms to describe their character. They likened sailors to "rubbish" and "offscourings."[134] One officer on the blockade complained that his crew consisted of "God forsaken-looking ex-ministers, school masters, lawyers," "idiots," and recruits who were like "children."[135] The low tenor of most sailor recruits proved such a problem that officers sent numerous pleas specifically demanding "good men."[136] David Dixon Porter, commander of the Mississippi Squadron, expressed the frustration felt by many officers when he wrote to Rear Admiral Andrew H. Foote: "They send us all rubbish here; we want good men."[137]

To a great extent, when officers referred to sailors as "bad men," "rubbish," and "offscourings," they were making value judgments partially rooted in class outlook and ethnic prejudices: the working class and working poor were lazy; the Irish were drunks and fighters; and so on. There existed a wide social chasm between naval officers, who tended to come from the middle and upper classes, and sailors, who emanated from the working classes of American society. This gulf between officer and sailor was much greater than the gap between officers and soldiers in the army.[138]

More difficult to discount, however, were the observations of fellow sailors. Their observations ran from bad to worse. Seaman John Wirts called his fellow crewmates on the *Lancaster* "bad men."[139] Israel E. Vail concluded that Union sailors consisted of "men of very little principle."[140] James Birtwistle worried that his crewmates were "composed chiefly of hard characters"—so hard, in Birtwistle's estimation, that he wanted to get off ship.[141] Seaman George Clark called his mates "as hard a set as one would care to be among." "What a collection of men there were," he growled, "the gambler, the thief, the clerk, the landsman, sailors . . . and the low browed."[142] Landsman Milo Lacy concluded that his mates were "composed mostly of the 'scum' of Boston and New York."[143]

Without question, many recruits resembled the skulkers, drunks, and reprobates of maritime mythology.[144] Many admittedly had led the "wild life" and had already dissipated their chances at success through alcohol, gambling, laziness, and crime.[145] Union crews, in the opinion of William Wainwright, a coal heaver on the *Kearsarge*, seemed to harbor an inordinate number of men who were "too lazy to work." William Keeler, a paymaster on the *Florida*, wrote to his wife that more often than not whiskey was "the cause" of men becoming sailors.[146]

Much of what made Union sailors unique and bad in the eyes of their critics was their puzzling behavior. Within the strong framework of their class consciousness, they wove a belief structure that centered on individualism and personal freedom. They flexed their own definitions of those core values and fiercely protected themselves from any entanglement that might jeopardize personal expression.[147] Sailors had little use for self-control, self-denial, and self-discipline.[148] By extension, any regimen that smacked of the restraint of the workplace, whether it was temperance, religion, or a rigid schedule, was seen as aristocratic, intrusive, and threatening.[149]

This attitude triggered charges that sailors were impulsive, wild, and unmanageable. According to William Rounesville Alger, Union sailors were "creatures of impulse," which he saw as their biggest character flaw. From this weakness, he opined at a National Sailors' Fair in Boston in 1864, all of the other vices and virtues of sailors flowed.[150] Union tars were the sort of men who ate food if they saw it, took a drink of whiskey if they wanted it, and stole something if they spied it. Lieutenant Francis A. Roe, who had spent the war with sailors, attempted to summarize the thought processes of the typical Jack: "He is violent, rapid, direct in all his acts and thoughts."[151]

Yet, in many respects, sailors consistently exhibited contradictory behavior. Extremely conscious of money, they spent every dime they had. Suspicious of religion, they howled when prayers and the divine service were dropped during the war. Intensely autonomous, many lived dependent on alcohol. Nothing spoke so strongly to this contrarian streak as their decision to join the navy, a service with a history of repression and depersonalization. In the navy, men exchanged their names for numbers. These numbers determined where they worked, ate, and slept. Every facet of their lives, from sunup to sunset, was overseen, measured, and regulated. Even stranger, once in the service, sailors routinely exhibited outright contempt for officers while tacitly accepting naval hierarchy. In order to reconcile themselves to their circumstances, sailors intensely channeled their individualistic impulses collectively. In fact, the collective exercise of their behavior, which often defied polite society, paradoxically created a cohesive sailor society with strong bonds of friendship. The conflicting nature of their behavior can easily cause one to lose sight of the fact that much of their violent, impulsive, and antisocial behavior served as signs of solidarity with fellow sailors and bound them tightly together.

In their social comportment, sailors were rough and loud. Whereas goodmen were expected to act gently, use polite language in benign conversations, abstain from tobacco, and imbibe moderately, Union sailors tended to swear, chew tobacco, and drink to insensibility. They routinely engaged in playful violence, drinking bouts, and verbal sparring matches laced with obscenities. Both sensitive and proud about their working-class origins, many sailors used boisterous behavior to assert their masculinity, defend their honor, and trumpet their origins.

This sensibility crept into almost all facets of their speech and manner. Sailors had a habit of teasing, joking, and mocking each other incessantly about everything and anything—which they called "making sport."[152] Making sport utilized sarcasm—bitter, withering, and relentless. Sarcasm stood apart from the sentimentality embraced by the middle class. Sailor speech and tone often came across as antisentimental, cynical, and cruel. The slightest mistake brought howls, catcalls, and merciless taunting.

For the most part, sailors showed little sympathy toward one another and laughed at the accidents of others.[153] They played tricks on almost everyone, including children, and on animals. Boy Charles Mervine marveled that the crew members on his ship were so mean that they did not assist or comfort the women who came aboard during choppy waters and fell into seasickness. "I guess they thought Sailors was a sett of heathens," Mervine penned in his log, "the way they laughed at the delicate creatures."[154]

Roughhousing proved vitally important. Free fighting, consisting of hard slapping and hurtful punching—called "fistanna" by sailors—was common even among friends. Sailors were likely to fight viciously when provoked and were quick to throw a punch or pull a knife when riled.[155] "I am going to rip your guts out" was one of their favorite expressions. It was not an idle threat. Daily use of knives to cut and splice lines aboard ship made sailors lethally handy. So handy were some Boston recruits that the officer on the receiving ship at Charlestown asked each recruit to hand over his knife before boarding. The officer would then jab the dirk into a deck seam and give it a sharp kick to break off the sharpened point. He did so knowing that it would take an industrious recruit another six months to reshape a deadly tip.[156]

Such levels of violence jarred even rough-and-tumble soldiers. Sailors on ship and on land proved susceptible to massive and chaotic fights of enormous scope and violence. In May 1862, 260 sailors from Boston literally took apart the town of Cairo, Illinois, during one massive brawl.[157] On the island of St. Thomas, 150 sailors from the *Powhatan*, on liberty for the first time in months, killed three and wounded many more English sailors in massive fights called "riots" by one seaman. The *Powhatan* sailors had engaged in an almost continuous round of fights during a twenty-four-hour period and had even driven back to their forts the Danish soldiers called in to restore order. Off Bird's Point, Missouri, Private Charles Wills marveled that the navy would not let its gunboat sailors on land for fear of their fighting: "They are such cusses."[158]

Seaman George Clark recalled a night when a draft of sailor recruits pulled alongside the receiving ship he was on, the *Allegheny*. The new recruits arrived on board with plenty of liquor. After ten minutes of hard drinking, Clark recalled that "one of the hardest fights took place that I ever witnessed." In describing the melee, Clark wrote, "Imagine, if you can, seven hundred men striking each other for the fun of the thing; when one saw a head he hit it, laughing, swearing, and fighting at the same time." Eventually, the marines and some soldiers were called in to quell the fight. As the soldiers stood with their bayonets fixed, staring at the sight of men pounding each other senseless for no reason, they quaked. Sensing their fear, one six-foot-tall Yankee sailor bellowed over to the phalanx of advancing soldiers: "Go away, soldier, or you'll get hurt."[159]

Sailors' impulsiveness also can be seen in their attitudes toward money. Overall, sailors did not possess the market mentality and its emphasis on working feverishly to accumulate property. Lieutenant Francis Roe stated that sailors were nothing like the rising class of "business men" in the North who subordinated all to the pursuit of money.[160] This was not to say that Union sailors did not like money; they loved it. But, for them, money was only a means to an end and not an end in itself. The Protestant work ethic of feverish accumulation and deferred gratification simply did not appeal to these men.

Consequently, sailors sought money only as far as they needed it, and they spent it as fast as they could get it. Many Union sailors embodied what one historian calls the sailor creed toward money: "What I had I got, what I spent I saved, and what I kept I lost."[161] Joseph Osborne, who had served a stint in the army before he enlisted in the navy, marveled at sailors' attitudes about money. "There is plenty of Greenbacks and the sailors are a liberal set they care nothing for money."[162] In fact, "liberal" was the most common term used to describe sailors' attitude toward money. "Some of these fools would buy any thing," Fireman George Geer wrote to his wife, "if they only had the money."[163]

The attitude of sailors toward money was reflected in enigmatic behavior that swung from stealing everything in sight to great acts of charity.[164] In fact, petty thievery and wholesale stealing proved serious wartime problems. Purposeful sailors could empty a seized blockader, a warehouse full of cotton, or a private residence in minutes.[165] Even though thieves were scorned, shamed, and punished viciously, stealing seemed to be the custom on every ship, gunboat, steamer, and tug of the Union navy.

Sailors routinely stole from each other. Former soldier William Van Cleaf moaned that he was on the ship no more than a few minutes when his pocketbook and stamps were stolen. Seaman Tim Finn wrote that "you had to be on the lookout all the time or they would steal the Shirt off your Back." Theft aboard his ship proved so rampant that Seaman Carsten B. DeWitt fumed: "One cannot lay any thing down for a few minutes, but it is gone in the twinkling of an eye, which makes it very disagreeable, if you lose any thing, and endeavour to find out where it is gone to, the Answer from most of the men is that it is the Custom about every Man of War."[166]

Sailors balanced their meaner impulses with an altruistic impulse, called "sailor generosity." Sailor generosity proved very strong and often prompted sailors to put down their jagged, crusty exteriors and extend to others great singular acts of charity.[167] An encounter with someone less fortunate than they were almost always triggered this impulse. Someone's misfortune could remind crews of their rough circumstances, and there were sailors who believed, selfishly, that such gestures functioned as a form of atonement. As the older sailors told John Wirts aboard the *Lancaster*, "Charity covers a multitude of sins."[168] This marked benevolence baffled more business-minded types. Lieutenant Francis Roe recalled, "I never knew of an instance of a sailor hesitating to put his name to a charity subscription, or to share his purse even with a viscious comrade."[169]

Women, children, white refugees, and escaped slaves often found that Union sailors, when confronted with tales of woe or misfortune, could be quite generous. Reverend William Alger marveled that, as rough as Union sailors were, there was nothing quite "as tender as a sailor's tear."[170] Charles Mervine, who had witnessed drunkenness, massive fights, and stabbings, also witnessed something else: Union sailors' great capacity for charity. Mervine recalled that when Seaman James Young died from a fall off the topsail yard, the crew raised a subscription of $964.50 to send to his widowed mother. The better-paid officers contributed only $113.[171]

Seaman John Dempsey recounted to his sister a story about an Irish orphan who had stowed away aboard the *Kearsarge* in order to escape to America to find relatives in Boston. Despite his efforts to remain hidden, officers eventually found the boy and summarily ordered him ashore. Before leaving the vessel, thwarted in his attempt to go to Boston and rejoin what was left of his family, the young stowaway broke down and sobbed. The sailors of the *Kearsarge* were immediately moved to pity—so moved, according to Dempsey, that "we raised him $35 dollars in gold to pay for his passage to America."[172]

Sailors were struck at the wretched circumstances in which they found poor whites and escaped slaves along the coastal areas of the blockade and the lower Mississippi. Time and again, the hordes of escaped slaves and white refugees along the blockade and Western rivers discovered that they had no better friends in their hours of need than sailors. More often than not, Union sailors were willing to give a ride, offer food, and provide clothes to the war's dispossessed. Seaman James Henneberry, who had witnessed sailor thievery on the Mississippi, was also surprised at the many countervailing examples of sailor generosity. On the Red River in Louisiana, Henneberry wrote of the hordes of white refugees, "Here is a fearful many of them not having a bite of food and no means of getting any." He was amazed that his fellow mates refused to turn a blind eye to the misery they witnessed daily. Instead, Henneberry wrote, "The boys show their '*Sailor Generosity*' as far as they can."[173]

Integral to shaping the image and behavior of Union sailors was the small but influential number of lifelong sailors who, owing to their seafaring skills and potent personalities, seized the imaginations of most new recruits. Their behavior and mannerisms originally shocked and cowed the unfamiliar. Fireman George Geer wrote to his wife that he was "completely disgusted with Saylors. . . . They do not seam to know anything but Whores and Rum."[174] "I dont like the amusements that they go to," wrote Fireman John Taylor, "nor the company that they keep."[175]

While some recruits may have been completely disgusted with the ways of sailors, many quickly latched on to their mannerisms and ideas. They did so because a ship, aside from the naval duties it demanded, paradoxically promised a larger measure of personal freedom. Below deck and out of sight of officers, men could indulge their vices and do what they wanted to do in a sort of subsidized "never never land"— smoke, drink, fight, spit, and swear without fear of social repercussions. The navy was not interested in saving souls or in sobering them up.

In short, ships permitted men to act like sailors.[176] Understanding sailors' unique belief system and behavioral patterns is crucial to our grasping how Union sailors reacted to and adapted to the Civil War aboard ship. The lore and everyday practices of sailors partially explain how recruits endured basic training, naval inequities, and the unhealthy environment of a ship. Insight into the beliefs and backgrounds of sailors is also critical in understanding their responses to the larger issues of the war from distillation of religion in the military to the lasting implications of freeing the slaves. In the final analysis, to know Union sailors, one must know their habits. For the new recruits, the landsmen, the introduction to sailors' habits began as soon as they boarded ship.

## Any Man Can Become a Soldier
### The Making of Union Sailors

Most recruits had little idea of what to expect when they shipped.[1]
Many had never been on a ship, much less a man-of-war. More than a
few believed that they were going on an excursion or a romantic cruise.[2]
Others thought they had chosen an easy service. By most accounts, recruits' notions about what it meant to be a sailor proved completely
wrong. Instead, what men discovered was that becoming a sailor was
an incredibly difficult process. Unlike soldiers, who only had to make
a few primary adjustments within a familiar physical and social environment, sailors discovered that in order to assimilate they had to
make fundamental adjustments to their bodies as well as to their minds.
Yankee seamen not only had to leave land; they had to live within the
tight confines of a ship without family, friends, and most importantly,
women. As if this were not enough, recruits also had to acquire the technical skills necessary to navigate a ship, the essential task of a seaman,
and learn to fight on one, the essential job of a sailor.

The process was especially difficult for most Union recruits since
few joined the navy with any experience.[3] In fact, the Rendezvous Sample indicates that 78 percent of sailor recruits possessed absolutely no
skill or experience in things nautical. Stated another way, only a little
over 22 percent of recruits joined the navy with any previous experience as mariners, sailors, boatmen, seamen, or watermen.[4] As a result,
in both the East and the West, on blockade and river squadrons, most
Union sailor volunteers shipped into the navy, in the words of historian
John D. Milligan, as "a veritable set of landlubbers."[5]

All men entered the navy under the same mustering procedure. After
recruits signed the enlistment book at the rendezvous, they reported to
large decommissioned wooden vessels, called receiving ships or "guardos," located in Atlantic ports and Western river stations. Guardos func-

tioned as basic training stations and crew disbursement centers.[6] On receiving ships, navy physicians administered rudimentary physical examinations. Doctors rapped men on the chests to test for tuberculosis, whispered in a low voice to test hearing, and asked them to turn and cough to uncover hernias.

After the recruits had passed physical inspection, they swore the oath of allegiance prescribed by Congress.[7] The last administrative matter that sailors had to perform during mustering was the reading and signing of the shipping articles. Shipping articles functioned as a contract detailing the terms of a sailor's service with the navy. They set forth such critical information as rating, monthly wages, wages advanced, and term of service. After signing the articles, the recruits received their uniforms, blankets, and eating utensils.[8]

For most men, stepping onto these guardos represented their first time aboard a ship. Seaman Tim Finn remarked that most recruits "had never seen Salt Water." Men's experiences on these vessels usually proved distasteful and were a first signal that sailoring was not the adventure they had heard about. Guardos were crowded, dirty, and uncomfortable.[9] One sailor on the *Ohio* said, "There was little for us to do."[10] An officer called them a "floating hell."[11] Since receiving ships were not their final destinations, men did not settle in. They ate standing up and slept outside on the decks.[12] First meals consisted of such fare as rice and a heavily salted, canned beef which sailors derisively called "salt horse."[13] Many landsmen who enlisted in the navy hungry gobbled up their promised rations. Tim Finn marveled: "The way they could get away with grub was a wonder to old sailors."[14]

Sailors usually only spent a few days on receiving ships. When a crew was needed, officers drafted a portion of men on deck and organized them into manageable groupings approximately the size of crews. Very often, officers tried to separate the few friends and family members who had enlisted together. As officers called off names and vessel assignments, men would jump back and forth between groups in order to join crews in which they knew someone.[15] Sailors drafted from receiving ships in the New York, Boston, and Philadelphia naval yards usually sailed south on their assigned vessels or were transported on ships disbursing crews along the blockade cordon.

The real training began when they arrived at their assigned vessel. The simple act of boarding their ship often triggered the first realizations that sailors were being confronted with a physical world vastly different than the one they had left on land. A sailor on the *Ino* marveled that all his life, he was used "to going up and down stairs on a slant." He expressed shock that in order to board his ship he had "to be rowed in a small boat to a Ship's side, & suddenly find himself under the necessity of making a perpendicular ascent." [16]

Men marveled at how hard the decks felt under their feet. It was not like walking on earth or grass. Walking, even on the so-called "soft sides" of deck planks as sailors comically referred to them, hurt feet and body alike.[17] "After standing about for a while," the sailor on the *Ino* wrote, "you think, what a soft floor you left at home in your Mother's kitchen." [18]

The roll and pitch of the ship as it reacted to the waves also compelled these nascent seamen to reconfigure other bodily functions. When they tried to walk on deck as they had on land men ended up rolling and falling all over the deck.[19] New sailors found that they could no longer stroll with their legs close together in firm precision. In order to maintain their balance, recruits widened their walking stances as their environment moved beneath their feet. One eighteenth-century writer observed that sailors "swing their Corps like a Pendulum," when they walk. This adjustment gave sailors their distinctive gait that lent legs a bandied, bow-legged appearance.[20] This new way of walking appeared awkward but effectively allowed sailors to walk the decks without succumbing to the tossing of the ship.[21]

Recruits also had to adjust to the fact that ships were chronically wet. Sailors lived and worked in a constantly damp, musty, and wet home. Soaked clothes, humid hammocks, and moldy surroundings became facts of life. The cold, damp decks and the constant stream of humidity above and below deck rendered a mini-weather system where throat infections, colds, pneumonia, and tuberculosis thrived.[22] Sailors tried to offset this constant state of wetness by waterproofing their clothing with tar—the origin of the nickname "tar" for a sailor—and by shedding clothes. Despite their efforts, these measures did little to keep sailors dry and warm. Instead, they lived in an uncomfortable state of wetness, beset by fears that "the conditions," according to prevailing theories of disease, would wreak havoc with their health.[23]

This chronic dampness coupled with the large amounts of food in the holds also made ships ideal breeding grounds for vermin.[24] The most dreaded pests were rats, and they were everywhere. In fact, there were so many rats in a ship that one man marveled that if a flying fish fell on deck, rats would devour it within seconds before he even had a chance to reach for it.[25] Rats munched through books and bedding and regularly bit sailors' hands, arms, and legs while they slept. Rats were not the only pests. Roaches crept into everything from food to beds. One sailor commented that roaches "were fearful in numbers—they are in every place about the vessel."[26] "As to cockroaches," wrote Seaman John Swift, "I have become so used to them that I can go to sleep while they are performing pedestrian tours up my legs & over my body generally." If a man took a drink out of a glass or did not check his food he most certainly would receive a mouthful of roaches before anything else. Sailors routinely complained that their pork and beans should be renamed "roaches and beans" owing to the dominance of pest over pork.[27]

Sometimes, men learned the hard way. One night Landsman Rowland Stafford True awoke and not feeling well took a sip from a cup containing medicine the surgeon had given him. Anxious to get back to sleep, True did not light a match to check his glass. "I swallowed it," True wrote, "but something was in the glass besides syrup." To his horror, the objects in his mouth were moving. As he emptied his mouth, True recoiled: "I spit out about a half a dozen cockroaches."[28]

Bluejackets' disdain for personal cleanliness made matters worse. Their unkempt bodies proved inviting hosts for armies of lice and fleas, which infested hair, clothing, and bedding. "Judging from appearances," wrote Charles Mervine of his mates, "they look as if they never had an introduction to mr. soap and water." "This is an awful dirty hole," groused Seaman Joseph Collins to his mother and father. "It is nothing to see five or six lice drawn up in a line of battle on a fellow's back."[29] "The crew have been Lousy and dyrte," Charles Hart wrote from the Flying Squadron located somewhere off the coast of Cuba. "We have found shirts in the Hammock netting all alive and pantloons walking off on deck."[30] Symmes Browne summed up the awful infestations that the average Union sailor endured aboard ship: "The fact is the boat is actually alive with roaches, and rats, mosquitoes and flies, gnats and bugs, of every description."[31]

As detrimental as the chronic wetness and the vermin were, no factor eroded sailors' overall health like the foul air they inhaled. Edward Everett, famous orator of the nineteenth century, in a speech to raise money for a national home for sailors stricken with poor health, argued that the air below deck ultimately "hurt Jack" the most. In an address delivered before the 1864 National Sailors' Fair in Boston, Everett declared, "A man might as well breathe the air of the black hole of Calcutta as that of a small vessel between decks."[32]

Although vessels varied in the navy, in large sailing vessels on the blockade, sailors ate, slept, and relaxed in the forecastle, located in the front of the ship. The forecastle was below deck and with the cramped space and low ceilings it tended to collect smoke, vapors, and moisture.[33] Seaman George Clark groused, "The odor of bilge water, cooking, tobacco, and bad air, was constantly assailing our nostrils." The air in the forecastle routinely reeked of smoke from burning candles and tobacco, mold, and mildew.[34] Moreover, vapors emanating from the water, tar, and waste products collecting in the ship's bilges — large holding areas in the front of a ship — also tended to filter into the forecastle and into the sailors' berth deck. Worse yet, hydrogen and carbonic acid gases often seeped out of poorly constructed ventilation systems, especially in monitors.[35]

While it is unclear whether there was a direct correlation between the poor air quality and the spread of disease, there appeared to be some detrimental relationship between the air below deck and general sailor health akin to the long-term bodily harm caused by cigarette smoking or air pollution. In short, breathing the dirty air below deck seemed to inflict long-term damage on the health of sailors. Men often developed hacking, persistent coughs.[36] Tars also noticed that as time passed their skin assumed an unhealthy appearance. Although some of the skin changes were caused by an increased exposure to the sun, their skin did not take on a healthy glow. Instead, it developed a wrinkled texture and a yellowish hue that resembled parchment.[37]

Moreover, whatever the actual physical effects rendered by the air they breathed may have been, many sailors came to believe that the air below deck hurt them. After breathing in air that was "so thick with smoke at times we could scarcely see to do our work," young Alvah Hunter plainly called it "bad air."[38] Crew member Samuel Powell believed the combination of all of these debilitating physical factors dogged him years after he left service. "For fourteen years, with scarcely any respite, that sickness, aggravated by the heat, the lifeless air, and the ill-adapted food on ship followed me," Powell wrote, "and has done so at intervals ever since."[39]

One of the most formidable changes that new sailors confronted was a lack of space.[40] Enlistees, even from densely populated, urban areas, had lived their previous lives accustomed to almost complete freedom of movement and open spaces.[41] Now, they not only had to contend with the fixed dimensions of a ship but also with a drastic reduction in personal space. With sixty other sailors, men slept and ate in berthing compartments that were thirty feet long and forty feet wide, and their hammocks measured—even when fully extended—no more than nine-teen inches wide.[42] "Being used heretofore to considerable exercise, in a cool climate," Frederick Clarke of the *Blackhawk* wrote, "and suddenly changing it to a confined position in a hot one, has thrown me into a high fever."[43]

On the outside looking in, ship dimensions seemed ample and space not a problem. The average ship on the blockade was 375 feet long and 20 feet wide. The gunboats in the Mississippi Squadron averaged 175 feet in length and 50 feet in width.[44] Some recruits looking at the size of their ships initially thought they guaranteed plenty of space. Seaman Joseph Osborne remarked to his brother Elias that the *Vandalia*, which was 345 feet long, provided "enough room to walk around and [one] can get tired of walking before night."[45] Nevertheless, the hard truth was that sailors were not truly free to roam their fixed environments.[46] Naval regulations granted little of the available room to ordinary sailors. Sailors were not permitted in the officers' quarters or on the relatively spacious quarter-deck where the officers supervised the operations of the ship. If not at their quarters, on watch, or on work detail, sailors were confined to one of two places—the berth deck or the gun deck.

Sailors faced the issue of space deprivation as soon as they reached their receiving ships. Asa Beetham, a gunner on the Eastern Gulf Block-ading Squadron, complained to his sister that he shared his space with 1,400 men. "Lord only knows where they will put them," he opined. "If they Don't send some of us away to make room for them they will have to sleep standing."[47] Landsman Daniel Kemp wrote that when off duty, their "resting place" provided "little room."[48] On one ship, officers stuffed 400 men into a berthing compartment designed for 160.[49] Space also constricted when cold or stormy weather forced men below deck. Coal Heaver Charles Poole stated that when inclement weather struck, men "huddled together on the Berth Deck with no Room to lay down or sit down and no Room to walk about."[50]

The drastic reduction in living and personal space affected landsmen physically and psychologically. The first effect of restricted space was that many sailors began gaining weight. Men universally mentioned that they had "groan fat," or as one man phrased it, "getting fuller in the face."[51] The more pervasive effects of space reduction were mental. Extended confinement in close conditions increased anxiety, lowered efficiency, and caused manifest depression.[52] Captain Thomas Turner noted that cramped conditions caused his sailors much "suffering in their meals" and in their "space."[53] Seaman Joseph Brigham moaned that "it came pretty hard on me at first being under so much restraint."[54] Boy Alvah Hunter noticed that after ten days of close confinement on the monitor *Nahant*, the crew became "depressed."[55]

This immersion into a watery, dirty, cramped, and mentally challenging environment vividly underscored for recruits the onslaught of adjustments necessary to assimilate into the navy. Physical and psychological adjustments, however, represented only one phase in becoming a sailor. Those men who shipped between 1861 and 1865 also found themselves submerged in a new, singular society: one gender, male; one set of men, sailors; and one society, the ship. There were no women, no social groups, no churches, no other places to eat, and no other places to drink. There were no choices of neighbors or co-workers.[56]

Sailors suffered an almost complete severance from civilized society. Once aboard ship, sailors did not have the opportunity to venture outside the formal and informal organizations of their service and renew contacts with civilian society. Sailors rarely received furloughs or liberties to visit families and friends. When they were in port, they did not get one-day passes to leave the ship to eat and drink at local taverns or attend theaters or churches of their choice.[57] Although this jarred sailors at first, their radical disconnection from society on land was to manifest its most pervasive effects over time.

The entry of new sailors into ship society was not as simple as donning a bluejacket and cap. Among sailors there existed an established hierarchy. Skill, years of experience, and rating established a man's status in this society. As soon as a man enlisted, the commanding officer of the receiving ship examined him to determine skill level. After a few questions, officers garnered a solid idea of a recruit's experience level. Based on the results of the examination, the navy designated for each man a rating, which was the same as a rank in the army. A rating, however, meant much more than a rank since it expressed more than just a slot in the naval pecking order. A sailor's rating denoted his level of experience in sailing ships. From his rating sprung a man's tasks, salary, and social status aboard ship.[58]

Recruits whose answers bore the markings of four or more years of experience enlisted with the rating of able seaman.[59] Able seamen represented the pinnacle of the sailing craft and usually worked in the topmasts of sailing vessels. Technically sound and armed with invaluable experience, able seamen knew how to sail the ship. They reigned supreme in sailor society. One rating below the able seaman stood the ordinary seaman. Ordinary seamen possessed at least two years of ship experience and could do some, but not all, of the duties that able seamen could perform. What skills they had in common with able seamen, they did not do as well.[60] For services rendered to the navy according to their rating, the navy paid able seamen $18 a month and ordinary seamen $14 a month.[61]

Men over seventeen years of age and without experience mustered in as landsmen. Since landsmen enlisted with no skills, they performed most of the menial, labor-intensive tasks aboard ship. Landsmen shouldered the loading and unloading of the supplies and did most of the cleaning.[62] Moreover, since ships required nearly continuous repairing, landsmen expended a great deal of time painting, scraping barnacles, and plugging leaks. While landsmen found the maintenance tasks onerous and boring, they could perform these tasks with little training and supervision.[63] Landsmen received $12 a month.

At the bottom of the sailor ratings were "boys." Usually boys were just that—recruits who enlisted very young. Boys served as apprentices and were to learn the workings of a ship. They performed servantlike tasks aboard ship for officers, such as laundry and cleaning. During combat, they ran black powder from the ship's magazine to the guns, whereby they earned the nickname "powder monkeys." The navy subdivided the rating into first, second, and third class, with corresponding salaries of $10, $9, and $8 a month.[64]

The incorporation of steam machinery also created a new type of sailor, one more mechanically inclined. This new class of sailor served below deck and in the engineering division. The task of these engineering sailors—called firemen and coal heavers—was similar to that of deck hands. Instead of working the sails to propel the ship, coal heavers and firemen worked the steam engines. Firemen supervised the operation of the boilers and controlled the fires in the boilers, which produced the steam that generated power to the engines to propel the ship.[65] They had to know how to manage fires properly, using different types of fuel, and to repair steam machinery with blacksmithing tools.[66]

Coal heavers climbed into cavernous bunkers and heaved mountains of dusty, dirty coal into the boilers. Their jobs were filthy, dangerous, and hot. C. W. Fleyne worried that he regularly breathed air "like that coms from a furnace."[67] Temperatures typically soared above 120 degrees, causing the walls to sweat and the metal to turn so hot that men had to grasp handles, levers, and rungs with canvas mittens or risk searing off the skin of their hands. George Arnold said that his fire room was so hot "you can immagen how a crab would feal in a pot of hot watter."[68]

Ratings also structured the seemingly bizarre patterns of socialization that occurred as seamen and inexperienced sailors intermingled on deck. Before gaining admission into sailor society, novices were compelled by grizzled seamen to undergo certain rites of passage. These rituals marked the stark progression from civilian to sailor. Union sailors, following in the traditions of the sea, wrapped formal and harsh initiation practices around the more difficult transition events. In short, veteran seamen made the assimilation process much harder by subjecting landsmen to a hazing process designed to baptize them into their new society.

The earmarks of the initiation proved unmistakable and the first few days were the worst. As soon as fresh recruits arrived, sailors greeted them with a shower of unwelcome grumblings and unfriendly warnings. Landsman Daniel Kemp recalled that he and his fellow novices were met by catcalls and howls such as "Oh! you fellows will be sorry you ever came here."[69] Boy Alvah Hunter remembered that his first day aboard a monitor started with an old sailor coming up to him and warning, "You'll go to the bottom in her, youngster, there's where you'll all go."[70]

A man's first night below deck undoubtedly proved the most terrifying. As recruits quickly discovered, ships made no room for mattresses. Instead, sailors had to sleep in hammocks that took up little space and effectively minimized the roll and pitch of the ship. Landsman Daniel Kemp was shocked when he gazed on "the plain piece of canvas" that was his new bed.[71] Sleeping in a hammock was a practiced art. They were not easy to get into and, once in, even more difficult to stay in. New sailors routinely spent that first night climbing in then roughly falling out of their hammocks, much to the delight of other sailors.[72] During that first night, landsmen already wrestling with uncooperative hammocks often found themselves tossed out or kicked out by mischievous mates. In order to heighten the terror, more devious tars slashed hammock riggings with their knives as landsmen slept, sending more than one man crashing down from heights as high as five feet. Landsman Hugh Burns remarked that he was "nocked Sencless" by his fall. "When I recovered my head was in Such pain that I dident no where I was."[73]

Older tars also teased and ridiculed new hands relentlessly. Seamen called new recruits "farmers," "hayseeds," "lubberly sons of seacooks," and worse.[74] They mocked their dress, the way they spoke, and the way they ate. The use of a civilian term to describe something nautical—

such as when landsmen called "lines" "ropes" or referred to the starboard and port of the ship as right and left—drew immediate howls.

Playing tricks figured prominently in the breaking-in process. Seaman George Clark marveled that the typical landsman "jumped at every bait that was held out to him."[75] Some sailors spent quite a bit of time, on the counsel of older sailors, looking for "sea stamps" in which to mail their letters home. One favorite trick was to give landsmen a hook and send them on mail buoy watch. Only after a few hours of standing mail watch, coupled with the muffled snickers of older salts, did embarrassed landsmen grasp that the mail came by steamer and not in buoys scattered over the ocean.[76]

Another favorite prank was to announce that a sea-bat or other exotic creature had been captured and caged on deck. As the victim bent over to peer at the creature, his crewmates would bash him in the rear with a broom scaring the man nearly out of his wits. One Dutch landsman made the mistake of telling some of the veteran seamen that he had never seen a skate-fish. That night, while he slept, his berth mates suspended a skate-fish, which was horribly misshapen and ugly, over his hammock. When he awoke, he saw the creature staring him in the face. George Clark recalled the ensuing scene: "With a yell of rage, he grasped the queer fish by the tail, and be-labored every man who came in his way, shouting,—'Who hung the devil over my hammock? Take that, you bean eater; what for you scare me so much?' His anger cooled as his devil wore out, and at last, only the tough tail remained in his hand."[77]

Throughout the taunting, veteran sailors kept a keen eye out for recruits who looked a little green. What they were looking for was any evidence that a new sailor was succumbing to seasickness. Seasickness— or as sailors called it, "heaving of the dog"—represented the first true test for untried sailors. Seasickness was a temporary malady caused by the motion of the ship.[78] Sometimes it struck on the first day, sometimes on the third, but it was always certain to occur. Usually, the first onset of rough seas caused seasickness.[79] As the ship tossed from wave to wave and bobbed up and down men began to feel dizzy. Seaman James Collins likened the awful rolling sensation to being "tossed around like a cradle."[80] Joseph Osborne wrote that he was "not used to bobing up and down on the Sea . . . I tell you it made me disy the first day."[81]

Dizziness soon gave way to nausea. Slight repetitive sounds increased the nausea's intensity. Seaman Israel E. Vail, serving on the *Massachusetts*, recalled being "tortured by the sound of rattling crockery in the wardroom pantry, and the sliding back and forth of chairs."[82] The nausea eventually increased in violence and led men to vomit repeatedly. Landsmen suffered the affliction for a day or two, sometimes three, vomiting usually every half-hour. Charles Poole's bout made him so sick that he begged his crewmates to "throw me overboard."[83] Seasickness among new sailors on the steamer *South Carolina* proved so debilitating that many men wailed "loud and fervently" that "if they got home once more the country could go to the divel."[84] It was not uncommon for so many sailors to be sick at one time that vomit collected in heaps on deck.[85]

Seasickness initiation rites varied. Since new recruits possessed no idea how to end the misery, more seasoned hands laughed and taunted the greenhorns as they staggered around the deck looking for some sort of relief.[86] Some offered remedies they knew would not work or make sick men feel worse. "Chew crackers; drink tea; drink coffee; get drunk; stay in bed; keep walking around; eat a lot; eat a little; don't look up; and don't look down" were standard, empty suggestions.[87] Others tried to make seasick recruits queasier by mentioning various types of disagreeable foods such as pork, molasses, and fat. During widespread bouts of seasickness, the greasiest meals available often made their way to mess tables. The most bitter practice, in the opinion of Seaman John Wirts, was when sailors leaned over to the side of seasick men and disingenuously whispered that "the disease is not dangerous, and that *no one ever been known to die of it.*"[88] Eventually, these green hands learned, with a little help from kinder hands, that drinking warm water or sea water and taking salt water baths often ameliorated the effects of seasickness. Complaining, not eating, and drinking coffee did not.[89]

The onset of seasickness and the rough reactions of sailors, though mean spirited, constituted a critical initiation rite. Older salts considered overcoming seasickness—along with the hazing—the "first principle of seamanship."[90] To endure the taunting of fellow crewmates while seasick, called "gaining one's sea legs," was an important initial step in winning the acceptance of the crew of a ship. Such an ordeal represented a test of manliness. Experienced seamen sought to know how new recruits would hold up under painful and humiliating circumstances. They also wanted to impress on green hands that they could not gain acceptance into the crew and brotherhood of the sea until they had gone through the rough experiences every seaman had to encounter.[91]

As traumatic as these adjustments were, they paled in comparison to the embarrassment, trouble, and sweat expended by recruits in learning both to work like a seaman and to fight like a sailor. The dual nature of sailors' training was what prompted an exasperated Secretary of the Navy Gideon Welles to emphasize the fundamental difference between soldiers and sailors. Faced with a Congress that refused to exempt veteran sailors from conscription, Welles wrote, "While every able and sound man of proper age can be made a soldier and put into immediate service, there are comparatively few of our population who can be employed as sailors."[92]

Sailors were skilled laborers who knew how to work the maze of lines and sails that harnessed the wind to move the ship. While orders concerning ships' maneuvers and actions on deck came from officers, men with years of sailing experience understood instinctively the meaning of every order and the name and function of every piece of equipment aboard ship. More importantly, good sailors possessed an intuitive sense—called a "nautical frame of reference"—that grasped the fragile relationship between their ships and the sea. This frame of reference enabled sailors to know, at all times, the relationship of their ship to wind, sea, and land and the relationship of every place, role, and action within the ship to themselves.[93] Tested sailors could read the sky for weather changes, smell the air for shifts in favorable winds, and interpret wave patterns.[94] They worked well with officers who used their judgments to navigate the ship. Much of this was born of experience. It was also difficult to teach.

Since most recruits shipped as landsmen, they had much to learn. Because Union officers used steam only as auxiliary power, most sailors received a traditional education in wooden ship sailing. The first instruction men received was learning the names, functions, and locations of hundreds of lines located throughout the ship. "Marlinespike seamanship"—the art of knowing how to knot, splice, seize, and rig lines—consumed a large part of their early education.[95] New sailors spent hours tying and untying lines and knots bearing such mysterious names as "Turk's Head" and "Half-Hitch."[96]

Once men grasped a working familiarity with lines, they used that knowledge in learning the technicalities of working the sails—the primary skill of top seamen. Sailors spent hours making, taking-in, reefing, and furling sails. By reading the wind and changing the position of the ship's sails to catch it, sailors moved the ship.[97] A sailor's educational process also included tying vessels to docks, lowering and raising small boats for ingress and egress, and acquiring a working knowledge of tackle, purchase, and anchoring.

New sailors typically stood in awe and completely lost amid the over-whelming sight of men engaging lines, sails, spars, and wood. Sails flapped, lines were tied and untied, and men scurried up and down rope ladders as if they were born on them.[98] Inexperienced sailors re-marked that at first glance a ship looked like a "labyrinth of ropes & cordage."[99] The obvious degree of technical education staggered re-cruits as they watched the few seasoned tars weave and bob through a maze of cords, ropes, and sails with effortless precision, grace, and strength at dizzying heights. Recruits observed that some men bounded down ladders and climbed masts that made them dizzy just looking at them. "You look up at tall masts, and down the hatchway into the dark hold," wrote one cowed recruit, "and feel as if you don't want to climb any just yet, & had little rather not go down it the hold, at present."[100]

Although many recruits had seen old salts amble on land, most had never seen them at work. Young Charles Post wrote that one seaman named "Wash" seemed "to take a delight in mystifying me by the mirac-ulous way in which he twists a rope about and finally evolves a stupen-dous snarl, which he calls by a stupendous name."[101] Seasoned sailors sputtered their own argot and exhibited a rhythm all their own as their language and bodies instinctively responded to the needs of the ship. They endured the dizzy rushes aloft and latched onto every mast and line as if "every finger was a fish-hook."[102] One landsman described the spectacle: "Your eyes and ears are greeted with a string of technicalities which would puzzle St. Paul, & your eyes that *Jack* (rough as he looks), does seem to understand his own language. Spry as a 'cat,' tough as a 'rhinocerous,' versatile as a 'monkey,' he manages to attain heights, as-sumes postures, throws himself into attitudes, & does things generally, which you never before *reflected upon*, even though you may have seen them laid down in the book."[103]

Sailor training proved awkward and demeaning. Novice sailors often suffered a constant barrage of yelling and corrections from officers and the few seasoned salts. Officers seemed to think that the best way to school their charges was to scream at them mercilessly. "The Officers, bawl at the sailors, as if they were all deaf, & had done something wrong," wrote one man.[104] Officers admitted using such tactics. Lieu-tenant Cornelius Schoonmaker of the *Minnesota* wrote to his brother that "it was uphill work at first, but I blustered around them giving them no rest until I had things my own way."[105] Many officers screamed at new sailors not only to address shortcomings but also to break their spirits. Many officers believed that sailors would never obey orders unless their spirits were broken.[106]

Former soldiers experienced tremendous difficulties under naval training. Contrary to their expectations, the ordeal proved tougher than army training. Soldiers rebelled at humiliation handed out by officers, and many petitioned to return to the army. Landsman Cosam T. Bartlett, who had left the army for sailoring, regretted to a friend that "a sailor's life is a hard one in every sense of the term." Nimrod B. McPherson, a soldier from Company A of the 101st Illinois Volunteers, begged General Ulysses S. Grant to relieve him and his company from further naval service. "Every man of the Company," McPherson wrote to Grant, "is dissatisfied at the treatment received at the hands of Naval officers."[107]

Part of the frustration over their treatment stemmed from the underlying presumption held by officers and old tars alike that unskilled sailors could do nothing right. Landsmen received constant criticism about the quality of their work, even if it was something as small as the manner in which it was done. Seaman Bartholomew Diggins grumbled that he could not stand the way new sailors worked. To his dismay, faced with "so much work," he wrote, "the newer hands thought it all natureal and work on cheerfully."[108] "A Boy or landsman was always in the wrong on errors," piped Seaman Charles Alexander Schetky.[109] In *Two Years before the Mast*, Richard Henry Dana summed up what many Union landsmen likely felt as they spent their first few days aboard ship. "There is not so helpless and pitiable an object in the world," Dana wrote, "as a landsman beginning a sailor's life."[110]

Union landsmen did little to hide their shortcomings. The navy expected green recruits to exhibit a number of basic qualities inherent in "good sailors," namely, promptness, intelligence, quickness, attentiveness to duties, and respectfulness to officers.[111] Instead, many recruits showed slowness, dullness, and disrespect. They proved slow at grasping orders and in accomplishing basic sailing tasks such as tacking, climbing masts, and reaching their stations.[112] As was to be expected, landsmen spent a great deal of time fumbling with their hands and tripping over their feet. Many lacked what one officer politely termed "an active turn of mind" necessary to discharge the duties of their ratings.[113] One officer simply called his men "idiots." Commander Charles Green, after surveying his sailors on the *Jamestown*, remarked, "The crew are the most ignorant set of men I have ever seen on board ship."[114]

Fellow sailors concurred with the assessments of their superiors.

Seaman Harry Browne, trying to convince his brother Symmes that a lack of experience and skill was no impediment to joining the navy, wrote, "If you are ignorant, it is nothing more than is the case with everyone."[115] George Clark stated that the average Union landsman was "lost in amazement at everything he saw and heard."[116] "The great majority of the crew," groaned Seaman John Brogan, "could go no higher than our hammock nettings." The landsmen on Seaman Tim Finn's ship proved so error-prone that even the salty veteran was moved to pity. "Poor devils of landsmen," he observed, "could not get into their hammocks and they could not lay on deck very long or they would get Drowned. . . . I pitied them though there was many Laughable Scenes."[117]

Some of the scenes that took place would have been comical if landsmen's lives had not been made so miserable by the experience. A landsman on the *Kearsarge*, serving on lookout, had difficulty counting and spotting sails. One night, he spotted some objects in the water and called out, "There is two sails in sight." "Can you make them out[?]" cried the boatswain. "One I can see and the other I cant," the confused sailor replied to the supreme irritation of the boatswain.[118] Watching one landsman fumble around in the topmast, a patience-exhausted officer exploded with a barrage of criticism. The boatswain, a petty officer who functioned as the foreman of the crew, dryly commented to the officer, "That's a farmer up there, sir; he don't know that he's on the crosstrees, say *haymow* and he'll jump overboard."[119] Captain Charles Davis marveled at the lack of sense shown by some recruits: "A man was killed in the mortar fleet this morning in a curious way. He had a cylinder of loose powder over his shoulder and a lighted cigar in his mouth. His head was blown off. These mortar men are said to be very careless."[120]

On strictly a performance level, officers routinely complained that Union sailors were, for the most part, "inefficient."[121] A number of factors inhibited sailor training and efficiency. First, recruiting officers and unscrupulous agents often rated landsmen as seamen in order to fill seamen quotas in crews. Officer Richard Worsam Meade III railed that unskilled landsmen, "incompetent to perform the duties of the rating," routinely filled skilled positions of seamen and firemen.[122] Second, prevailing naval guidelines recommended that, in order for a sailing vessel to function efficiently and safely, the crew contain no less than 25 percent able seamen and 25 percent ordinary seamen.[123] On average, Union crews featured about 80 percent landsmen and less than 20 percent seamen.[124] Officers and veteran seamen were likely overwhelmed by the sheer numbers of landsmen coming aboard ships at the same time. Such an intense concentration of inexperience probably affected the efficiency of all sailors and clouded the overall perception of the efficiency of landsmen.

Third, conventional wisdom held that no less than four years of service and training were necessary to transform civilians into able seamen. Unfortunately, the shortage of seamen coupled with the need to place as many vessels as quickly as possible into service meant that most sailors did not receive extensive training. Officers often gave their new sailors only days to become familiar with their new tasks.[125] Although the learning atmosphere differed from ship to ship, most men only received what can best be described as on-the-job training.[126]

As a result, most sailors learned by watching and doing. Henry Browne wrote that most crew members on his boat "have to pick up gradually as we see."[127] Samuel Powell stated that he learned by "watching others a few times till I saw just the thing to do, the next opportunity was taken of trying the awful thing."[128] Another sailor described the landsmen training process as follows: "You stay where you are, & keep your eyes and ears open, and very likely your mouth too."[129]

Lastly, veteran seamen did not willingly assist landsmen in their education. Overall, their demeanor cowed new recruits. They confidently and silently ambled around deck.[130] "One could easily recognize the thorough-bred seaman," observed George Clark; "he was quiet and wary of everybody."[131] Hard-bitten, underpaid, and unwilling to give away the only wealth they possessed—their experience and know-how—topmen and sheetmen purposely excluded newcomers from the learning process.[132] Although the unwillingness of veteran sailors to assist novices functioned as another fundamental rite of passage from civilian to sailor, many seamen also felt that landsmen should learn the ropes the hard way, just as they did. Suspicious, unhappy, and mean-spirited, they enjoyed the sight of seeing nervous and lost greenhorns fumble with sails, lines, and knots.[133]

Officers, too, contributed greatly to novice sailors' difficulties. Experience levels among petty and commissioned officers ran thin on the blockade and on the rivers.[134] The practical problem was that if an officer was unsure of how to run a ship, he was of little use in teaching novices how to sail. With landsmen overrunning most crews, the navy needed lots of teachers. Instead, the navy featured nonsailors serving as seamen learning—by making mistakes—from officers giving incorrect orders because they did not know what they were doing. With the trained sailors unwilling to help and some of the officers wanting in technical expertise, it was no wonder that many landsmen had difficulty learning the skills necessary to function as effective sailors.

Because Civil War naval service did not require a great deal of open sea sailing, the lack of experience among Union sailors hindered, but did not cripple, naval operations.[135] What ultimately bridged the experience gap were the efforts of officers who swallowed their pride and tapped the only reliable source of seamanship available: the small but highly skilled bloc of recruits who enlisted with experience.[136] Both career and volunteer officers realized that in order to train so many apprentice sailors they had to maximize the precious amount of available talent. Green officers admitted that they often barked out meaningless orders to knowledgeable sailors and then followed them around to watch how they carried out the orders. New officer Edmund Ellis explained to his mother how he learned his job from experienced sailors: "I told the sailor the best I knew how; To reef the jib-boom spanker *she-bang*. He said he didn't know what that was! (nor wonder) Well then says I, go on the Hurricane deck and fix whatever you find wrong up there. He said the spanker-rang was too slack. I followed him up to see what it was, and this is the way I have to learn everything, give my orders as I get and then follow up and see what they do."[137]

Experienced sailors, fully aware they were being used, complained continuously about ill-trained and poor sailing officers. William Van Cleaf growled that his executive officer "dont know what a davit is nor the starbord from the port side of the ship."[138] After being ordered to heave anchor twelve times in one day, Seaman Freeman Foster fumed, "There is considerable talk among the men about the officers."[139] George Clark howled that "I have never seen officers of the Navy, choice young upstarts, who did not know how many ropes there were in a ship, who could not draw up a day's work, keep a log, or steer a ship."[140]

What eventually emerged was an unspoken arrangement between officers and sailors: in exchange for giving lessons in seamanship, the few experienced sailors aboard were granted by the officers a wide berth with regard to their on-deck duties. Seamen focused their energies on the highly technical needs of the ship while the landsmen did most, if not all, of the menial labor.[141] Officers had little choice. The older salts were critical in the first stages of the war in exhibiting seamanship for landsmen and untested officers.[142] Seaman James B. Collins described this forced accommodation: "We have got the run of the officers so that we manage to keep out of their way . . . and the officers have got so now they pass by us and start others to work cleaning decks etc. while we stand bye calmly observing how nicely they do it."[143]

Even with the contributions of seasoned sailors, the navy still had to turn most of its recruits into sailors. To make sailors out of civilians, the navy immersed recruits into an atmosphere of rigid routine, continuous drill, and harsh discipline. Officers assigned each sailor to one of five divisions: master, engineering, powder, gun, or surgeon. Within the respective responsibilities assigned to their division, all phases of Union sailors' lives were tightly scheduled. These activities were also arranged so that each task rolled into the next without break. Boy Charles Mervine sighed that a sailor's life was nothing but "regulated." "Its original outlines are the same day after day."[144]

The daily schedules of sailors were consistent throughout the navy. Crews' days began early, usually between 4:00 to 5:30 A.M., with the shrill pipings of the boatswain's whistle rousing men from their hammocks. This rude awakening was also accompanied by hoarse shouts of "turn out" and "all hands, tumble out, lash and carry." Sleepy sailors tumbled out of their hammocks, washed themselves out of a bucket, bundled their clothes, and swore busily as they filed out of the berth deck. Officers expected sailors to rise, dress, and stow their hammocks within eleven minutes. More exacting officers demanded this exercise be done in seven minutes.[145]

After rising, sailors cleaned the ship. Cleaning was one of the most dreaded parts of a sailor's day. In a 24-hour period, men walking, spitting, and working created quite a bit of debris on deck. Cleaning, sometimes called "swabbing the deck," found men scrubbing the dirt, garbage, and coal dust out of decks using mops and salt water. The most tedious part of cleaning was a process called "holystoning." Holystoning consisted of sailors dragging large flat stones or wooden blocks tied to ropes back and forth across the deck to punish dirt and grime out of planks.[146] Its name came from the Royal Navy, where it was said that English tars often used pieces of semisoft stone broken from church monuments to clean their decks.[147] The method proved effective but was extremely hard and boring work. Union sailors hated the exercise and tall swearing usually accompanied the task.[148]

Ship cleaning preceded breakfast, which occurred between 6:00 and 8:00 A.M. Breakfast featured men choking down coffee, usually weak, and hard biscuits, always stale.[149] Cosam Bartlett wrote that the biscuits ran so stale that even with "a strong knife you can cut it about as easily

*"Holystoning the Deck": Every morning sailors pulled a block of wood attached to ropes back and forth across the deck as part of their cleaning duties. The process was called "holystoning." Harry Simmons Sketchbook, courtesy of W. L. Clements Library, University of Michigan.*

as you could seasoned oak."[150] As bad as breakfast was, on most days meals were sailors' only bright spots. Charles Nordhoff believed only breakfast helped him make it through cleaning. "If you will rise at six, get a thorough wash, and walk the poop-deck in your shirt-sleeves till eight, you will find that breakfast is also an event."[151] As one sailor summarized, "When breakfast's done, the next thing I look forward to is dinner, and when that's done, I look for supper time."[152]

Meals proved so important for Yankee sailors that the men who ate together quickly formed the most important social unit in their lives. Removed from families, friends, women, and other social organizations available on land, sailors looked to their companions to fill the void. Although they had been plunged into an instant society aboard ship, the hierarchy among sailors coupled with the large number of strangers inhibited immediate cohesion. As a result, the custom of preparing and eating meals within small groups, called the "mess," assumed a vital importance in sailors' lives.

A mess consisted of five or six sailors on the Western rivers to ten to twenty sailors on the blockade. Mess members usually held the same rating and worked the same watch schedule. The men shared a common mess chest, a small tub called a "kid," which contained their plates, spoons, and forks. Mess mates cooked their meals under the supervision of a trained cook and ate all of their meals together.[153] The meals were placed on a mess cloth, which was usually nothing more than a tarred piece of canvas laid between two guns or on chests on the berth deck. Although the mess chest contained forks and spoons, sailors typically used their own knives to cut and eat their food. Mealtime conversations proved brisk and bawdy.[154]

In their messes, sailors told their troubles and related jokes. Mess mates were there, whether they wanted to be or not, in the good times and the bad. It was a man's mess mates who were to help him when he fell into trouble. In fact, naval rules stated that when a sailor became drunk, his mess mates, not officers, "were to take charge of him."[155] When a sailor died, it was his mess mates who prepared his body for burial, built his casket, and commended his body to the sea. The mess became for all intents and purposes a sailor's family aboard ship. Coal Heaver Charles Poole called his time with his mess mates "the most important hour in the day."[156]

Some of the worst hours sailors spent were during inspection. Every day, after breakfast and before the noon meal, crew members assembled in rigid lines on the quarter-deck for inspection.[157] Naval regulations required that crews be "strictly clean."[158] This required that men bathe daily and brush their teeth, new experiences for most. Seaman Frederic Sherman complained to his mother after he joined: "Send me tooth brush they make us keep clean hear."[159] The presence of a dirty sailor provided officers with the opportunity not only to instill the importance of personal hygiene but also to reinforce the repercussions of ignoring the navy's system. If inspection revealed a sailor with dirty hands, unkempt hair, or general slovenliness, he was dragged out of line and roughly stripped. Five or six of his crewmates then proceeded to scrub him with soap, sand, hickory brooms, and brushes. The spectacle, as intended, left a vivid impression on the reluctant bather as well as on the rest of the crew. "It wasn't often a man needed a second scrubbing," remarked Landsman Rowland True.[160]

A sailor's dinner, around noon, constituted his largest meal of the day and featured heavier foods such as salted beef or pork, beans, rice, bread, pudding, and pickles.[161] Dinner also separated morning from afternoon drill, which varied depending on the day of the week. Drill represented the heart and soul of sailor training. Drill developed teamwork and unity of action so that every sailor knew his station and what needed to be done at that position. Drills nurtured quickness, agility, and reflexes.[162] They also taught sailors to perform designated tasks

*"All Hands Up Anchor": One drill that required teamwork was raising the anchor. Sailors had to respond to the boatswain's whistle to "All hands, up anchor" with teamwork and precision. Charles E. Stedman Sketchbook, courtesy of the Boston Athenaeum.*

with crushing sameness, no matter what their intellectual level. Each sailor had a station for every drill and either played an active part or stood at his station waiting to be assigned in relief.

Basic drills consisted of general quarters, fire drills, rescue drills, man overboard, and abandon ship.[163] Sailors also practiced a number of specific operational and combat exercises during the week. On Mondays, crews practiced lowering, raising, and rowing the small boats used to enter and exit the ship and target practice with the ship's big guns.[164] Tuesdays meant small arms drill using rifles and pistols. Thursdays and Fridays usually focused on fire drills. On the coast, officers routinely ordered general quarters drills in order to increase response times to blockade runner chases. In the river squadrons, officers concentrated on repelling boarders and quelling fires. Officers practiced

*"Small Arms Drill": Sailors had to learn to use both pistols and rifles as part of their training. This was to ensure the efficacy of small arms fire from the ship during close naval combat and the boarding of hostile vessels. Harry Simmons Sketchbook, courtesy of W. L. Clements Library, University of Michigan.*

these general drills at specified times but often called them during meals or in the middle of the night. Nighttime and mealtime drills functioned to keep sailors on edge and always mentally ready. Captains monitored the readiness of their crews by clocking and comparing response times.[165]

General quarters—also called "battle stations"—was the most practiced and important drill.[166] This exercise required that sailors drop whatever they were doing, prepare the vessel for battle, and run to their assigned spot in the ship as if under attack. Once sailors reached their stations, they practiced fighting and shooting the ships' guns. Proficiency in loading and firing the large caliber cannon—called "great guns" by sailors—represented the single most important combat skill sailors could develop. Some crews exposed to daily drill at general quarters became expert gunners. Surgeon Samuel Boyer marveled at the improvements wrought by continuous drill. "Some shots were splendid."[167]

General quarters started with the roll of the drum. Well-trained crews could wake, lash and stow hammocks, and be assembled at battle stations within ten minutes.[168] There was much to do in that ten min-

*Sailors and officers at "battle" or "action" stations aboard the USS* Kearsarge.
*Sailors sometimes had to stand at their stations for hours until the "All clear"*
*signal was given. Courtesy of the U.S. Naval Historical Center.*

utes. To be ready at general quarters meant that sailors had to unstow
side arms, boarding hatchets, revolvers, and cutlasses and cut loose the
heavy guns. Tarps had to be placed over all the hatches. Sailors had to
open the powder magazine and begin relaying shells and gun powder
to the gun deck in canvas bags and boxes, and then return to their stations.[169]

Although some sailors grumbled at the exercise, the gun and combat
drills could prove quite exhilarating. Creative officers sometimes took
guns ashore and fired shots near the vessel so the ship and crew could
"pretend to be under attack."[170] Officers barked out such orders as "pass
and load," "run her home," and "run out the starboard gun and fire!" In
response, sailors worked the guns, trained, loaded, and mimicked fire.
One sailor described the spectacle: "The second hand scarcely sweeps
over a quarter hour of its dial before the men have crowded around the

*"The Eleven Inch Gun": The most important combat skill a sailor could acquire was the proper use of the ship's big guns. Sailors drilled at the big guns constantly. Charles E. Stedman Sketchbook, courtesy of the Boston Athenaeum.*

port bulwarks, and are slashing the air with a most Quixotic fury—then crouch on bent knee, to make ready their pistols."[171]

General drill readiness varied from ship to ship. Finely tuned crews, like the one on the *Fort Hindman*, could close every porthole, unravel every fire hose, unstow every smothering blanket and fire ax, and ready every boat for abandoning ship, all components of a successful fire drill, in twenty-three seconds. The crew moved so fast during one drill for Rear Admiral David D. Porter that he did not have time to get out of the way of the spouting fire hoses and to the amusement of the crew became "somewhat wet."[172]

Union sailors hated drill and it showed.[173] "Few of them had ever been in the Navy before," Bartholomew Diggins observed, "and needed much drilling and instruction to fitt them for their several stations."[174]

*"Drilling at the Mortar": One of the most dreaded types of duty for a sailor was mortar boat duty. The mortars let loose a ferocious recoil that pushed the boat below the waterline and made such noise as to deafen many men.*
*Harry Simmons Sketchbook, courtesy of W. L. Clements Library,*
*University of Michigan.*

Charles Poole observed that his crewmates routinely did so poorly during drills that they often had to stand at stations two-and-a-half to three hours while the captain inspected "to see if they knew where their respective places was and if they knew what they had to do in action." William Wainwright commented that during a usual general quarters drill at least half of the crew had no idea what to do. "Some had lost a boot others couldnt find their cap and there was running hither and tither."[175] Samuel Powell, a sailor on the Gulf Blockading Squadron, concluded that "Jack has such a contempt for drill he will never perfect himself in its minutiae." "So the despised 'sojer,' if thoroughly drilled, can always beat him in quickness—the very point on which he plumes himself."[176]

While sailors hated drill, it schooled into the collective psyches of a set of strongly autonomous men the importance of order and the legitimacy of the naval authority structure. In addition, repetitive drill proved the most effective way for unskilled recruits to learn to work and fight as sailors.[177] Despite the rush of physical, psychological, and social accommodations, through drill and naval routine, landsmen inched closer to becoming sailors. They adjusted to the motion of the ship.[178] Their physiologies made allowances for the foul air and rampant disease that ensued from throwing men together into a cramped, dirty, and vermin-ridden place.[179] Men began regularly washing, brushing their teeth, and grooming their hair in short crops.[180] Their feet callused, their skins tanned, and their lungs coarsened. They slowly began grasping some of the basics of seamanship or at least learned to move across decks and up and down masts without getting dizzy.

Novice sailors also slowly began to talk and think like sailors. Men began tossing about terse, precise, analogy-ridden, technical terms, laced with profanity, in their everyday speech. Recruits who just a few weeks ago used to "get up and make their beds" now "heaved out and triced up." Instead of "passing gossip" sailors exchanged "scuttlebutt." Left became "port," and right became "starboard."[181]

Clipped acknowledgments recorded the metamorphosis. Seaman Charles Alexander proudly recalled that he had become an "expert in swift dodging."[182] James Glazier admitted to his girlfriend that "I am used to the graceful motion of the ship."[183] Men often acknowledged that they felt a "sea change" within themselves, whether they were on a ship at sea or on a river gunboat.[184] Coal Heaver George Arnold wrote to his brother, "I am altred boy from what I was once." Ed Goble, serving on the *A. O. Tyler*, confidently wrote to his uncle that after all the drilling and discipline, he felt "much like a sailor."[185] For better or worse, the navy had made an imprint on the thousands of recruits who joined the sea service. As the blockade dragged on and the river war became ugly, how deep of a mark remained to be seen.

# 3

## Ships of Fools
## The Sailor's Experience
## on the Union Blockade

The majority of men who shipped into the United States Navy during the Civil War served on the blockade of the Confederacy, a 3,800-mile cordon arching from Cape Charles in Virginia to the mouth of the Rio Grande in Texas.[1] Although many had enlisted to serve on the blockade under the promise of spine-tingling chases of blockade runners and unlimited prize money, what sailors failed to realize was that the blockade was not traditional sea service. Instead of action and travel, sailors languished on ships, for months at a time, at fixed points in sweltering heat watching and waiting for blockade runners to make dashes out to the open sea. Like typical sailors, Union Jacks suffered societal isolation, unhealthy living conditions, and the tedium of ship routine. Unfortunately, blockade service was anything but typical. Rather than a few weeks, blockade sailors suffered months and sometimes years of stark isolation and crushing monotony. Over the long term, for sailors, the blockade deteriorated into a war of nerves and voyages of endurance.

At the outset, the blockade service did not appear particularly onerous and—with the promise of prize money—even potentially lucrative.[2] The average blockade sailor did not have to travel very far from shore or navigate treacherous open seas. Once they reached their assigned vessels, sailors could expect to venture no more than six to nine miles from land. Moreover, the service did not involve the degree of peril that attended traditional naval battles or Civil War military campaigns. Since the blockade's policy was to catch—not destroy—pitched battles and sailor casualties proved rare. All the navy asked of blockade sailors was their exertion in sighting and seizing blockade runners leaving and entering Confederate ports.

The devil, of course, was in the details, and it was the details that made the blockade so slyly miserable. The first detail was that the block-ade was nearly round-the-clock service and much of it at night, owing to the reality that it was easier for runners to slip the blockade under cover of darkness. Yeoman Isaac Bradbury observed that only blockade sailors possessed the unique ability to "turn night into day."[3] Practically, this meant that no sooner had sailors finished their daily chores and drills, tapped out their last pipe, and spun their last yarn, they were called back to work. As a result, although sailors were piped to their hammocks around 8:00 P.M. every night, they rarely slept long. Every time a runner or unidentified ship was spotted, sailors were roused from their hammocks and ran to their stations to begin preparations for a chase.

The around-the-clock nature of blockade service caught most men by surprise. Sailors complained that they spent their nights in "a state of constant watchfulness."[4] Seaman Frederic Sherman was amazed at the nocturnal nature of his schedule. He wrote to his mother that his routine consisted of working all day and then being on duty eight hours each night.[5] An exasperated James Collins wrote to his mother and father that the blockade's travails kept him and his brother John at "work all day" and on "watch at night."[6] Edward Saltonstall groused in April 1862 that because of the nightly alarms, "I havn't had all my clothes off but once since I left New York Oct 16th."[7] One sailor wrote to Dr. Wil-liam F. Thoms, who headed a sailor benevolent society in New York, that he had to work "all the time and had no time to get any rest." "For three days and nights," the sailor wrote, "I did not close my eyes."[8]

Although scanning the broad expanse of ocean or the narrow inlets for small ships proved difficult, it was nothing compared to trying to do so in the dark. Except on moonlit nights, blackness enveloped the seascape and shut out the shoreline. Sailors complained that nighttime duty on the blockade was essentially "blind work" because it turned out to be almost impossible to see objects on the water. Even on clear nights, Charles Post wrote to his father, "you can see about 50 yards on each side of the ship."[9] Moreover, it proved nearly impossible for Union sail-ors to see and hear even friendly ships since Union vessels effectively cloaked their location by closing all hatches, extinguishing all lights, and refraining from talking, making noise, and smoking below deck.[10]

The problem for sleepy sailors was that when peering into such dark-ness everything looked menacing. The combination of night blindness, sleepiness, and tiredness from the day's work bred in blockade sailors a state approximating paranoia. Nightly, fatigued lookouts screamed,

"Sail, ho!" to every unidentified object they saw on the water.[11] More often than not, sailors proved to be their own worst enemies as most of these alarms turned out to be false. Sometimes, it was a foreign vessel straying too close to the blockade cordon. In other instances, it was a nearby friendly ship. Other times, Union sailors sounded the alarm over and over, not realizing they were looking at the same ships sighted hours before.

Sailors hated these false starts because they made them work all night and robbed them of sleep. During especially active periods, blockade sailors often raced to battle stations three to four times a night in reaction to alarms. Nearly every ship's log was filled with nightly accounts of "strangers" and false alarms.[12] The problem was that after being called to stations crews had to stand at the ready for two to three hours until the senior officers pronounced the situation safe.[13]

The results were often comical. Francis B. Butts recalled that one midnight, the lookout aboard the *Flag* noticed a floating object bearing down on the ship. Sailors groggily racing up from the berth deck heard the boatswain scream, "Back her, back her for God's sake back her; she is right under our bows." Fearing that a torpedo was about to detonate, sailors hit the deck fully expecting to take, as one sailor said, their "next breath among the stars." As the ship backed its engines, it let loose a shot that sliced the dreaded torpedo in two. Sailors listened but heard no explosion. As the relieved sailors took a closer look at their vanquished enemy, embarrassment soon replaced their fear as a mass of severed seaweed mockingly floated by.[14]

False or not, the drill for blockade sailors was always the same. Within minutes of the "making of a strange sail"—the term used by sailors when they sighted an unidentified vessel—sailors fled their hammocks, stumbled through dark decks to their quarters, and prepared for action. Seaman Augustus Van Gieson wrote to his sister that each night "everybody must get to their places on the guns or wherever they are stationed."[15] Sailors slipped anchor cables, latched onto their guns, and pushed the ship's engines to full steam waiting to see whether friend or foe approached.[16]

Not surprisingly, crews often had trouble slipping the chain and anchor in the dark. Hammers were misplaced and the pins in the anchor's chain often stubbornly fought back. Sailors howled as their unknown quarry gained valuable time. "Confound the chain! will it never unshackle?" sailors swore as they struggled to get the ship moving.[17] It was all "rather confusing," said one man.[18]

Sailors scrambled to general quarters not knowing what to expect. As they hit the gun deck, they often saw sudden flashes of rockets and signal lights from other blockaders. This "single white defining light" presented the only fleeting glimpse men received on the way to their stations. Men feared in those first few moments a number of possibilities, most of them bad. Sailors' imaginations ran wild in the brief period of suspense and wonder. Paymaster William Keeler memorialized the fears of the sailors jabbering around the *Florida* as they raced to their stations. Blockade sailors fretted aloud: "Is she a friend? Will she answer our challenge? Or is she a foe ready to sweep our decks with grape & cannister as soon as she can make us out? Or is she an unarmed blockade runner anxious only to escape the vigilance of our cruisers?" [19] The first few moments of an alarm constituted the most dangerous time for sailors aboard a blockader.[20] After the cry of "Sail ho!" all eyes fixed their sights on the response to the quarter master's query, "Where away?" Once they fixed on the general location of the intruder, gun crews readied the appropriate batteries of the ship. If the lookout determined the vessel off the starboard beam, sailors manned and loaded the starboard batteries. In the open waters around the blockade, crews challenged the approach of an unknown vessel with the burning of a clear red light followed immediately by a quick white flash. The failure to return the proper response signal—four crisp flashes of white light—usually brought an immediate response from gunboat cruisers.[21] Sometimes, even if the proper signal was returned, a sister ship failed to see the signal causing it to open its guns on a friendly vessel.[22] Yeoman Isaac Bradbury said that it was not uncommon for blockaders to shoot at each other at night. If a signal was "not answered immediately," Bradbury wrote, "crash goes a shell through us." [23]

The proliferation of alarms caused other problems. When ships weighed anchor at night to sniff out a runner or change positions, they frequently lost their place in line. Even though crews signaled other vessels when they became lost or disoriented, often ships had drifted so far out of line that their location signals went unseen. Ships also veered too close to other blockaders and caused accidents. In fact, collisions with other ships at night proved relatively commonplace.[24]

Seaman James Collins recounted to his mother and father that one night the night watch thought their ship had fallen out of position. The crew set off the customary signal lights but received no answer. They presumed they were four miles from the shore. When morning came, the sailors awoke in horror to find their ship resting under the gun barrels of a Confederate battery. Collins estimated they were not more than a "pistol shot" from the fort. Seeing this, the crew nearly panicked. The captain, in little better shape, rushed onto the quarter-deck, half dressed, giving rapid orders to back the ship out of gun range before the men in the fort woke up. The crew, scared out of their wits, succeeded in backing the ship out in ten minutes when the task should have taken them a half an hour.[25]

Not all alarms were false. After many trials and errors, sailors honed their sighting skills by learning the conditions that helped to predict legitimate runs. First, blockade runners usually attempted to give Union vessels the slip at twilight where the setting sun tended to blur the horizon. Second, blockade runners avoided moonlit nights. Instead, the onset of moonless and cloudy nights encouraged blockade running since the absence of nighttime light further paralyzed Union sailors' ability to see.[26] Third, fog and heavy drizzle often precipitated runs by rebel cruisers through the blockade. Fourth, sailors also noticed that when a blockade runner lurked, partisans on shore lit fires on the beaches to guide the vessel to safety.[27]

The most important lesson learned by sailors was that it was often easier to hear rather than see runners.[28] Sailors came to appreciate that, oddly enough, if they could see an object clearly, it was probably not a runner. As a result, once conditions appeared favorable for a run, instead of looking, blockade sailors began listening for runners.[29] They often initiated a chase based solely on sound.[30] Crews listened in the night winds for the sounds of paddle wheels splashing in the distance. Next, they strained for the sound of a steam whistle, even if ever so faint. After they ascertained the general area from which a sound was coming, crews often sped off in search of a runner not knowing which way to turn or which way to chase.

If visual confirmation was made, pulse-pounding chases ensued. Owing to the speed of blockade runners, officers and seamen had to make split-second decisions as to the direction and course of their vessels. Crews tried to maneuver their ships as quickly as possible into firing range in order to discourage the vessel from fleeing. For the most part, Union blockade vessels proved slower than the sleek, steam-driven runners.[31] Whenever possible, Union sailors used the coast as an ally by trying to trap runners between the coast and the warship. By angling runners along the coast, slower Union ships hoped to compensate for a lack of speed by trapping the runners in shallow waters or disabling them on the shoals.[32]

The confrontations between Union blockaders and blockade runners consisted of flat-out sea chases. The longer chases extended from ten to twenty nautical miles and hours on end.[33] For Union sailors, pursuing a blockade runner was the single most exciting experience in the navy. Men dashed from one side of the ship to the other listening and looking. Sailors tripped over each other trying to make their way in the dark, all the while receiving orders from officers and chattering instructions to their mates. Shots flew in all directions at both blockade runners and friendly ships. During longer chases, gun crews often leveled over 100 shots at a single blockade runner.[34]

Sometimes, in order to pick up additional speed, officers ordered crews to toss overboard heavy objects such as coal and sandbags. In the middle of a chase, deck sailors took down yards, masts, and anything else that slowed ship speed.[35] Below deck, coal heavers and firemen threw shovelful after shovelful of black dust, hyped by oil, grease, and pitch, into furnaces in order to bring the ship to full steam as quickly as possible.[36] Charles Post recalled that during one such chase the increase in steam made the ship so hot "suspicious little spots of red" began to show in the ship's iron where it was "heated red hot by the solid flames" leaping from the boilers. "The ship was trembling from stem to stern," Post wrote, with the men "working like demons."[37]

Seasoned sailors could discern the distance between their ship and a runner and could formulate quick estimations on how fast they had to perform countermeasures in order to catch up. The measuring of these actions in time and distance, called "intervals" by sailors, often confirmed the frustrating distance between blockader and blockade runner. Sailors continuously evaluated the effects of their efforts to bridge the distance. They groaned when the ship, yawing to fire, lost distance.[38] The typical chase, as described by Joseph Canning, consisted of "all officers on deck all the crew and all looking for a Blockade Runner—all talking—all ordering and all quite daft and crazy."[39]

Until 1865, the typical chase ended in failure. One sailor lamented to his mates, "If disappointments make philosophers, we ought to rank with Diogenes."[40] Based on the huge number of blockade evasions and disappointments, Union sailors should have become earnest philosophers. Although Union blockaders managed to seize 1,149 blockade vessels and destroy 355 others, more than 7,500 Confederate runners eluded the blockade cordon between 1861 and 1865. Only in early 1865 when the war was nearly over, did the blockade become "effective," with the capture ratio rising to one out of every two ships.[41]

The comments of Union sailors confirmed the ineffectiveness of the blockade. For most of the war, many sailors believed that unless a blockade violator literally ran into a Union vessel, it could get through safely.[42] Union vessels rarely caught ships running in. Samuel Powell, who served in the Gulf Squadron, concluded that "captures of vessels running in were very rare."[43] Crews rarely caught runners heading out. In September 1861, Ralph Chandler penned in his journal: "I say boldly & without hesitation that there was has [sic] not been a night during the last three months that a steamer could not go in & out of Charleston harbor without fear of molestation."[44] By 1863, the situation on the Atlantic blockade had not markedly improved. Charles Post observed: "As far as I can see, if they do not stumble upon us by accident, they are pretty sure of running by."[45]

Men took hard the many escapes made by rebel runners. Sailors grumbled and complained about the chases that ended in failure and the seeming futility of their efforts. The number of fruitless chases left men feeling despondent and ineffectual. Sailors wanted to catch every runner. The morning after a failed chase, sailors typically filled their discussions with growls of "ifs," "ands," and "buts."[46] Sailors masochistically rehashed each part of the failed chase attempting to assign to the disappointment some defined causation. At mess, at work, or while relaxing, mates argued among themselves that if this order had been performed more quickly or some neglect remedied, the outcome would have been different.[47] Men opined that their ships were too slow or were stationed too far out to do much good. They cursed the moon for not being out and the clouds when it was.[48] Others rationalized that their squadrons did not have enough ships or that the chases had rightfully aborted when they veered too close to Confederate forts. A month of failed chases worked hard on Charles Post. After another fruitless night, Post lamented: "I am going to bed with a heavy heart. Two more guns have just been reported. I suppose it will be the same all over again to-morrow. I wonder if we shall ever be *really on top!*"[49]

Sailors' grievances sprang from a number of factors. They did not like spending the night away from their hammocks night after night with no results. They were practical-minded men who thought that with the proper execution of orders they should be able to apprehend these "rebel pirates." In addition, there was also a certain amount of pride that seamen wanted to take in their service. Sailors were aware of all of the negative stereotypes that made the working, watching, and waiting necessary in maintaining the blockade seem unheroic, unmanly, and

soft. Crews knew there was little chance on the blockade to earn lau-
rels through battle service. Blockade sailors longed for opportunities to
distinguish themselves. "All we ask for, however," sighed one seaman,
"is a fair chance to run them down."[50]

Although officers ran the ship, the success of the blockade rested on
the ability of blockade sailors to detect and react. The frustrating nature of the blockade made sailors feel powerless. One sailor wrote that
blockade runners "do not care a fig for the West Gulf Squadron, for they
know precisely where to find them."[51] Sailors took it personally when
rebel shore guns—certain that a runner would elude their ships—let
loose a volley "as a sort of bravado" to let the blockade sailors know that
a vessel was going to make a run.[52] Sailors viewed the failure to catch a
blockader as a battle lost and a personal failing. A sense of impotence
pervaded many Union crews, who became frustrated at their inability
to perform the job they were sent to do. Seaman Henry T. Rommel wrote
to his mother and father, "A schooner came in and the men on her Put
theire finger to their nose . . . So you See that is the way that things go
here."[53]

Sailors and their ships became a target for newspapers, politicians,
and impatient Northerners, who labeled the blockade squadrons "negligent."[54] Bluejackets became very sensitive to the negative press and the
public's perceptions concerning the blockade. Critics made the navy's
inability to prevent vessels from leaving and entering the blockade
fodder for their constituents.[55] Isaac Bradbury on the *Cambridge* tried
to correct the sad image of the porous nature of the blockade held by his
friends by maintaining that the blockade was as "effective as it can be
possibly."[56] Landsman Charles Post snorted, "I wish that some of you
people in New York, who are so fond of talking of the negligence of the
blockade could be here some of these dark nights and see how we are
situated. . . . Your wonder would then be how we ever stopped any of
them."[57]

Sailors themselves castigated the suspect nature of the blockade by
coming up with analogies that projected the haphazard nature of their
service. Joseph Canning viewed blockade service as being "in the fashion of a spider watching for flies." To Seaman Henry Clay Taylor, sitting on a ship waiting for a faster, sleeker vessel to run by was akin to
being "a cat at a mouse hole."[58] The seemingly innocent metaphors reflected the frustration and shame many sailors felt. Sailors kept track of
which ships among their squadrons possessed better records for catching blockade runners. James B. Collins stated that a crew's reputation

depended solely on the number of runners seized. In fact, their reputation was deemed "ruined" if they let runners by.[59]

Personal shame and lack of sleep aside, the greatest sense of loss suffered by Union sailors in letting blockade runners escape their dragnet was pecuniary. Plain and simple, when blockade runners slipped the grasp of Union crews, sailors felt that it cost them money, prize money.[60] A proportionate share of the cash value of blockade runners seized by sailors' ships, prize money quickly became the sole objective of many Yankee sailors and their greatest source of disappointment.[61]

The starry-eyed recruits who had enlisted believing prize money was a way out of financial distress fell particularly hard. Theirs was the disappointment felt by someone who thought he had purchased a winning lottery ticket. "Boys were thinking they had lots of prize money coming to them," wrote Tim Finn.[62] Others thought prize money was a sure-fire way to a comfortable life. Calvin G. Hutchinson wrote to his wife that such thoughts even pierced seasickness. Hutchinson, serving on the *Commodore Morris*, was suffering from a severe bout of seasickness when he spied a runner. "I forgot all about my seasickness," Hutchinson wrote, "& jumped round the deck eager enough to secure my house & lot on a good street in Roxbury."[63]

Sailors thought about prize money all the time. Every sighting of a potential prize set off a flurry of thoughts about newfound wealth. Landsman Milo Lacy gushed in his log that he thought about "getting a prize" all the time and that he and his crew fell into "visions of prize money" at the start of every chase.[64] As soon as a crew had a potential prize in sight, crew members immediately began speculating on their potential shares in order to gain quick currency. "Shares of prize money were quoted at various rates & a variety of speculations were undertaken," wrote William Keeler, "on the strength of what some thought was already in the pocket."[65] Men offered to sell their shares of potential prize money for twenty, ten, or five dollars. Sailors strapped for cash offered to sell their shares for as low as fifty cents. "But," as one tar recalled, "would-be-salesmen of their shares are far more numerous than buyers."[66] Those not speculating their share of the prize money were placing bets. Charles Post recounted that in the middle of a blockade chase off the port of Wilmington, "every one from the captain to the humblest side boy had a bet, in prize money, which loomed before us like a fortune."[67]

The lure of prize money proved so intoxicating that it frequently altered the way officers and sailors conducted chases. Crews frequently risked losing runners rather than sinking them. Charles Post called this accusation "an infamous falsehood" but the conflict between higher duty and filling one's pockets was a problem among sailors on the blockade.[68] Union ships sometimes began chases without signaling nearby vessels so they could seize a prize alone and not have to share a prize capture. This practice, called "covering the signal distance," meant that crews—in direct violation of navy orders—chased runners alone instead of notifying other blockaders within signal distance.[69] According to law, all navy ships within the signal distance of the vessel making the capture—roughly six miles—and in a position to render assistance if required, were entitled to share in the prize.[70] Vessels, in greedy attempts to secure the sole share of a prize, extended chases in order to lose slower vessels outside the signal distance.[71] Once they had isolated a potential prize from other Union ships, soldier-turned-sailor Samuel Powell wrote, "they swooped upon their prey, gobbled her up, and shut the rest . . . completely out."[72]

Union crews engaged in strategies that relegated the destruction of runners to a secondary motivation. Gun crews often lobbed single shots or fired rounds of blank cartridges across the bows of unidentified ships in order to subdue, not destroy, blockade runners. Crews were fearful of damaging the runners' precious cargoes of cotton, tobacco, and liquor. Only when absolutely necessary did some Union crews destroy blockade runners.[73] Sailors joked that their ships served as instruments of "salvation" rather than "destruction."[74]

Blockade runners sensed the greed of blockade crews. They quickly learned that some ships would rather seize a portion of wet cargo than risk losing a whole ship in a doubtful chase. During close pursuits, runners would toss bales of cotton—called "waif"—into their wake knowing that Union vessels would often slow down to pick them up.[75] The taste for these precious dumpings ran so intense that if more than two blockaders were engaged in a chase and a runner dropped bales into the water, blockade crews sometimes stopped the chase and struggled among themselves for the dumpings of the runner. Paymaster William Anderson recalled that "what a struggle there was between boats of the different ships in the rear of the chase, for the possession of this consolatory flotsam."[76] After an aborted chase, the decks of blockaders were often littered with the "derelict cotton" which had bought a free pass through the blockade.[77]

The degree to which many ships put prize money over patriotism rose to such levels that Gideon Welles suggested in December 1863 that Congress abolish the practice of awarding prize money and instead award bounties for destroying—rather than salvaging—blockade runners. Under Welles's plan, officers and sailors would divide the bounties in the same manner as prize money.[78] Although Congress never adopted Welles's recommendation, only when officers and sailors realized that the war's end would quicken with an efficient blockade did they finally adopt a preference for destruction. In a May 1864 letter from the steamer *Osipee* patrolling off Mobile Bay, Seaman Edward Blue wrote: "The rush for prize money has died out in a great measure and we are only anxious now to sink, burn & destroy."[79]

Sailors' dedication to self-interest quickly bubbled to the surface when they boarded prize vessels. Eager to turn a profit during their service, many sailors found looting irresistible. Looting became routine even though, if a crew was found to have looted a captured prize, it would forfeit its share of the prize money.[80] Some sailors even risked their lives to preserve the prize ship and its cargo. On one occasion, a sailor was so fearful that a disabled prize would sink before its cargo was extracted, that he tied a halyard around his waist, swung over the bulwark, and plugged his leg into the shot hole in order to keep the vessel from going under.[81]

Union officers did little to discourage looting. Semi-organized plundering traditionally functioned as part of sailors' wages during wartime.[82] The heavy presence of liquor on blockade runners only intensified looting.[83] After the sailors on the steamer *Cambridge* subdued and boarded the prize *Dee*, they proceeded to loot everything on the vessel and drink whatever they could. "We might have saved more of her cargo only our men would get drunk," wrote Isaac Bradbury, "as the whole vessels deck was covered with Brandy & wine in bottles."[84] Paymaster William Keeler described the wild looting committed by sailors on the *Calypso*: "Here a jack tar is rushing across the deck, his arms full of pieces of calico when his eye is caught by an unopened box just thrown out of the hold, down goes the dry goods upon the deck among coal, water, oil and molasses & catching up a heavy hammer he brings it down upon the box with a force which not only crushes the top but drives it to the bottom through bottles of quinine with which the box is filled. Catching up a bottle—'damn the medicine'—& in he jumps half up to his knees in quinine, completing the destruction which the hammer had commenced."[85]

A partial explanation for the intensity and frequency of looting by blockade sailors may have been their disappointment over the lack of prize money. For a number of reasons, prize money became a myth for sailors.[86] First, the difficulty in catching Confederate runners meant that many Union crews did not even catch a prize in which to share. Many sailors grumbled that the difficulty in catching runners made reliance on prize money extremely difficult.[87] Second, the statutory share of prize money allocated to ordinary sailors proved small. The navy distributed prize money incrementally with the largest group, the sailors, receiving the smallest percentage.[88] Seaman Tim Finn left the service in 1862 solely because he felt he had been cheated out of his expected prize money: "When the government got its half and the Commissioned officers there Share there was but little left for the petty officers and the men it was like Sifting it through a 24 foot ladder all that Stuck to the Rungs the petty officers and Crew got I left the Navy thourgly disgusted with the Service."[89]

Third, the procedures for adjudicating prize ships were time-consuming and not universally understood by sailors. Consequently, those crews who seized prizes received their shares long after the initial capture and in amounts smaller than they expected. Some men received their shares years after the war ended.[90] In short, prize money was parceled slowly or not at all. Sailors came to feel great hostility toward the navy about the issue. Seaman Joseph Collins groused that a sailor's prize money was "pretty hard to collect."[91] Many felt cheated. "I have got prise money to me," wrote Coal Heaver George Arnold, "but I dont know as I will ever get enny or not."[92] Fourth, most sailors believed that officers kept the prize money rightfully belonging to seamen. The hostility and disappointment over prize money became so pervasive that it was rumored that before battle sailors sometimes mockingly prayed "that the enemy's bullets may be distributed the same way as the prize money is, *principally* among the officers."[93]

Resentment over prize money also stemmed from the growing frustration that many sailors felt about the blockade. Many men began to look to prize money not as a windfall but as hardship pay for the awful quality of life they endured.[94] Although blockade sailors did not suffer the battle casualties of soldiers, march knee-deep through mud, or sleep on hard ground, they did go through a shipboard experience unlike anything most had ever known or could have possibly imagined even in their worst nightmares.

The everyday enemies that sailors faced on the blockade were not traditional. The real war for blockade sailors was not the frustrating battle between the blockaders and the runners. Instead, it was the psychological war endured by sailors as they struggled to deal with extended exposure to the most negative aspects of living on a ship, namely the thumb-twiddling monotony of shipboard routine and the wrenching isolation from society on land. The blockade service confirmed for sailors the truth of a prewar observation that warned when the average sailor was sober he would "tell you that he hates the sight of blue water, that he habitually hates his ship, hates his officers, hates his messmates and despises himself." [95]

Isolation and monotony had always formed the bulk of sailor gripes. Yet, to a great extent, the limited duration of naval and merchant cruises had masked the debilitating effects that ships worked on the mind. Typically, sailors traveled from one port to another able to withstand the crushing sameness of ship life because they knew that they would reach landfall in a specified number of days. On cruises that reached or exceeded the specified number of days, anxiety among the crew gradually rose past a healthy level. Men forced to remain on a ship too long typically became depressed, unruly, or mutinous. [96] Sailors' free time on land, aptly called "liberty," functioned as the critical safety valve for releasing the anxiety generated by weeks aboard ship. Once in port, sailors released the accumulated, unhealthy anxiety generated by the conditions aboard ship by "letting off some steam" quickly and aggressively through binge drinking, riotous fighting, and paid sexual indulgences. [97]

Owing to the threat of desertion, blockade sailors rarely went ashore. Because of a shortage of recruits to spell them, they infrequently received liberty. [98] It also mattered little if a sailor's term of service had expired. If the navy needed him to plug a hole in the crew, he had little choice but to stay. Two days before Christmas 1864, an exhausted and depressed Seaman Oceolo Smith wrote to his mother that his time was up in three days. It did not matter, he said, for there was "no hope of getting out." [99]

As a result, the average blockade sailor served six, nine, or eighteen months without breaks, without leaving their ships, and without renewing their contacts with civilian society. [100] This unnerved many men. "We are not allowed to go ashore," Seaman Francis McKey grumbled in August 1863. [101] Over time, their perilously long stints aboard ship placed many sailors on the slow descent into despair and made overcoming mental stress the single greatest challenge Union sailors faced on the blockade. [102] Many shared the feelings of Seaman Israel Vail. After eight consecutive months aboard ship, Vail moaned, "We had almost reached the conclusion that the government intended us to remain here alone until the close of the war."[103]

For the nineteenth-century sailor, life on any ship was dull. Instead of romance and action, most sailors found the bulk of their daily lives immersed in collective acts of boring and tedious work. Those men who dreamt of leaping aboard a blockade runner with a saber in one hand and a pistol in the other often found themselves fighting the Civil War with a mop and bucket.[104] Such dull work over the short term was boring and irksome. Over time, during the Civil War, the realities of life as a sailor in the United States Navy, where crews performed their jobs at the same times, on the same days, day after day, and week after week, while eating the same meals and looking at the same faces, converted traditional sailor fidgets into something worse than boredom: monotony.[105]

The logs and letters of Union sailors reveal monotony as the most common complaint on the blockade. Seaman John Van Nest wrote to his mother that the blockade "is a very dull lazy life and I am sick of it." Landsman Joseph Fry called his service "rather dull business."[106] "During the last week," Joseph Osborne wrote to his girlfriend, "I have seen enoughf of the sea. . . . I am not sea sick but I am sick of the Sea."[107]

As time progressed, monotony lent a bizarre quality to blockade sailors' lives. Each day sailors knew how the contents of their day would unfold and at what exact times. "Variety is the spice of life," moaned Seaman Edwin Benedict, but "not on the Blockade." "I am getting well tired of the service," Elisha Hansen wrote, "and I wish was out of it." Nineteen-year-old Charles Post tried to explain to his mother the mindlessness of blockade life: "I told her she could get a fair idea of our 'adventures' if she would go on the roof of the house, on a hot summer day, and talk to half a dozen hotel hallboys, who are generally far more intelligent and agreeable than the average 'acting officer.' Then descend to the attic and drink some tepid water, full of iron-rust. Then go on the roof again and repeat this 'adventure process' at intervals, until she was tired out, and go to bed, with everything shut down tight, so as not to show a light. Adventure! Bah! The blockade is the wrong place for it."[108]

The travel paths of blockade ships worsened the feeling of monotony. In the more isolated stations, sailors sat on ships that went nowhere. "We have to lay in one place about all of the time," wrote Frederic Sherman.[109] On the most active vessels, sailors traveled back and forth between the shore and the blockade line over and over, literally in circles.

The fact that blockade sailors rarely strayed from their assigned stations constructively negated one of the more positive aspects of ship life, the constant change in scenery.[110] Seaman Bartholomew Diggins, who had served as both a merchant mariner and a sailor before the war, found the situation troublesome. "Blockading was not the most agreeable duty," he wrote in his journal, "an unfriendly shore on one side of us, and the great waste of water on the other."[111] Sailor William Miller concluded, "A more dreary place I have never been in."[112]

Since they had no access to current newspapers, books, and other people's news, sailors immediately lost touch with Northern society. Steamers brought mail to ships semi-regularly but not consistently. Crews often went for weeks without receiving any.[113] By the time the mail steamer did arrive, the news was stale, the foodstuffs spoiled, and the letters dated. William Keeler lamented that crews received "no papers, no letters, no news, *no nothing*."[114] Mary Osborne immediately noticed the difference of trying to communicate with her brother who had previously served as a soldier. Now that he was a sailor, Mary wrote, he did not "hear from home & friends as often as you did in the Army."[115]

Not surprisingly, sailors fretted about the lack of communication. Tars routinely expressed fears over being "cut-off" and "shut out." Joseph Osborne expressed to his girlfriend Louise the isolation felt by sailors on the blockade, "Here we are shut out from all the world." "All hands are getting very impatiant," Fireman George Geer wrote to his wife, "to hear from the World."[116]

For sailors, the greatest source of isolation was their prolonged separation from the land-based society. Prior to shipping, every sailor had grown up, lived, and interacted in a complex social environment consisting of family, friends, acquaintances, and strangers. To pull them out of this world and place them into an environment bereft of traditional relationships and the possibility for new ones proved highly traumatic.[117] A ship in theory promised freedom from societal control, but simultaneously that freedom meant a severing of ties that afforded security and a sense of belonging. Not only did these men miss the feeling of being on land; for them the ship lacked the basic accoutrements of land-based society on which they unconsciously had come to depend.

Sailors missed their friends. Charles Poole complained from the decks of the *Kearsarge* that he felt a "longing to see kind Friends far away."[118] Other sailors longed for the informal social associations and groups they used to frequent. They missed the complex web of commonplace social connections that comprised daily life from family and friends to mere acquaintances. They missed their familiar haunts such as boarding houses and taverns. Landsman Milo Lacy bemoaned "the contrast between my mode of living then I was at home in Iowa, and had all the heart could wish (almost)." All he had to do now was "only think of it, and then weep."[119]

Most of all, blockade sailors missed women. "I miss Ladies society," wrote Joseph Osborne to his girlfriend, "*yours* especialy." "Was it not for that I would be contented here."[120] Any time a woman was within visual reach of a spyglass, sailors quickly found her. When it was sounded that "real-alive young ladies" were coming aboard, the crew of the *Brazileira* went into a "state of mild phrenzy."[121] Sutlers often hired women to work on the "bum boats" that brought obscenely priced articles from shore. Sailors would pay any price for tobacco or liquor, especially if the item was attached to a "petticoat," wrote one man.[122] Lonely tars tattooed dancing girls on their forearms so that they could watch them while they worked.[123] Seaman Israel Vail wrote that he had almost forgotten what a woman looked like until a steamer arrived with women on board: "The sight of a woman had been denied us for eight months, and we had only dim recollections of how they looked, and the sudden appearance of several of that sex upon our station, nearly prostrated us with astonishment and delight; and a general effort was noticed among all hands, to appear as attractive as possible in case the ship came near enough for the ladies to observe us."[124]

Moreover, in normal society, men could change their circumstances and their companions to lift their spirits. On a ship, they could not. Although they were homesick for family, friends, and women, the most important feature of living that sailors missed was the ability to vary the content of their lives.[125] On land, people, with some limitations, could change the scenery, the environment, their situations, and even their mood with a walk, a ride, or a short trip. On a ship, there were no places to go. Men could not saunter off to a pub if they felt like it. They could not switch groups or friends. "Unlike land," wrote Seaman Edwin Benedict, a sailor "cannot change company or circumstances to cheer oneself."[126] "It is not like being on land where you can saunter out if you have nothing to do," wrote Charles Poole, ". . . but instead you have to stay (one hundred feet being the extent of your travels) in one place."[127]

Blockade sailors did take some constructive measures to combat monotony and anxiety. They bonded tightly within mess groups. They developed practices and behaviors designed to release stress. On the blockade, an important means of battling isolation was to engage in conversations about everything. This constant state of talking ranged from idle chatter and gossip—called scuttlebutt—to the most important form of talk: stories, called "yarns" by sailors. Stories functioned not only as a way for sailors to vary the sameness of their lives but also as a critical socialization process.

When they landed on the decks of ships, sailors did so surrounded by groups of men they had never seen before. Not knowing anyone, sailors had to socialize themselves anew. "What then brought you here?" was the most common query in the early days of the blockade. In the days, weeks, and months that followed, sailors recounted their life stories and how they ended up aboard ship. It was through these initial dialogues that sailors became acquainted. Usually the juiciest tales surfaced first. Men talked of families, friends, and women left behind. John Wirts, a seaman in the Pacific Squadron, stated that it was typical for new sailors to talk of abandoned families and wives. "It was strange to hear husbands, who had deserted their wives speak most rapturously of their wives as the paragons of their Sex." In more contemplative moments, they spoke of economic woes and troubled times.[128]

The stories of Union seamen were riveting because, as one sailor emphasized, there "were no moral scruples to restrain" one from drawing on "the unexplored regions of the imagination." Old sea dogs and harder elements of the crew often spun vulgar and violent yarns designed to astonish and terrify. Some bragged of numerous women in numerous ports fraught with amorous adventures. Other men spoke of lives defined by great fines, murder trials, and estrangements. Such stories proved "instructive" and "amusing," wrote Landsman Cosam Bartlett, "but the greater part were dark with crime, & vice, red with blood."[129]

The darkest yarns were likely entwined threads of fact and fiction. Union sailors had a peculiar habit of confirming the veracity of the most jaw-dropping stories with "oaths of truthfullness." Nevertheless, these stories, many of them heart-rending, provided—along with their mess groups—the fundamental building blocks in helping sailors find common ground, form groups, and establish confidants. Sailors sharing similar tales usually broke off into subgroups called "sets," thus forming cliques within the larger ship community. The failure to assimilate into a set carried severe social consequences. Not only did it deprive sailors of friends in an unfriendly environment; it also meant that they risked additional isolation in a situation where they already felt intense loneliness.[130]

*"All Hands Scrub Clothes": Nothing illustrated the organized monotony of a ship
like the Saturday ritual of washing clothes for Sunday morning inspection.
Sailors scrubbed at their few articles of clothing with brushes and soap
in a silent hum of activity. Charles E. Stedman Sketchbook,
courtesy of the Boston Athenaeum.*

Without question, there were gradations in the isolation and monotony on the blockade.[131] Moreover, in small doses and tempered by
breaks on land, sailors probably could have withstood the stress. However, most men, not being sailors before the war, did not know how
to deal with the mental burdens that the blockade placed on them.
Old salts also did not possess techniques for combating the ill effects
of prolonged voyages. For the most part, Yankee sailors could and did
handle the futile chases, the false alarms, and poor living conditions—
with aplomb, grit, and determination.[132] What they had difficulty overcoming were the psychological effects resulting from living aboard ship
too long.

The longer blockade sailors remained in their ships, the worse the effects of living in a ship became.[133] Sailors began complaining of over-whelming feelings of nothingness, purposelessness, and anger. Stephen Blanding said that at times he felt "insignificant."[134] Another unhappy sailor labeled the situation as "weeks of listless waiting, doing nothing, seeing nothing, hearing nothing."[135] Joseph Watson recognized in 1863 that what he and others were experiencing was worse than just sheer boredom. Watson called blockade life "worse than monotony: it is the absolute weariness of spirit."[136] As one worn-out sailor wrote in July 1864, "Blockade duty is perhaps a harder test of this love [of country] than actual field service; and as months pass on, it becomes almost unendurable."[137]

Like the aimless crew on the mythical *Ship of Fools*, the nursery-rhyme quality of blockade sailors' lives—living in cramped, dirty ships, under all kinds of weather, drilling the same drills, performing the same tasks, eating the same moldy food, and on ships that went nowhere, except backward and forward, or sometimes in circles, chasing ships they knew they would not catch—seemed empty and meaningless, like death.[138] Many sailors associated blockade living with death.[139] George Bright likened the blockade service to nothing short of "living death."[140]

Sailors' letters and journals strongly suggest that many of them fell into various phases of depression while on the blockade.[141] As a result, men grew listless. Work rates slowed appreciably. Coal Heaver William Wainwright said that on some days he grew so despondent that he could barely carry his lucky bag—a bag containing a sailor's personal belongings—from one deck to another. Seaman John Van Nest was so mentally drained after one summer on the blockade that he feared he would not survive the next. "I hope I shall not have to spend another summer down on this coast," Van Nest wrote to his mother, "for it will use me up."[142]

Lively faces and vigorous grumbling acted as accepted signs of good sailor mental health.[143] Content sailors were obvious. They growled, snapped, and howled at every perceived slight, indignity, and hardship. Depressed bluejackets sported long, hollow faces, spouted deep moans, and became uncomfortably docile. Boy Charles Mervine observed in the dog days of August 1863: "I seen several very long faces on, on some of the men whose times of service have expired. . . . Muttering curses not loud but deep."[144]

The onset of silence in a crew indicated trouble. Sailors who did not grumble, gripe, and complain were showing sure signs that they had lost their grip. Samuel F. Du Pont, commander of the North Atlantic Blockade Squadron, who had kept the same crew on his flagship, the *Wabash*, for a year and a half without a break, sent them North on liberty only when he noticed that his tars had ceased complaining. In his opinion, a silent crew meant their "flesh and blood could stand it no longer." As the misery of the blockade worsened, "the men have never uttered a grunt," Du Pont explained, "and this is one reason I send them."[145] In many instances, only when sailor depression reached dangerous levels would officers relent and send sailors on liberty.[146]

Deterioration in the ability to sustain conversations served as another barometer of flagging spirits. Colorful stories and banter among sailors weakened by depression turned threadbare. Discussions degenerated into conversing about which way the wind would blow tomorrow. Other telling verbal signals could be noted when sailors began talking seriously about the details of the naval enlistment office where they now believed—as they looked back—they had signed their lives away.[147] Samuel Powell recalled that the discussion among his mates grew so "interminable" one afternoon that they began asking, "Were there eight or nine desks in the office of the Navy Agent at New York when the ship sailed?"[148] Officer A. T. Mahan recalled that on the blockade "the largest reservoir of anecdotes was sure to run dry, the deepest vein of original humor to be worked out." Topics of discussion became so pitiful on Mahan's ship that tars were reduced to reciting nursery rhymes such as "Mary had a little lamb."[149] "There were few things either in heaven or hell," sighed Charles Post, "which we did not talk over."[150]

The strange tenor of sailor conversations projected the mental stupor. Cut off from the thoughts, actions, and sights that held their attention ashore, sailors turned their thoughts to darkly introspective and morbid matters.[151] They dwelt on certain issues, great and small, again and again. "A place on ship board furnish him facilities which could no where else be found," mused Cosam T. Bartlett, "as every phase of life is here portrayed naked."[152] Tars silently and openly rehashed the state of their lives from birth to their decision to join the navy. Sailors pondered life-altering mistakes and people left behind. Left to their own devices, Charles Nordhoff explained, sailors on the blockade were forced to "expend their energies and thoughts upon matters of infinitesimal account."[153] This state of mind partially explains the diminished quality of their conversations, which took on a simplistic, repetitive tone, eerily similar to their navy life. "I have never seen a body of intelligent men reduced so nearly to imbecility," A. T. Mahan wrote, "as my shipmates then were."[154]

The psychological decline that many sailors experienced corrupted social relations. Men suffering from depression typically made poor company. Many sailors stopped caring about how they comported themselves. This attitude, coupled with the fact that they were already sick to death of seeing the same faces for eighteen straight months, eroded any semblance of collegiality, camaraderie, and civility. Living in a space so contracted at times that they could not move but continually had to touch, sailors took to dissecting the many flaws of their mess mates and berth mates. "There is no place where you will get better acquainted with a man," growled Seaman Patrick Meade, "than in one of those ships."[155]

There was plenty of fodder for irritation. Denied the company of women, fresh food, and sleep, it was not difficult for sailors to find something, many things, to annoy them about their ship mates. Whether provoked by skin color, place of birth, poor hygiene, the way food was chewed, or snoring, sailors, the longer they stayed on the blockade, harbored thoughts—bad thoughts—about their crewmates. "If you want to find out what a man really is," groused Noel Blakeman, "go spend a year with him on the blockade and you will discover what kind of stuff he is made of as well as what kind of fellow you are yourself."[156]

While this social breakdown was partially understandable, given the good deal of time blockade sailors possessed to dwell on the imperfections of their mates, its effects proved far-reaching and disruptive. Often, the fragile social relations that sailors had just recently formed to ward off the isolation of the blockade fissured.[157] Men stopped sharing, and thefts increased. Discipline lapsed. Moreover, the discharge of ship duties suffered as the coordination that came with deferring to another's knowledge and skill disappeared. Every request, piece of advice, suggestion, and interaction now became a point of argument. "Arguments seem to predominate," wrote Charles Poole in May 1864.[158] The exhaustion of minds and bodies only seemed to intensify their growing animosity toward one another. Milo Lacy observed that "everybody appears to hate everybody, and himself."[159]

William Wainwright called the increased combativeness among crew members the time for the "devil to pay." During this time, sailors attempting to ward off severe depression drank more heavily and fought continually. By 1 March 1864, William Wainwright observed that one-half of his crew was regularly drunk and fighting.[160] Fist and knife fights among sailors became relatively commonplace, some deadly.[161] Coal Heaver George Arnold, who had been in two major fights in one day, remarked, "i never interfear with enny one except they commense it." In his second fight, if his opponent's friends had not stepped in, Arnold crowed, "I would have nocked seven bels out of him."[162] Robley D. Evans described the violent results when the mood grew dark on the blockade: "Our men were kept on board so long, and we were under steam, that they became very irritated and ugly. Fights were of daily occurrence, and some of them serious . . . Several men lost their lives in this way."[163]

George Bernard Shaw once quipped that the longer men stay aboard ship "they become crazy, crazier and crazier."[164] Indeed, the observations of bluejackets indicate that the mental strain of the blockade did break many a sailor.[165] These nervous breakdowns resulted from the unchecked exhaustion, sleeplessness, and depression rendered by the blockade.[166] Back then, however, a nervous breakdown meant nothing more than a sailor being unable to get himself out of his hammock for duty one morning, then the next, and the next.

Although sailors possessed little understanding of what was happening to them, they devised numerous ways to describe the horrible malady. William Wainwright wrote of feeling "played out," "heart broken," having "crossed the line," and suffering from "low courage."[167] John Van Nest likened the sensations to being totally "used up."[168] Gussie Van Gieson fretted that "I dont know what to do with myself."[169] William Miller described how he broke down when he awoke on the morning of 14 December 1861. "I was so bad that I was not able to be at any duty . . ." he wrote to Dr. William Thoms, "I had to give up all together."[170]

Alvah Hunter, a boy on the monitor *Nahant*, recalled that one morning he awoke feeling unable and unwilling to get out of his hammock. Hunter knew something was wrong but he was at a loss since he felt there was nothing physically ailing him. Unsure of what to do and worried, he decided to see the ship's surgeon. After examining the boy, the doctor angrily snapped his conclusion that the lad was not sick. "I know that, Sir," Hunter snarled, "I'm just broken down!"[171]

The reactions of sailors varied. Some were allowed to rest. Young Alvah Hunter was permitted to recuperate for a few weeks off the ship and recovered.[172] Other bluejackets—fearful of continued exposure to the blockade—sought, and in some instances demanded, discharges and reassignments. One sailor, seeking an immediate discharge, wrote to Secretary of the Navy Gideon Welles, "I am a poor, weak, miserable, nervous half-crazy boy . . . everything jar[s] . . . upon my delicate nerves."[173]

A small number of sailors did go insane.[174] Some bluejackets thought about suicide. A depressed William Wainwright despaired in his log that "I should like to see the man that wouldn't either be heart broken or put an end to himself by committing Suicide."[175] Others tried to end their own lives. Fifteen-year-old Charles Mervine awoke one night to the cries of the night watch on the *Powhatan* calling for help in trying to stop the bleeding of a sailor who had cut his own throat. When the man regained consciousness, he only murmured that "trouble was the cause of his so doing." A soldier traveling on the steamer *Arago* watched in horror as a sailor, unable to handle the life on the blockade, decided to take his life. "One terrified man rushed above deck, stripped off his coat," wrote Lawrence Van Alstyne, "said 'Good bye, all' and jumped directly in front of the wheel."[176]

The sailors who overcame the disappointment and psychological pressures of the blockade did so by developing a strain of mental toughness uniquely tailored to combat the blockade's war of nerves. To be courageous on the blockade meant that men had to accept, adapt, and overcome every annoyance and daily hardship that the navy and ships forced on them. As one man phrased it, sailors, in order to survive, "had to get used to it."[177]

Blockade sailors had to get used to living within the isolation and the monotony. Sailors steeled themselves to the around-the-clock service, the sleeplessness, and the disappointment over failed chases and lost prize money. Lastly, Union sailors had to come to grips with the hidden toll that living on a ship exacted from their bodies and their minds. Such a toughening required—as sailors recalled—the "greatest endurance."[178] Yet, endure these men did. Lieutenant Percival Drayton attempted to define the mettle required of sailors on the blockade: "The publick give credit for feat of arms, but the courage which is required for them, cannot compare with that which is needed to bear patiently, not only the thousand annoyances but the total absence of everything that makes life pleasant and even worth living."[179]

# The Devil's Own Purgatory
## The Experience of Gunboatmen
## in the Mississippi Squadron

Monotony was not a problem for the sailors who served on the Western rivers in the Mississippi Squadron. The men and the war they fought between 1861 and 1865 proved vastly different than their counterparts on the blockade. While riverine service lacked the crushing sameness of blockade sailoring, its proximity to shore and ability to strike into the Confederate interior thrust sailors into the land war and into contact with terrified Southern civilians. Complicating matters, river sailors featured some of the meanest men the Union navy recruited during the war. Their ill tempers, however, proved well suited for the irregular war they waged. River jacks—called "gunboatmen"—not only assisted the army in land-based operations, guarded transports, and patrolled rivers; they also became embroiled in a nasty guerrilla war.[1] This guerrilla war proved so brutal and so destabilizing that it blurred the lines between stealing and foraging, civilians and combatants, and acts of war and murder.

The Union's plan to neutralize Confederate resistance in the West weighed heavily on wresting control of the Mississippi, Cumberland, and Tennessee rivers. In order to accomplish this, the War Department, under the navy's guidance, improvised an inland navy composed of converted steamboats originally called the "Western Flotilla." This flotilla, later rechristened the "Mississippi Squadron," consisted of a "heterogeneous lot" of over 200 "makeshift conversion jobs," loosely referred to as "gunboats." These gunboats consisted of wooden gunboats (the *Tyler*, *Conestoga*, and *Lexington*), mortarboats, ramming vessels, and half-armored boats called "tinclads."[2]

The backbone of the Mississippi Squadron was eight ironclad gunboats designed by Samuel Pook and constructed by St. Louis salvager James B. Eads. Named mainly for the river cities they sought to protect,

*The crew of the USS* Cairo, *a gunboat of the Mississippi Squadron.*
*Contrary to myth, these vessels were ungainly and unreliable. They were*
*so hot and dirty that sailors called them "federal bake ovens."*
*Courtesy of the U.S. Naval Historical Center.*

the *St. Louis, Carondolet, Louisville, Pittsburg, Mound City, Cincin-*
*nati, Benton,* and *Cairo* were not wind-driven. They were flat-bottomed
river boats, with no sails, propelled by a reciprocating steam engine
fueled by coal, and clad with iron.[3] In fact, the *St. Louis* was actually
the first U.S. ironclad, predating the more famous *Monitor* by several
months.[4]

Although by December 1863 the Mississippi Squadron featured
5,500 sailors, when the war started the fleet had none.[5] As it had done
on the blockade, the navy erroneously believed that once it had constructed the boats, experienced rivermen and flatboatmen would flock
to this new squadron. It proved a bad assumption.[6] Rivermen joined the
army rather than the river navy.[7] In fact, so few men turned out to enlist
for the river fleet that by October 1861, after months of heavy recruiting
in Cleveland, Cincinnati, St. Louis, Detroit, and Milwaukee, only 100
men had shipped.[8]

The nature of the vessels of the fleet played a role in discouraging enlistments. The woodclads, tinclads, mortarboats, and ironclad gunboats that made up the squadron were all steam powered. Steam power still represented a somewhat risky method of water travel, and rivermen mistrusted its use even before the war. Woodclads could be shot to ribbons by bullets. Tinclads were covered lightly with armor and contained plenty of exposed wood. Mortarboats recoiled so violently each time they fired that they were prone to sinking and deafening the crew.

While the ironclad gunboats represented a technological advance, they were coarse, untested, and unsafe vessels and their designs concealed a number of flaws. These boats contained more than 120 tons of iron plating and the navy knew the boilers could cause a great many deaths if punctured, but it underplated the middle and rear of the boats.[9] The bulk of the iron plating, sometimes two to two-and-a-half inches thick, only covered the forward part of the boat since the navy erroneously believed these boats would fight headfirst. Thinner plating covered the center of the boat where the boilers and engines were housed, leaving them underprotected.[10]

The navy knew the ironclad gunboats were unsafe. In June 1861, John Rodgers, the first commander of the Western Flotilla, admitted to Secretary of the Navy Gideon Welles the potential pitfalls of these boats. "The boilers and engines can not be defended against cannon shot," Rodgers wrote to Welles. "We must take our chances."[11] River sailors did not need a detailed explanation to understand that these boats were unsafe. Lieutenant Seth Ledyard Phelps complained that recruits did not want to join the Mississippi Squadron because of a firm belief "that the service on Gunboats will be exceedingly dangerous."[12]

Gunboats looked ungainly and downright unsafe. Seaman John Swift called them "queer looking articles." "I guess you open your eyes if you saw one," he wrote to his girlfriend.[13] Landsman Daniel Kemp recalled that his gunboat, the *Cincinnati*, "looked in the distance like a big turtle moving on the water."[14] After inspecting the monitor *Ozark*, Seaman De Witt C. Morse wrote home, "She looks to me like a clumsy and unhandy vessel."[15] Acting Assistant Paymaster William Wesley Barry wrote that old rivermen watching as he prepared to board the *Reindeer* muttered: "You will never come back the river is so narrow in places the limbs of trees will hit your boat and perhaps your smoke stacks, and when you get above these narrow places the rebels can easily fell large trees into the channel."[16]

Confusion as to who would be best suited to man these boats also hindered recruiting. The War Department was unsure of the type of training river sailors would need or whether sailors were required at all. Blue-water officers and sailors scoffed that ugly steamboats crawling down muddy channels were unsuitable places for men used to fluffy white sails and clean, open waters. "I cannot conjecture what they want of Sailor men on these Gun Boats for," railed Seaman Frederic Davis, "for there is no Sailoring to do."[17]

This uncertainty explained why the Western Flotilla found itself originally under the control of the War Department. Army and navy officials toyed with the idea of crewing gunboats with soldiers and applying army, not naval, regulations when training recruits. Eventually, salt water officers realized that—despite the lack of brine in the river water—gunboats demanded sailors and naval training tailored to the realities of the Western rivers and the mechanical nature of the gunboats.[18]

Unable to attract recruits, the navy scoured men from every possible source. It lowered standards at rendezvous, sought castoffs from the army, and accepted men deemed unfit for blockade duty. In fact, the core group of these "brown-water" sailors consisted of two groups: sailor rejects from the blockade and soldier transfers from the army. One can only imagine what the 600 men from the blockade must have been like for the navy to send them west rather than onto its undermanned blockade vessels. "Gunboatmen"—the term often used for river sailors—proved so undisciplined that by war's end the best of the lot consisted of escaped slaves and Confederate prisoners of war who agreed to enlist rather than spend any more time in a Northern prison camp.[19]

The first indication of the unhinged quality of river sailors surfaced as soon as some blockade rejects landed in Cairo, Illinois, the center of operations for the Mississippi Squadron. Almost immediately, these recruits took to drinking in the many saloons that dotted Cairo. One night, 260 of them began brawling in the streets after oversampling the local spirits. Some men drank so much that they died from liquor overdoses.[20] Rear Admiral David D. Porter, later commander of the Mississippi Squadron, was so disgusted with the quality of average blockade transferees that he called them no better than "rubbish."[21]

Soldier transferees were not much of an improvement. Desperate for men, Commander Andrew H. Foote had written to Assistant Secretary of the Navy Gustavus Fox that he would take any soldiers—"even if they are without brains, I only ask for muscle."[22] With the Forts Henry and Donelson campaigns looming, the War Department responded to Foote's plea and transferred 600 soldiers from the Western armies.[23]

The idea was a disaster. The army, taking Foote at his word, sent its offscourings. The average soldier transfer was usually a "malcontent" seeking a release from the guardhouse and a man of "intemperate habits."[24] Brigadier General Ulysses S. Grant had specifically instructed his officers to transfer soldiers in the guardhouse for "desertion, disorderly conduct etc." to the gunboat service. Furthermore, he wrote, "I would suggest, in view of the difficulty of getting men for the gunboat service, that these men be transferred to that service; also that authority be given to transfer unruly men hereafter."[25]

David D. Porter complained that most of the solders transferred to his boats were men who had led an "irregular life." He ordered his sailors to hold them down, disarm them, clean them, and then give them a good shave before joining crews.[26] One such soldier transferee was Private Charles Wash. Wash had been languishing in a military prison for attempting to murder his lieutenant when he received the option of standing court martial for attempted murder or transferring to a gunboat. He chose a gunboat.[27]

Moreover, although soldiers voluntarily transferred to the river fleet, they did not adjust well to the regimented life of the river navy.[28] Carpenter's Mate Herbert Saunders complained that some of the soldier transfers he met were "soft."[29] Upon sizing up the new soldier recruits, Commander Foote wired to Gideon Welles, "We want no more from the Army. . . . I prefer to go into the action half manned than to go with such men."[30]

The core group of soldier transfers and blockade misfits was joined by smatterings of recruits from all over the Midwest, former slaves called "contraband sailors," and, after 1862, men seeking to avoid conscription into the army.[31] They resisted attempts at naval discipline and training and possessed a penchant for drinking and stealing that outdid, in many respects, the worst antics of their brethren on the blockade, no small feat.[32]

Worse yet, their ranks seemed to contain inordinate numbers of men prone to pushing beyond accepted parameters of wartime behavior. Officer Seth Ledyard Phelps summed up what many officers thought of river sailors when he complained to John D. Rodgers that "the river material is very poor."[33] Rodgers had his own ideas for breaking this swarthy, untrained bunch: "I shall read the articles of war every Sunday until they know them, and get a parson at them whenever I can so as to break down their spirit—and let their wives come on board to lecture them on weekdays. With all these helps and hard drill they will have no time to give trouble."[34]

Arrival at the newly christened naval station at Cairo, Illinois, represented the start of a river sailor's service. Due to its strategic location at the confluence of the Ohio and Mississippi rivers and the terminus of the Illinois Central Railroad, Cairo became the most strategic Civil War port on the Mississippi River. The war had transformed this "rough sort of hamlet" into a swimming mud hole teeming with soldiers, sailors, animals, and peddlers. Fights were commonplace. Liquor dealers and prostitutes found ample customers. Weeds choked the streets, which were most of the time impassable. Worst of all, the place stank. One newspaper correspondent wrote that "Cairo smells bad": "A tumulous and disorganized rabble of stinks . . . assails the nostrils."[35]

Sailors, who had come from similarly mean places in New York and Boston, were universally shocked at what they found. "We have got into the worst place I ever imagined," wrote Frederic Davis as soon as he landed.[36] Seaman John G. Morrison, just off the train from the battlefields of Virginia, called Cairo "a dirty, swampy hole, no sidewalks, and mud knee deep."[37] To add to this foreboding atmosphere, the seasonally rising waters of the Mississippi subjected the city to intermittent flooding.[38] Seaman William Van Cleaf wrote home that "I would not live there if they would give me the whole Citty. . . . [T]he river is high now and the Citty is all under water so that they have to pump it out with a steam pump."[39]

The viciousness of Cairo gave sailors a taste of what lay ahead. Like blockade sailors, gunboatmen had to make the lifestyle switch to a ship. However, these river boats were not sailing ships, and they presented a whole range of different challenges for men new to them. River gunboats lacked the majestic beauty of ocean-going vessels. Moreover, these boats afforded less space and were much hotter than wooden sailing ships. Sailors often had to sling their hammocks wherever there was room rather than on a designated berth deck. In fact, these gunboats were so small and so hot that river sailors called them "federal bake ovens."[40]

In addition to being smaller and more cramped, gunboats were dirtier and noisier than blockade vessels. In order to be constantly ready to move, vessels, even at night, kept their boilers at half-steam. The revolutions of the engines reverberated and rattled the boat's planks, plating, and crew.[41] Constant firing of the engines consumed 6,000 pounds of coal a day.[42] As a result, the smokestacks belched coal smoke almost continuously. This left a thick black frosting all over the boat. Below deck, the engine's boilers generated enormous amounts of heat in both the boiler room and throughout the boat. Coal heavers and firemen had to endure daily temperatures in excess of 100 degrees.[43]

While the routine, regimen, and drill proved essentially the same as on the blockade, river sailors' boat training was different.[44] Gunboats did not demand that sailors learn how to work sails and spot weather patterns. Although hired pilots bore responsibility for charting a boat's course through narrow river channels, gunboat sailors confronted the peculiarities of river navigation.[45] It was a formidable task made more so due to the fact that—like blockade sailors—almost none of the men had nautical experience.[46]

Additionally, Western rivers were not easy stretches of water to navigate. Such rivers as the Cumberland, the Tennessee, and the Yazoo featured shallow, narrow navigable channels and serpentine courses. Depending on the time of year, rivers rose and fell, often to impassable depths. Turns proved sharp, water depths changed continuously, and objects floated everywhere. Crew member W. W. Barry concluded that the Cumberland River was "so crooked that sometimes a steamer a half a mile ahead of us would be apparently coming directly in the opposite direction and suddenly turn around a bend and lo' she proves to be going up the river."[47]

In many stretches, Western rivers resembled muddy creeks and bayous more than navigable waterways. Even the mighty Mississippi proved difficult and unpredictable. "You will see the old Mississippi, she looks & is tough," wrote Seaman Freeman Foster.[48] Seaman E. W. Goble called the river the "stormy Mississippi."[49] Safe passage often literally depended on as little as yards and inches in water depth or river width.[50] River banks proved so narrow in places "that sometimes our boats would be so tightly wedged between two trees that we'd have to get the trees up by the roots before we could proceed," commented 18-year-old landsman Daniel F. Kemp. "It was really like traveling thro' a woods that had been flooded," he marveled.[51]

The small margin of passage led to frequent collisions with trees and overhanging branches. Tree trunks, roots, and limbs punctured smokestacks and smashed holes in the sides of boats.[52] On the Cold Water River, George Yost's gunboat tried to squeeze through a six-yard passage between two large trees. The crew misjudged the gap and the resulting damage ignited the roof and almost blew up the vessel.[53] Near Mound City, Illinois, a single tree crashed onto the deck of the *Carondolet* and almost sunk the boat and its crew. Seaman John G. Morrison described the intense shock from just one tree: "Everything was darkened and bits of wood and glass flying in all directions. The boat quivered and shook in every point at this shock . . . After awhile I went on deck and found that the hammock nettings were broken down in several places. The hog chain and stanchions that supported it were carried away, her seams were opened and gaping in several places, and in consequence of the breaking of the hog chain, she had sank about 7 inches on the starboard side."[54]

The shallowness of the currents combined with the weight of gunboats produced numerous groundings on river bottoms. Men who developed a quick eye and a presence of mind for river depths and widths became valued river sailors.[55] Gunboats rubbed hard on the bars of the rivers, which loosened the caulking and caused vessels to spring numerous leaks.[56] If a gunboat struck bottom and got lodged, the weight of its iron-plating made it extremely difficult to free. Crew members sometimes spent hours and days freeing boats from the muddy bars and shoals of Western rivers.[57]

The sharp currents and whirling eddies of the Western rivers swung boats back and forth in the water. One crew member commented that such currents would often "ketch a ship and swing her to one side she would then come back to her old place."[58] This swinging of a boat from stern to stem also forced sailors to read the currents in the river and attempt to maintain the vessel's course with the use of anchors, ropes, and chains.[59] Moreover, Western rivers were often crowded with troop transports, gunboats, and supply ships. Gunboats swinging wide into other navigation lanes caused smashes and numerous accidents. Only trial and error taught officers and sailors when and where to drop anchors in order to keep a boat from swinging from one side to the other.

The placement of the heaviest of the iron plating around the forward part of the boat also created another problem. The concentration of the weight caused the front of the boat to sink downward when moving through the water. With the boat arched like a hog's back, the sinking in the front made the vessel more susceptible to groundings in the riverbed. Sailors remedied this by attaching from front to back a thick, movable chain, called a "hog chain." Only by making sure that the hog chain was taut could sailors keep the boat level and moving through shallow channels.[60]

Many anchors found their way to the bottom before river sailors learned what they were doing.[61] Yet, as a result of all of these challenges, river sailors became more technically oriented and more machine conscious than blockade sailors. They became handy at repairing and replacing engines, boilers, iron plates, and smokestacks and maneuvering pulleys, stanchions, and chains. In short, the gunboat service forced these men to become literally "jacks of all trades" in order to keep their boats afloat and moving down the Western rivers of the Confederacy. River sailors had little free time and lots of hard work. Seaman George Vance wrote home that after a few weeks on the *Peosta* he was "worn out" and in a "stupor."[62]

Of all the differences that distinguished the situation of river sailors from that of sailors on the blockade, none was more consequential than the accessibility to land. River sailors prowled inland waterways with shores close on each side. On most days, they were a few yards from shore. River sailors could see clearly the events and people on shore, and those on shore could see them clearly.

This nearness to land molded the river sailors' experience in a number of ways. It allowed crews to participate in the major military operations of the Western war. River sailors provided heavy gun support, transport, and amphibious capabilities during the campaigns of Fort Henry, Fort Donelson, and Vicksburg. They served on ramming vessels, mortarboats, and shore batteries. This proximity also enabled river sailors to assist in the emancipation of slaves and in the feeding and clothing of white refugees in war-torn areas of the South.

Most significantly, however, the proximity of sailors to shore coupled with the mobility of their craft in shallow waters enabled them to penetrate deep into unprotected areas of the Confederacy. This produced two consequences. First, it rendered a devastating psychological shock to Southern citizens, who did not expect to see Yankee vessels steaming outside their farms and homes. Second, it set loose men with few scruples and little discipline into slave-populated and cotton-rich areas. The result was a very personal and very violent war between sailors and Southern civilians and guerrillas unmitigated by the conventional rules of warfare.

Gunboats and river sailors penetrated areas of the Confederacy thought unreachable because of a lack of good roads. Union river sailors, not soldiers, were often the first ones to penetrate the key areas of the Western Confederacy. The quickness with which sailors and their boats arrived as well as the little amount of water they needed to sail amazed Southerners. Vessels patrolled rivers that, David D. Porter observed, "no one would believe that anything in the shape of a vessel could get through."[63] Young Eliot Callender marveled that "these boats could go anywhere the current went."[64]

This unexpected vulnerability created in Southerners an almost "pathological fear" of gunboats.[65] Commander Andrew Hull Foote wrote to Gideon Welles that Southern citizens "feared the gunboats, and only the gunboats."[66] In fact, this fear prompted Confederates to concoct every possible type of obstruction to block, sink, or slow the progress of the Mississippi Squadron. Rebels strung chains across banks, sent burning scows down rivers, and seeded river beds with thousands of floating mines called "torpedoes."[67] Confederate use of torpedoes and rams—considered to be impermissible weapons of war —stemmed from the desperation and shock that Union gunboats engendered in the hearts and minds of Southerners.[68]

It was hard to blame them. When a gunboat appeared, there was no time to prepare and no time to flee. Many Southern farmers located in backwater areas of Mississippi, Tennessee, and Arkansas awoke to the sound of the whirring and chugging of gunboats landing practically in their back yards. Private Charles Wills, an Illinois soldier, stated that the gunboats were so terrifying to Southerners because "they go at them as though they were going right on land."[69] Daniel Kemp sought to put words in the mouths of Southerners whose faces he saw as gunboats crawled through the woods and through their property. "They would probably say," Kemp figured, "the Yankees will make gunboats that will sail on a wet sponge one of these days."[70]

The terror created by gunboats easily outdistanced their tactical effects.[71] Southerners viewed gunboats and their crews as akin to a Viking invasion, spreading fear and instability into the internal areas of the South. The arrival of gunboats often prompted slaves in the area to leave their enslavers and head to gunboats seeking freedom. Some of these slaves even joined the Mississippi Squadron as crew members adding to the anguish of already harried Southerners. Gunboats and river sailors ultimately became symbols of societal unrest and slave-stealing.[72]

The approach of a gunboat and river sailors instantly threw Southern communities into hysteria. Lieutenant Commander Le Roy Fitch observed that "when a gunboat heaves in sight, all the citizens are thrown into a state of excitement, close their houses, and hurry their negroes back into the country."[73] Emily Caroline Douglas described for her fellow Southerners the scene in Natchez, Mississippi, upon the approach of the *Essex*: "[Brother Kirtland] found wild confusion, men rushing out their horses at full speed women with bundles children crying all in the greatest terror, and no wonder for upon the defenseless city whose terrible instruments of death were flying in all directions."[74]

Sailors understood this because they saw firsthand the reactions of Southern citizens. Gunboatmen eventually came to relish the fear they helped create.[75] Eliot Callender wrote that the gunboats "struck terror to every guilty soul as they floated down river."[76] Seaman James Morrison stated in his diary that when they steamed past a community along the Red River he saw "the men scowling at us and the women would put their hands to their faces and look at us through open fingers." Morrison was further surprised when "one woman put her thumb to her nose and her fingers performed several maneuvres for our edification."[77]

Confederate regulars despised the gunboats as well, particularly when they had to flee in the face of them. Seaman De Witt C. Morse wrote to his cousin that as they passed a levee at Memphis, a group of rebels shrieked, "Oh! you d——d tin clad. . . . We're enough for you, any of you," all the while keeping their bodies covered from sight.[78] Soldier Charles Wills watched in pride and awe at the effects rendered by the *Carondolet* on rebel shore batteries. "We could see every motion of the Rebel gunners plainly, and they worked like men until the boat got within about 300 yards of them, when they broke, and I tell you they used their legs to their advantage."[79]

After gunboats had forced the evacuation of Baton Rouge, Louisiana, Seaman James Henneberry found a deck of playing cards as he sifted through the camp belongings of rebel soldiers. As he peered at the deck, Henneberry found on the back of the deuce of clubs a message left by a Confederate who had little doubt that a sailor would latch onto a deck of cards. "You D——d Yankee Son a b——s," the message read, "only for your Gun boats we would see you in h–ll before we would give up this place."[80]

Fear and hatred of gunboats also triggered daily guerrilla warfare along the Western rivers.[81] Guerrillas—called "freebooters," "farmers," and "bushwhackers" by sailors—helped spearhead this war. Guerrillas operated in bands of 3 to 1,000, usually on horseback, and under such colorful names as the "Arkansas Jayhawkers" and the "Feather Bed Rangers."[82] They fired at sailors from masked shoreline batteries, sharpshot at Union gunboats, and seized passing unarmed commercial vessels.[83] Guerrillas also attacked unarmed contraband camps.[84]

Speed, surprise, and trickery were their most valuable assets. Guerrillas adopted a number of disguises. One day they would appear to be a part of Confederate regulars; then the next day they would claim to be white refugees and begged sailors for food and water. At other times, they played the part of loyal Unionists willingly signing oaths of allegiance. Then as soon as sailors turned their backs, guerrillas slipped their disguises and would attack relaxed and isolated crew members. In fact, sailors often found guerrillas killed in clashes still bearing signed loyalty oaths in their pockets.[85]

Sailors, owing to their visibility on deck during the day, their responsibility of standing watch at night, and their initial willingness to help white refugees, suffered the brunt of guerrilla attacks. Daniel Kemp recalled that the "guerrillas kept up a continual fight to pick off our men."[86] During the day, guerrillas ambushed, wounded, and killed members of sailors' foraging parties and those sailors who responded to calls for help from the banks. Any sailor who looked out of a port (an opening through which cannon were pointed) risked being shot. At night, guerrillas rowed silently out to gunboats and tried to overtake the night watch.[87] In order to discourage foraging, they poisoned water wells and granaries.[88] The following poem vividly illustrates the mindset of river guerrillas:

> Whenever the vandal cometh,
> Press home to his heart your steel,
> And when at his bosom you can not,
> Like the serpent, go strike at his heel.
> Through thicket and wood go hunt him,
> Creep up to his camp-fire side,
> And let ten of his corpses blacken
> Where one of our brothers hath died.
> In his fainting, foot-sore marches,
> In his flight from the stricken fray,
> In the snare of the lonely ambush,
> The debts we owe him pay.[89]

Guerrillas could be quite brutal.[90] Seaman Frederic Davis believed that guerrillas lived by the creed, "Dead Men Tell No Tales." Landsman Daniel Kemp recalled that sailors did not dare venture onto the spar deck in guerrilla-laden areas because "as soon as a man made his appearance he was fired upon by some sharp shooter skulking along the bank."[91] In one particularly grim instance, guerrillas kidnapped two sailors on a foraging party from the *Gazelle*. Their crewmates, joined by soldiers, quickly formed a search party. Eventually, the two sailors were found. The rescue party, however, recoiled in horror when they saw what had been done to the two. The kidnapped sailors had not only been murdered; they had also been, in the words of the search party, "horribly mutilated" by the guerrillas.[92]

Being in hostile territory and often detached from military support, sailors operated under the assumption that guerrillas were always watching them whenever they were on deck or on shore. Guerrillas did seem to appear at the most vulnerable times.[93] Whenever only a few men went ashore or a vessel became disabled, guerrillas seemed to materialize out of thin air. Officers and sailors routinely complained that the banks of almost every river seemed literally "alive" with guerrillas.[94] "Only they come upon a fellow," Frederic Davis wrote to his parents, "when he dont know it."[95]

The navy adopted a number of measures to protect sailors. Boats shifted anchorage every night so that they were not stationary targets. Crews were barred from showing any lights at night and from striking bells. Crews adopted silent signals to communicate with other vessels instead of whistles.[96] Sailors were prohibited from congregating on the deck in the daytime. Lastly, sailors were barred from landing ashore in areas not secured by the army.[97]

Although often a single shell lobbed from a howitzer was enough to disperse guerrillas, river sailors, as tough as they were, proved unprepared for this sort of irregular war. They did not understand why men who were trying to kill them would flee from a pitched fight. Western sailors were unprepared for the use of deceit, treachery, and torture. These tactics not only violated rudimentary American notions of fair play but created a tremendous amount of fear and frustration. What were sailors to do with men who did not stand up like men? Not surprisingly, gunboatmen came to view guerrillas and their methods as cowardly, unmanly, and uncivilized. George Yost labeled such behavior not war but "assassination." "They are our bitterest foe," wrote Frederic Davis, "so cowardly, so ignorant and taking up every unfair means to make our numbers less."[98]

After a number of unprincipled encounters, gunboatmen soon firmly believed that guerrillas were criminals. Seaman De Witt C. Morse called guerrillas "thieves and highwaymen."[99] Seaman John Swift wrote that "they have the most diabolical unshaven countenances you can imagine."[100] Rumors circulated that guerrillas ate soup from the skulls of murdered soldiers and sailors.[101] One sailor aptly summarized the malevolent environment that guerrillas created on the Western rivers: "If any man believes there is no purgatory—let him come into this Western Flotilla—& then he'll believe it. For with the rebels on one side & the guerrillas on the other—& the '*damned Mississippi*' forever bothering & biting us—its the devils own purgatory."[102]

Nothing fanned sailor anger over guerrillas like their purposeful blurring of the lines between innocent civilian and armed partisan.[103] Sailors liked it even less that guerrillas used civilians as cover for their actions. In fact, guerrillas often disguised themselves as ordinary civilians in order to lure boats to shore. Other times, they intimidated civilians into using their homes for bases of operations in order to disguise their whereabouts. Guerrillas used their horses, seized their food supplies, and confiscated their cotton. These techniques made it nearly impossible for sailors to distinguish between guerrilla and civilian.

The guerrillas' tactics also bred an instinctive distrust of all Southern civilians save contrabands. Officer Le Roy Fitch concluded that "I am forced to believe no man living with these guerrillas."[104] Seaman De Witt C. Morse described the intermingling of guerrillas and civilians as warfare on a "defenceless people": "They go mounted upon the best horses their victims can raise for them, in parties of from three to a dozen. . . . Some of them manage to get the confidence of their nearest neighbors in order to find where there cotton is hidden, or if sold, where the greenbacks are; (which latter they are always eager to get;) and then hang the owners to the first tree."[105]

The rising number of sailor casualties goaded the river navy into implementing a scorched earth policy with regard to Southern communities in the vicinity of guerrilla attacks. Rear Admiral David D. Porter had seen enough to know that guerrillas had effectively co-opted civilians, even nonbelligerent ones, as screens for their operations, at the cost of sailors' lives. In October 1862, Porter issued General Order No. 4, which mandated that in the event a gunboat was fired on from shore, every sailor was to "destroy everything in the neighborhood within reach of his guns," even the innocent.[106]

The navy and its crews believed that even if shoreline communities were not directly involved in guerrilla activity, they bore responsibility for suppressing it. "Should innocent persons suffer it will be their own fault," reasoned General Order No. 4. This was done in order to "teach others that it will be to their advantage to inform the Government authorities when guerrillas are about for certain localities."[107] Seeing an opportunity to further co-opt civilians into their war, guerrillas took advantage of this new approach by firing at boats from innocent residences. Surgeon Fayette Clapp stated that numerous houses and farms were burned to the ground as a result of such acts. As time went on, any firing aimed at a gunboat from a residence, Clapp wrote, was usually "against the will of the parties owning them." In one particularly sad incident, Clapp watched as a gunboat crew leveled a home while the father, mother, and their ten children stood nearby and wept.[108]

Surrounded by a hostile civilian population and moving in an unfamiliar terrain, crews needed little prodding to implement Porter's antiguerrilla policy. After the issuance of General Order No. 4, as soon as a vessel or foraging party was shot at, even once, sailors exacted immediate retaliation; they shelled and then leveled buildings, farms, and small towns. After guerrillas had attempted to kidnap a small foraging party of sailors off Fort Pillow, George Yost wrote that forty heavily armed sailors went back on shore and burned up "all the houses, barns, and everything combustible near the scene."[109]

When guerrillas attacked the gunboat *Fairplay* outside Caseyville, Kentucky, sailors moved in and seized every man in the town, confiscated the goods in all the stores, and ordered that unless a ransom of $35,000 was paid in twenty-four hours, the sailors would fire the town and carry the men south to points unknown. The ransom was quickly paid.[110]

In response to guerrilla activity in Arkansas in October 1862, Lieutenant Commander Richard Meade Jr. wrote that his sailors destroyed "all houses and cornfields for miles along the river. . . . The inhabitants of the place were given half an hour to remove necessary articles from the houses, when buildings, and fields were laid in ashes."[111]

By 1864, official levelings of guerrilla havens were being supplemented by acts of individual vengeance. In some cases, gunboat crews adopted an "eye for an eye" policy and began summarily executing guerrillas. In fact, some boats began dropping placards in guerrilla nests announcing that they would shoot any guerrilla prisoners held after the murder of any crew member. One such placard dropped ashore matter-of-factly announced the "determination to shoot a prisoner in my possession, or whom I might capture in the future, for each person killed by rebels firing on transports."[112]

Sailors' expeditions sent ashore to net guerrillas often ended not in captures but in acts of retribution.[113] Sailors, and soldiers too, routinely did not grant guerrillas the protections typically afforded prisoners of war.[114] Once sailors captured guerrillas, they showed little mercy.[115]

Seaman Charles Schetky recalled that when a forage netted a guerrilla, the tars tied the man's feet to his horse's underbelly and bound his arms. With a start, sailors would then slap the horse's backside and watch as the mount dragged the man over rocks and soil. After a terrifying ride and if the man survived, sailors would ask if he would agree to take the oath of loyalty to the United States. If he agreed, the guerrilla would be taken on board to fulfill the oath. If he did not, there were more such rides until the guerrilla agreed or died.[116] Seaman John Swift related to his girlfriend how he treated the ten guerrilla prisoners he stood guard over one night. "I had the pleasing job of being compelled to shoot one of them & give another a poke with a bayonet," Swift chuckled.[117]

One of the most vicious examples of retribution took place on 18 June 1862, on the White River in Arkansas, when a masked guerrilla battery fired a shot into the *Mound City*. The shot entered the steam drum, disabling the boat, releasing a lethal blast of steam, and killing all but fifteen of the crew, who jumped into the river to save themselves. The guerrillas who fired the shot jumped onto the sinking vessel and began to pillage its contents at the same time they shot at the men fighting to stay afloat in the swirling currents of the river. Sailors on nearby vessels watched in horror as guerrillas picked off their mates struggling in the water.

Immediately, officers on surrounding vessels ordered their sailors to retake the sinking boat. As sailors leaped onto the *Mound City*, officers gave the outlaw order of "no quarter," meaning that boarding sailors were not to spare the lives of the guerrillas who were now looting the stricken vessel. Enraged gunboatmen needed little encouragement. Seaman William Van Cleaf wrote home that, after the order, Union sailors carried out a "general slaughter": "one man killed thirteen men by himself alone the rebels got down up on their knees and beged for quarters. and we could see our men knock out their brains with the but of ther muskets. the water was only up to our neck where the boats was disabled and the rebels were so buisiy trying to board and take her a prise that they did not have their arms and our men killed them like sheep."[118]

The unprincipled violence of the guerrilla war, in which Southern guerrillas intimidated, stole from, and killed Southern civilians, seemed to legitimize every sort of illegal and immoral behavior on the Western rivers from Cairo to New Orleans. Part of this change stemmed from the escalating brutality of the war itself, which quietly began authorizing any behavior short of killing unarmed white noncombatants.

For river sailors, the guerrillas' removal of the line between civilian and combatant transformed all Southerners, not just Confederates, into potential aggressors and targets. Caught up in this ambiguous atmosphere, Western sailors began to lose whatever discipline had been instilled in them and surrendered to brutality. Once this degenerative cycle was thrown into motion, it became difficult to police and next to impossible to stop.[119] The erosion of discipline became such a concern that Rear Admiral Porter began encouraging officers to keep their crews aboard out of growing fear about what would happen if sailors were unleashed.[120]

One of the more evident signs that river sailors were losing their discipline was that, as they moved further South, they began plundering civilians' homes and farms with reckless abandon.[121] Although such acts were specifically banned by the naval articles of war and squadron regulations, gunboatmen proved to be excellent pillagers. On a broad scale, river sailors often stripped Southern farms of crops and livestock. Daniel Kemp marveled that the men on his boat, the *Cincinnati*, went to one plantation and stole 150 chickens, 600 pounds of bacon, a young bull, some geese, and a couple of guinea hens. "I did not know our men were permitted to plunder in this fashion but it was done just the same," he wrote.[122] Seaman John Morrison wrote that on his boat "a good many of the men went ashore and brought off several trophies in the shape of pigs and chickens and several other kinds of notions not laid down in the articles of war."[123]

What they could not carry back to their boats, they often simply destroyed. Landsman Milo Lacy observed that those men who were not pillaging were "wantonly destroying property" around Port Hudson plantations. The thievery and destruction by river sailors grew to such alarming levels by 1863 that Rear Admiral Porter began seizing pilfered livestock and threatened to shoot thieves and pillagers on sight.[124] Sailor William Bock wrote home to his father that he had never seen "such another place for swindlers, cottonthieves." He concluded, "Every kind of crime is committed on this river."[125]

Nothing, however, fanned the passions of river sailors like cotton. As the Mississippi Squadron moved into the cotton-rich areas of Louisiana and Mississippi, sailors quickly realized that cotton was gold. They had heard stories from former slaves regarding how slaveholders had subjugated an entire race in order to exploit it. Sailors witnessed guerrillas intimidate and kill innocent civilians for cotton. They had watched their officers salivate over it. Sailors had witnessed "businessmen" attempting to bribe boat captains to allow their vessels to pass upriver laden with cotton.[126] Seaman De Witt C. Morse wrote to a friend that his boat had protected a man getting his cotton to the bank. Morse watched in envy as the man came back from the bank "with $30,000 he had made in cotton."[127]

Not all sailor thievery, particularly with regard to cotton, was the result of a lack of discipline. The matter was more complex. It was a problem of the war and a problem of human nature. Just as it had muddied the issue of lawful killing during wartime, the guerrilla war played a conducive role in loosening the distinction between authorized foraging and punishable stealing. In effect, guerrillas legitimized stealing from civilians under the cover of contributing to the Confederate war effort. In reality, many guerrillas profited from their activities; they rode expensive horses, were handsomely armed, and possessed lots of money. River sailors uncovered the source of that wealth when they seized guerrillas' stores and found bales and bales of cotton. Many blamed guerrillas for single-handedly igniting the illicit cotton trade on the Western rivers. David D. Porter wrote that "it is well known that cotton can not be got out without the connivance of guerrillas."[128]

This criminal relationship between cotton and guerrillas became so entrenched in the minds of many crews that when they saw cotton they often thought of guerrillas and when they saw guerrillas they thought of cotton. Once this association became rooted in the minds of sailors, the line between authorized seizure of Confederate matériel and theft of Southern goods quickly blurred. Consequently, when tars saw any cotton on the Western rivers, they seized it. Most sailors knew it was likely stolen from innocent Southern civilians, but they also knew that, if it had not yet been stolen, it would probably end up in the hands of guerrillas anyway. Rather than seizing cotton later, many thought it would be better to act now and save themselves time and trouble.[129]

This is not to say that river sailors did not have their own self-serving motives for seizing cotton. They did. Many had enlisted solely for financial reasons. For those who had been poor and struggling to get by or who were simply fiendish-hearted, in the words of Seaman Hiram Martin, "cotton in those days was worth big money."[130] By March 1864, two bales of cotton fetched between $700 and $800.[131] Sailors showed their infatuation by meticulously noting every bale of cotton they saw.[132] Ultimately, the guerrillas' seizure of the property of Southerners provided river sailors an excuse to steal cotton from innocent civilians.

Moreover, as the war lengthened, river sailors became angry that, unlike blockade sailors, they were not entitled to prize money. Many felt short-changed: while they were battling mosquitoes and guerrillas and freeing contrabands for only their base salaries, blockade sailors lounged aboard ships raking in prize money. The myth of prize money on the blockade made many river sailors unhappy. They began to grumble that if they had it to do all over again they would only ship for the blockade.[133]

The lengths to which river sailors would go in their quest for cotton was vividly illustrated by the theft of cotton money by two sailors on the *Baron DeKalb*. On the night of 23 September 1862, Seamen James Kincaid and Henry Coyne flawlessly executed the theft of $9,600 from the paymaster's safe. The money represented the proceeds of the sale of cotton seized aboard the rebel steamers *Jeff Thompson* and *Beauregard*. The sailors broke into the paymaster's office, pried the safe from the bottom of the boat, and lifted it up to the top deck. From the top deck, they dropped the safe over the side of the vessel onto a smaller boat. The two then traveled down river and tore the door of the safe open wide enough to squeeze out $9,600. The sailors paddled back to the *Baron DeKalb* with the money stuffed in their pants, reboarded, and stealthily returned to their hammocks. Flush with cash, the two later deserted and were caught in New York City.[134]

River sailors and officers proved extremely prolific in seizing cotton up and down the Mississippi.[135] For the most part, gunboatmen shouldered the work in locating, baling, and transporting cotton back to their boats. They also shared in the value of the captures.[136] Sailor cotton forages were by no means small operations.[137] Their expeditions often spread seven to eight miles inland as they combed plantations and farms. Sailors commandeered slaves, wagons, and mule teams and transported the cotton to nearby gins. If the gins were operational, they began baling. If they were not, officers sent mechanics from nearby vessels to repair the gins and put them back into operation. At these sites, gangs of sailors ginned and baled the fluffy material like experts.[138] Western sailors' proficiency in processing cotton grew so impressive that Rear Admiral Porter was purported to have remarked that "Jack made very good cotton-bales."[139]

Since sailors often seized cotton from Southern civilians, it was not clearly earmarked as Confederate matériel. Crews quickly concocted a clever remedy to convert any doubtful seizures into prize money. Sailors crafted stencils of the letters "C.S.A." and "U.S.N." and marked any captured cotton with "C.S.A." on one side of the bale and "U.S.N."

on the other.[140] Other times, in order to make it appear that the rebels themselves had stamped "C.S.A." on the bales, sailors would stamp "C.S.A." first and then over those letters brand "U.S.N."[141] These measures, they hoped, would certify their claims of ownership. As Lieutenant Commander Thomas O. Selfridge commented: "The legal difficulties of establishing non-Union ownership of captured cotton led my crew to resort to an expedient while not entirely ethical, may have been justified by the special conditions."[142]

The prowess of sailors in seizing cotton bred a great deal of hostility between the army and the navy and between soldiers and sailors. Initially, soldiers laughed as sailors branded cotton bales with the letters "U.S.N." two feet high instead of the usual two-inch-size identification letters in order to legitimize their larceny. They grew demoralized, however, as they saw sailors cart off cotton as a prize of war and every gunboat weighed down with cotton, while they received nothing.[143] One army officer called the actions of sailors nothing more than "a big steal."[144] The hostility grew to such levels that during an uncomfortable dinner disgruntled army colonel James G. Wilson sardonically asked Rear Admiral Porter the meaning of the sailor-stenciled letters "C.S.A./U.S.N." Porter continued eating and replied that he had no idea. To which Wilson snorted that it stood for the "Cotton Stealing Association of the United States Navy."[145]

"Cotton mania" hindered naval operations.[146] The volume of cotton seized often forced sailors to attach to their boats empty coal barges in which they stored their cotton. If they ran out of barge space, Hiram H. Martin recalled, they stuffed the cotton "between the decks."[147] Gunboats stuffed with cotton in their holds often became too heavy to float. In the failed Red River Campaign, every gunboat had cotton stuffed in the holds. In order to avoid sinking their boats in the currents, sailors frantically jettisoned their precious bales of cotton overboard, only after they had tossed the gunboat's protective iron plates.[148] In fact, the navy even lost one boat above Yazoo City owing to the preoccupation with cotton foraging. In April 1864, the captain of the *Petrel* left his fellow boats and attempted to run by a Confederate battery for no apparent reason. Without support, the boat was an easy target. Once the fieldpieces disabled the *Petrel*, Rebel soldiers seized its guns and destroyed the vessel. The crew fled without properly firing the ship. Commander Robert Townsend arrested the *Petrel*'s captain and blamed the destruction of the vessel on a "desire to procure cotton, rather than the noble ambition of advancing the public service."[149]

Landsman Daniel Kemp recalled that during the failed Deer Creek, Mississippi, expedition, sailors placed lust for cotton over their mission and in some instances even over their own lives. As Confederate artillery pushed the fleeing sailors back to their vessel, in a retreat Kemp called worse than Bull Run, he watched as his mates "loaded all the gunboats with cotton as we retreated then burned the gins and all the cotton we couldn't carry." It was "disgraceful," he concluded.[150]

Even when Union sailors lost campaigns, they still managed to cart cotton back to their boats. After the Deer Creek expedition, Landsman Daniel Kemp counted as much as $25,000 in cotton loaded on the gunboat *Cincinnati* on 20 March 1863. Between 8 April and 13 April 1864, Seaman Alexander Miller counted 504 bales of cotton—worth roughly over $200,000—loaded onto his gunboat during the Red River Campaign.[151]

Not all sailors agreed with the pilfering of cotton from Southern civilians. Some questioned the steady stream of cotton being loaded on gunboats and wondered how the navy could legally seize cotton since it was not considered a prize of war.[152] "There is something wrong someplace," William Bock wrote to his mother. "Cotton is not a legal prize for the navy—at any rate—they can not claim anything which is not afloat as prize money."[153] De Witt C. Morse snarled to his friend back home that "there is a certain kind of business carried on along this river that I don't exactly approve of, though very likely it is none of my business, viz: that of cotton dealing."[154]

This is not to argue that river sailors operated unilaterally in their cotton campaign. Officers ordered, supervised, and profited from sailors' acts. Naval officers manipulated sailors into vigorously seizing cotton as prize money. Without question, naval officers like David D. Porter and Thomas O. Selfridge winkingly approved of sailor appropriations.[155] It was even rumored that the ill-fated Red River campaign was instigated solely for the purpose of gobbling up cotton.[156] Moreover, the worst case of cotton fever was exhibited by an officer, not a sailor. On 4 September 1864, Captain Daniel W. Glenny attempted to sell his boat and his crew on the *Rattler* to the Confederates for $250,000 and 100 bales of cotton. The plot failed, but the cotton operations continued.[157] By April 1865, between 6,000 to 7,000 bales of cotton had made their way to Cairo naval courts as prizes of war.[158]

The experiences of Western sailors strongly showed the social and economic repercussions produced when a military force bearing new technology was unleashed into a civilian population. One would think that it would have been easier for river sailors to patrol undefended back waters of the Confederacy. Instead, their task proved difficult and volatile because it was ambiguous. The fear and hatred created by sailors aboard ominous-looking war machines near homes and farms instantly destabilized the Southern social structure. Families became frightened. Slaves ran away. Rougher elements of these Southern communities struck back violently, using unaccepted guerrilla tactics. Guerrillas profited from the panic by bullying, stealing from, and murdering their frightened neighbors.

Although they had helped trigger these scenes, Mississippi Squadron sailors sat literally in the middle. In the middle of rivers and streams, in the middle of civilians and guerrillas, and in the middle between foraging and stealing and between acts of war and murder. "We are right where we see it," wrote Frederic Davis to his father.[159] The results proved ugly, and the dangers feared from serving on gunboats came from unexpected places. It was daunting to try to separate guerrillas from Southern civilians when they were all dressed in plain clothes, they were all sneering, and they were all hostile. Who were the guerrillas? Were they only criminals on horseback conducting semi-disorganized operations at night? What about the simple farmer who had just seen his harvest seized and in desperation lifted his rifle at a Union gunboat as it drifted by his farm?

The fact that most Southern civilians sympathized tacitly or openly with guerrilla forces did little to help river sailors in their decision-making processes. Scared themselves, surrounded by a hostile people, and traveling through bogs and swamps, eventually Mississippi sailors lashed out at the guerrillas, Southern civilians, and their property. The problem was that the insidious nature of the guerrilla war made it too difficult to distinguish between civilian and guerrilla and between war matériel and personal property. Ultimately, the ferocity and pecuniary nature of the guerrilla war along the Western rivers enabled Western sailors to exercise their baser natures and greedier impulses in a war environment tailor-made for stealing, mayhem, and murder.

# 5 All Hands Drunk and Rioting
## The Maritime Culture of Union
## Sailors

The image of the jolly jack tar, a drink in one hand, a woman on his arm, quick with a story as well as a knife, has achieved a sort of mythical notoriety in the American memory.[1] While accurate in its caricature of the outgoing personalities of sailors, this stereotypical characterization packs little in the way of explanatory power. In crude terms, Union sailors seemed every bit the drunk and riotous seamen of maritime mythology.[2] In many ways, they appeared worse. Union sailors drank to wretched excess, stole everything in sight, fought, railed, chafed, and rebelled against any institutional and personal constraints placed on them by the navy. Their behavior reflected many realities. One was that men run amok when released from society's rules. Another was that the navy's attempts to domesticate, discipline, and sober up sailors only angered them and created a backlash culture spiteful of officers and naval hierarchy.[3]

Stereotypes of the behavior of sailors have long circulated as cultural currency with little or no explanation from historians. Even today, most people to varying degrees are aware of many of the—mostly negative— caricatures of sailors' behavior. Such phrases as "drinks like a sailor" or "swears like a sailor" immediately conjure up clear, descriptive images of behavior that is distinctive, colorful, and strange.[4] Many of the works churned out about sailors generally and Union sailors specifically are anecdotal narratives that seek to describe, rather than explain, their behavior and culture.[5]

Maritime historians have focused on the environment and the nature of ship work as determinative factors in shaping the distinctive look and behavior of sailors. These influences helped mold Union sailors, who looked, moved, and talked like typical sailors. Ruddy cheeks worn by the sun and wind, scars from working with wood and metal, and clothes tarred for waterproofing all found their impressions on their bodies and faces. Moreover, the collective nature of shipboard details lent an unmistakable rhythm to their movement.[6] They communicated using precise, technical terms, peppered with colorful, often obscenity-riddled analogies. Sailors made their points quickly, often drawing mental pictures with their words. Phrases like "learning the ropes" and "versatile as a monkey" achieved a certainty of expression, unmatched on land.[7]

However, environment and vocational marks told only part of their story. The culture and characteristics of Union sailors reflected more than mere outward behavioral patterns engendered by work. While the labor requirements of the ship and the sailors' battles against nature certainly played a significant role in helping influence their behavior, the culture of common Union sailors—broadly defined as the pattern of behavior and standardized social characteristics embodied in thought, speech, customs, and actions—derived from the collision of their working-class beliefs with the stern and sober strictures of the wartime United States Navy.

The fundamental problem was that the free-spirited impulses of recruits, borne of class beliefs and ethnic diversity, which made them naturals for the physical demands and risks of the seafaring life, clashed with the service realities of the United States Navy. The navy was an aristocratic institution steeped in hierarchy and overseen by native-born, middle- and upper-class officers. The navy was stricter than the merchant marine, which allowed seamen more leeway when it came to personal behavior. Merchant captains did not pay a great deal of attention to the personal habits and moral development of their crews. Merchant sailors could drink, be dirty, sing songs, and swear while they worked, as long as they got the work done.

The wartime navy was an altogether different service. Combined with the confining nature of ships, the overregulated life mandated by the navy clashed deeply with the personalities of sailors. Old sailors resented the long nature of their cruises and the navy's reform agenda. New sailors felt trapped, crowded, and disillusioned. Any illusions of unconditional freedom dissipated in the stifling atmosphere of regulations, duties, and the oversight of officers.

Moreover, the navy's social structure featured a rigid system of moral and behavioral supervision in a fixed hierarchy presided over by career and volunteer officers.[8] In the 1850s, reformers had convinced navy officials and congressmen that sailors were men in dire need of behavioral correction. The navy embarked on an intrusive program designed to elevate the lives of its sailors through religion, education, and sobriety. By 1861, the "behavior of American naval seamen was minutely regulated." Wartime legislation made the situation worse.[9]

As a result, even though they eventually adapted their behavior to the navy's regulations and tacitly acknowledged its authority structure, sailors did not totally capitulate. Instead, tars reacted by forming a culture that pushed against the limits of naval regulations wherever possible. The culture of Union sailors reflected their working-class backgrounds, time-tested maritime rituals, and the reality that these men had been freed from the constraints of civilian society. Two dominant principles informed this culture. The first was the desire to escape the confining atmosphere of the ship through any means possible. The second was the urge to resist.[10]

Escapism was the first dominant principle behind the culture of Union sailors. Aboard ship, men engaged in a number of escapist activities. While much of this entertainment proved self-destructive, the much ballyhooed love of mirth often was nothing more than an attempt by sailors to suppress the sense of confinement.[11] Any activity that could take a sailor's mind off of the ship was extremely popular.[12]

Sailors liked to tell jokes, stories, and anecdotes.[13] Seaman George Clark recalled that the "top-gallant forecastle was the favorite place to tell tales of love, wreck, and the joys and perils of a sailor's life."[14] They enjoyed the theater and all sorts of entertainment from dancing to musical instruments. Sailors also engaged in competitive, physically challenging games, from tag to wrestling. Baseball proved extremely popular. James Henneberry commented that "it is now played with a good deal of earnestness on each side."[15]

Crews loved to gamble at anything from checkers and dominoes to card games such as Forty-five, Euchre, and Old Sledge. Seaman George Clark described a typical night of escapist entertainment aboard a Union ship: "Every kind of song was sung; rough jokes played; feats of strength, quickness, and elasticity displayed; jig dancers footed it out by the hour; cards, dominoes, and tee-totums, came in play; crack-a-loo and gambling were carried on slily, and the men tried every way to kill time."[16]

Union sailors also engaged in more individual forms of escapism. Men enjoyed writing letters home, even if they did not have the money for postage to mail them. George Bright marveled that it was a soulful sight watching a whole crew's eyes focused, "diligently scratching at sheets of paper laid flat on the deck." Seaman Edwin Benedict at-

*"Six Bells in the Dogwatch": A sailor's drill typically ended at around 5:00–6:00 P.M. Once freed from their daily duties, sailors enjoyed dancing since it combined physical exercise and music. Charles E. Stedman Sketchbook, courtesy of the Boston Athenaeum.*

tributed such concentration to the fact that writing to people on land allowed him to go there mentally.[17]

The same sentiments lay behind sailors' well-known attraction to fishing. The secret was that sailors loved fishing partly for the sport, partly for the food, but mainly for the relief it provided. When fishing, men could block out their annoying crewmates and overbearing officers for hours by focusing on the blue water. Seaman Israel E. Vail described the activity's allure: "When all else fails, fishing seems to offer the refuge from despair; and the quiet contemplation of the bob, in constant expectation of its disappearance below the surface, or the thrilling anticipation of the jerk, in absence of the bob, seems to bring rest to an unhappy mind. With a knowledge of this happy fact, fishing was carried on from morning until night over the sides of the ship."[18]

The ultimate form of escape for seamen was desertion. Traditionally, desertion had functioned as the way for seamen to change bad situations.[19] Like the generations of sailors who had gone before them, when

*Sailors enjoyed any activity that could take their minds off their ships. One of the most popular activities was making music. This is the sailors' band aboard the USS* Wabash. *Courtesy of the U.S. Naval Historical Center.*

sailors became tired of their shipmates, their ship, or the drudgery of seafaring life, they slipped off ship as soon as it landed in port. When granted the opportunity, tars proved ingenious at desertion—adroitly leaping through portholes, disguising themselves as civilian workers, or tying hammocks together and then rappelling down the sides of the ship. No hatch or port was too small or too disgusting. Officers often had to place marines at the head's exit hole or risk losing their crews.[20]

The problem for Yankee sailors was that the navy effectively negated opportunities for desertion by restricting liberty to absolute necessity and keeping men at sea and away from ports for most of their terms. Although 6 percent of all navy enlistees did manage to desert during the war, which was less than the percentage of army deserters (9.6 percent), far more would have deserted had the navy given them the chance.[21]

With desertion a limited option, Union sailors opted for the most effective way to escape their surroundings without ever leaving the ship: they drank. This, too, was not a new practice among sailors. The Royal Navy had attached such importance to the use of alcohol aboard

*"Splicing the Main Brace for the Last Time in the U.S. Navy": Union sailors loved to drink. During the first part of the war, the navy, continuing a tradition adopted at its inception, provided a grog ration twice a day. Congress abolished the practice on 30 August 1862. Charles E. Stedman Sketchbook, courtesy of the Boston Athenaeum.*

ship that it formally instituted the grog ration—rum and water—for seamen.[22] The American navy had also established the practice, although it substituted whiskey for rum because whiskey was cheaper.

The distribution of the grog ration—called "splicing the main brace" by sailors—functioned as one of the most important and anticipated parts of a sailor's day.[23] Twice a day, before breakfast and before supper, sailors received their grog ration. It was done in formal fashion. Upon the boatswain's whistle, men stood in a single-file line and impatiently waited for the ship's steward to ladle finely measured servings of grog into their own grog mugs. Sailor Stephen Blanding described the anticipation surrounding the event: "When the Boatswain piped for grog time, the crew fell into and marched in single file, before the ships steward, who dealt out each share as he came up. Each man received one gill in a small round measure. The boys often tried to trick the steward by falling into line again and thereby getting a double ration, but they were not always successful in this, for the steward, master at arms, and a marine stood by to see that each man got his ration and that no man was served twice."[24]

The grog ration was an integral part of the work day. Alcohol slaked thirsts and motivated men to perform unpopular and filthy work details such as coaling the ship and holystoning the decks. It was so effective in prompting sailors to work that Boy Charles Mervine commented, "If you want a Sailor to work give him his whiskey and he is true to the letter."[25] Its withholding was used as vital form of punishment.[26] Sailors believed that the liquid helped in maintaining morale by regularly promising a few hours of pleasure in a dreary, depressing environment.[27] Sailors so looked forward to their grog that they often awoke in the morning chanting: "Pipe to breakfast, heave the Log, Strike bells eight and roll to Grog."[28]

The problem was that the living situations of Union sailors proved so miserable that most recruits overreacted and relied on liquor exclusively to help them through the day. Heavy drinkers to begin with, Union sailors did not drink in moderation. "All are great smokers and drinkers," wrote Seaman Harry Browne.[29] Sailors drank on Christmas, Saturdays, and whenever they went ashore.[30] Alcohol was used to brace, calm, and restore men's nerves before and after combat.[31] Union sailors drank to alleviate their physical maladies, such as when they were too hot or too cold. They drank when they were thirsty, bored, lonely, or sad. "Rum," wrote Landsman Cosam T. Bartlett, "lay nearest the sailors heart."[32]

Clearly, the navy attracted a significant number of men who liked to drink alcohol. For many, drinking was a significant part of their prewar life. Such men were used to drinking—and drinking heavily. For some, the exercise functioned as a competitive outlet whereby they buttressed their manhood and bonded with male peers by drinking other men under the table. Drinking and the social accoutrements that surrounded it formed a vital center in their world and was a vital way to bond. These types of men tended to work in aggressively masculine and competitive working-class occupations that encouraged the consumption of alcohol. They were some of the roughest men working in some of the meanest labor environments in a country, that as a rule, drank a lot anyway.[33]

Others were alcoholics. It should not be surprising that since the navy offered a liquor ration twice a day, it attracted men addicted to drink. Paymaster William Keeler was so convinced that alcohol was the key ingredient in luring recruits that he wrote to his wife, "It is amusing to listen to the history of the lives of some of our men & learn how they started in life—what they were once & what they are now—in most cases whiskey is the cause."[34]

Many men drank because initially the navy did not prohibit them from doing so and alcohol seemed for a time to raise their spirits. Coal Heaver William Wainwright defended his decision to begin drinking as a last resort. "I dont know as anyone could find any fault for there is very few young men could withstand the temptation that was held out to me." Faced with the loneliness, the boredom, and the isolation of the ship, Wainwright had succumbed to the temporary escape offered by liquor. "I felt as though I had been transported into another world," he rationalized.[35]

The introduction of large numbers of men who liked to drink into an environment that encouraged drinking, overseen by an institution that subsidized it, created a large number of alcoholics and turned the Union navy, in the words of one officer, into a "drunkards' asylum."[36] George Geer, a fireman on the *Monitor*, wrote home to his wife, "I believe that Liquor in the Navy has made many [a] Drinkard."[37]

The debilitating effects on sailor performance and health surfaced everywhere. It was not unusual to see sailors hung over and staggering serpentinely on the decks of ships. William Wainwright penned in his log that—more often than not—his crewmates were "so tired [drunk] that they could lay down a great deal better then they could stand up." Seaman Edwin Benedict wrote that symptoms of alcohol abuse proved so prevalent that his mates regularly suffered "sore heads" and "plug noses."[38] Seaman John Simpson wrote that on Union ships "Liquor and not King cotton reigned supreme."[39]

Naval physicians railed against the medical consequences of the men's lack of restraint. Samuel Boyer, surgeon aboard the *Fernandina*, said that the liquor problem was so "acute" that Union vessels on the blockade had become "floating grogshops."[40] Doctor William Whelan of the Bureau of Medicine and Surgery wrote to Commander John Dahlgren that the use of alcohol to ward off depression actually made life

*Alcohol abuse not only affected sailors physically; it disrupted discipline. When sailors reached shore on "liberty" they usually drank to excess like the besotted "liberty man" above returning to the ship. The original caption reads: "Justly Incensed Commander to Liberty-Man Returned on Board: 'Here—come here, you—sir—what's your name?' Inebriated Mariner: 'Name? Lor bless yer, I aint got no name—it was shot away at Mobile.'" Charles E. Stedman Sketchbook, courtesy of the Boston Athenaeum.*

more depressing for sailors. Whelan argued that the biggest problem in sailors' use of liquor to raise their spirits was that alcohol's escape was only temporary. After sailors experienced the well-being initially brought on by consuming alcohol, Whelan confided, "depression soon occurs." This high followed by a worse low was what made repetition necessary and dependence inevitable.[41]

Men deprived of liquor for longer times than their bodies would permit experienced delirium tremens and other withdrawal symptoms. Hardened alcoholics often visibly trembled on deck. Landsman Milo

Lacy wrote that on his ship it was common to see drunk men "excelling the hags in their slovenliness" and then "lying back in it." Seaman Charles Kember recalled the awful effects of his withdrawal. "A few days after that I lay on the gun deck with the horrors from the effects of drinking when I came too I came to the conclusion I would not drink anymore." [42]

The temporary stimulation rendered by spirits proved their greatest allure. The longer men stayed aboard ships with no respite, the more depressed they became, and the more they sought liquor to alleviate the depression. The more they used liquor to alleviate depression, the more they depended on it to help get them through the day. As a result, men who shipped as hardened drunks drank more. Recruits who may have been impulsive drinkers before now became habitual drinkers. Men who had never touched a drop, when faced with the prospect of endless days aboard ship, soon saw liquor as the only form of escape. One recent convert aboard the *Sabine*, charged with drunkenness, begged his commander to disregard the charge, pleading that he was "not a drinking man. . . . I have a wife who will become crazy when she learns that one . . . to whom she had always looked up with respect, has in an unguarded moment . . . blighted his future prospects." [43]

The increasing dependence of Union sailors on alcohol disrupted naval operations. George Bright, after taking a group of sailors to Hilton Head, South Carolina, was aghast that, although on shore for less than an hour, his men came back and fell "dead drunk in the bottom of the boat." They were so drunk that they could not even navigate the small boats back to their ship. The whole crew, including Bright, almost drifted out to sea. [44]

Drunk gun crews misfired or missed their targets. Often, sailors who boarded a captured blockade vessel usually sought out liquor to the exclusion of all else. When the steamer *Florida* ran the runner *Kate* aground, her sailors wasted no time in sniffing out alcohol. "They went on board," wrote William Keeler, "all hands got drunk, had a fight & came off without accomplishing their purpose." [45] During a routine boarding of a seized blockade runner, the sailors aboard the *Brooklyn* became so drunk and unruly that an officer restored order only after slashing a man's throat and a marine discharged his rifle in a scuffle, killing a drunk sailor. [46] Union Jacks' propensity for alcohol abuse grew to such mythical proportions that George Bright marveled: "Jack is a terrible fellow for smelling out liquor, however well it is concealed. I believe a party of sailors, set ashore on a desert island in the middle of the sea, would contrive to get drunk in less than two hours without even looking for anything to eat."[47]

Moreover, alcohol abuse acted as the single largest contributor to disciplinary problems aboard ships and on shore.[48] When sailors became drunk they were more prone to fight, steal, and disobey orders; sometimes all at once. On the Mississippi Squadron, intoxicated sailors ran continuously amok in Cairo. The worst episode took place on 22 April 1862, when after drinking five barrels of whiskey, sixty men died from liquor overdoses, drownings, and suicides. In recounting the night to his father, Frederic Davis wrote, "You would not believe one half that I could tell you. . . . God forbid my ever passing another such a night." "It is awful to see what degredation some sailors will sink for the sake of rum," young Charles Mervine penned in his log.[49]

One of the more shocking incidents of sailor drinking occurred on 18 June 1862 in the aftermath of the explosion of the *Mound City*. During an attack on the St. Charles' Batteries in the White River campaign in Arkansas, fifty-nine members of the crew died, many of whom burned to death when guerrillas fired a shell through a steam drum. The rest drowned in the currents of the White River. Before the guerrillas boarded the vessel, those sailors who survived the explosion did little to earn their new lease on life according to Jonathan Duble, first master on the *Conestoga*:

> I beheld with extreme disgust a portion of the few men who were uninjured, drunk. A portion of the crew of the *St. Louis*, a portion of the crew of the *Conestoga*, also some of the soldiers of the *New National* were in the same beastly condition, and while so acts most scandalous were perpetrated on board. Men lying in the agonies of death were robbed of their monk bags, money purses. Rooms were broken open, trunks, carpet, sacks etc., pillaged, and their contents scattered around and destroyed. Watches of the officers were stolen, and quarreling, cursing, and rioting, as well as robbing, seemed to rule. Liquor was put in water casks, with water and ice, for the relief of the wounded, but these men had buckets full, pure, who drank for the purpose of debauch.[50]

A solid year and a half of officer reports of rowdy, drunken behavior by sailors prompted both houses of the United States Congress, under pressure from reform groups, to pass legislation imposing more rigorous behavioral standards on U.S. ships.[51] On 17 July 1862, Congress passed *An Act for the Better Government of the Navy of the United*

*States.* The act, while outwardly amending the navy's administrative regulations, sought to curb the misbehavior of sailors. Such activities as cruelty, swearing, lying, gambling, "scandalous conduct tending to the destruction of good morals," provoking with reproachful words, and exhibiting contempt for officers became punishable offenses. The linchpin of the reform plan was the decision to ban all alcohol aboard ships as of 1 September 1862.[52]

To put it mildly, the Reform Act was not well received. Not surprisingly, the prohibition on drinking drew the most fire.[53] Seaman Franklin Smith wrote that when Secretary of the Navy Gideon Welles's order to prohibit alcohol was read to his fellow mates aboard the *Bienville*, it was greeted with "disgust."[54] George Geer noted that "the men take it to heart very much, and swore they will never come in the Navy again."[55] Men in the North Atlantic Blockading Squadron immediately drew up a petition to have the law repealed. The unilateral extinguishment of the right to drink was called "an act of tyranny."[56] Others snarled that the "Country would go to the Dogs."[57] Seaman John Simpson penned in his journal that the crew on the *Brooklyn* grew so "indignant" as the order was read that the captain had to order a grog ration as soon as its reading was finished or risk a riot.[58]

Sailors believed that the prohibition of alcohol violated the terms of their enlistment.[59] Sailors' anger over the banning of spirits made its presence felt in the penning of songs like "Farewell to Grog."[60] The outrage was memorialized in poems. In "Jack Ratlin's Lament," Seaman James Eggo constructed a fictional dialogue between an old sailor, Jack Ratlin, and a new sailor, Bill Frill. In the poem, Ratlin cites a litany of sailors' grievances, the greatest of which is prohibition:

> But the greatest cause of all my woe, I am just about to mention,
> It's another abolition scheme, of their black heart's invention.
> You know that day by day we drank our Uncle's health in whiskey,
> Which kept us our weary way, contented, gay, and friskey.
> But those d——d abolitionists to gratify their passion,
> Not content with freeing contrabands, they've stopped the spirit ration;
> But if they'll just take my advice, though they may treat it slightly,
> They'll give the sailors back their grog, give the niggers hell or Hayti.[61]

Many tars wept at the last formal distribution of the spirit on 31 August 1862.[62] Some murmured that they would "go crazy if they cannot get Liquor." Others vowed to drink more.[63] Sad sailors watched with heavy hearts as casks of whiskey were rolled ashore.[64] Seaman Stephen Blanding recalled the feelings of his mates on the end of the grog ration: "I well remember the day we received the news that grog was abolished. . . . Curses not so loud, but deep, were indulged in by old tars, some of whom, had seen years of service, and who, by custom, had become habituated to their allowance of grog, that very expectation of it was accompanied by a feeling of pleasure. It was a long time before the men forgot the actions of congress, and in fact, they never ceased to talk about it."[65]

While the overindulgence of alcohol had undeniably triggered a host of problems, its abolition did not stop drinking among sailors. The measure only stemmed subsidized drinking. Sailors may have drunk more after the outlawing of liquor than before. After naval prohibition, men would do almost anything to get their hands on liquor. Many sailors spent their entire wages on "Rot Gut" and "Red Eye" now sold at exorbitant prices by sutlers that steamed out to Union vessels. Prices ranged from $2 to $10 per bottle for "the most wretched stuff worth perhaps 10 cents," one man wrote.[66] Yeoman Carsten DeWitt marveled that the high price for liquor "does not make any difference with poor Jack, who will pay for everything they want."[67]

Sailors smuggled liquor aboard ships in unmarked jars and cans marked oysters or navy sherry. They often forced boys to steal it aboard.[68] When they were out of money, they stole liquor from surgeons' dispensaries and officers' quarters.[69] Drinking among sailors proved so pervasive after prohibition that William Keeler, paymaster on the *Monitor*, was moved to decry the profusion of alcohol: "There are three great evils in both our army and navy . . . the first is whiskey, the second is whiskey, and the third is whiskey."[70]

On a profound level, the Reform Act struck at the heart of the culture of Union sailors. Most recreational and social exchanges among common sailors centered around formalistic, communal rounds of drinking. Sailors constructed songs, danced, and played music while drinking. For others, imbibing was a potent holdover from their prewar cultures, in which festive drinking represented an integral part of funerals, weddings, elections, and holidays.[71]

Furthermore, drinking, swearing, and rowdy excesses functioned as measured payments for sailors' submission to the miseries of a ship and the rigidity of the navy. For good or ill, alcohol and the culture that grew up around it helped sailors overcome hardship in the absence of other sources of comfort. Banning alcohol absolutely dealt a severe blow to already sagging morale. The measure managed to offend almost every segment of the sailor population from working-class toughs to recent immigrants, without effectively curbing alcohol abuse. The only success the prohibition could claim was that it almost universally made sailors angry at the navy, their officers, and Congress.[72]

Strict application of the Reform Act by officers further fanned sailor anger. Viewing the measure as a license to correct all of the distasteful behaviors exhibited by sailors, vigilant officers, with renewed vigor, routinely reproached crews for every personal flaw from swearing to snarling to spitting. After 1862, Union sailors became even more measured, gauged, probed, and restricted. Men who thought they had escaped mainstream society's rules and expectations regarding acceptable behavior now found themselves subjected to around-the-clock personal scrutiny.

Instead of making sailors more obedient and more sober, the Reform Act hardened the contrarian impulses of Union sailors into passive acts of resistance; while they outwardly adapted their behaviors to the rigid strictures of the navy, they subtly defied them. It was a tightrope act since there was a fine line between accepted defiance and chargeable insubordination. As much as Union sailors valued demonstrations of their liberty, they were not going to indulge in them at the risk of spending the war in irons. As the war dragged on, sailors crafted a peculiar behavior that featured subtle, yet contrary, patterns of responding and performing. Union sailors, in an environment that demanded ultimate compliance, after 1862, became compliantly noncompliant.

This behavior manifested itself through a series of mini-rebellions designed to impede personal intrusions. Confronted with naval minutiae aimed at personal reform, sailors adopted a general attitude that scrolled in a rough equilibrium between sullen compliance and open defiance.[73] Tars did their duties, but they controlled the way they performed them. The language of this attitude rebellion was the grumble. Deep and guttural, sailors responded to any request, inquiry, or order with an indecipherable growl. Sailors "grumble at anything," marveled surgeon Theodore Lyman.[74]

The beauty of grumbling was that it was loud and demeaning enough to register a sailor's discontent but not sufficiently intelligible that a crewmate or officer could understand it. George Bright explained to his father that the sailors he encountered were "always growling about something even when perfectly good natured."[75] They growled when they worked. They even grumbled when they were not working. Seaman Joseph L. Brigham found on the steamer *Pocahontas* even when lying still "everyone growling because they have to lay around so." George Geer was amazed to realize that the grumble was the essence of a sailor—so much so, he wrote, that it "is part of them."[76]

Grumbling performed a number of functions. It was not civil, it was not friendly, and it was not nice. But it was not whining. Grumbling and growling were mean and instantly disarming. Older sailors raised the practice to an art form and used it liberally from complaining about the food to demeaning a green hand. William Wainwright marveled that old sailors "growl more than any other persons aboard the ship."[77] Sailors, through this device, exercised chronic contempt for everyone and everything aboard ship. Nothing proved sacred. Everything—from mess mates and friends to navy regulations and officers' foibles—was mocked, derided, and devalued.[78]

Furthermore, grumbling helped sailors create space aboard ship: when leveled at fellow shipmates they did not like—such as contraband or immigrant sailors—the discomfort it created kept listeners at a physical and psychological distance. When rained down on new recruits it cowed them immediately. Landsman Daniel Kemp remarked that the first thing he heard as he hit the deck of the *Clara Dolsen* was sailors scowling, "Oh! you fellows will be sorry you ever came here." The sound of it, Kemp admitted, instantly made him feel "blue."[79]

Sailors mined the content of almost every act looking for an angle from which to scorn. New recruits who volunteered to perform details or help officers could expect to be greeted on their return with the panting and barking of their mates who let the errant sailor know he was acting like a trained dog. "But there must be somebody to make Fun of," explained Charles Poole after he and his mates finished tormenting a young sailor. Such antics not only made for good teasing but served as gentle rebukes designed to stifle acts and values deemed incompatible with sailor behavior. Plus, as Poole explained, "it will soon blow over and he will have his chance the same as the Rest."[80]

More importantly, grumbling permitted sailors to vent their frustrations in a combative and masculine manner. Sailors loathed the mindless minutiae and attention to detail that the navy foisted on them. They resented officers' abuse. Sailors quickly became aware that many of these officers had never wielded any power before. They recognized when discipline was thinly disguised sadism. Sailors also realized that officers who paid attention to the letter rather than the spirit of the law brought them no closer to winning the war. Every time sailors polished the brass in the rain, scrubbed the deck of a ship while coal dust fell, or suffered reprimands for spitting or swearing, they growled, scowled, and grumbled. Grumbling all at once mocked, questioned, and rejected the details of navy life that most of the time seemed meaningless.[81]

Officers' inability to understand sailors made them easy prey. Seaman John Simpson recalled that when his ship faced a shortage of food, the commander reduced the men to half-rations. The commander, obviously out of touch with the sailor's mind-set, decided he would couch the unpopular order in patriotic terms. He explained that sailors must make this sacrifice as part of their patriotic duty to the cherished republic. When he dismissed them, he did not call them "men" or "crew" as they were usually called. Instead, he addressed them as "citizens." As soon as the boatswain piped them down a few minutes later, Simpson recalled, "a unanimous laughter took place among the men," as they chortled about the commander's sentimental pandering.[82]

A fanatical devotion to his limited sphere of rights was a sailor's measuring stick for grumbling. Woe befell those persons who trampled, ever so slightly, on the rights of sailors. Union sailors were always on the "bright lookout" for those who slighted their rights. This attitude was not all the result of navy regimentation. Indeed, checked and restrained on board a man-of-war so densely crowded, it was understandable that most came to guard their rights selfishly. Officers' intrusions into their personal lives only made this behavior more pronounced. *Naval Duties and Discipline*, an 1865 manual designed to aid officers in understanding the mind-set of Union sailors, warned: "The sailor is the most profound stickler among men for what he conceives to be his *rights*. He will not bate a jot of them; he will fight to the bitter end for them. It is not because his pay is so small; it is because that little, to the quarter cent, is his; his by divine and human right."[83]

Subtle variations of disrespect permeated sailors' behavior. Sailors crafted these affects into a dizzying display of subtle resistance, primarily aimed at officers. They drew on a whole spectrum of attitudes specifically calculated to frustrate. On the mild end, a titter, a sneer, a look, or simply responding with hands firmly planted in his pockets registered a sailor's contempt. Men would often slowly respond to officers' orders, making them wait ten to fifteen minutes before they appeared. This form of foot dragging was called "sogering." Sailors when sogering would procrastinate by knocking things over and cleaning them up or attending to something else. Men would do anything to force an officer to ask twice or three times to have an order carried out.[84] When they did appear, sailors could marshal a great number of excuses to test an officer's patience. Crew members argued that they did not hear the order, were asleep, or that they had appraised the value of the order and subsequently determined that they "did not see anything that had to be done."[85] The sharpest of these sailors were called "sea law-yers" because of their ability to offer a myriad of plausible but untrue excuses.[86]

Such actions drove officers mad. To heighten the effect of the irritation, sailors adopted a surly demeanor. One officer complained that sailors displayed cold, "irritating indifference" to the discharge of their duties.[87] Others railed that sailors routinely discharged their orders "caustically" and with bitter "sarcasm."[88] Such tactics included repeating orders in a tone bristling with mockery and contempt. Sailors proved particularly irritated when officers asked them what they were doing. More often than not, sailors responded with such barbs as "I will let you know" or "None of your damn business."[89]

Boatswain Thomas Smith recalled one such incident when he ordered Seaman James McConlogue to clean the spit boxes. Smith watched, beside himself with anger, as McConlogue delayed, wandered, and inch by inch literally dragged his feet to the task. Only when Smith confronted him face to face did McConlogue finally attend to the order with a sneer, "I guess you will get it done."[90]

Through these acts, sailors made every order from officers an exhausting contest of wills. Grumbling and contrived confrontations with officers were peppered with healthy doses of profanity. Officers proved easy targets since they tended to emanate from the polite classes where such language was frowned on.[91] With their use of profanity, sailors attempted to right the imbalance of power between officers and enlisted men by deflating any pretensions officers possessed. Calling an officer a "son of a bitch" or responding to an order "to come here" with "I'll be damned to h–ll if I go up there" proved highly popular. If sailors could not gain equality in condition, they would at least achieve it through speech.[92]

Men aimed aggressive profanity at officers when their honor or manhood was questioned. Typical of a slight that might draw a sailor's wrath was the reaction to a rumor heard by Seaman E. W. Goble on the *Forest Rose*. Having gotten wind of a story that David D. Porter had said that "he could not trust Western men that they would not fight," Goble let loose on his captain at the first opportunity. When the captain requested volunteers for a risky expedition organized by Porter, Goble exploded: "I told him no that I would see the Admiral in h—l befour I would do it after the remark he had made the d——d dirty Son of a B——, I hope that a 64 [pound shell] will wipe out his a— befour he gets back."[93]

The dexterity with which Union sailors rattled off obscenities and vulgarities shocked new sailors, officers, and civilians. Seaman Thomas McNeil complained that many of his crewmates used God's name in vain with frightening regularity. William Miller fretted that he was constantly assaulted by foul language and songs. Milo Lacy remarked that "the curses uttered excell anything in that line I ever heard."[94]

While it was not unusual for rough men to use rough talk, the use of foul language possessed social implications.[95] Profanity allowed working-class sailors to let off steam in a familiar and collective manner. It reflected the reality that family, women, and polite society were not around to correct them. The only people to offend were their shipmates, and it was clear that they were men who would require a great deal more than swearing to vex. Profane swearing, vulgarities mixed with God's name used in vain, also highlighted the coarsening tendencies of the ship and the growing distance of the sailors from polite society since it carried obvious antichurch and anti-institutional overtones.[96]

Irreverence, impiety, and a strong antiauthoritarian flavor also crackled beneath the surface of their maritime rituals. On both the river and blockade squadrons, Union sailors—with the encouragement of more seasoned tars—borrowed time-tested maritime practices to release tension and loosen the stern character of the navy. The most popular was a ritual called "skylarking." Skylarking was a sort of organized free-for-all during which sailors did exactly what they wanted, freed from every rule and regulation. They did not have to listen to officers or remain sober.[97] In addition, skylarking allowed sailors to transfer conflicts from messes and tension from naval routine into rough play.[98]

The ritual commenced when the boatswain's whistle piped "all hands to mischief."[99] Many sailors struggled with their newfound freedom. Some men wandered around, while others burst into spontaneous acts of wild dancing and ill-coordinated music making. Others wrestled, played tricks, jumped, or made strange noises. Seaman James Henneberry recounted that on the *Benton* skylarking featured all hands "running jumping wrestling and all kinds of games enjoyed as men only knows how to enjoy the luxury of shore when cooped up for 4 months on board a boat."[100] While skylarking took place, officers did not—

*"Skylarking": The most popular form of releasing stress, besides drinking, was skylarking, a sort of organized free-for-all that allowed sailors to drink, fight, and generally raise hell without disciplinary restraint from officers. Charles E. Stedman Sketchbook, courtesy of the Boston Athenaeum.*

would not—interfere. Sailors often baited officers by taunting or dousing them with water.[101] Peaceful skylarking consisted of ordered athletic contests and feats of strength. Men sang songs, smoked, or just sat back and relaxed.

Other sailors, less playfully inclined, turned skylarking into melees by beating the hell out of one another. One favorite event, enjoyed by the harder elements of the crew, was a game called "Fox and Geese." Those who wanted to join in the fun took a handkerchief and tied it around a hammer or anvil. They then blindfolded themselves and chose someone to be "it." That sailor received control of the weighted hankie. The object of the game was for the person who was "it" to make hard contact with another player who then became "it," and so on. Frank Judd commented that the game continued "until all get tired & then they nock off." He wonderfully understated that the contest "is fun to look on but 'a horse of an other color' to join."[102]

In violation of the Reform Act, sailors carted out the grog tub. They guzzled down as much whiskey as they could. Not surprisingly, skylarking usually became wilder and more bizarre after the unmeasured drinking of grog.[103] Older sailors subjected landsmen to a quasi-religious experience called "ducking." Ducking—called a "new baptism"— was a critical initiation rite for green hands as it represented an immersion into a new society with a new set of rules and priorities.[104] It was not, however, a Christian ritual and in fact lampooned Christian baptism since it was involuntary, rough, and characterized by drunkenness and ribaldry.[105] In order to baptize the unwashed members of the crew, sailors seized them and tied them to a stick suspended over the ocean. Landsmen grappled with sailors to free themselves, usually to no avail. They soon found themselves nearly drowned, doused in salt water and gasping for air as the impromptu dunking machine submerged them three times rhythmically in and out of the ocean.[106]

For sailors, doing what they wanted to do with no supervision was the best aspect of skylarking. According to Charles Poole, "enjoying ourselves in a maner to suit our own taste" was what he enjoyed the most.[107] The ritual represented a critical method of venting discomfort. Aside from allowing sailors "to let off some steam," skylarking allowed men to build solidarity. Skylarking reversed the balance of power on a ship since officers stepped aside and sailors took control. This reversal of order called attention to the fact that although officers gave the commands, without the efforts of sailors the ship could not function. Moreover, these theatrical chastenings warned officers of the potential dangers of pushing too far men armed with knives, caged in a ship, and making $14 a month.

Unfortunately, many officers failed to comprehend the gloved fist behind the customs of sailors.[108] Sailors accepted the notion that in order to win the war or at least operate the ship, they would have to do what they were told. They subscribed to naval hierarchy and their subordination within the navy's system. Sailors recognized that what often mattered on a ship was not skill but appearance, not intelligence but the system, and not freedom but drill. They had renounced enough of their personalities to suffer endless salutes, intrusive inspections, hours at stations, numerous insults, and a thousand pettifogging details. They had learned which things were necessary and which were not.

Union sailors became less tolerant of matters that they had come to believe were unnecessary and had no connection to winning the war. As the war progressed, crews grew very hostile to the social reforms implemented by the navy, especially the induction of contrabands and the abolition of liquor. They also came to loathe what they perceived as their systematic mistreatment by officers and the navy.[109]

Much of this animus flowed toward officers. Even though the relationship between officers and their crews differed from ship to ship, officers too often treated their charges like the "carefree, simple, grog-and-tobacco Jackys" stereotype of folklore and misused their power.[110] Officers insulted sailors and treated their rights cavalierly. They rarely addressed sailors by their names and exhibited little interest in their health and well-being.[111] Cosam Bartlett snarled that the average sailor "almost forgets his name, so seldom is he called by it." Worse yet, officers routinely denigrated sailors by calling them "scum," "felons," "damned useless articles," and "niggers."[112]

Granted, sailors brought their share of problems to these relationships. Like officers, they were burdened with false stereotypes; to them, officers were snooty and effeminate and owed their commissions to connections rather than to skills. While some sailors respected the men under whom they served and some officers took good care of their crews, the potential for such mutual respect withered under the widespread indifference displayed by officers, both in their personal relations with their men and in their application of unpopular naval policies.

This insensitivity to the well-being of crews was highlighted by the officers' loose handling of two rights deemed fundamental by sailors: pay and term of enlistment.[113] Because the navy thought sailors wasted money and as an incentive to keep them in the service, it failed to pay sailors their monthly wage. Naturally, sailors loathed not being paid. Many wanted to have money in their pockets to gamble and to buy food and liquor.[114] Some wanted to send money home. Sailors would sadly approach the paymaster day after day asking for money, only to be told that there was no money aboard ship. They obsessively followed their balances. Ultimately, they concluded that the navy was trying to cheat them. Fireman George Geer wrote to his financially strapped wife, "What a swindle the Navy is." "I always was afraid that they would cheat us," Fireman John Taylor groused to his family, "and so it has turned out."[115]

The only thing sailors hated worse than not being paid was being forced to remain aboard ship after their terms of enlistment expired.[116] Most sailors had signed on for three-year terms. However, the Reform Act gave officers the power to detain indefinitely seamen whose terms had expired.[117] Union officers exercised the power liberally. Although the navy had done this because of the lack of sailors and awarded sailors a one-quarter increase in their salary while detained, crews complained that such a regulation traditionally had only applied to special cases on foreign waters where acquiring a new crew was simply not feasible. They argued that it did not apply where vessels were within easy travel of home naval stations.[118]

Sailors called this forced service "impressment." Impressment was the dreaded practice by which navies forced sailors to serve the state without their consent. The United States had gone to war with Great Britain over the issue in 1812. Seaman Jacob Cochran railed that "it is plain to be seen pressed men, which is contrary to the constitution and the laws of the United States."[119] Sailors viewed it as another example of poor treatment. It became the chronic source of sailor insubordination.[120] The exasperation felt by many sailors was expressed by the crew of the *Hartford*, who pleaded in the *New York Herald* that they had spent eighteen consecutive months "locked up." They asked for two things: "Give us our liberty and one-half of the money that is due us."[121]

Perhaps the indifference shown would not have resonated so strongly had officers not reinforced the inequalities in living conditions between sailors and officers. William N. Bock groused that on board a naval ship "the officers get the Benefit and the Men go a begging."[122] Although much of this inequity was institutionalized by the navy, which mandated that officers sleep, eat, and work in separate quarters, naval officers took few pains to play down their advantages—that they lived in nicer surroundings, ate better food, and went ashore more often.[123] An example of this attitude was the practice of keeping livestock aboard ship to assure officers fresh meat.[124] On New Year's Day 1862, Seaman James Henneberry fumed as he cleaned up the mess left by the cows and chickens wandering on the decks of his gunboat. They were to be enjoyed by the officers later for dinner. "All the chickens and roast beef that I will get for dinner," he wrote as he sidestepped the livestock, "will be salt junk and hard bread."[125]

Further weakening the relationship between sailors and officers was the reality that officers lived without the new moral restraints imposed on sailors. In fact, the relations between sailors and officers might not have been so strained had officers hidden or shared their violations of the Reform Act. Instead, sailors regularly saw officers drunk, swearing, stealing, and generally living beyond the bounds of the reform-minded program. Lieutenant Commander H. K. Davenport confided to L. M. Goldsborough, the commander of the North Atlantic Blockading Squadron, that many officers think that "'buttons & lace' constitute a license to commit any impropriety of conduct."[126]

The frustration felt by crews prompted a number of responses. Some sailors attempted to redress their grievances through the use of petitions and letters to newspaper editors, but these efforts yielded few results.[127] Instead, Union sailors took other measures to vent their discontent.[128] On both the Blockade and the Mississippi Squadron, peaceful uprisings typically consisted of work slowdowns, sick-outs, and work stoppages. When sailors worked slow, they reduced their pace until officers made changes or at least recognized sailors' grievances. Sick-outs involved whole crews lining up at the ship's surgeon's door and feigning illness. Sick-outs were of limited effectiveness, though, since surgeons were aware of such tactics and often nipped them quickly by pronouncing allegedly sick men fit for duty.

Work stoppages proved more serious. They occurred when a single sailor, sensing the frustration of his crewmates, incited them to drop their mops and pails.[129] On other occasions, sailors planned ahead and dropped their tools at a designated signal or at the refusal of a demand. A stoppage of this kind erupted on the *Cincinnati*. Angry because they had not been paid in fourteen months, a portion of the crew marched up to the officers and demanded their wages. When the officers denied their request, the whole crew dropped their mops.[130] On 9 April 1863, twelve sailors approached the officers on the *Carondolet* and announced that, according to their calculations, their terms of enlistment had expired. The Mississippi Squadron was in the middle of the Vicksburg campaign; so the officers declined to release them. On hearing this, the crew refused to work any longer.[131]

Tactics such as these had been used not only by merchant sailors but also by the working class. They functioned as a form of collective negotiation designed to secure attention and change.[132] The problem was that such acts during wartime—considered strikes in the private sector—were punishable by death in the navy. In February 1863, unhappy with conditions aboard ship, the crew of the *Western World* informed the captain that they would not return to their stations until they had secured a change in command. The captain refused their demand outright. He then assembled everyone on board and read to them the Articles of War, which pronounced the penalty of death by hanging for all mutineers. The crew quickly rescinded their demand.[133]

On ships where conditions had seriously deteriorated, sailors openly defied their officers. A sailor's refusal to obey any order had serious consequences, but refusing to man the guns, a direct assertion by sailors that they would not defend the ship, was the most important order a sailor could disobey.[134] In these situations, officers would often give sailors a chance to recant by asking them a second time. In January 1863, when the crew of the *Benton* refused to go to quarters, the officers piped all the crew members to their hammocks. Immediately thereafter, each man's name was called and the question was again put to each man individually, "Will you go to work?" Surgeon Fayette Clapp, who witnessed the proceedings, recounted in his diary that he sat amazed when each mutineer responded to the officers' query with a bold "No sir." "Their punishment will surely come," he concluded.[135]

Those crews who believed that officers denied sailors their fundamental rights were prone to unplanned and violent outbursts. Oddly, seemingly trivial events, like the failure to provide mess chests and hammocks or when officers ate food donated to sailors, which would wound their egos, blew the lid off tense ships.[136] For Union sailors, a bruising of their pride was almost as serious as overcrowding. Crews could tolerate the inequalities, the poor living conditions, and the monotony. What they could not tolerate was being treated as less than free men.[137]

An example of the repercussions borne by officers' arbitrary disregard for the rights of sailors was the near-mutiny that took place on the *Brooklyn*. At sundown on 8 May 1863, the boatswain piped all hands to man the cat fall, a chain used in hoisting the anchor. During the drill, the master's mate caught hold of a man for no apparent reason and sent him to the mast for punishment. When the commodore began interrogating the sailor, a fireman who had witnessed the incident stepped forward and defended the accused sailor. The fireman stated that the accusation was groundless because the alleged transgression existed only in the imagination of the master's mate, who was drunk. The accused sailor also confirmed that he had done nothing wrong and pleaded that he had been wrongly accused. The commodore summarily dismissed the fireman's testimony as false, ignored the sailor's plea, and then sent him to solitary confinement.

The crew was stunned. John Simpson remarked that "this made a deep impression on the men who thought it a great injustice and was the cause of much grumbling." As soon as the master's mate returned to duty, the crew hounded him with a constant barrage of catcalls and hoots. A few minutes later when he turned his back, a sailor threw a chain chalk after him. The master's mate immediately reported to the first lieutenant that a mutiny was afoot. The lieutenant placed the marines on emergency, mutiny alert. No mutiny ensued; but, owing to the continuing threats made by sailors, the master's mate kept a cocked and loaded pistol at his side for days after the incident.[138]

The most violent rebellions were those that spontaneously erupted from a potent mix of festering of officer and sailor relations, an event that temporarily destabilized the ship, and liquor. Mutinies of this sort took place on the *Fernandina* and the *Hartford*.[139] On 4 April 1862, several crew members aboard the *Fernandina* became drunk and took to brawling. When rebuked by the captain, the ringleader, Seaman John Hillman, kicked the captain in the face, drew his knife from its sheath, and proceeded to slice him up. The crew, seeing the captain go down under the strokes of the mutineer's blade, did not rush to their captain's aid but instead took the opportunity to go on a "general melee." Only when the captain was able to wrestle his Colt revolver from his holster and blow a hole through Hillman's abdomen while slashing open the throat of another sailor did the debacle abate long enough for the marines to restore order.[140]

A similar uprising took place on the *Hartford*. Seaman Bartholomew Diggins recounted that one night a city detective came aboard the vessel returning a man who had deserted the ship in New Orleans. The desertion had been one of many stemming from severe overcrowding in the berth deck. Sailors had begun deserting after the captain revoked an order allowing sailors to use some of the quarter-deck to ease the overcrowding. Even though they saw the forcible return of the sailor who had left the ship to escape the dreadful living conditions as an affront, this alone did not provoke the crew. Only when they saw the detective receive a cash reward for what he had done did sailors' hearts darken. The sight of seeing a price placed on the head of one of their own and done right before their eyes overwhelmed their emotions.

Unwisely, the detective, before leaving, decided to take a tour of the vessel and examine the shot holes it had received in battle. Not only did this further infuriate the crew, but it also gave them an opportunity to strike back. When the detective reached the berth deck, a fireman named Gallant struck him and hurled a division tub filled with water at this head. The detective cried for help. By the time the marines arrived, the throng of angry sailors was beating the detective. The marines rushed at Gallant with drawn cutlasses. The sailors quickly relieved some of the marines of their weapons and began turning them on their former owners. During the scuffle, the detective crawled on his hands and knees to safety. After much fighting and with the aid of some reinforcements, the marines eventually subdued the rioting sailors.[141]

Officers and marines usually quelled rebellions with a show of force and some hand-to-hand fighting. However, as the war dragged on, disruptions by Union sailors grew in regularity and scope. Whereas once only a few men would cause trouble, after 1862 whole crews began defying orders and threatening ship safety. While this change stemmed from sailors' growing intolerance for their living situations, soldier transfers and a growing number of unprincipled recruits disrupted crews and the harmony of many ships.

The standard punishments for mutineers consisted of the loss of two months of pay and the wearing of double irons. In serious cases, the navy sent mutineers to prison.[142] The ultimate punishment was hanging. However, the problem of rebellious sailors grew to such levels that the navy began cowing mutinous sailors by adopting the extreme measure of using gunboats to quell mutinous crews. This remedy proved very effective since it psychologically paralyzed mutineers. Rear Admiral Samuel P. Lee, in charge of the North Atlantic Blockading Squadron, wrote to Gideon Welles that gunboats exercised a great "moral effect" on mutineers.[143]

One of the largest rebellions took place on the *Benton*. In January and February 1863, river sailors had staged two large uprisings amid a series of sick-outs and work stoppages. The February mutiny had erupted among new sailors when they refused an order to man the boat's large guns. Rear Admiral David D. Porter did not waste time doling out individual punishments. Instead, he ordered the surrounding gunboats to prepare for a full assault. Several of the largest gunboats of the Mississippi Squadron steamed up to the sides of the *Benton* and leveled their guns directly at the heads of the mutineers. Marines in small boats rowed to the sides of the vessel, loaded their guns, and brandished their bayonets. The rebellious crew lost its nerve and surrendered. Surgeon Fayette Clapp, who had witnessed the whole scene, wrote that it was easy to see why: "The big guns of other vessels pointing at us, looked formidable, I assure you"![144]

These disruptions reflected a number of truths. The peaceful rebellions showed the influence of the working class among Union sailors.

Work slowdowns and strikes had functioned as modes of resistance to unhealthy work environments and ruthless bosses. The more violent responses highlighted the rowdiness of Union sailors. Without question, the occurrence of documented and undocumented uprisings reflected the reality that Union sailors were a rough and tumble lot who often lost their tempers when their pride was pricked or when they had a bellyful of the navy and their officers. The odd scenario of the navy abolishing their free ration of grog and at the same time turning a blind eye to sailors buying expensive, poor quality liquor only worsened the mood and the situation aboard ships.

Whether as a result of stereotypical thinking or indifference, many officers failed to understand the tensions behind sailor rebellions. They did not understand the grumbling, the drinking, and the violence. Moreover, they did not appreciate the culture of resistance that sailors crafted and the different values sailors held. The result was a social dissonance that placed officers and sailors on the same ship in two different worlds. The dissonance crippled officers' ability to understand why Union sailors were angry and—more often than not—caused them to misinterpret why their sailors were drunk and rioting.

## Saving Jack
## Religion, Union Sailors, and the
## United States Christian Commission

In his work *For Cause and Comrades: Why Men Fought in the Civil War*, James M. McPherson contends that, as products of the Second Great Awakening, "Civil War armies were, arguably, the most religious in American history."[1] Many soldiers, he contends, marched off to war with Bibles in their pockets. Not so for Union sailors, who "with few exceptions" were more prone to throw their Bibles aside.[2] Overall, most men who served as Union sailors in the Civil War seemed to lack the religious dedication McPherson attributes to their brothers in arms. Unlike the experience of soldiers, that of sailors in the navy during the Civil War lessened, rather than encouraged, a genuine and expedient reliance on prayer, conventional religious practices, and faith in God. Much of the blame for failing to save "Jack" falls on the navy, which took actions that effectively discouraged religious expression aboard ships. The navy failed to provide enough chaplains, worked sailors on Sundays, and abandoned a prewar policy of mandatory attendance at Sunday services. Stirred by charges of Sabbath desecration and a perceived erosion in religious sentiment aboard ships, the United States Christian Commission launched a vigorous campaign to reclaim sailors' souls. The Commission sent ministers and Bibles to ships on the blockade and gunboats on the Mississippi. Their efforts raised the morale and awakened the religious sensibilities of some sailors, but those efforts were belated and meager.[3] The Commission could not overcome the spiritual vacuum of Union ships.

Social scientists, psychologists, and historians have identified religion, whether it is defined as prayer, a belief in God, or ritualized practice, as a critical resource in helping men confront the hardships of military life and the horror of combat. Samuel A. Stouffer's groundbreaking 1949 work, *The American Soldier*, confirmed for many what historians, sociologists, and clergy had already believed for generations—that "there are no atheists in foxholes."[4] Stouffer and his staff discovered that 84 percent of infantrymen and 71 percent of enlisted men in other branches of the service responded that prayer "helped a lot . . . when the going got tough" in World War II.[5] Moreover, the conflict also seemed to intensify religious convictions. Seventy-nine percent of enlisted men with combat experience, and 54 percent of men without combat experience, responded that their army service had increased their faith in God.[6]

Although fighting eighty years earlier, Union troops also evidenced a sincere reliance on prayer, faith, and religion to deal with the death, destruction, and inhumanity of the Civil War. Civil War historians have discovered that ordinary soldiers used religion to overcome the hardships of army life and the psychological shock associated with combat. Based on the letters and diaries of ordinary soldiers, scholars have found that not only did religion help soldiers survive the war, but it also ultimately made them "better" soldiers. Religion, in both simple and complex forms, gave Northern soldiers the courage to fight and the confidence to handle the physical and psychological effects associated with service adjustment and combat.[7]

Religion's resiliency among soldiers stemmed from two factors. First, Union soldiers enlisted with a strong core of religious beliefs and practices. Charles J. Stille wrote that Union soldiers were "young men of character, intelligence and courage such as had never made up the rank and file of any army."[8] Second, whether or not Union soldiers were the most religious in history, Northerners, unwilling to see their sons, husbands, and brothers succumb to the evils of camp life, insisted that religious experience not be lost as millions of men left home for the first time. As a result, even though away from their small towns and living in an army camp, Union soldiers regularly had access to the rudimentary elements of religious expression. The army provided for chaplains while Christian organizations sent literature and ministers into camp. The army erected chapels under tent awnings in order to give men a sanctuary from the army. In these makeshift chapels, chaplains conducted weekly Sunday services and weekday prayer meetings. The open space of camps and their proximity to civilian society also lent soldiers an opportunity for their own private devotions or a chance to attend local church services, if they desired.[9]

The role of religion and its importance for Union sailors during the war proved more uncertain. Unlike the hallowed glow associated with soldiers, wartime attitudes characterized Union Jacks as anything but religious or moral. Part of the image problem arose from lingering pre-war stereotypes that routinely labeled sailors as immoral and irreligious.[10] In fact, the notion of sailor irreligiosity proved so pervasive during the war that Mary Osborne chastised her brother for joining the navy instead of the army on just such grounds. "I hope as you have turned sailor instead of soldier," she wrote, "that you will not be contaminated with vice."[11]

Union sailors did seem less susceptible to religious expression and less inclined to use religious practice to fortify themselves during the war. The recorded observations of sailors, chaplains, and officers from every major naval squadron, and the delegate reports of the United States Christian Commission strongly indicate that the average sailor exhibited little interest in expressions of religious practice and spiritual matters. Furthermore, until early 1864, sailors' experiences in the navy seemed to lessen, rather than increase, their adherence to spiritual beliefs and participation in religious practices. This conclusion is also based on the comparatively little space that sailors gave to the general subject in their letters, diaries, and journals. Little is known about religious beliefs among sailors—even superstitious ones—because they did not mention them. If Union tars thought about life, death, salvation, prayer, God, or their souls, they rarely recorded such thoughts.

Although no one kept statistics on their moral and spiritual standards, many Union sailors joined the navy already in a state of "quiet unreligiosity."[12] In 1861, a "religious sailor" proved difficult to describe. On the one hand, the term likely denoted someone who faithfully subscribed to a mainstream Christian denomination, attended church every Sunday, prayed daily, and lived a moral life. On the other hand, a Christian sailor could be someone who had accepted Christ as his savior and promised to lead a good life.

Religious sailors naturally noted, in shock, the low levels of religiosity and the small number of Christians among their shipmates. Seaman C. W. Fleyne complained to Dr. William Thoms, head of the New York Nautical School, that out of eleven officers and 100 crew aboard the *Commodore* there was "not one Christian among them."[13] One sailor serving on the gunboat *Daylight* counted one Christian in a crew of 200.[14] Chaplain Joseph Stockbridge, chaplain on the *Lancaster*, counted only three "professed Christians" among his crew. He reported in 1863 that out of a wartime force of 51,500, there were only "hundreds of professedly religious sailors."[15] The incidence of religiosity, from complex to simple, proved so low among Union tars that the appearance of five, ten, or twelve religious sailors in a crew of 150 was often enough to characterize it as a Christian crew.[16]

The relationship between religious beliefs and sailors proved, in many ways, an enigma. Without question, the Union navy had its share of sailors who lacked dedication to mainstream religious beliefs and practices.[17] A great many sailors likely resented and ignored the teachings and strictures of organized churches and clergy. Much of the ignorance stemmed from a lack of "moral training," wrote one sailor. Many, in the estimation of the Reverend William Rounesville Alger, possessed a "lack of piety."[18] "I do not profess, and am not religious," Seaman Frederic Davis wrote to his parents. "I have not seen the inside of a Church for sometime."[19] Some hard characters, such as Seaman John G. Morrison, exhibited an open hostility to religious intrusion. After encountering a street preacher in Cairo, Illinois, Morrison scoffed, "What gammon it [religion] is. It is only time and money wasted."[20]

Nevertheless, the attitudes of most Union sailors, even ones labeled irreligious by chaplains and religious sailors, did not fall into such neat categories as religious or profane. Part of the problem in ascertaining the attitudes of sailors toward religion was that sailors were a varied set of men from more diverse cultural, religious, and economic backgrounds. They exhibited a complex range of attitudes concerning religion from sincere personal belief to doubt, ignorance, disbelief, distance, and skepticism. Moreover, many Union sailors decried accepted displays of piety and brought unpopular Catholic ideals and rituals as well as elements of evangelicalism into the navy's traditional Protestant enclave.[21]

Furthermore, it is difficult to obtain a clear picture of the attitudes of sailors toward religion because sailors often borrowed religion and Christian beliefs when it served their interests. For example, many Union sailors marked themselves with tattoos of crosses and crucifixes on their forearms and chests. Although traditionally viewed as an outward sign of religious fervor, Union sailors—aware that certain churches demanded a proper land burial—tattooed themselves with such religious symbols in order to increase their chances of securing a shore burial.[22] Union sailors used religion as a pretext for venting their general dissatisfaction with the navy, especially when they believed naval practices violated Christian principles. Religion then arose in the form of a complaint. Sailors invoked Christian practices that worked in their favor, such as Sabbath observance, fair treatment, and objections to physical abuse. They decried their application when used to change sailor behavior.[23]

It is unclear whether the navy drew men of a profane bent or whether ships "dechristianized" sailors. While the navy did attract men having little interest in religion, many of the conditions blamed in the past for curbing religious practices proved prevalent on Union ships. Reformers thought the disgusting physical conditions aboard ships fouled sailors' souls.[24] Ministers, such as William Rounesville Alger, argued that sailors came to dismiss the importance and power of God after winning too many battles with the sea. "Too constant contact with phenomena calculated to awaken awe and submission," Alger opined, "hardened sailors to the power of God."[25]

Other realities made Union ships spiritual vacuums. Because of a lack of space, there were no chapels and no privacy for personal devotions. Because the navy did not purchase enough, Bibles and religious literature were scarce. Yet, while the effects of a lack of chapels and literature were points of debate in explaining the religious vacuum on ships, ministers, politicians, sailors, and their families did agree on one overriding factor: isolation. William Alger believed the isolation weakened the sailor's religious impulses by "exempting him from society."[26] Once a ship went to sea, water effectively severed sailors from the influence of society's primary religious institutions: churches and ministers. Sailors immediately noticed the effects of not having those institutions to turn to.[27] They also became acutely aware of the absence and the opportunity to go to church. "We have no church to go to no social meetings no meetings for singing same as we have in New York," lamented William C. Miller.[28]

More importantly, however, the isolation rendered by a ship separated sailors from the secondary sphere of religious influence—families and friends.[29] Family, particularly female family members, traditionally had played a key role in reinforcing religious beliefs and practices.[30] The transition to a ship represented the first time that many men had ventured outside the reach of these circles. Mary Osborne worried that her brother Joseph's severance from society would make him doubly susceptible to erosion of his faith and the "dangers of the inexperienced sailor."[31] Sailors' isolation was exacerbated by the fact that they did not receive mail regularly.[32] Away from the religious network of churches and families and confined in an environment where traditional recourses to religion failed to exist, sailors often spent lengthy periods of time in a religious vacuum.

Socialization into the society of the ship also inhibited the development of religious sentiments. In those first few weeks in the navy, men, unsure in their new environments, sought to prove their toughness and masculinity as they assimilated into crews. Reliance on religion, particularly prayer, was not an admirable trait in the all-male atmosphere of a ship. The successful, admired sailors were ones who were able, through their own skill and self-reliance, to weather storms, win fights, hold large quantities of liquor, and overcome any hardship.[33] According to sailors' lore, only a sinking ship should contain sailors who pray.[34]

Moreover, the hard characters often seized control of the moral tenor of crews through mockery, threats, and physical violence. These men openly scorned religion and disrupted attempts at its expression.[35] Evangelical sailors were more a source of amusement than of effective religious instruction.[36] Isolated from land and desperate to fit into shipboard life, most men quickly jettisoned the outward practices and utterances of religion. In fact, during the war, tars admitted that they often were afraid to voice religious sentiments and participate in religious services in the presence of other sailors. "I am alone," one sailor dejectedly wrote from the blockade.[37]

Critical to and symbolic of this "dechristianization" process was the overpowering use of swearing, profane jests, and ribald songs. Union sailors swore constantly and used God's name in vain with abandon, especially on Sundays.[38] For these men, wrote Seaman Patrick Meade, "every word was an oath" and "every thought was blasphemy." Thomas McNeil complained that many of his crewmates used God's name in vain with great frequency. Seaman William Miller fretted, "We have go to stop on board and listen to profane songs & jests."[39] Such rough talk not only offended proper societal mores but also possessed distinct antichurch overtones. Profanity had traditionally been the vocabulary of blasphemers.[40] In fact, sailors swore so much that officers began punishing men for uttering profanities, and Congress banned the practice by law in 1862.[41]

An old maritime religious tract had warned sailors, "A tongue that swears does not easily pray."[42] To the religious few, the stream of profanity must have seemed to be a fitting voice for the immoral environment in which they now lived. Although isolated from land, sailors on both the blockade and river squadrons did, however, manage to import every conceivable form of vice and immoral behavior onto their ships. Below deck, men regularly drank to dissipation, assaulted each other with fists and knives, stole from each other, and caroused with prostitutes whenever they were available. "I think I have seen something of the world," Frederic Davis wrote, "but I never knew so many different things or men, as there is here."[43]

The immersion into an immoral environment cowed the few professedly religious and nominally religious sailors almost immediately.[44] They quickly sank into spiritual ineffectiveness and despair, and many were so disheartened that they wanted to leave ship.[45] "I have never been so impressed with the dreadful reality of sin as I have been here," wrote Seaman Joseph Osborne to his girlfriend from the decks of the *Vanderbilt*.[46] Sailors often referred to their ship as hell or purgatory.[47] Yet, away from land, religious sailors could not avoid the atmosphere of sin. They had to live and work in the middle of a vice-ridden atmosphere that they never would have been exposed to on shore. Such exposure to an immoral environment led Thomas McNeil to lament, "There is a grate many temptations on the water."[48]

In April 1861, the navy knew three things about the religious needs of sailors at sea. First, the service knew that ships tended to become religious vacuums once they left port. Second, the navy understood that religion helped sailors overcome the isolation of the seafaring life and the hidden wounds generated by hardship and combat. Third, the navy knew that chaplains aboard ship had functioned as the primary means of guaranteeing the exercise of regular religious practice among sailors including the preservation of Sundays as holy days. Navy clergy led divine services, held morning and evening prayers, and provided guidance to the spiritual lives of sailors.[49] Moreover, chaplains shouldered the responsibility for the moral and spiritual education of sailors, many of whom were young or unexposed to any previous religious education.

In 1854, the U.S. House of Representatives had rejected an effort to remove chaplains from the navy. One of the overwhelming justifications for retaining clergy was Congress's explicit recognition that a ship became devoid "of all means of moral and religious culture" while at sea. In determining that the navy needed chaplains to preserve religious practice aboard its ships, the House concluded: "The navy have still stronger claims than the army for the supply of chaplains: a large portion of the time our ships-of-war are on service foreign from our own shore . . . If you do not afford them the means of religious service while at sea, the Sabbath is, to all extents and purposes, annihilated, and we do not allow the crews the free exercise of religion."[50]

Any plans the navy possessed for preserving religious life aboard ship during the Civil War unraveled because of a shortage of clergy. The service started the war with only twenty-four chaplains, but in December 1861 retirements shrank their number to nineteen.[51] During the war, the number of active chaplains never exceeded nineteen. Meanwhile, the number of sailors in the navy leaped from 7,600 to 51,500.[52] The dramatic rise in enlistments left the navy in the predicament of having fewer chaplains to minister to more men. In 1861, there was, on average, one chaplain for every 320 sailors. By 1865, the ratio of chaplains to sailors had fallen to one chaplain for every 2,450 men.[53]

Owing to this shortage, the navy placed most of its chaplains at navy yards and not on ships; the rationale was that chaplains could assist more sailors at a naval station than on a ship. The ramifications of this decision proved enormous. For most of the war, Union sailors had no chaplains on their ships. As of April 1864, the whole force of sailors on the blockade from Fortress Monroe in Virginia to the mouth of the Rio Grande in Texas served without the guidance of a single chaplain.[54] The Mississippi Squadron featured one chaplain, and he was stationed at the naval base at Cairo, Illinois.[55]

For their part, chaplains did not rush to serve in the navy. Many failed to volunteer because of the harshness and isolation of naval service, particularly on the blockade.[56] Navy chaplains also sensed a resistance to their enlistment from senior officers and from the navy's administrative leadership. Those few chaplains willing to serve often were turned away by captains. Sailors dryly noted that captains had difficulty "hunting up" chaplains they approved of.[57] Strangely enough, however, facing an obvious shortage of chaplains, some officials believed the navy already had too many. Gustavus Vasa Fox, Assistant Secretary of the Navy, actually objected to a proposal to appoint more chaplains. In a letter to Superintendent of the Naval Academy George S. Blake, Fox groused, "We have more chaplains in the navy than can be used, and are about to appoint a few more." When the proposal for more chaplains received approval, the new appointments inexplicably found themselves assigned to the Naval Academy, not aboard ships.[58]

Traditionally, a chaplain serving shipboard proved to be a difficult fit.[59] The mere presence of a clergyman served as a nettlesome reminder of the awkward reconciliation between the realities of war and the demands of Christianity. Although many Northern clergy became zealous supporters of the cause, at root, a chaplain's message of peace and mercy seemed incompatible with the purpose of war.[60] Sailors, too, probably possessed their own reservations about chaplains. Tradition-ally, mariners had regarded them as bad luck because they believed the devil owed them spite.[61]

Chaplains also posed practical problems. On a ship at sea, every sailor had two or three tasks to perform. Chaplains did not. Nothing irri-tated sailors and officers more than watching a chaplain stroll the decks while the rest of the men worked. To make matters worse, when chap-lains did work, they seemed only to interfere. Sailors noticed that the mere presence of a chaplain on board dampened the potential for de-bauchery—on the part of both officers and sailors.[62] If sailors forgot that the chaplain was aboard, he appeared all too happy to remind them. Chaplains routinely criticized men for bad habits, bad language, and bad living and filed written reports with the navy on all that they wit-nessed. Although chaplains were statutorily required to file reports, this kind of moral overseeing created a good deal of tension and won few friends aboard ship. Officers and sailors resented the prying by chaplains into their daily lives and called them "tell tales" and "spies."[63]

Chaplains raised so much trouble by their omissions and commis-sions that crews loved to retell the yarn about two sailors, one old and one new, sitting around the scuttlebutt after a day's work as the chaplain walked by. As he paced away, the younger sailor asked the older one, "What does the chaplain do?" At this, the older sailor's face screwed up into a half-grimace and a half-grin. "He does nothing six days a week," growled the older tar, "and disturbs the peace on Sunday."[64]

True to the point of the yarn, chaplains did most of their disrupting on Sundays. They did so in two ways. First, chaplains vociferously ob-jected to any work performed on Sundays. Throughout the war, chap-lains rebuked captains, privately and publicly, for working sailors on Sunday. This criticism placed captains in an awkward situation since their primary duty was the proper operation of a vessel. Captains would not sacrifice the safety of their ships or suspend naval operations to keep the Sabbath holy. Captains ruled absolutely and resented any in-trusions into their authority. Moreover, captains historically had not permitted a religious-driven calendar or holidays to alter a ship's work schedule.[65] Chaplains, on the other hand, firmly believed that Sunday was their day and, of course, the Lord's.

Sunday clashes ensued. After witnessing Sabbath violations on the *Potomac*, Joseph Stockbridge preached the following Sunday on the "duty of properly observing the Sabbath." Furious about a public rebuke and challenge to his authority from the chaplain, the captain issued

Stockbridge a written reprimand.[66] When the chaplain on the *Independence* sermonized on his ship's Sunday violations, the captain cut him off in mid-sentence and closed the service.[67] During the Civil War, captains threatened and muzzled chaplains and would confine them to their cabins to keep them out of the way.[68]

The second difficulty surrounding navy chaplains was that their denominational affiliations proved ill-matched with the men they sought to serve. Although naval regulations vaguely commended chaplains to "instruct in the principles of the Christian religion," the official Sunday service aboard ships was that of the Episcopal denomination, the dominant religion among chaplains.[69] By 1861, the nation's religious affiliations had greatly diversified.[70] In addition to the swelling numbers of Methodists and Baptists, German and Irish immigrants had also radically altered the religious landscape since many of these new arrivals were Catholic.[71] In 1854, the three largest religious groups in the United States were Methodists (4,209,333), Baptists (3,130,878), and Roman Catholics (2,040,316). Episcopalians numbered 625,213.[72]

The composition of the chaplain corps only partially reflected these changes. Of the twenty chaplains who served between 1861 and 1870, there were eight Episcopalians, seven Methodists, four Baptists, and one Presbyterian.[73] The navy did not have a Catholic chaplain until 1888.[74] The specific problem for the navy was that proportionate numbers of Methodists, Baptists, and Catholics likely enlisted during the war. Moreover, foreign-born sailors constituted 45 percent of Union naval volunteers, many of them from heavily Catholic places in Ireland, Germany, and Canada.[75]

More importantly, events in the 1850s had made the navy particularly sensitive to the divisiveness that chaplains could generate among religiously mixed crews. In 1853–54, some Baptist chaplains had touched off a furor called the "Prayer Book Controversy" when they openly objected to the use of the Episcopal liturgy aboard ship. These same chaplains had delivered sermons to crews—containing Catholic and Episcopal sailors—that attacked Catholic and Episcopal teachings on infant baptism and apostolic succession.[76] The events had triggered a minor religious war aboard certain ships, angered Catholic and Episcopal sailors, and created hostilities among Protestant sailors of other denominations. Many of these wounds had not healed by 1861.[77]

To make matters worse, many of the chaplains who had precipitated the controversy were still in the navy or applied for reinstatement when the war arrived. This fact, coupled with the regulation adopted in 1860 that allowed chaplains to use the formal service of their avowed denominations, convinced the navy that chaplains were a divisive force.[78] With such a potentially volatile mix of religious views among Union sailors, the navy and its captains were not about to let chaplains destroy crew cohesion by aggravating religious divisions. It was not surprising then, that those few chaplains that did make it aboard ships found their influence checked and the content of their sermons curtailed by wary captains.[79]

The absence of chaplains shaped the religious lives of Union sailors in numerous ways. The largest consequence was that their absence let captains assume firm control over the dissemination of religion aboard ship. From 1861 to early 1864, captains dictated the content, format, and regularity of religious practice on most vessels, from the utterance of prayers to weekly divine services. Suspicious of the potential pitfalls that religion presented, Union captains adopted a traditional, conservative approach, which maintained the formalities of religious practice while downplaying spiritual meaning. The practice of religion outwardly remained the same. Although most sailors were not Episcopalian, captains retained the Episcopal rite as the official liturgy of the Sunday services, called the "divine service."[80] The continued adherence to the Episcopal rite was understandable since over 40 percent of officers were affiliated with that denomination. The Episcopal service, derived from the Book of Common Prayer, had also been the official liturgy of the navy since its inception.[81] Although they led their sailors through the same prayers chaplains had used in the past, captains refashioned their tenor: Sundays and divine services became an added exercise in naval obedience rather than a religious education and a source of comfort and strength.[82]

On Sundays, captains bound more tightly together the physical inspection and the performance of divine services.[83] Although the back-to-back schedule was mandated by naval regulations, with the captain overseeing both as naval and religious authority, the compulsive nature of the captain's power, epitomized by the inspection, spilled into Sunday services.[84] Sailor Amos Burton, who had joined the navy in 1860, noticed the change almost immediately: "How different our Sabbath now is to what it was a few months ago."[85]

Inspection commenced at 9:30 A.M. with officers forming sailors into a line on the port side of the quarter-deck. Standing orders required that sailors on Sundays dress in their best uniforms and be fully clean.[86] As their names were called, sailors had to pass through a gauntlet of

*Sunday morning inspection on board the gunboat USS* Metacomet. *The rigid Sunday inspection provided little inspiration for the "divine service" that immediately followed. From* Harper's Weekly, *10 December 1864, courtesy of the U.S. Naval Historical Center.*

marines and officers standing on the starboard side of the quarter-deck. Sailors were expected to remove their caps respectfully while senior officers examined their appearance.[87] If a sailor or his uniform proved unclean, marines stopped the offending man at the mast where officers berated him. Sailors listened to comments like "Jones, why are your shoes not blacked?" and "you are a filthy beast, a disgrace to your shipmates." Officers then ordered crewmates to strip and scrub dirty sailors hard with brushes, sand, and hickory brooms.[88]

All of this constituted a less than inspiring prelude to the divine service, which followed promptly at 10:00 A.M. At the tolling of the church bell, sailors hoisted the church pennant on the flagstaff and assembled on the port side of the quarter-deck in their best suits, hats doffed.[89] Enlisted men sat on overturned buckets or cross-legged, called "sailor style," on the hard planks of the deck. Officers usually sat on the other side of the deck on camp stools. Fresh from inspection, the captain led the divine service. The liturgy varied, depending on the captain, but usually started with the captain's rumbling through a few chapters from the New Testament. The captain then recited the formal liturgy from

*"Sunday Morning—Reading the Articles of War": As part of the Sunday inspection, officers read out the array of potential infractions that could land sailors in shackles, the brig, or a naval prison. Charles E. Stedman Sketchbook, courtesy of the Boston Athenaeum.*

the Book of Common Prayer.[90] Sailors remained quiet, looked at the sea, and responded to the end of each prayer with quiet amens.[91]

Ambivalent in his role as chaplain and untrained in the nuances of theology, a captain would hammer away in his sermon on a few basic themes. One was to remind sailors that their mothers, sisters, and wives were at home praying for them and acting as guardians of moral conduct.[92] In Civil War America, men equated women with religion and a moral life. The association proved so strong that the mere ringing of church bells could immediately conjure up feminine images for soldiers.[93] Sailors made the same connection. Coal Heaver William Wainwright commented that thoughts of church stirred up images of sharing prayer books with "rosey cheeked girls" and the chance of accidentally

*Sailors and officers at divine service aboard the USS* Passaic. *Sailors sat
on the port (left) side of the ship, officers on the starboard (right) side.
Sailors sat cross-legged, while officers sat on chairs.
Courtesy of the U.S. Naval Historical Center.*

touching hands in moments he described as "electric."[94] Captains invoked the feminine image to call sailors to a more orderly life.[95]

The use of the feminine image by captains also reflected their underlying discomfort with the role of chaplain. To Northerners, religion
largely remained the province of women and was commonly thought
to cause one to soften and civilize—traits believed to be undesirable
in both soldiers and sailors. Thus captains feared that religion would
weaken the fighting spirit of their sailors. In order to negate such a danger, captains altered beyond recognition the religious content of their
services. As one captain readily admitted, "If it did no good, it could do
no harm."[96]

In order to contradict any feminine qualities associated with their religious role, captains often herded their men to services using profanity.[97] After discovering a sailor missing from divine service, one captain erupted, "Put this man in double irons, d—n him!" "I'll teach him to come to his prayers."[98] Swearing during sermons and prayers was not uncommon. One captain in giving a sermon on hypocrites called them "damn rascals."[99] Another captain, leading a service before the assault on Fort Fisher, when informed that his ship would not be in the fight that day, ended the service abruptly. Throwing down his prayer book violently, he exclaimed, "Well! I'll be G–d d——d if I'm going to pray if we aren't going to fight."[100] His sailors erupted in laughter. Although profanity may have protected a captain's masculinity, it did tend to make a mockery of services by deriding them. Further, the use of profanity and its antireligious overtones left no misunderstanding as to the captain's true thoughts on the subject and only encouraged sailors to treat religion as an undesirable exercise.

Obedience constituted another popular theme of captain-styled divine services.[101] For this purpose, the prayers of the Episcopal service seemed to mesh nicely with captains' underlying message of obedience and control. Many officers, arguably, had no problem booming out prayers to sailors that called on them "to submit . . . to my governors . . . to order myself lowly and reverently to all my betters and to do my duty."[102] The import of these prayers, when combined with the intrusive and demeaning nature of the inspection before services, was not lost on the men. Sailors felt that religion was being used to break them.[103] In the unlikely event that sailors overlooked the message of obedience and subordination emanating from divine services, a captain would often reinforce the lesson by ordering such backbreaking work as coaling and loading stores immediately after the service.[104]

When the captain held divine services, Union sailors seemed to make an attentive congregation. Certainly, the inspection before helped to temper their spirits. The fact that the captain controlled every facet of their lives and that he was giving the sermon likely played a large role in commanding their undivided attentions. Certainly the craving for social excitement also led religious and irreligious sailors to be very attentive listeners on the Sabbath.[105] Whatever the reason, Coal Heaver William Wainwright observed that sailors were better behaved and more attentive than civilian churchgoers. "I have never seen so much quiteness and attention paid to the word of God as I have seen on board this ship."[106] Chaplain Donald McLaren recalled that the war

*"Morning Prayer": Some ships permitted morning prayers, but this
practice receded dramatically as the war continued. Prayer meetings
organized by sailors themselves became the most popular form of
religious expression for religious sailors. Harry Simmons Sketchbook,
courtesy of W. L. Clements Library, University of Michigan.*

increased the intensity and attention of both sailors and chaplains at
Sunday services.[107] Surgeon Edward Pierson remarked that a divine service attended by sailors after battle, with their faces "black as your hat
from the Powder" and grumbling amen at the end of each prayer, "was
the most solemn sight I ever witnessed."[108]

Sailors laughed at the captain's acting as chaplain. On a deeper level,
however, Union sailors rejected the captain as a religious figure; they
viewed his assumption of religious duties as the ultimate intrusion into
a personal sphere.[109] In addition, seamen quickly saw through their captains' thinly disguised motives and lack of piety. Landsman Milo Lacy
called his captain-minister "a wolf in sheep's clothing." Some sailors
laughed to themselves watching a captain "put on a parson's face, as
far as he knew how."[110] In their eyes, putting on a parson's face did not
make a person religious. William Wainwright complained, "There is no
more religion in him [Captain Winslow] then there is in my old boat."[111]

Worse yet, the captain's performance delivered little in the way of
entertainment value. "The sermon is the same, year in and out," wrote

Charles Mervine. One sailor complained, "It is tiresome tho, as the Captain is rather long." William Wainwright concluded that divine services held no attraction for him since "I dont like to go to hear a man that cant preach any better than myself." Overall, Seaman Amos Burton concluded, the captain as chaplain left "a very unsatisfactory feeling."[112]

Captains and the navy took other measures that discouraged religious expression. First, the navy did not provide sufficient numbers of Bibles so sailors could read and pray in their own manner. In 1864, with the number of Union sailors at an all-time high, the navy purchased seventy-five Bibles.[113] Second, although navy regulations mandated that divine services be held "whenever circumstances and weather allow," captains regularly failed to hold divine services.[114] Some captains routinely omitted services if they felt there was pressing work. Others dropped services if they did not care to have them.[115] One sailor commented that divine services were "uncommon at sea."[116] James E. Henneberry marveled that his boat, the *Essex*, did not have a religious service until November 1862.[117]

Surprisingly, religious and nonreligious sailors expressed ill feelings over the lack of regular services. In their letters and diaries, they meticulously recorded the absence of church on Sundays and holy days.[118] Obviously, some irreligious sailors used a lack of services to vent their general unhappiness over the navy. Given the choice, even irreligious sailors would rather pray than work. "At 10 A.M., instead of divine service, we hauled up along the bank and took in 40 cords of fence rails," John G. Morrison groused, "and instead of praying we fiddled (on the rails)."[119]

Protestant or Catholic, religious or not, nothing raised sailors' ire like working on Sundays. Union sailors used to chant the following rhyme when they toiled on Sundays: "Six days shalt thou labor and do all thou art able. On the Sabbath Day holystone the deck and scrub the cable."[120] Most sailors—whether based on religious belief, cultural tradition, or self-interest—had internalized the cultural practice of not working on Sundays. For Americans in the nineteenth century, Sundays meant rest, relaxation, and religion. The sacredness of the Sabbath and its crucial role in preserving the rhythm of an individual's holy life extended back to the seventeenth century.[121] Although captains had already substantially dampened the religious spirit of the day, sailors still wanted to retain the rest and relaxation.

Granted, the Union navy could not have waged a six-day-a-week blockade or suspended river operations on Sundays. Sailors accepted the reality that fighting and some operational work had to be done around the clock and on the Sabbath. Nevertheless, sailors did vehemently object to work performed on Sunday that they knew was non-essential.[122] One sailor growled that scrubbing the decks and polishing all of the ship's brass work on Sunday was nothing short of "shameful."[123] Fifteen-year-old Charles Mervine, after helping loosen, make, and shake out the sails one Sabbath, complained, "Such is a sailors Sunday. . . . I wonder if the Hon. Sect'y of the Navy allows such work as this to be carried on."[124] The few chaplains who did manage to get ship-duty observed—to their dismay—that Sunday morning was often one of the "busiest mornings of the week in cleaning ship insides out."[125]

The overall result proved dispiriting. To a man, sailors admitted that Sunday became the most lonesome day of the week. Seaman Edwin R. Benedict summed up the melancholy effect the day had on the emotions of sailors. "The day was a rather lonesome one," he noted in his diary, "as nearly all Sabbaths in the Navy are."[126] It was not that sailors were avid churchgoers. The reason for the loneliness of the day was that sailors directly associated Sundays with home and home with church.[127] It was on Sundays that sailors wistfully recalled women, friends, and community.[128] Sailors remembered watching people wrestle with itchy collars and whispering to friends. Some, probably few, even missed passing the collection plate.[129] In violating this focal point of weekly Christian cultural and religious practice, many men likely felt that the navy was further isolating them from home.

Without question, sailors themselves broke the Sabbath by gambling, getting drunk, and playing music.[130] Nonetheless, the impact of being forced to work on a day traditionally reserved for rest demoralized men and squandered an opportunity for the navy to foster religious feeling, or at least raise morale, by playing up the day's vivid connection to home and family. In the process, Sundays became less sacred and more depressing. Seaman Edwin R. Benedict lamented, "Another Sabbath day so sacred in many localities (but far different here)."[131] Charles A. Poole wrote that while scrubbing the decks and polishing the brass work one Sunday, "I could not help thinking of the difference between my Sundays now and when I was at home. The same work has to be done today that is done every day."[132] Religious sailors regarded such measures as a callous disregard for their consciences and a government "wink" at men of "bad conscience."[133] Even men of bad conscience did not want to work on Sundays. In short, the captains' harshening of an unpopular Sunday service coupled with increased labor on the Sabbath managed to offend just about everyone, lowered morale, and squashed religious sentiment among sailors on the day most favorable for nurturing it.

The special needs of sailors when it came to religious instruction and the obstacles encountered in attempting to meet those needs goaded the navy into making changes. Since 1799, the navy had compelled sailors to attend divine services aboard ship no matter what their faith or lack of faith.[134] As much as the navy valued conformity and the Episcopal leanings of its officers, it placed a higher premium on recruiting sailors. In order to increase harmony and decrease tension over religion, the navy decided to abandon its policy of mandatory attendance at divine services in favor of a voluntary form of religious practice. On 17 July 1862, Congress passed *An Act for the Better Government of the Navy of the United States*, which "earnestly recommended" but did not compel sailors to attend divine service. The act also ended the requirement of daily morning and evening prayers.[135]

The navy had adopted these policy changes as a concession to the increasing number of Catholics, Baptists, and Methodists joining the service since the 1850s.[136] The movement toward voluntary attendance had started before the war. In 1860, the navy had begun excusing Catholic sailors from divine service in order to, in the words of Secretary of the Navy Isaac Toucey, "respect the religious convictions of the Catholics."[137]

Moreover, the navy's action reflected a universal trend taking place throughout the Northern military. The Lincoln administration had made a conscious effort to defuse religious tensions by making concessions to all religious groups, even unpopular ones. Lincoln arranged to have Catholic and Jewish chaplains in the army even though, before the war, the chaplain law provided only for the appointment of Protestant clergy.[138] The underlying message conveyed by these measures was simple. Religious factions were expected to ignore their divisions for the good of the Union, and the government would do its part by granting members of differing denominations some measure of autonomy.[139] It was in this spirit that the navy's decision to drop mandatory attendance should be seen.

The navy's adoption of voluntary attendance at divine services immediately altered the spiritual practices of sailors and the religious environment of Union ships. At 10:00 A.M. on Sundays, sailors now had a number of options. Men could attend the official Episcopal service, not attend services, or worship as they wished. Catholics took advantage of the change by performing their own services, using their own prayers from their own prayer books.[140] Black sailors also benefited from the new atmosphere. Continuing a tradition that had its roots in the prewar maritime culture of African American seamen, the navy encouraged some measure of religious autonomy for black sailors.[141] Aboard ship, black sailors conducted their own services.[142] If close enough to shore or in port, officers allowed African American sailors to go ashore and attend their own church services—a concession not granted to white sailors.[143]

Even the navy's sacred burial traditions gave way in light of the new policy. Where once funerals for sailors had been headed by the captain and subject to navy—not religious—procedures, funerals now could conform to the religion of the deceased.[144] Captains now permitted Catholic sailors to be buried according to the Catholic burial rite; if possible, officers sought out a priest to conduct the liturgy and secured burial plots in Catholic cemeteries.[145]

Christian sailors used their newly granted freedom to construct a less formal style of worship. They did this by organizing small prayer meetings aboard ship. Officers permitted men to hold these gatherings on their own time. Prayer meetings consisted of a few sailors gathering on the open deck or in cramped corners of the ship. Sometimes, the meetings were held by men huddled together while on night watch. In these meetings, sailors recited prayers, read scripture, and unburdened themselves of their troubles.[146] An article appearing in the June 1863 issue of the *Sunday School Times* described how one sailor, after finding only one other Christian in his crew of 200, started a meeting on the *Daylight*: "The next day about ten o'clock he got his hymn-book and Bible, and took charge of the 'right wing' of the ship to begin his meeting. It was a very solemn service; an invitation was given to all those who felt their need of Christ to express it; twelve men knelt and asked the two to pray for them. Several of these found the 'pearl of great price.'"[147]

After July 1862, prayer meetings became the most popular form of religious expression among sailors. Interest in these meetings proved so great that Christian sailors gathered four to seven times a week. On one ship, prayer meetings were held every night for ten months. As the war progressed, the numbers at prayer meetings easily surpassed attendance at regular Sunday services. Religious seamen seemed to respond to the democratic, less formal, and heartfelt nature of these meetings.

As a result, commented Chaplain Joseph Stockbridge, "many sinners were awakened."[148]

Although many sinners may have been awakened, most of them fell back to sleep. Despite the growth of prayer meetings, their impact proved limited. Overall, the most significant impact of the jettisoning of compulsory attendance was that most sailors stopped going to any type of service on Sundays.[149] Seaman James E. Henneberry, serving on the Mississippi Squadron, noted that shortly after voluntary attendance commenced, only one-half of the crew on his boat attended divine service one Sunday.[150] On both the Mississippi and blockade squadrons, attendance progressively dwindled among sailors and officers.[151] Some Sundays there were only a handful in attendance.[152] A lieutenant serving on a James River gunboat, sadly observed that just one sailor answered the church bell on a Sunday after the adoption of voluntary attendance.[153]

Predictably, irreligious sailors happily stopped attending services. Catholics and evangelical-leaning Protestants had theological reasons for not attending. Men who had never formed the church-going habit, or who were not religiously inclined, quickly concocted all kinds of excuses for not going. Sailors rationalized that they received nothing out of the service, that they could not hear the captain, that it was too hot, or that they were too busy.[154] William Wainwright offered a glimpse into the Sunday morning decision process for sailors not inclined toward religion: "I started on deck with the intention of going to church. but before I got on deck my mind changed. I have no doubt but it would be better for me to go but has [sic] long as I dont take any interest when I do go. I think I might as well stay away."[155]

The navy's intentions in allowing voluntary attendance at services were practical in scope and represented a balance between extreme positions on religion. By abandoning compulsory attendance and allowing for a divergence in practice, the navy had merely acknowledged the religious diversity of its crews. However, the government's attempt to let irreligious and religious sailors decide for themselves which form, if any, of religion to practice in a harsh environment lacking clergy and churches effectively discouraged most formal religious practice. "Sailors like soldiers," Chaplain Edmund C. Bittinger explained, "will only do what is required of them."[156]

Clergy and religious leaders quickly attributed growing sailor irreligiosity to the abandonment of compulsory attendance at divine services. The sharp decline in sailors' attendance at Sunday services prompted chaplains and Northern religious groups to protest. In fact, the furor surrounding navy and army actions with regard to the Sabbath had initially prompted leaders of various religious groups in New York City to meet with President Lincoln on 13 November 1862. At that meeting, they called on him and the heads of all military departments to ensure a better observance of the Sabbath.[157] Although he did not re-institute compulsory attendance, on 15 November 1862, Lincoln issued a general order demanding that Sunday labor in the navy "be reduced to the measure of strict necessity." Lincoln assured Northerners that the measure had been taken to protect the sacred rights of Christian sailors and as a sign of deference to the "best sentiments of a Christian people."[158]

Lincoln's order did little to reinvigorate the Sabbath and religious practice among sailors. "The repeal requiring the presence of the Ship's company at divine service has given a strong impetus to Sabbath desecration," complained Chaplain Stockbridge to the Navy Department in May 1863.[159] Moreover, Chaplain Stockbridge reported that a host of new "customs" among sailors had arisen since the institution of voluntary attendance. These customs turned the traditional nature of the day on its head. Not only did sailors stop going to services; they engaged in all sorts of activities that defied the spiritual tenor of the day: they openly and lustily gambled, danced, and played music.[160] Except during work periods, Sundays used to be rather quiet aboard ship. Now, Seaman Joseph Osborne observed, Sunday nights had grown "lively."[161] Captains seemed to view the new policy of voluntary religious practice as a vindication of their earlier attempts to work sailors on Sunday. They now forsook holding services altogether and worked sailors harder than ever. Chaplain Joseph Stockbridge warned that unless the navy adopted some "counter-action" to stem the erosion of sailor attendance, "our Sabbath is gone."[162]

One could argue, as some citizens did before the war, that the navy had no right or constitutional basis for administering religion to men.[163] However, from a practical standpoint, the navy knew that sailor morale declined in a ship atmosphere overcome with immorality and irreverence. While the extreme situations of sailors during the Civil War made the preservation of religious practice more difficult, such conditions also made them more necessary. What Union sailors needed were tailored religious services and moral instructions designed to lift their spirits and to provide a link to shore.[164] Officers noticed that collective services and prayers helped sailors, even if they did not want them.

An officer serving on the *Lackawanna* admitted, "The service of the Church had always an excellent influence."[165]

Chaplains noted that the navy's well-intentioned but wrongheaded measures ultimately "demoralized" sailors.[166] By early 1864, sailors' letters and journals rang with this demoralization. Many complained of chronic depression, fatigue, and lack of purpose in their service.[167] The cumulative effect of the navy's actions was that sailors did not use religion to buoy their morale under trying conditions.[168] Living in the religious vacuum that the navy helped to create, most sailors did not turn to religion on their own. Instead, they wilted and then fell back on alcohol and other forms of escape to get them through the war.[169]

The navy's problems in addressing the spiritual needs of sailors eventually prompted religious organizations to expand their efforts at outreach by launching a campaign to bring religion aboard ships of the blockade and gunboats on the Mississippi. Before the war, organizations such as the Missionary Society for Seamen, the American Bible Society, and the American Seaman's Friend Society had labored to bring religion to sailors by supplying scriptures and religious tracts to seamen. They had even constructed floating chapels in places like New York harbor.[170] These groups also sought to improve the living conditions of American sailors and had been in the forefront of the fight to abolish flogging as a means of punishment in 1850 and the campaign to prohibit alcohol on ships in 1862.[171]

The Civil War caused these reform organizations to intensify their efforts. On 15 November 1861 in New York City, members of the Young Men's Christian Association (YMCA) organized the United States Christian Commission. Organizers formed the commission to inspire soldiers and sailors to live "faithful, consistent Christian lives" while away from home in the service. Its members, called "Christians," attracted strong support from Methodist and Episcopal churches.[172] The work of the commission was to be carried out by 4,886 commissioned agents called "delegates." These delegates promised to function as "moral police amid these national convulsions." Although the army was their first priority, the commission eventually saw the large numbers of navy volunteers as a unique opportunity to reach a group of men once thought physically and morally unreachable.[173]

The commission did not intend merely to preach at sailors. The organization realized that it had to meet the men's temporal wartime needs before the sailors would listen to a religious message. The commission molded its approach around the traditional view of charity as a religious obligation and primarily "alleviative in nature."[174] The commission's preachers believed their primary responsibility to be the alleviation of the suffering and hardship of sailors and not sermonizing on the message of salvation. Commission delegates hoped that if they tried to aid sailors' physical welfare, they might also save their souls.[175]

In order to "hunt out" Christian sailors, commission members developed a four-pronged plan of operation. First, commission members brought clothing, fresh fruits and vegetables, and lemonade. Second, delegates planned to establish personal contact with sailors by making individual visitations. Personal contact with psychologically and physically ailing sailors, they believed, was pivotal to achieving success.[176] Third, delegates volunteered to lead Sunday services and prayer meetings aboard ship.[177]

In trying to understand the religious problems of sailors, the commission concluded that the greatest factor impeding religious practice stemmed from isolation. As a result, the fourth and final part of the commission's strategy was to attempt to reconnect sailors to Northern society. To accomplish this, the commission adopted two critical approaches, one old and one new. The first measure the commission took was to hire dispatch boats to make bimonthly rounds through the squadrons, distributing thousands of Bibles and religious tracts.[178] An officer on the receiving ship *North Carolina* reported that the commission sent so many Bibles that every member of the crew had at least one copy.[179] Easy to read and sensibly written, religious tracts played up spiritual themes, good stories, and temperance morals. Such titles as "Come to Jesus," "The Little Captain," and "Where Is Jesus?" were designed to spark religious curiosity before delegates arrived and maintain it after they left.[180]

The second measure that the commission took was to do whatever it could to revive a chain between homes and ships.[181] This chain would not be established by abstract references to mother and family as captains had done in their sermons. Instead, the commission took practical approaches to establishing bonds between sailors and shore by bringing any reminder of home they could, from local newspapers to gossip.[182]

More importantly, delegates encouraged sailors to write home. Letter writing, however, proved costly and expensive for sailors. The navy did not provide men with pencils, paper, envelopes, and postage to write home. Sutlers often charged as much as forty cents for a single sheet of paper and an envelope.[183] Commission delegates brought writing supplies for sailors and mailed their letters free of charge.[184] If a man was unable to write because of an injury or illiteracy, the commission member would write the letter for him. By subsidizing the exchange of letters, the commission enlisted the assistance of family and friends, particularly women, in the campaign to save sailors from Satan's reach on board ship.

The navy, not surprisingly, was skeptical. Although the commission's chairman, George H. Stuart, extended the commission's offer of assistance in 1861, delegates did not begin visiting sailors until 1864. Only when sailor morale plummeted in 1864 did the navy let delegates aboard ship. In Stuart's opinion, Gideon Welles had looked with a "jaundiced eye" on its offer to assist with the spiritual lives of sailors. According to Stuart, Welles had only cautiously accepted the commission's offer to assist by saying that the navy would accept only "legitimate means to promote the welfare (present and future) of all who are in the service."[185]

According to the commission, the navy feared that too much religion would make sailors "effeminate" and deprive them of courage.[186] Furthermore, although many denominations were represented among the commission's delegates—including the Methodist, Baptist, and Congregational churches—they were heavily Protestant and not at all timid. Most preachers were evangelical and of the "blue flame sulphureous order," as one sailor commented.[187] In order to gain access to sailors, the commission buried denominational and doctrinal differences for the cause of the Union. It promised to conduct its campaign under the guiding principles of "Catholicity," "Nationalism," and "Voluntariness."[188]

Once begun, visitation work proved extremely difficult. The task of reaching sailors was logistically problematic since delegates had to travel to where sailors lived—on ships and boats of the blockade and Mississippi River fleets. Reaching soldiers was not so difficult. In army camps, the commission established "stations" where the men could come and worship, visit, and receive literature.[189] Although delegates did establish permanent stations in places like the Brooklyn Navy Yard and the Navy Yard at Charleston, these places were merely pass-through points, where if recruits had time—much less the inclination—they grabbed a handful of literature and went on their way.

To facilitate the commission's efforts, captains permitted ministers to preach to sailors on the berth deck. The berth deck was one of the few places aboard ship where sailors could relax or sleep. The berth deck was also the favorite place for sailors to steal, drink, and beat one another. Delegates often read prayers aloud to sailors as they lay in their hammocks. For rough and tumble sailors, it must have seemed strange to have a minister read prayers to them as they went to sleep. One delegate recalled, "I stood by the swinging hammocks, and read to them from the Book of Books, concerning God's wonderful love to them."[190]

To their displeasure, delegates found that ships made poor churches. The noise, the crowded conditions, and constant buzz of activity made holding services difficult.[191] Furthermore, jumping from boat to boat under the scrutiny of captains and entering hostile environments loaded with nonbelievers required tough men. J. D. Wyckoff reported that he visited quite a few gunboats in the Mississippi Squadron before he encountered any religious sailors. On more hospitable ships, he met one or two religious sailors among crews of 150 to 200 men.[192]

Despite all of these obstacles, commission delegates brought certain elements to religious services that captains had not, including fervor, piety, and most of all sincerity.[193] Seaman John Eliot Parkman noticed the difference immediately when the Reverend W. L. Tisdale preached to sailors one Sunday: "A man of excellent intentions I have no doubt, but badly clothed and clammy, with a tendency to burst as he warms to his work. He preached on the berth deck and as it was no more than six inches above his head it proved a wonderful Sounding board as he hurled and writhed in the telling points of his discourse—He has gone, but the deck still rumbles and my head is cracking."[194]

Surprisingly, Union sailors seemed to accept grudgingly the efforts of commission delegates. Without question, they mocked the "Holy Joes" that came across their decks for their religious fervor and boisterousness. Sailors likely cringed and growled when ministers belabored the evils of drink, wanton women, and tobacco, or handed them unempathetic tracts such as "Hell and its Miseries."[195] Nevertheless, unlike their objections to navy-dispensed religion, sailors did not complain about the commission's visits. Sailors believed its ministers to be sincere in their mission and accepted them as a genuine source of religious and spiritual comfort.

One of the reasons for sailor empathy was that commission delegates received little compensation for their work. Sailors seemed genuinely impressed that someone would board a ship to work for less than they did.[196] In addition, for men feeling put upon and abused, the free distributions of foodstuffs, reading materials, and mailing supplies were most appreciated. Seaman John Swift, who had not been to church in some time, expressed gratitude for the literature: "I have one of their bibles which does as well."[197] Sailors also tacitly thanked the commission for the free writing supplies and postage by engaging in the very act of writing home. Since Sunday conjured up the strongest feelings for friends and families, it was not surprising that whole crews often feverishly used the day to write letters to friends and family back home.[198]

Most importantly, commission delegates adapted their demeanor and the content of their services to meet the specific religious needs of sailors.[199] Gone were the calls for obedience, the captain's railing about sailor lowliness and hypocrisy, and dry readings from chapters of the New Testament. In their place, commission ministers used kind words and invoked images of Christ as the Good Shepherd who would "bring us through our *Warings* to honorable peace" and would shield them in "every hour of Danger Battling with the Foes of our government."[200] Other ministers restyled familiar psalms to accommodate the unique situation of the sailor. "Thou shall not be afraid for the Terrors by night nor the *Shell that Flieth by Day*," assured Minister E. B. Turner to sailors on the *Onondaga*. Fully aware that seamen loved to sing, the commission also employed hymns tailored to sailors' special circumstances and trials. Hymns such as "Look Aloft," "A Home beyond the Tide," and "Far at Sea" echoed familiar themes of loneliness, storms, and temptations.[201] A particular favorite, the "Sailor's Hymn," called out:

Tossed upon life's raging billow
Sweet it is, O Lord to know
Thou didst press a sailor's pillow
And canst feel a sailor's woe.[202]

Minor incidents revealed the subtle impact that the commission made on individual sailors. The Reverend J. D. Wyckoff, a Congregationalist pastor who performed services for sailors on the receiving ship at Cairo, recalled a story concerning Seaman John Jones. Wyckoff had noticed that during the meetings, Jones had not participated. Afterward, however, Wyckoff recalled that Jones approached him and sheepishly asked for a copy of the *New York Observer* and a Bible for "a mate." Wyckoff thought this strange but complied with Jones's request. As Wyckoff turned to leave, Jones again approached the minister and, with his right hand extended and partly closed so as to conceal from his crewmates what it held, said, "I want to do something for Christ; won't you take this for the Commission?" As Jones hurried away, Wyckoff looked down at his hand and saw five dollars.[203]

On 14 June 1864, the steamboat *Eclipse* exploded on the Mississippi

River killing and severely injuring many on board. Amid the frightful burns and broken bones, one sailor, who had been severely scalded, recognized the voice of a commission delegate from meetings on the receiving ship at Cairo. Even though he admitted that he was not a religious man and that he had, in fact, been afraid to participate in the Cairo meetings, the sailor cried out that he wanted "to see the Christian Commission man." When the delegate responded, the man said to him, "I've been a great sinner, but I'm seeking repentance and forgiveness. . . . I'm not ashamed to ask Christians to pray for me now."[204] These incidents, although individual in nature, do speak to the type of collective impact the commission made on religious and nonreligious sailors alike. Seaman John Swift summed up the contribution that the commission had made to sailors' lives. "There is a Society in this Country," Swift wrote his sister, "which supplies all who are fighting under its flag, with food for body & soul."[205]

The Christian Commission's efforts did seem to awaken the religious consciences of some sailors.[206] Observers recalled that the commission's services worked a positive effect on the men. Levi Hayden concluded that they created an atmosphere of "Pathos Love and reverence for the Deity unity and good fellowship" even in sight of the enemy.[207] Other sailors acknowledged that they felt the "benison" and comfort of these prayers all the day long.[208]

Proof of this awakening was the increase in voluntary attendance at divine services that often followed a dissemination of literature and visits by the commission's delegates. Both the delegates and the officers credited the distribution of literature for the rise in service attendance by sailors. On ships where only a few of the crew had previously attended divine service, after a distribution of literature and a visit by delegates, over a hundred would appear at the ringing of the church bell.[209] When an officer notified the commission that only one sailor attended a divine service one Sunday, it sent a supply of literature. The very next Sunday, 100 men attended the service. As a result of the literature, the officer marveled, "There is a great change among the crew."[210] Some men even altered the tenor of their lives by signing temperance contracts under which they agreed to forego alcohol, swearing, "wicked companions," and the "wild life."[211]

Yet, in 1865, as the war drew to an end, the commission sadly concluded, "Work for Christ on our gunboats, and among sailors generally, is very peculiar work . . . it might be termed difficult."[212] By its own account, the commission met with frustration and mixed results in its mission to aid Union sailors. To be certain, the commission did achieve some successes. Its literature reportedly reached 580 ships and over 34,000 officers and sailors.[213] In many small ways, the commission's efforts also alleviated some of the hardships suffered by sailors aboard ship.

What is unclear is how much of an impact the commission made in planting the seeds of religious practice and faith in the souls of a group labeled "irreligious." Ministering to men not prone to expressions of faith and denominationally divided, with no chaplains and isolated on a ship, was a daunting task. Moreover, the commission's work among sailors was hampered by its late start in 1864 and by the isolation of ships from land and from each other, thus making collective, sustained religious awakenings extremely difficult to achieve. Not surprisingly, despite the commission's efforts, no large-scale revivals took place among sailors during the Civil War comparable to those that took place in the ranks of their army counterparts.[214]

The troubled tale of religious expression among Union sailors reveals much about the difficulties of maintaining spiritual practice and belief in the church-free, cosmopolitan environments of ships. The religious dimension in the lives of Northern sailors during the Civil War was distinctly different from that of Union soldiers. The obstacles to embracing a vigorous spiritual faith on board a navy vessel in the 1860s suggest a model for examining how religious ideals and practices may fare when sailors, as well as soldiers, are separated from the reinforcing influences of families, clergy, and organized church communities. For naval volunteers, many of whom were not traditionally religious, the ships on which they served formed a spiritual vacuum, which was amplified by the antireligious tendencies of the institutional navy and the assertively profane atmosphere that veteran seamen nurtured. Recognizing the religious problems faced by men when they go to sea should cause historians to reassess stereotypical notions concerning the irreligiosity of sailors and broaden our understanding of the spiritual complexities faced by men when they head off to war, be it on sea or on land, far away from the reach of clergy, family, and friends.

# Frictions
## Shipboard Relations between White and Contraband Union Sailors

The study of the Civil War has become so romanticized that many of the complex issues that made the event a seminal one in American history have become obscured. This is partially understandable because the war's soldiers and sailors endured such tremendous hardships and performed such Herculean feats that, viewed in retrospect, they leave one astounded. What happened when former slaves joined white soldiers and sailors has been one of the complex issues that remains obscured. The few analyses available tend to treat the induction of blacks into the armed services as an inexorable process in which a policy decision was made, implemented, and embraced despite most white combatants' harboring various degrees of racial hostility toward African Americans in general and slaves in particular. While former slaves functioned well with whites in the army and navy, their assimilation was not simple, unchallenged, or bloodless.[1] For the most part, white sailors rejected contrabands as sailors. They did so owing to a tangled mix of racial prejudices, unflattering stereotypes that equated sailors with slaves, and working-class people's fears of blacks as labor competition. The combination of all of these tensions eventually triggered a social war—referred to as "frictions" by sailors—as whites racially harassed, sometimes violently, former slaves serving alongside them.[2]

The presence of slavery in their republic provided a constant marker by which Americans measured their freedom. Slavery forged in the nation's consciousness certain negative characteristics—such as dependence, illiteracy, and powerlessness—that came to be associated with slaves. In the nineteenth century, the reality of slavery proved so potent that whites whose lives swung close to the lives of slaves risked inviting comparison. Concerns over the independent nature of the nation's citizens had found fresh evidence in the aftermath of the market revolution, in which a decline in the need for skilled labor and an increase in worker dependence on wages irresponsibly foisted on the laboring classes the inaccurate label of "wage slaves." Additionally, the market revolution not only called for the assessment of the republican credentials of the new working class but also rekindled latent fears about other marginal groups once thought to be no better than slaves. One of these groups was sailors.[3]

Part of the impetus for this comparison was the "situational slavery" of sailors.[4] Aboard ship, sailors lived in an oppressive environment where they performed menial labor, considered beneath free men, under the constant threat of coercion. Sailors, like slaves, lived beholden to one master, the captain. On a ship, captains ruled absolutely and arbitrarily and wielded power nothing short of despotic. They routinely abused their authority, as masters did in regard to their slaves.[5] Moreover, although the navy had abolished flogging in 1850, officers corrected sailors for offenses, great and small, with brutal and humiliating punishments. The life of a sailor rankled so much like forced servitude that, beginning in the 1830s, reformers and seamen missionaries explicitly compared sailors to Southern slaves, except, as Harold Langley asserts in *Social Reform in the United States Navy, 1798–1862*, "slaves emerged better by comparison."[6]

Formidable American writers who had served as ordinary sailors powerfully disseminated the idea of the slavelike existence of men at sea. Richard Henry Dana Jr. in *Two Years before the Mast*, Frederick Law Olmsted in *The Cotton Kingdom*, and Herman Melville in *White-Jacket* graphically illustrated the slavish qualities of a sailor's life. All three dramatically highlighted the common bond between sailors and slaves in gripping retellings of floggings aboard ship.[7] In *Two Years before the Mast*, Dana describes a horrifying scene in which Captain Frank Thomas reveals to his crew, after gleefully flogging a man, the true station of a sailor aboard ship: "You see your condition! You see where I've got you all, and you know what to expect! — You've been mistaken in me — you didn't know what I was! Now you know what I am! — I'll make you toe the mark, every soul of you, or I'll flog you all, fore and aft, from the boy up! — You've got a driver over you! Yes, a *slave-driver — a negro driver*! I'll see who'll tell me he isn't a negro slave."[8]

Thomas's assessment was also significant because it revealed a second bias against sailors; sailing was a profession not only for slavish individuals but for black people as well. Although sailors in the antebellum United States Navy were overwhelmingly white, African Americans had been permitted to serve as seamen. The navy was willing to accept free blacks owing to a ship's separation from land that permitted more social flexibility. So many African Americans sought to join the navy that by 1839 the navy had placed a 5 percent ceiling on monthly and weekly enlistments.[9] In spite of this limitation, the allowance—when compared to explicit directives that banned blacks from enlistment in the state militias and the United States Army—doubly damned sailors as slave-tempered and black-hearted.[10]

Together, these factors—situational, fictional, and demographic—fomented a powerful American cultural perception before the Civil War that sailors were, in fact, not much better off than slaves. Cultural and social notions that equated sailors with blacks and slaves ran so deep that Americans began ascribing the negative behavioral stereotypes from each group to sailors. Jesse Lemisch concludes that Americans thought of "Jack Tar as jolly, childlike, irresponsible, and in many ways surprisingly like the Negro stereotype."[11] Even sailors referred to themselves as "vassals" and "slaves of the lowest cast." One sailor, Christopher Slocum, sadly summarized the shared bond that knit sailors and slaves together: "And now I ask what slave at the South suffers more hardships or feels more keenly the bitterness of oppression than the poor care worne sailor."[12]

So potent and so rankling were these stereotypes that by the late 1850s few self-respecting white men would join the merchant marine.[13] More importantly, when the war started, white recruits did not rush to the navy—they headed to the army. Although racial perceptions did not compel white recruits to join the army, the notion that sailoring was a service that welcomed blacks and subjected men to situational slavery certainly weakened the navy's ability to attract recruits. The strength of this association proved so strong that W. Jeffrey Bolster surmises that if one were to "substitute 'Negro' for 'sailor' and 'race' for 'vocation,' . . . few Americans at mid-century would have missed a beat."[14]

When the war began, consistent with previous practice, the navy allowed free blacks to enlist.[15] Even though some considered sailors the equivalent of slaves, there was still a considerable leap between culturally equating sailors with slaves and allowing them to serve on Union men-of-war. Yet, surprisingly enough, the navy enlisted former slaves as early as July 1861. While originally the navy had no intention of tapping this resource, the crew shortages resulting from a lack of white recruits compelled the change. Slaves had also forced the shift in practice.

As soon as Union ships penetrated Southern coasts and rivers, former slaves—called "contrabands"—began flocking to navy vessels seeking freedom and offering their services.[16]

Every day found a steady stream of black refugees—men, women, and children—beckoning at the sides of ships from crude rafts, commandeered water craft, and nearby riverbanks. Initially, officers did not know what to do with them. Vessels were too small to house and food supplies too limited to feed hundreds or thousands of refugees. Moreover, a naval ship was no place for women and children. As a result, some captains returned them to shore. However, even if not antislavery in sentiment, most officers and sailors did not want to return contrabands to slavery. Most commanders allowed contrabands to remain aboard until the navy decided how best to handle them.[17]

Although most officers were willing to keep contrabands on board until guided by a formal policy, they were unwilling to allow contrabands to remain unemployed. While waiting for the navy to arrive at a contraband policy, officers began putting contrabands to work performing routine chores around the ship.[18] Male contrabands performed manual labor and servantlike tasks.[19] Women scrubbed the officers' and crew's laundry, cooked, and sewed. Children did what they could.[20] It was during this time of uncertainty that some officers decided that the most promising male contrabands should stay. "A few were selected from among the best men," wrote Seaman Israel E. Vail, "and were retained on board as a part of the ship's crew."[21] Those not accepted for service received transport to contraband camps and military stations.

On 25 September 1861, Secretary of the Navy Gideon Welles announced that the navy would enlist male contrabands with the rating of boy, the lowest position aboard ship.[22] Granted, the navy's long history of using blacks and the cultural association between sailors and slaves likely helped the navy brook some of the squeamishness about such a monumental move. However, without question, part of the reason why officers and the navy decided to experiment with contrabands as crew members was the initial reaction of white sailors. White sailors peacefully accepted black refugees aboard ship and did not object when some male contrabands joined their crews. To be sure, officers had crossed their fingers when allowing contrabands to board since everyone acknowledged that white crews featured some of the roughest, ill-tempered, and violent recruits in the Union war effort.[23] The navy was so worried that ornery sailors would pounce on these refugees that the service promulgated regulations ordering that contrabands not be "ill treated by the rest of the crew" and "discouraged imposition upon them."[24]

Yet what happened when slaves called at the railings of blockade vessels and river gunboats amazed officers and sailors alike. Union sailors looking into the faces of people they resented on sight—given their racial dispositions—did not turn them away or stage ragged protests. Instead, they helped them aboard. More often than not, it was a white sailor who tied off contraband crafts to Union vessels and helped them aboard, fed them, and gave them dry clothes, usually a blue sailor suit.[25] Although sailors did not give the orders aboard ship, they wielded a great deal of practical power since they were the eyes and ears of the ship. They could have made contraband journeys to ships difficult or nearly impossible. Sailors could have refused to recognize their boats, sounded their arrival as a threat to ship security, or returned them to the water. They did not. Instead, white tars helped these fugitives aboard their ships night after night, often at the risk of their own lives.[26]

This does not mean that white sailors were glad to see gangs of contrabands streaming toward their ships. To the contrary, white tars often snarled about their appearance. These men were trying to fight a war and had not planned on dealing with a flood of former slaves. White sailors grumbled about contrabands because they created a tremendous amount of additional work. Although sometimes a handful of contrabands arrived every night, in areas with large black populations like the lower Mississippi Valley and the South Carolina coast, the numbers of contrabands flocking to Union vessels were enormous.[27] Seaman James Henneberry wrote, "Every night we receive 6 or 8 negroes on board."[28] So many came aboard Northern ships that George Clark said that they "were in every one's way."[29] Sailors routinely complained that contrabands quickly grew to be a "nuisance."[30]

Sailors had a reason to gripe. Contrabands, particularly on the Mississippi Squadron, overran the capacities of the fleet's largest gunboats. In some instances, river sailors had to attach large barges to the stern of their boats in order to house them.[31] On these barges, contrabands—ranging from 700 to 1,000 people—literally established small towns. Thomas Lyons commented in his journal that the barge attached to his boat, the *Carondolet*, was so large that during one afternoon there was a wedding taking place at one end, a prayer meeting on the other, and a baptism in the middle.[32]

Some of the hostility expressed by white sailors also stemmed from deep-seated prejudices—prejudices that sometimes bordered on sheer hatred—for people of color generally and slaves in particular. Based on their letters and diaries, the overwhelming majority of Union sailors harbored every vicious, condescending prejudice ruminating in American society concerning blacks in the mid-nineteenth century.[33] Overall, white sailors seemed to share the dominant Northern opinion, which painted blacks as childish, meek, subservient, passive, clownish, care-free, and irresponsible. They—like many other Northerners—believed that blacks lacked manners and intelligence and could aspire only to very limited social, economic, and wartime roles.[34]

Their views of slaves proved to be even more prejudiced. In racial assertions, sailors argued that the only thing worse than being black was being a black slave. White sailors called the contrabands that came aboard "lazy," "dishonest," "impertinent," "stupid," and "disgusting."[35] Landsman Rowland Stafford True's racial attitudes ran the gamut from romanticized racism to white supremacy. "They were usually good na-tured and full of fun," he wrote, "but sometimes were ugly and disobe-dient."[36] Other sailors thought of them as "animals."[37] White sailors like Seaman William H. Price considered African Americans not equal to whites. His brittle interpretation of the Declaration of Independence excluded them by omission. "It does not seem say anything at all con-cerning the niger or the black man," he opined, "or whether he is nearly a man at all or not."[38]

Although predisposed against these former slaves, white sailors did not want to return them to their masters. Their motivations for accept-ing them lay in a mixture of basic empathy, pragmatism, and romantic racism. Their antislavery impulse did not arise from strong ideological convictions about the equality of men. Union sailors witnessed first-hand the worst effects of slavery since their ships were able to penetrate deep into the South. Most slaves, in a pitiful state to begin with, arrived at Union ships even worse off because of the toll that the effort to escape had taken. They had been on the run for some time and had suffered a great deal in order to get to a ship or gunboat. White sailors often found slaves huddled on the banks waving furiously to get their attention as if their lives depended on it. "Destitute" was how one officer described the condition of most contrabands.[39] This condition played right into the sympathies of white sailors because it meshed neatly with most pre-conceptions held about slaves. This state of dependence made it easier for white sailors to accept contrabands aboard ship.

The horribly exciting stories contrabands brought with them proved particularly effective in winning sailors' acceptance. Sailors were captivated by stories and especially sad ones full of adventure, woe, and hardship. They loved hearing how contrabands fought the surf, shoals, and tide in dugout canoes and rafts to reach blockaders.[40] Fear-riddled tales of paddling down a river clutching to a piece of driftwood dodging river snakes and rats while guerrillas and locals armed with guns and torches prowled on the banks gripped the listeners' attention.[41] Accounts of whippings and the display of scars angered them.[42] Many could identify with being hungry and on the run.[43]

The stories of contrabands fed right into sailors' renowned weakness for persons in worse shape than they were in. This elusive soft spot, called "sailor generosity," represented one of the few pathways into sailors' souls.[44] Freeman Foster marveled that the four contrabands his mates took aboard said that their lives as slaves were so hard that "they would not go back & they said they would sooner jump into the river." Three contrabands told sailors aboard the *Mount Vernon* "that if they should be returned they would be murdered."[45] Calvin G. Hutchinson, serving on the *Commodore Morris*, recounted one such heartrending story on the Rappahannock River:

> I said to the boy. Do you want to go on board the gunboat?
> Yes Massa! he answered Why? said I.
> Kase I wants to get free! was his reply.
> Why do you want to get free? was my next question.
> The child said Massa John Tolifer done sends me after soft crabs and when I dont done get no soft crabs den he beats me.[46]

It would be more romantic to say that white sailors ultimately accepted black refugees because of their gut-wrenching stories. Alternatively, it would be even easier to attribute white sailors' acceptance of contrabands as crew members to their belief that the use of contraband sailors was strictly a war measure and an appropriate way to strike back at Southerners. Historians have concluded as much about soldiers.[47] Unfortunately, sailors' acceptance of contrabands was not that high minded. Despite the stories, despite the heart-wrenching condition of contrabands, and despite their own beliefs, white sailors initially accepted the shipping of contrabands as crew members primarily because they would shoulder some of the work aboard ship.

In their own words, sailors welcomed contraband sailors because they were "short of hands."[48] Overworked sailors accepted anyone who could help with their never-ending list of shipboard duties. In fact, as soon as contrabands arrived they began assuming most of the backbreaking, tedious, and dangerous work that white sailors did not want to do. Many white sailors shared the feelings of William H. Price who accepted contraband sailors only because of the critical manpower shortage. "I had just as leaf have a little white jack as I would black," Price penned to an enraged friend, "any port in a storm as jack tar says."[49]

Another factor conducive to the initial assimilation of contraband sailors was that the navy charged white sailors with the task of cleaning, instructing, and supervising them. Naval regulations warned that contrabands were "naturally negligent" and in need of improvement.[50] White tars gleefully participated in this improvement process as it gave them the chance to put their racial dispositions into action. Under the rules mandating that the crew pay "great attention" to contrabands' appearance, white sailors cut their hair, scrubbed their skin hard with soap and brushes, and taught them how to keep their persons and uniforms clean. Every morning under the supervision of officers, white sailors rigorously inspected contrabands to make sure that they had washed themselves and cleaned their uniforms and that their bags and bedding were in navy order.[51]

White sailors pushed their black mates hard about their work habits and personal shortcomings. Sailor George Clark called them "large, fat, indolent men."[52] Seaman John Swift wrote to his sister that a "lazier, more impertinent & dishonest set of men I never saw."[53] All of these constant criticisms had a positive effect on contrabands in the view of many white sailors. George Clark marveled at the transformation that contraband sailors underwent as a result of the "new ideas infused into them."[54] White sailors paid so much scrutiny to contraband sailors' perceived foibles that one exasperated contraband complained that he never had "so many bosses" in all of his life.[55]

Although some contrabands complained about "rough" treatment by white crews, teasing and making sport were traditional rites of passage for new recruits.[56] Part of the zeal with which white sailors rode these new recruits formed an integral part of the initiation process. As they had done to previous raw recruits, Union sailors quickly set to teasing their new shipmates. Current sailors roughhoused and taunted them. "All sorts of pranks were played on them," recalled George Clark. They mocked the seemingly "happy-go-lucky" characteristics of some and the physical features of others. "Such ones generaly make good sport for the men," wrote Coal Heaver Charles Poole.[57]

Overall, the barbs turned out to be racially motivated. Name-calling was popular. Sailors called contrabands "niggers," "wolly heads," "monkies," "Nimrods," "mokes," and "Gideonites."[58] They mocked their physical appearance, from hair to eyes to teeth. Men poked fun at the way contraband sailors talked and acted.[59] Landsman Rowland Stafford True's crewmates on the *Silver Lake* called one contraband "Lippy," because, as True recalled, "I never saw such thick lips on a human being."[60] Lieutenant Louis Kempff recorded some of the racial taunting endured by contraband sailors as white sailors scrubbed them: "their hair (rather their wool) was cut off close and I am told that *elephants* ½ inch long were found on them."[61]

White sailors' acceptance of contrabands as refugees of war was one thing; permitting them to live and work in close proximity with white crews was another matter entirely. Naval officials were aware of the potential unrest presented by mixing white toughs with former slaves in a tight space. The navy initially sought to forestall potential unrest by incorporating blacks into white crews under a number of pointed limitations.[62] These limitations, the navy hoped, would help create comfortable zones of social and labor distance enabling white sailors to coexist peacefully with former slaves as sailors.

The first measure the navy took was to rate contraband recruits no higher than boy no matter what their age or level of maritime experience.[63] By giving them a rating specifically intended for children, the navy accomplished three implicit objectives. First, stamping a contraband as a boy neatly crystallized white prejudice: the lowest rating was a perfect marriage of naval rank and racial stereotype. Romantic racial caricatures of blacks in the nineteenth century often characterized them as no better than children.[64] The designation was also acceptable to white sailors because "boy" was a pejorative term commonly applied to black men. Second, a man's rating effectively dictated his social and professional position in the ship's hierarchy. The rating of boy firmly ensconced contrabands in the lowest possible social stratum among sailors.[65] Third, this rating restriction limited the maximum wage of contraband sailors to $10 per month, the lowest salary paid to crew members.

Much to the delight of white sailors, the rating of boy also conferred on contraband sailors the dirtiest, most strenuous, and most physically demanding jobs that had to be done on board. Since most sailors did not want to work in the hot and smoky engine room, contraband sailors became the preferred choice for coal heaving and furnace firing below deck, especially in the Mississippi Squadron and West Gulf Blockade

Squadron. "They did all the coal heaving, fired the furnaces, and helped the engineers," wrote Rowland Stafford True.[66] Contraband sailors also assumed much of the back-breaking physical labor aboard ship, such as coaling, loading stores, and transferring ammunition from shore to ship. Additionally, officers and crew members often ordered contraband sailors to row ashore to forage for fresh fruits and vegetables, sometimes at great risk. Others found themselves dispatched on hunting expeditions to rake oysters, hunt game, and catch crabs for the rest of the crew.[67]

Initially, white sailors expressed little discomfort with contraband sailors serving in an unskilled capacity partly because such a menial role meshed neatly with racial prejudice. Such prejudice relegated blacks to performing slavelike tasks such as cleaning and repetitive manual labor. Like boys, contrabands could perform work that was physically demanding but that did not require the discretion, judgment, and responsibility typically expected of seamen. Furthermore, the salary differential comforted white sailors since it confirmed in their minds the belief that their labors were worth more because of their whiteness. For many, work performed by white hands implied a higher quality of workmanship. Lastly, white sailors derived pleasure in seeing contraband sailors shouldering the bulk of the hard labor that they used to perform. Such jobs, many whites thought, were inherently beneath them. Some probably derived a feeling of power since they often supervised the efforts of these new crew members. Many believed that contraband sailors were working for them.

The second measure the navy took had far-reaching consequences not only during the war but after the war as well. Beginning in 1861–62, the United States Navy, for the first time in its history, tacitly allowed officers to implement local policies of racial segregation aboard ships.[68] Segregation, while practically allowing the navy to enlist unlimited numbers of contrabands, effectively ended decades of nominally equal treatment for whites and blacks on U.S. ships.[69] After 1862, officers segregated contrabands based on their own needs and prejudices. The result was an inconsistent and complex system of segregation, which varied from squadron to squadron and from ship to ship.

On segregated ships, contraband sailors worked and drilled in their own groups. Often, officers took them on shore for small arms drill rather than allow them to engage in such training in front of white sailors.[70] The navy also insulated black sailors from white sailors' living arrangements. Since the mess was the most basic social group among sailors, the navy specifically demanded segregation of cooking and eating matters. Contraband sailors could mess only with other contraband sailors, eating food cooked only by black hands.[71]

On the blockade, where vessels were large and isolated from land, the policy was less severe and consisted of soft social segregation in mess groups and some cultural activities.[72] Even among ships on the blockade, segregation policies differed. Some officers freely intermingled contraband sailors in white living arrangements and work details. Other officers clung to the concept of racial separation and created segregated labor shifts called "checkerboard crews," with whites and blacks performing different duties on different parts of the ship at different times.[73]

The Mississippi Squadron was the strictest enforcer of racial segregation. Some river officers, such as Andrew Hull Foote and David Dixon Porter, feared that the sight of integrated crews on Western gunboats as they prowled the interior of the Confederacy would inflame Southern civilians. Racial fears were so pronounced in the squadron that at the time the blockade squadrons were poised to enlist contrabands, Foote had stamped out any such thoughts in the Mississippi Squadron. "As there are objections or difficulties in the Southern country about colored people," Foote wrote, "we do not want any of that class shipped."[74]

Moreover, many officers, including Porter, shuddered at the prospect of integrating former slaves among rough-and-tumble river sailors within the tight confines of river gunboats.[75] Many of these men came from the Midwest, where hatred of blacks ran the strongest in the country, save in the South, racial interaction was scarce, and belief in white supremacy strong. A firm belief in black inferiority and fierce resistance to bestowing political and social rights on black people proved to be a common thread in sailor attitudes.[76]

In fact, the Mississippi Squadron did not even permit contraband enlistment until 30 April 1862.[77] When it did, the squadron established strict parameters of social and labor segregation. In 1862, Porter issued an official edict mandating that contrabands "not . . . be mixed up with the crews of the vessels."[78] Further, regulations instructed that contrabands "be messed by themselves and also kept in gangs by themselves when at work."[79] This led to a situation in which black and white sailors worked in their own groups, ate in their own messes, and slept in color-coded shifts. The system of segregation on the Mississippi Squadron, while not perfect, was systematic when compared to the blockade.

Rowland Stafford True wrote: "There were about thirty Negroes aboard the Silver Lake. . . . Their mess and mess cook was entirely separate from ours."[80]

Segregation in the Mississippi Squadron grew out of the strict adherence to separate watches and work details. Whenever possible, officers on the Western rivers tried to keep contrabands apart from white sailors by working them in the boiler room.[81] When this was not feasible, white and black sailors worked in separate shifts. Since crew members ate and berthed in watches with the same men with whom they worked, color-coded shifts effectively established social segregation. Through the use of rotating white and black watches, the races were separated by keeping them apart performing different activities at different times.[82] Consequently, when not working, black sailors slept and ate in the same places as white sailors, while white sailors worked. When contraband sailors worked, white sailors would then eat and sleep. In this way, black and white sailors were technically working and living together on the same boat but did so separated by race and time of day.

For those who believed that segregation could be attained in the navy, Union blockaders and Western gunboats turned out to be poor places to draw color lines. Racial segregation was difficult in an environment where skill and knowledge, not color, bestowed status and privilege.[83] The fine lines dictated by segregation did not work in the closely confined, teamwork-driven, singular society of ships. There was simply not enough room. The inherent realities of shipboard life regularly demanded that sailors break color barriers when faced with collective tasks such as chasing a blockader, fighting a gale, or working guns in combat. Most of the time, it was simply impractical to have exclusively black or exclusively white crews working in the engine room or in gun crews. The rigid policy of having all-black or all-white cleaning crews may have muzzled racial tensions, but such an arrangement did not get the ship clean as fast as all men pulling together. Consequently, for all of the posturing about and planning for segregation, on most ships whites began routinely sharing duties with blacks in gun crews, daily chores, and labor details.[84]

The integration of shipboard duties was only one of several obstacles to racial separation. Although the extent differed from ship to ship, as soon as they entered the service, contraband sailors began participating in certain elements of sailor culture. The reason for such inclusion was partly utilitarian and partly rooted in the social realities of the ship. Union sailors, owing to their isolation, lived in a singular society and culture.[85] While some thought that the navy could create two societies aboard one ship—one white and one black—such hopes were illusory. For all practical purposes, the navy's decision to let contrabands aboard ship, no matter what its official policies, in effect admitted African Americans into sailor society.

The decision to permit contraband sailors to partake in the daily grog ration was the most important social concession achieved by contraband sailors. Group consumption of alcohol was the core of sailor culture, and the grog ration was sacrosanct. Partly to provide men a good slap against foul weather and to lift sagging spirits amid the drudgery of the naval work day, the grog ration functioned as an integral aspect of sailors' lives. The ration was part of their wages, elemental to their culture, and served as an important bonding ritual.[86]

The inclusion of contrabands into the ritual of the grog ration was significant. Black and white tars stood together in the same line, at the same times, to partake from the same tub of grog. Contrabands received the ration from the same ladle and drank from the same grog cups, just like manly sailors. Although neophytes to naval culture, contrabands quickly ascertained the significance of their participation. George R. Durand marveled about the elevation in social status denoted by the inclusion. "The contrabands have grog served out to them twice a day, same as the crew," Durand wrote, "which seems to mean them much."[87] It also meant much to white sailors, who probably resented the intrusion into their culture by former slaves.

A more significant integration occurred, however, when officers—out of necessity—began inserting contraband sailors into skilled positions. The navy had generally instructed officers to encourage contraband sailors "to learn anything they may show a disposition for." Some officers construed this directive to allow contraband sailors to develop technical and nautical skills aboard ship, regardless of their formal ratings. As a result, contraband sailors began handling such jobs as pilot, ship carpenter, and fireman.[88] Beginning in 1862, some officers incorporated contraband sailors into gun crews and night watches. Officers did not want to take this step, but they would not compromise the safety of the ship to preserve segregation. Even noted segregationist David D. Porter yielded in this regard. In the clipped prose typical of a sailor, he explained, "Owing to the shortness of my crews, have to work them at my guns."[89]

Like the inclusion in the grog ritual, the seemingly rapid incorporation of contraband sailors into gun crews and night watches sent shock waves through white crews. Serving in gun crews represented the fundamental martial skill of sailors; it was a realm traditionally reserved for whites. As did soldiers, many sailors believed that the Civil War was a "white man's war" and the use of blacks at the navy's great guns represented a radical break from that ideal.[90] To white sailors, the navy was not simply employing slaves to perform the scut work around the ship; now the navy was making sailors out of slaves.[91] Although irritated, white sailors had grudgingly accepted the induction of contrabands to perform menial tasks. This new degree of assimilation was much more difficult to accept: it placed contrabands on the same plane as whites. Seaman William Price thought the arming of slaves unthinkable and not justified by the mood of the country. "A niger bearing arms with the majority of the people in this country," Price wrote to his friend, "appears to be contrary with us to all civilize nations."[92]

The most important encroachment of contraband sailors by far was their limited insertion into night watches. The night watch, called the "lookout," was the most vital watch of the day. On lookout, sailors maintained a vigil scanning the horizon for blockade runners, other vessels, and possible attacks from shore. The task required a keen, discerning eye and a sense of judgment about what one was observing while on watch. At night, lookouts assumed virtual control over the entire ship since the lives of their sleeping crewmates—as well as the safety of the vessel—depended on their discretion and judgment. For these reasons, not all officers had permitted the assignment of blacks to watches along with the rest of the crew.[93] The change in policy was momentous since it meant that blacks possessed the same discretion, judgment, and intelligence as whites, so much so that they could be inserted into positions of responsibility. Moreover, the inclusion of contrabands in watch duties also placed white sailors in the position of depending on contraband sailors.[94]

It was even more troubling for white sailors to see that officers were not acting out of a sense of paternalism or indulging in a kind gesture to a downtrodden people. To the contrary, contraband sailors began working with white sailors in work details, in engine rooms, and on watch because, by most accounts, they had proved themselves to be good sailors.[95] Contraband sailors seemed to assimilate quite well into work and naval details. Up until the end of 1862, white sailors also noted that, unlike themselves, contrabands seemed to like their new stations. Daniel Kemp, a landsman from Buffalo, wrote home to his mother, "The Negroes we have taken on board seem to like their new life first-rate."[96]

Generally, contraband sailors were enthusiastic, hard working, and, most importantly, better disciplined than white sailors. Albert S. Barker commented, "To their credit be it said they were as a rule, a very well-behaved set of men."[97] They deserted less frequently.[98] In combat, contraband sailors fought, with a few exceptions, courageously and became proficient in working the great guns of ships. In 1863, the army's adjutant general, when trying to decide whether the army should form black artillery units, observed, "The experience of the Navy is that the Blacks handle heavy guns well."[99] For these reasons, most officers—including those who intensely disliked blacks—wanted contraband sailors in their crews. Even David D. Porter, who detested using blacks in the river fleet, commended their performance. "I could get no men," Porter explained, "so I work in the darkies. They do first-rate, and are far better behaved than their masters."[100]

The cracks in the color barrier and the incorporation of contraband sailors into the fundamental aspects of a sailor's life helped erode any nascent goodwill that white sailors may have felt. Many white sailors now saw contraband sailors as a threat to their positions aboard ship. This threat was magnified because, as the war progressed, the number of contraband sailors grew steadily, and they began to form sizable blocs of strength on ships. By late 1862, many ships' crews soon featured one-quarter to one-half black sailors. In extreme cases, contraband sailors dwarfed the white complement of the crew. For example, in February 1863, the gunboat *Glide* had a crew of only eight whites and thirty contraband sailors.[101] At war's end, over 18,000 African Americans—roughly 15 percent of the total number of recruits—served in the Union navy during the Civil War.[102]

The army's aggressive campaign to recruit former slaves also heightened racial tensions since it altered the way the navy recruited contrabands. When the army finally permitted the enlistment of contrabands, it did so at a higher monthly wage. By 1862, contrabands no longer sought out ships as the only road to freedom. When given the choice, they headed for the army and the higher wages. Faced with a drop in the number of contraband recruits, Union ships began making specific landings to enlist contrabands. White sailors watched as the entire dynamic of receiving contrabands changed. No longer were sailors agents of mercy helping refugees reach a better life through a chance encounter. Instead, sailors were actively seeking to enlist former slaves for the same positions on which they once held a monopoly.

This interservice competition forced the navy to abandon the rating and salary restrictions for contraband sailors. In response to pleas from squadron commanders, on 18 December 1862, the secretary of the navy effectively equalized salaries by allowing contrabands to enlist as landsmen. Although the new policy did not allow contrabands to ship as seamen, after demonstrating the required proficiency, they could ascend to the higher ratings of ordinary and able seaman, the same as whites.[103]

The removal of color-based rating restrictions had immediate economic effects.[104] Circumstances varied. Owing to the earlier placement of contrabands in positions like coal heaver, fireman, and gunner, contraband sailors, who before had made $10 per month, now received between $20 and $30 for performing the same jobs.[105]

Since most white sailors had originally entered the service as landsmen, they felt the impact of Welles's decision most profoundly. The announcement that former slaves could come straight from the fields and enlist as landsmen, the same rating that most whites had received when they joined, triggered a number of thoughts—none of them comforting. The first thought that could have crossed their minds—that the prejudices labeling blacks as inferior were wrong—did not surface. To judge from their letters and diaries, if the thought of black equality crossed sailors' minds, it did not linger long. The men surveyed here did not evidence any change of heart regarding black equality.

Instead, the inclusion of slaves in their rating, in their society, and in their war stirred up a whole host of uncomfortable thoughts among white sailors about themselves. Situationally, Union sailors lived like slaves, and their living situations made them feel like slaves.[106] They inhabited cramped, filthy conditions in a public space that denied them privacy, much less personal dignity. Much of their shipboard work was menial, physically demanding, and performed thoughtlessly like the backbreaking work performed by slaves. Although the navy had abolished flogging in 1850, the standard punishment—for even minor offenses—was the shackling of hands and feet with what were called "double-irons."[107] In nineteenth-century America, men shuffling around the decks of a ship while shackled could not have evoked any image but that of slaves.

Contrabands serving as seamen seemed to confirm prewar stereotypes that equated sailors with slaves. Family, friends, and civilians reinforced the comparison by calling sailors "black" and "slaves." Typical of the reaction of civilians were the comments of a friend of Seaman William Price. In a teasingly nasty letter, the friend charged that the navy's use of "black jacks" had not elevated contrabands; it had turned Price's "sole black."[108] Officers too used the term "nigger" when referring to white sailors. Indeed, officers seeking to degrade white sailors could choose no more explosive phrase than "nigger."[109]

Moreover, the working-class origins of white sailors made them extremely sensitive to the label "slave." Many Americans had distrusted the rise of the working class and its dependence on wages to make a living and derisively referred to the working class as "wage slaves."[110] As a result, many white sailors who had suffered the unflattering comparison in the past now heard it again. This time, however, they heard it while staring into the faces of former slaves who were working alongside them in the same positions.[111]

The working-class backgrounds of white sailors made them extremely sensitive to all forms of labor competition.[112] By the mid-nineteenth century, the white working class harbored a great deal of animus toward black laborers. They viewed free black labor and slaves as a competitive form of unskilled, cheap labor and a genuine threat to rising wages. The fact that dock owners had used black laborers to break wage strikes in New York, Boston, and Chicago had only escalated these fears. Contraband sailors coming aboard ships to compete for the same positions and work for the same wages aroused anew fierce prewar feelings concerning displacement by black workers.[113]

Former slaves and so-called wage slaves working in the same place, competing for the same ratings, and making the same pay created a feeling of racial demotion among white sailors.[114] After the ascent of contrabands, Union sailors began using terms such as "freedom" and "slavery" to describe themselves and their service. In his log, Coal Heaver Charles Poole wrote that he longed to "be free of the Navy and my own Master again."[115] Coal Heaver George E. Arnold, writing from the *Nansemond*, did not hesitate to affix the label of slave to himself because he thought his position in the navy worse than that of a slave. He summarized what many white sailors felt after December 1862: "I long to be my own master again to go whare I like and to do as I like. . . . I dont like to be a slave nor I never will be again this is worse than slavery a blody site."[116]

The feeling of racial demotion created by the induction of contrabands was vividly illustrated by the fictional dialogue contained in Seaman James Eggo's poem "Jack Ratlin's Lament." In one of its verses, Seaman Jack Ratlin grumbles to Landsman Bill Frill, expressing the anger and hostility felt by white sailors:

This abolition Congress, Bill, they've raised the very devil,
They've put themselves, and all of us, down to the negro's level;
They've said that you and I, Bill, won't have the least objection,
To fight along with negro slaves, regardless of complexion;
They've passed a bill to free them all, and ship them in the navy,
They mean to give them all the meat, and leave old Jack the gravy,
But hang me, Bill, if that big gun, although it were ten times bigger,
Will e'er again be served by me, alongside of a nigger.[117]

The anxiety of white sailors swelled with President Lincoln's announcement of the Emancipation Proclamation on 1 January 1863. Although the navy had been constructively freeing slaves since July 1861,
the government's official endorsement of a war to end slavery intensified white anger. While the measure had also stirred a negative reaction
in the army, most Northern soldiers eventually came to accept emancipation as a war aim.[118] Like soldiers, some white sailors did peacefully accept emancipation. Yet those who accepted the policy did so
guardedly. Sailors like Joseph Gregory recognized the economic and
societal disruption caused by releasing the Confederacy's unpaid labor
force. Even then he was quick to add, "I am no abolitionist."[119] William
Price justified the measure on historical precedent. "England would
have armed the slave against his master that would have ended the war
before now," he wrote.[120]

Most Union sailors, never, even grudgingly, accepted emancipation.
The demonstrations of expertise and dedication shown by contrabands,
so critical in securing their peaceful acceptance in the army, did not
sway sailors. When Seaman James E. Henneberry heard that Lincoln
had freed the slaves he initially refused to believe it. "No, No," he wrote
in his diary. "Were he to do so the souls of 200,000 who have already
offered up their lives for their country would appear before him and
denounce him as a traitor to them."[121] Indicative of the angry mood
of white sailors were the comments made by Seaman Joseph Collins.
"That [the Emancipation] is the begining," Collins wrote home to his
mother and father, "we will see where the trouble will end."[122]

The "beginning" and the "trouble" to which Collins referred was
the deterioration of relations between white and contraband sailors.
White sailors—already fretting about the implications of changing relationships between blacks and whites—simply could not accept eman-
cipated slaves coming aboard ship serving in the same capacities.
The end result was that after emancipation, white irritation, romantic

racism, and peaceful prejudice gave way to more heated and recurring racially motivated exchanges, called "frictions" by sailors. These frictions, which began to occur with increasing frequency in 1862, consisted of a wide range of abusive behavior from petty bickering and minor physical fights to coordinated acts of violence.[123]

In their letters, anger replaced the haughty superiority white sailors had once expressed toward contrabands. Seaman Joseph Osborne growled to his brother Elias that the Republicans would not be satisfied until "they free and steal all the nigers."[124] Many white sailors viewed emancipation as a clarion call to return whites and contrabands to their respective places.[125] Sailor attitudes bristled with violent threats. Seaman William Van Cleaf was so enraged at the thought of emancipation that he wrote to his mother when he had first heard about the possibility of freeing the slaves back in 1862, "I would have it to say that I helped to free their niggers I would cut my throat from ear to ear."[126] He was not alone. "If I had my way," Coal Heaver George Arnold vowed to his cousin, "I would cut every nigers throt in the united states."[127]

After emancipation, white sailors complained bitterly that contraband sailors overstepped traditional boundaries. They routinely accused those contrabands unwilling to play a servile, subservient role of acting "saucy" and "impudent."[128] Seaman Bartholomew Diggins grumbled that contraband sailors "took advantage" of the new situation. In Diggins's opinion, after emancipation, contrabands "grew in bad habits and at lenths became so unbearable. . . ."[129] Sailor John Swift believed contrabands had grown "impertinent" as a result of the measure.[130] "A white man cannot speak to one of them and receive a civil answer," wrote William C. Holton.[131]

It was unclear whether contraband sailors viewed emancipation as a mandate for demanding equal treatment by white sailors and the navy. Certainly, emancipation engendered a sense of pride among black sailors. "The contrabands in this part of the country," wrote Benedict Donohue, "appear to understand Abe's last proclamation pretty well." Some probably did challenge, in both moderate and bold ways, the parameters of their new status. What was clear, however, was that after the announcement of emancipation, white sailors became intolerant of any manifestations of equality by contraband sailors.[132]

After emancipation, white sailors came to believe that officers gave preferential treatment to contraband sailors. Bartholomew Diggins felt that "officers heard them with as more favor then did they did the crew."[133] This view proved so pervasive that some sailors believed that contraband sailors enjoyed conditions superior to theirs, even when plainly they were not. Many sailors bristled at the idea that the contrabands' new status was not earned by service but bestowed by a central government and a navy that now valued blacks over whites. James B. Collins wrote to his parents, "You would scarce believe the slack they have got lately."[134] George Arnold wrote, "They think more of a niger on this boat than they do of a white man . . . they even poot them over white men."[135] William Price also noticed the growing tendency. "As far as I see our army and navy offerces chooses black jack in preference I believe."[136]

So pervasive were white anxieties over the new social order that they soon projected themselves onto one of the more popular forms of sailor recreation—the theater.[137] On large vessels, sailors erected makeshift theaters containing a stage and audience seating. White sailors watched performances from hard wooden benches placed in front of the stage. Black sailors sat off to the side in their own section.[138] Boy Charles Mervine wrote that the carpenters on the *Powhatan* built an impressive stage dressed up "with flags of different nations as we intend to give a shine tonight called the 'Powhatan's Minstrells.'"[139] On the *Brazileira*, sailors rigged a platform on the quarter-deck, swung sails overhead so that the audience was entirely covered, and decorated the stage with flags and greens.[140]

Not surprisingly, the most performed type of theatrical production among white sailors were black minstrel shows.[141] These shows had become popular in the 1850s among the white working class in the United States in response to fears over their new dependence as wage laborers. They had helped assuage workers' fears that they were becoming de facto slaves by identifying and ridiculing physical, mental, and behavioral differences that distinguished blacks from themselves.[142] The purpose of blackface productions was to create an artificial distance—through ridicule—in order to stave off the reality that the situations of poor working whites and plantation slaves were strikingly similar. Likewise, after 1862, blackface minstrel shows became conduits through which white Union sailors projected worries concerning their similarities with contraband sailors. For white sailors, these blackface productions both reaffirmed sailors' commonly held racial stereotypes and functioned as a public forum responsive to their racial and status insecurities in the postemancipation navy.[143]

Numerous blackface plays made their way onto Union vessels in the period after emancipation. One play, *Bombast Furioso*, featured

*This photograph subtly illustrates the racial dynamics between white and contraband sailors. The contraband sailors aboard the USS* Hunchback *are photographed noticeably off to the side in their own group. A black sailor, however, is placed front and center with a banjo.*
Courtesy of the National Archives.

contraband recruits fumbling through military drills armed only with broomsticks and ample doses of stereotypical black stupidity. This play packed particular resonance with white sailors who enjoyed seeing blacks fail at military service. The "black" recruits in this performance proved to be much more popular than their real counterparts because they obediently clung to the white racial script and displayed little of the nautical prowess actually exhibited by contraband sailors. In *Nigger in a Daguerreotype Saloon*, instead of working well at a ship's large guns or in drills, a white sailor in blackface had the audience howling by "throwing somersalts, catching flies, & making faces." The white sailor "made an excellent Wolly head," remarked one tickled audience member.[144]

To the delight of white sailors, these blackface plays created as much distance between them and blacks as possible. In *Ethiopeana*, the black played a fool.[145] The play *Virginia Mummy* emphasized the childlike qualities attributed by white society to blacks.[146] White sailors enjoyed these skits since they, if only for a short time, returned contrabands to their perceived proper place. For a few hours, whites did not have to worry about the similarities between themselves and blacks and whether they were slaves, worse than slaves, or black-hearted. While such theatrics may have proven successful in assuaging the fears of whites, they heightened racial sensitivities once the curtain dropped. On the *Brazileira*, racial tensions rose so high that the commanding officer had to transfer his black sailors off ship.[147]

The animus reflected by these theatrical productions also surfaced in more sinister ways. Although the dynamic differed from ship to ship, after January 1863 white sailors on both the blockade and the Mississippi Squadron engaged in rough forms of social correction designed to reassert dominance over contraband sailors. These "corrections" assumed the shape of social punishments something akin to the charivari in the South.[148] Their object was not to injure contrabands but to reduce their status through formal rites of humiliation, force, and intimidation. They represented private acts of policing designed to reestablish in the minds of contraband sailors the social lines and boundaries beyond which a contraband would dare not go, no matter what Lincoln, the officers, or the navy said. Through these acts, white sailors hoped to reassert their interpretations of the proper roles for black and white people aboard Union vessels.

Refusals to accede to previously established racial lines led to incidents of reproach. Contraband William B. Gould recalled that when 300 black soldier transferees on the *Niagara* tried to eat out of mess pans— the traditional dinnerware of sailors—they "were treated verry rough by the crew."[149] Such rough treatment also consisted of contraband sailors standing for hours at a time bound with ropes or holding heavy objects.[150] William N. Bock wrote from the *Rattler*: "When one of them acts saucy or impudent he stands on the capstan a few hours with a large chunk of coal under his arm—Sometimes they stand on the pilot house all night."[151]

When the warnings carried in these punishments failed to work, white sailors resorted to violence. By their own admission, many white sailors often thrashed, shot, and threw contraband sailors overboard at any opportunity and for no reason at all.[152] On the *Penobscot*, when the first lieutenant sent a young contraband sailor on an errand, an Irish fireman stepped up and smashed him in the face.[153] Thomas Lyons recounted in his journal that several sailors on the *Carondolet* had been "condemned to ride the Hog-Chain for flouring a Saucy negro."[154] Fireman George Geer recounted to his wife what happened when one of the contraband sailors on his ship began acting "quite important already." Incensed that the contraband had begun "to think himself as good as a white man," Geer's crewmates looked for the opportunity to teach him a lesson. When no one was looking, "One of the saylors he had some lip to," Geer wrote, "gave him a smack over the mouth." According to Geer, the smack worked because "for the preasant," it "has learned him his place."[155]

James B. Collins wrote home to his mother and father that there was not much danger in beating contraband sailors "because when one strikes a nigger there is about two dozen of the boys ready to exercise themselves."[156] Sailors often looked for any pretext to provoke hostilities. Collins happily recounted what happened to a black sailor when he boldly walked through a block of white sailors dancing a quadrille. "As he came in the square wether by accident or design he stomped on my foot." While the intent of the seaman's stomp was murky, the reaction of Collins and his mates was not. After the black sailor's misstep, Collins and his mates soundly thrashed him. "I gave him a good biff," Collins boasted to his parents, "he got a pretty good tossing all around."[157]

At times, the beatings were severe and potentially lethal. On 16 January 1863, James Collins wrote home to his mother and father, "We came near killing a negro last night." In another attack, one sailor went berserk and proceeded to kick and thump any black sailor he got his hands on swearing that he would shoot them and "any damned officer that took their part."[158]

At other times, white sailors simply murdered black sailors. In January 1863 alone, the crewmates of James Collins shot and killed two black sailors on board the *Nansemond*.[159] In November 1863, Samuel Leslie, a coxswain on the *Lackawanna* anchored in New Orleans, returned from liberty and immediately confronted on-duty black Seaman James Johnson. Words were exchanged, and in a fit of rage Leslie proceeded to kill Johnson by crushing his skull with a blunt instrument.[160]

When all else failed, white sailors tossed their black crewmates overboard.[161] Seaman Bartholomew Diggins described one such involuntary bath aboard the *Hartford*. "One night some of the men cut the fastening of of [*sic*] allot of rigging and spars . . . under which they slept on the spar deck letting the whole come down with a rush upon them. . . . Several of them was injured," he wrote. "One of the most insolent of

*The sailors of the USS* Miami. *Again, the contraband sailors*
*appear to be arranged in their own groups, shuffled to the side.*
*Courtesy of the National Archives.*

them was caught by some of the men and thrown out of one of the forward ports overboard, the swift current carried him down to Vicksburg
where he made a landing and told a terrible story of cruel treatment by
the Yankees which was published in all the Vicksburg papers." Diggins
smugly remarked later that "this and other strong measures had a good
effect on the contrabands."[162]

Rear Admiral David G. Farragut reported that, although steadfast to
their obligations, many contraband sailors began deserting owing to the
intense racial hostility aboard many Union vessels. White sailors of his
squadron, Farragut wrote, "disagree with them so much that we are
oblidged [*sic*] to be very rigid with sailors in consequence."[163] Francis
Gifford wrote home to his parents about the awful state of race relations between white and black sailors on the *Release*. "My nigger Ike

has left me because the white sailors dont treat him well."[164] Officers, in response to the violent outbursts, often dealt with violence by whites on blacks severely. On the *Nansemond*, officers held public hangings of white sailors for killing contraband sailors.[165]

Even with the harsh sentences imposed on white sailors, interracial problems continued and in some instances grew larger in scope, threatening the safety of Union ships and naval operations. At Ship Island, Mississippi, white sailors on a gunboat were ordered to support the advance of a black regiment on the mainland. When the time of the assault came, instead of concentrating their fire on the Confederate troops, as the black soldiers launched their attack, the white gun crews turned their guns on the backs of the black soldiers. The reason for such an act was attributed to lingering hostility among white sailors after a recent racial altercation.[166] In fact, the collective violence against contraband sailors reached such levels that by 1864–65 race riots had occurred on some ships.[167]

The worst riots occurred in February 1865 aboard the *St. Mary's* in the harbor at Valparaiso, Chile. The vessel had previously made a stop in New York City on its way back to Panama to rejoin the Pacific Squadron. While in New York, the ship picked up a large contingent of black landsmen, many of them contrabands. The current crew consisted of some of the worst white recruits the navy could muster, namely "hard characters," "bounty jumpers," and "shirks." The entire crew, Boatswain Edward Hammond attested, resented deeply the prospect of "making sailors out of these contrabands." Many nursed an "intense hatred" of the black landsmen.[168]

Tempers flared as the crew began drinking heavily as the ship put out to sea. Shortly after leaving New York City, pitched battles began taking place on the fore-top gangway. In this part of the ship, some white members of the crew drove contraband sailors away from their stations by hurling gun chocks at their heads. Daily scraps between white and black sailors disrupted daily drills and the completion of work details. Tensions reached such a level and white sailor anger over the presence of contraband sailors in their crew grew so intense, that upon leaving Valparaiso white members of the crew—rather than serve any longer with contraband sailors—tried to run the ship aground as it left the harbor.[169]

What accounts for this violence that exceeded anything experienced by the army? Certainly some of the violence displayed by white sailors originated from issues other than racial animosity. Some experienced growing distaste for the navy, while others may have gotten tired of living on a ship for so long. As both a symbol and a cause of the war, contraband sailors served as handy scapegoats for sailors weary of the same food, the same faces, and the same disappointments. Contraband sailors, in some sense, paid for the collective anger and outrage felt by white sailors for the miseries they endured in the navy. White army personnel voiced similarly malevolent sentiments on seeing black soldiers.[170]

Yet, overall, soldiers' reactions to the induction of slaves into the army were relatively nonviolent, which can be partly attributed to the fact that they served in segregated regiments, enabling them to avoid day-to-day interactions with black soldiers. The unlimited space offered by land allowed the army to set up separate camps for white and black soldiers, camps in which black soldiers often suffered around-the-clock confinement in order to avoid white on black violence.[171] As a result, unlike sailors, white soldiers did not live, fight, work, eat, and sleep with former slaves in a cramped space for months at a time.

By comparison, white sailors angered by the contrabands' quick ascent and assimilation were not afforded such favorable buffers. The cramped confines of a ship prohibited sailors from side-stepping the racial and status issues that contraband sailors presented. Ultimately, ships forced men highly suspicious of one another into daily close contact. For men on the cutting edge of new racial relations a ship created "an atmosphere conducive to hostility between the races."[172] Deprived of the ability to interact, retreat, regroup, rethink, and retry racial interactions, white sailors confronted, day-in and day-out, the volatile issues festering between blacks and whites while working side-by-side, eating nearby, and sleeping in the same berths. It would have been nothing short of remarkable had whites and blacks gotten along in such a tight living space, given the pressures of their shifting social environment and the challenges to their expectations about race and class.

While troubling, the navy's tale of racial integration is nonetheless enlightening because the ship, as a sort of closed experiment, provides a valuable lens through which to view a larger issue engendered by the war: the assimilation of former slaves among a free white citizenry rife with racial prejudice toward blacks and slaves and filled with insecurities about their own places in American society. The ship-to-ship glimpses open the way for investigations examining, on a larger scale, how whites felt and reacted to former slaves in their midst, in both the North and the South. Violent uprisings in certain Northern cities seem to indicate that former slaves moving to the North provoked the same sort of hostility among laboring classes during the war.[173]

The shipboard experiences reveal the complex state of race relations in the North before and during the war. The violence generated by incorporating former slaves into the navy demonstrates that how one race feels about another is often not a simple Pavlovian response to skin color. The feelings and behaviors of white sailors toward former slaves lend credence to the assertion that race relations in the United States often hinged as much on how white people felt about themselves as on their feelings toward African Americans. As evidenced by the severe and varied reactions of white sailors to contraband sailors, white racial hatred often tapped into unseen class and color expectations, images, and past experiences and masked as well as projected the social, cultural, and economic stresses of the period.

# My Youthfull Emagination of Hell
## The Face of Battle for Union Sailors

Nowhere was the contrast between expectation and experience for Union sailors more pronounced than on the decks of ships during combat.[1] Although sailors expected to see some combat, the men who sought out ships rather than battlefields often did so under the assumption that sailoring was the "least hazardous and easiest."[2] Yet the Yankee seamen who ran the batteries at Vicksburg, survived the minefields at Mobile Bay, and endured the blistering fire at Fort Fisher found their assumptions forever smashed. The interplay between technology and improved firepower when combined with the reality that sailors could not flee made naval warfare deadly. While limited in scope, naval combat was bloody and psychologically terrifying. The "face of battle" for sailors was the emotional ride men endured as they fought and died in the wildly unstable environment of a ship.

At first glance, naval casualty figures seem to undercut these assertions. According to the 1866 *Report of the Secretary of the Navy*, combat wounded 4,030 Union sailors, 1,804 of whom died.[3] However, raw figures tell only part of the story, and they do not explain what sailors experienced during combat.[4]

Union sailors' experience of combat differed from the way that naval historians have traditionally conceptualized it and from the way it is reported in *The Official Records of the Union and Confederate Navies in the War of the Rebellion*, the official transcripts of what happened during battle. Battle for sailors was more than precisely noted damage reports, accurate notations of enemy sightings, and dry casualty reports. What sailors endured was neither uniform nor simple. Confronted with vivid realizations of their worst imaginings, sailors did not act without panic, without nerves, and without disorder.[5] The essence of combat for sailors lay in the emotional swings their minds endured as they became targets of fire, their mates suffered horrible wounds and death, and their ships began to come apart.

Since the Confederacy possessed a smaller navy and relied on stationary fortifications for coastal and river defense, the traditional naval combat experience—ships blasting at each others' broadsides—rarely occurred during the war. Instead, sailors spent much of their war watching and waiting for action to happen. Some crews took part in large operations like Vicksburg or Mobile Bay. Others saw none or spent the war engaged in limited, intense spurts of action on blockade vessels waiting for runners or chasing rebel privateers, like the *Alabama*. River sailors tended to see a great deal of continuous day-to-day action owing to their proximity to land. The most common combat experience mentioned by sailors, on both the rivers and the oceans, involved their ships attacking or attempting to run by stationary Confederate fortifications. These engagements were short in duration, limited in scope, and promised the greatest chance of dying.

Union sailors possessed a number of preconceived expectations about combat. Although romantic notions of charging to glory with a rifle in one hand and a flag in the other did not encumber most sailors' illusions, many labored under a host of other misconceptions. The first misconception held by sailors was that they were safe from outside attack. This belief stemmed from premodern notions concerning the effects of mechanization on offensive firepower and defensive capabilities. Early on, sailors clung to antiquated notions of naval warfare that equated only seeing the enemy with physical danger. Many sailors thought the distance from shore and the metal and wood of the ship guaranteed their safety. "We do not stand a chance of being hit by bullets," wrote William Bock. Typical of this mind-set were the comments of former soldier William Van Cleaf, who wrote to his mother, "I consider myself as safe in her [his ship] as in a fort."[6]

Sailors pinned a great deal of their optimism on the ship's iron plating. Crews on both the blockade and the river squadrons put a great deal of energy into learning about iron plating. They found out which parts of the ship were plated, examined how tightly it was fastened, and determined its exact thickness. Seaman William Price wrote to a friend that "we have just discovered that iron is useful. [T]hat its pretty hard when applied to the right purposes." The association between sailors and iron proved so strong that soldiers often greeted sailors with shouts of "iron sides & iron hearts."[7]

Initial engagements without serious injuries led many sailors to credit iron for their safety. After not being hit during the Battle of Island No. 10, Seaman William Van Cleaf attached almost a mythical quality to iron's powers. "I suppose they [shot and shells] thought there to much iron on us for them."[8] After his boat was hit five times without damage during the Battle of Port Hudson, Seaman James Henneberry concluded, "We were hit five times once perhaps in the same place where we got the shot at fort Henry but we this time had Iron to protect us."[9]

The second misconception was that their ships were safe environments in which to fight. Sailors failed to appreciate that wooden and iron-plated, steam-driven ships in 1861 were not entirely safe.[10] Many of their design flaws had not been addressed, much less recognized. Technological innovations had been slapped onto these ships without much inquiry into the threats they might pose to sailors.[11] Machinery lacked safeguards; the weight of the iron made vessels buckle and sink; and no one knew for sure what exactly would happen if shells and cannonballs hit the machines and boilers.[12]

The third misconception held by sailors was that deaths would be few and delivered by a human enemy. Three facts made this impossible. First, owing to the use of heavy guns, small wounds proved to be rare in naval warfare. Big guns delivered big shots and shells that inflicted large and mortal injuries. Second, vast improvements in naval ordnance heightened naval-gun killing power since it enabled Confederates to hurl heavy exploding shells over greater distances with greater accuracy. Although the fire did not sink many ships, it rendered a great deal of damage to those ships it hit. Third, the willingness of Confederate naval defense forces to use powerfully propelled inanimate objects—such as torpedoes and rams—forced sailors to confront the reality that the war would be impersonal.[13]

Union sailors were prepared for none of this. They were unprepared for the long-distance killing and the use of inanimate objects as killing machines. They were unprepared for collateral deaths caused by the dismemberment of their ships and the deadly mixture of technology and increased firepower. Most men were unprepared for the ship's transformation from home, mode of transportation, and workplace into a place of terror where the familiar rudiments of sailors' daily lives became hostile. Most of all, however, most men were unprepared for the grisly nature of death in naval combat and the fear that it produced.

The hard bridge between illusion and reality began the first time that sailors heard the order to "clear the deck."[14] Clearing the deck typically took place a day before a planned engagement. For the uninitiated, the order appeared to be another futile naval exercise designed to keep men busy. Those puzzled sailors who asked older salts the meaning behind all of the preparations were told that "all objects that might make projectiles" had to be removed from the main deck.[15] Upper spars and rigging came down and sand bags dotted the ship from stem to stern. Sailors watched as carpenters and their mates erected bulwarks around exposed spaces using railroad ties and heavy canvas.[16] Other sailors found themselves preparing plugs and patches to stop shot holes. Men stowed tools and lines. They hung netting, chain garlands, and, in some instances, their own hammocks over the starboard sides. After a while, almost every part of the ship was covered with tarps and netting.[17]

Other preparations fed apprehensions. Men were ordered to place buckets of sand and water around designated portions of the ship. When they asked why, they were told that the water would be used for men to drink when thirsty and to douse fires which erupted on lines and sails. The sand, they were told, would be scattered on the decks to absorb blood. Seaman John Simpson remembered being shocked when he was told the sand was "to receive the blood that was to be spilled." Sand had to be scattered immediately, sailors learned, otherwise men would slip on the pools of blood that tended to gather around the deck.[18]

The surest sign of a fight, however, remarked Seaman Bartholomew Diggins, came when the doctors and nurses placed "swinging cats at the main hatch for lowering the killed and wounded."[19] Once medical staff located these devices at hatches, seasoned sailors knew there was certain to be a fight. Untested seamen often became unnerved by the ship's chilling transformation. "Things began to look decidedly warlike, more so than ever before during the cruise," wrote a nervous George Bright to his father.[20]

The night before a fight, instead of resting, sailors typically would be tossing in their hammocks worrying about their fates. Because the darkness cloaked the movements of their ships, sailors had to rise to fight in the predawn hours.[21] A few hours before daybreak, the boatswain jarred sailors awake with fierce barks of "all hands to quarters," "all hands, tumble out, lash and carry," and "cast loose and provide." Apprehensive, sleepy, and barely cognizant, men moved more quickly than normal to their battle stations, in a frenetic, dreamlike state that sailors called "battle speed."[22]

Seaman John Morrison wrote that at the call to action at 4:00 A.M. all that he remembered were men confused, sleepy, swearing, rubbing their eyes, and putting their clothes on backward—all acts "incidental," he wrote, "to a lot of sailors being roused out of a sound sleep."[23] James Henneberry recalled that he was so nervous before combat that when he was called to battle stations for the first time, "I never got out of a warm bed of a cool morning sooner in my life." "I left everything but my pants and started on the double quick for my station."[24]

Bleary-eyed and scared, sailors admitted that the period before combat weighed heavy with nervous tension. William Van Cleaf admitted to feeling "skittish" as he waited for combat to commence. As his ship reached its destination, Seaman Edward Blue said he felt overcome with "anxiety."[25] Moods on deck swung back and forth. At times, men chattered excitedly at their stations almost to the point of sounding perversely cheery.[26] The next minute, it was so quiet on deck that E. W. Goble wrote, "All was as still as the Grave."[27] Calvin Hutchinson noted that before the attack on Fort Fisher, "the ship was stiller than a church; I noticed sounds of ropes cheeping, steam coughing, and water washing alongside which I had never observed before." Bartholomew Diggins recorded in his journal that "a salam stillness prevailed, all that could be heard between the thundering of our mortars, was the revolutions of our Engine."[28]

Other sailors worried aloud about friends and relatives serving on other ships, many of whom they had bade good-bye the night before.[29] On the *Hartford*, before the attack on New Orleans, Bartholomew Diggins observed that "men gathered in little knots about the ship talking quitely of our chances, and fixing their little affairs in case the worst should happen." Sailors asked mates to deliver saved money, photographs, and unsent letters to loved ones "if you get through."[30] Other tars worried down hot coffee and ate biscuits and moldy cheese to occupy their mouths and minds.[31] Many sailors grumbled that in such circumstances grog should be served to take the edge off.[32] Seasoned sailors did not wish mates good luck but instead quietly admonished fellow hands to "keep their chins out of the water" and "hope and hang on."[33]

The worst part of combat preparations was the waiting. Men had no idea what to expect or what was happening. Rumors abounded but were more often than not worthless. Landsman Daniel Kemp complained that sailors knew "there was some movement on foot but what it was, was something the crew knew nothing about."[34] Sailors' heads ran full of conflicting notions about the safe nature of naval service and the myriad of precautions they had undertaken. E. W. Goble wrote that before combat, "All hands waited in suspence to hear the first gun fire."[35] For Bartholomew Diggins, the worst hours before combat were the ones filled with uncertainty and anxiety. Waiting and worrying almost demoralized him. Before his first taste of warfare, he wrote: "this is the most depressing experience of a warrior's life, waiting to be engaged and under heavy fire from the enemy, one has nothing to do to occupy the mind[.] the mind runs on the great uncertainty about to take place untill it is a relief when the battle opens."[36]

Good captains heartily encouraged their charges before they heaved anchor. This was a notable occurrence since sailors rarely saw the captain discharge orders aboard ship. The first lieutenant almost always gave the orders and addressed the men.[37] The effect of the captain addressing them in a manner almost familiar did much to cheer nervous spirits. Captain Wainright of the *Hartford* knew that his sailors would undergo murderous fire from the Vicksburg batteries as they passed. Aware of this as well as the egalitarian leanings of sailors, he took the unheard of action of asking his crew's approval before starting. Although they knew their approval was inconsequential, the men responded to his democratic gesture with a roar of approval. "We will follow you anywhere," the crew cheered, "we go to Vicksburg." Bartholomew Diggins marveled that "this was the first and only time the men were consulted, as to any action the ship was to take part in."[38]

Some captains called on competitive themes. Before the Battle of Fort Henry, Captain Thomas Porter gathered the crew on the spar deck of the *Essex*, pointed to the rebel flag flying over the fort, "and told us we were going to take it down and put the stars and stripes in its place." It worked. James Henneberry explained that Porter's speech had an elevating effect on the sailors. "All hands went down and had a good song heaving the anchor."[39] Others tried to hearten their crews by minimizing the danger. Captain Bradly assured his men on the *Benton* before the attack on Grand Gulf that the rebel batteries were "nothing but little *pop-guns*."[40]

The initial suspense ended with the first flashes of signal lights and shots from rebel guns. Within seconds of a flash, sailors heard the sound of a shot and then felt an impact, as one man described it, "making the whole Earth tremble."[41] To another man, it was "as if Lightning" and "Thundering" had commenced. These early shots rarely made contact since rebel gunners were groping for the right range. The first gunfire surprisingly seemed to relieve the unbearable tension that gripped sailors. As they got to work loading and firing the guns, sailors' fears ebbed.[42] Men watched as their shells hit or missed their intended targets and gave cheers or groans. The excitement level rose dramatically as Union guns peppered a fort and shoreline batteries. If a shot found its target, crews cheered with exclamations like "Great shot!"[43]

Sailors also took heart in the fact that—true to their illusions—the first round of Confederate shots almost always missed their ships and by great lengths.[44] Seaman John Swift wrote to his sister, "One cannot help feeling easy under fire when although constantly exposed they never get hurt."[45] John Morrison wrote that most rebel shots "would invariably overreach or, falling short."[46] Surgeon T. M. Coan wrote to his sister that the combination of iron and the horrendously off-target shots that initially came from Confederate forces seemed to reinforce in sailors their false notion of security. In fact, during the early maneuverings in the Battle of Mobile Bay, he prematurely mocked others' fears: "I was so used to being fired at and missed that I had little idea that our ship would be touched; and laughed at the dodging of the men."[47] The first misfirings of rebel guns confirmed, Gunner Cornelius Cronin wrote, the belief that he and his crewmates had "immunity from fire."[48]

Such security proved short lived. As they drew nearer to the fray and rebel batteries pinpointed the location and speed of their vessels, sailors' confidence waned. The first round of missed shots was followed by silence and then a tighter progression of shots as Confederate gunners honed their aim.[49] Seaman John Morrison described the tense scene as "silence for about a minute (which seemed an age) when they opened on us with about a dozen guns." Once Confederates ascertained a ship's location and course, batteries launched concentrated fire that Morrison likened to "rain."[50]

After this, shots, shells, and shrapnel flew in rapid succession.[51] Shells splashed now more closely in the water and let loose a "crack, crack" if they glanced off the sides of the ship. Nervous sailors kept exact track of where and how shells and shots landed as they witnessed Confederate guns construct an ever-tightening circle of fire.[52]

A sudden crash into the ship and a flying cloud of debris meant they had hit their mark.[53] Soon shot, shell, and canister began landing directly on the decks. Landsman Stanley Campbell remarked that the sudden appearance of shot and shell aboard ship startled him.[54] It was easy to see why. Imagine the terror sailors felt as 130-pound shots and shells roared past their heads and exploded at their feet.[55]

Solid shots passed almost peaceably, whistling their way through ships and blasting holes in exposed parts. Most times, shots hit the ship, let out a puff, and then a report. By comparison, shells arrived less hospitably. They screamed and whined and landed on deck with a queer, silent thud.[56] Shells carefully nursed themselves on deck until they fully exploded. When they did, the air around them filled with a peculiar shrill sound that sailors likened to "violently broken glass."[57] One sailor remembered that shells "moving with a fiendish velocity within a few feet of a man, make the most hellish and disagreeable noise imaginable."[58] Seaman Charles J. Hill wrote that "their shreaks were enough to make one's heart melt within him."[59]

It was right about the time that Confederate guns located the exact position of a Union ship that the crew came to recognize one horrible truth—the ship was not safe. Wood and iron did not offer the invincibility that they once thought it did, and modern ordnance rendered iron plates susceptible to projectiles. In a matter of minutes, well-placed shots splintered wooden decks and masts, shattered armor plates, and knocked heavy bolts out of secure holes.

Every time a shot or shell hit, it rocked the ship violently and sent parts flying everywhere. Lines snapped, and sails collapsed. A marine stationed on the *Galena* complained that after one direct hit "the ship began to fly all to pieces."[60] Often lines, masts, and the ship itself caught fire.[61] Shot and shell furrowed the decks of ships. James Henneberry wrote that during battle his ship looked like it had been "plowed up" by an "Illinois farmer."[62] The sight of their home and workplace being taken apart rattled sailors' confidence, shook sensibilities, and produced a sort of "commotional shock."[63]

Seaman John Morrison expressed shock that his ship was a "target" and that it did not offer the protection he once thought. "Crack, crack, and again we are pierced," he moaned.[64] Daniel Kemp snarled that, instead of providing fortlike invincibility, "shot and shell would pierce our sides as if they were made of paper."[65] Seaman Asa Beetham, after his first taste of combat, wrote that many ships "ain't worth a cuss, a very little firing & they are all blown to pieces."[66] Boy Alvah Hunter described how he and his mates felt when they realized the truth about their monitor. "All of us were greatly depressed by our failure," Hunter wrote, "and the evident fact that the monitors were by no means invulnerable there was little disposition to eat supper."[67]

Once robbed of their security, sailors flinched at every flash as if dodging shadows. As Gunner Cornelius Cronin explained, "I thought every shot was within a few inches of my head, or aimed directly at me."[68] The dismemberment of the ship also had repercussions beyond its psychological effects. The impact of shot, shell, and grape canister into planks and armor sent shards of wood and metal into sailors' bodies. In the middle of a fight, sailors found pieces and parts of their once-friendly ship flying at them. Bolts, pulleys, and nails flew in all directions. The most dreaded projectiles were wooden fragments called "splinters"—a misnomer since they were not small pieces of wood lodged in a finger or toe. Splinters proved to be long and sharp, often three to five feet in length and ten to forty-two inches in thickness. They weighed as much as ten pounds.[69]

Large splinters soared through the air like spears, breaking arms and legs, severing arteries, and rendering tremendous shock to the body's nervous system.[70] The smaller varieties rained down in what one sailor likened to "showers."[71] Edmund H. Stevens wrote that after Mobile Bay a surgeon had difficulty removing his shirt "as it was pinned to my back by splinters."[72] The problem with smaller splinters was that they "bled you like a butcher," one sailor recalled, "but left no scar, alike disconcerting and inglorious."[73] Seaman Edward Barker stated that many sailors' faces became "terrible to look at" since they were bleeding and "black and blue" from flying splinters.[74]

These were the results of minor injuries. The most murderous sight was the mangling wrought by shot and shell as they made contact with sailors' bodies. The damage the ship suffered from being hit by naval ordnance paled in comparison. Although the battle casualties in the navy were slight in numbers, almost all battle deaths turned out to be grisly. Men struck by shot and shell, even off a bounce, rarely remained intact. Solid shots literally pulled apart sailors as they passed through. Marine Private Charles Brother wrote that "very few were slightly wounded, all were either killed instantly or horribly mangled."[75] Bartholomew Diggins noted that he watched one shot shatter to smithereens two men instantly. When the first sailor was hit, his upper portion was scattered "about the beams and the side of the berth deck." Surgeon T. M. Coan recalled that the wounded brought to him during Mobile Bay were "bearing lifeless forms." He could do nothing for them.[76]

Shells were worse. Men nearest the exploding shell died instantly. Even if shells did not make direct contact, they blasted off arms, legs, or cut men clean in two at the bowels.[77] Severe multiple wounds from the same shell killed men instantly and severely demoralized onlookers. James Henneberry wrote in his journal that the wounds were so "extreme I shall not attempt to describe it."[78] In action off Fort Caswell, North Carolina, Seaman James B. Collins watched in horror as a crewmate had a leg taken off at the hip and one eye put out by shell fragments. As he was taken below deck Collins heard him scream that "he cannot realize that he has lost a leg as well as an eye."[79]

Decapitations were common. At Island No. 10, former soldier William Van Cleaf recoiled when a seaman "had his head shot off as clean as you could cut it with a knife." Patrick Meade remembered seeing "one poor fellow at the forehead gun with his entrails all hanging out." The blood, brains, and bone fragments of the dead quickly festooned decks, ladders, and lines.[80]

The pain for those not killed instantly was excruciating. Many poor fellows bled to death before assistance could be rendered.[81] Surgeon T. M. Coan wrote that wounded sailors possessed a certain "look of terror" in their eyes that all at once denoted pain, destruction, and ghastliness.[82] Young Alvah Hunter recalled that when he saw his first combat casualty, a sailor whose head had been opened up by a shell, he shuddered. "Then, for a few seconds," Hunter gasped, "I wished I was back in Boston."[83]

The physical torment from major wounds proved so painful that men often pleaded with their mates to end their lives. Surgeon's Steward Sayres Nichols wrote to his mother that "the shrieks and groans of the wounded were heartrending."[84] Daniel Kemp painfully recalled a carpenter's mate who had been struck in the bowels and severed in two. Writhing in pain, the wounded sailor begged his mates to "chuck me overboard." Kemp also watched in horror as a pilot, struck by a bolt through his back, screamed out to anyone within earshot to "shoot me for God's sake, shoot me." Kemp recoiled: "I hope I may never see another such death."[85]

There were many types of incidents in combat that Union sailors came to dread. However, two stood out as the most feared ways to die: in a boiler explosion and in a torpedo attack. Sailors viewed either kind of death as shameful because they felt it was the wrong way to die and because the means involved were hidden dangers.[86] All the discipline in the world could not prevent them.[87] In particular, boiler explosions unnerved tars because they were random, unpreventable, and collateral to combat. Sailors did not know how to reconcile themselves to having an enemy that was not only as impersonal as a torpedo but also one ostensibly on their side. Newspaper reporter Charles Coffin, traveling on the *St. Louis*, noted that sailor deaths caused by their own equipment—like boilers and splinters—crippled the confidence of sailors more than deaths caused by enemy fire. "It is a good deal worse to have a gun explode," Coffin concluded, "than to have the men wounded by the enemy's shot, for they lose confidence."[88]

For all of the troubling sounds heard during combat, the last noise a sailor wanted to hear was the distinctive scream of a shell piercing the boilers from down below. Crew member Samuel J. Bartlett was of the opinion that the most terrifying worry during combat was the "danger of being scalded or being blown up if a shell should strike our boilers."[89] The sound of a boiler explosion was unmistakable. As a shell punctured the boilers, it let loose a sharp crack, followed by an intense rushing sound as the scalding condensation collided with cooler air. Sailors then heard a loud crash as scorching steam came searing up from the engine room. William Van Cleaf wrote that boiler explosions were so terrifying because "steam came out in all directions."[90]

Already in the engine room with no time to react, coal heavers and firemen absorbed the brunt of steam explosions. Men burned to death instantly from the heat.[91] Sailors were "actualy boiled by the Steam," wrote Seaman Tim Finn. As the steam reached the upper portions of the ship, men often threw themselves face down onto the decks trying to protect their lungs and eyes. Those that did not react quickly enough suffered the consequences. Steam arrived on deck with such heat and such force that it seared flesh and knocked out teeth. Sylvester Doss recalled after the rebel ram *Arkansas* smashed into his boat, the *Lancaster*, he was "scolded very Bad, my Right sholder broken left Ribbs Broken and my teeth Blowen out . . . lots of our crews dide that night, by being scolded." A single release could disable one-quarter of a ship's crew. James Henneberry wrote that after a boiler explosion during the Battle of Fort Henry the escaped steam scalded "nearly everyman that was on the Forecastle."[92]

The sailors who received the brunt of the steam writhed on deck tearing off their clothes in futile attempts to rid themselves of the burning. Many sailors jumped off their ships to soothe their miseries only to drown or be shot by rebel sharpshooters. The ship's log of the *Richmond* recorded that after a shot from the rebel vessel *Arkansas* pierced one of its boilers, "the scalded men jumped overboard, and some of them never came to the surface again."[93] Men who had inhaled the steam choked on swelled tongues, gasped for air with crippled lungs, or cried out for cold water and ice. Seared corneas left men either permanently or temporarily blinded.

Sailors tried to comfort the wounded by placing their scalded bodies on soft cotton and shielding their eyes from light. They administered chloroform and opiates to dull the pain. Symmes Browne, who witnessed the injuries inflicted by steam explosions on the *Mound City* and the *Essex*, wrote home describing the miseries of 100 scalded sailors. "I saw most of the bodies brought back," he wrote, "and indeed the sight was awful." [94]

Despite the fear generated by boiler explosions, nothing approximated the hysteria caused by torpedoes. In fact, the most dreaded whisper among Union sailors during combat was "torpedo." Torpedoes—which are now called mines—consisted of both simple and complex varieties. Crude torpedoes were composed of wooden kegs filled with powder that exploded when the ship made contact. Other torpedoes required a tug on a line by guerrillas sitting on the riverbanks. More complex torpedoes featured glass demiglobes filled with black powder that detonated when the hull of the ship struck the glass. Some even had crude clocks that at a designated time triggered a hammer that struck a cap sparking the explosion. [95]

Union sailors hated torpedoes. They universally assailed them and other mechanized objects of death as "infernal machines" and "monsters." [96] The strength of feeling caused by torpedoes came from a number of sources. First, torpedoes were effective. Secretary of the Navy Gideon Welles commented that torpedoes were "more destructive to our naval vessels than all other means combined." [97] Second, torpedoes worked quickly. Owing to an absence of watertight compartments below the waterline and the weight of the ship itself, properly detonated torpedoes could sink an iron-plated ship fast, much more quickly than a wooden ship. [98] Men only had minutes to escape. George Yost, a boy on the ironclad *Cairo*, marveled how much destruction these floating jars of gunpowder caused. "We were struck by a Torpedo which exploded under the Forward part of our boat crashing in the bottom of the boat so that in 5 minutes after the explosion took place whole forward part the Hold was full of water." [99]

Third, torpedoes completely destroyed for sailors the myth that their service was safe and that iron guaranteed their security. George Bright worried to his father that torpedoes were the only "vulnerable point" to "our iron war dogs." [100] Rear Admiral David G. Farragut believed that sailors' fear of torpedoes was so strong that it required "more than discipline to overcome." The anxiety about torpedoes proved so effective in unhinging sailors that crews often spent their waking hours devising schemes to neutralize the devils and their sleeping hours dreaming about them.[101] Alvah Hunter's reaction vividly illustrated the psychological effect created by torpedoes. "It is certain the moral effect of this torpedo-attack was very great. . . . To the end of the war there was a lively apprehension of further attacks."[102]

In places where Confederates had heavily seeded torpedoes, "torpedo fever" seized the minds of crews. Sailors became so jumpy as they peered into the water that almost any floating object came to look like a torpedo.[103] The crew of the *Sebago* spent the entire night of 14 December 1864 maneuvering around what they thought was a deadly torpedo. Two sailors, hoping to explode it, fired two shots into its side. Nothing happened. As the darkness lifted on the morning of the fifteenth, the crew lowered a small boat and warily rowed toward the object in the water. Much to their chagrin, the monster that had terrorized them the whole night was nothing more than an old scow, capsized, and proudly featuring two bullet holes in the planking.[104]

Death was the most immediate fear caused by torpedoes. Yet there was something more generated by torpedoes than mere lively apprehension. In fact, the use of the term "infernal machines" by sailors to describe these devices was revealing. On a basic level, sailors hated torpedoes because they viewed their use as sneaky, treacherous, and unmanly. Moreover, torpedoes robbed sailors of any feelings of control and reduced them to nervous spectators watching and waiting. Confederates often compounded these feelings by disguising torpedoes as flags of truce or other seemingly harmless objects like messages in bottles and driftwood.[105] Calvin G. Hutchinson expressed the disgust many sailors harbored toward these "infernal machines" when he wrote to his friend William Hill: "I am decidely opposed to this cowardly method of warfare; I had much rather be blown up by my wife than by one of these things."[106] Captain Thomas Craven summarized what many tars felt about the Southern use of torpedoes when he wrote to Secretary Welles in 1861. "If this is the use to which the enemy is to put the flag of truce," Craven sighed, "God help us from Southern chivalry."[107]

Furthermore, Union sailors saw in torpedoes the threats posed by nascent technology to their way of life. This is not to say that Union sailors were heirs to the Luddite tradition. Indeed, they seemed to exhibit a pragmatic approach to technology for their time. Many had emanated from the working class and had worked with machines before the war. As a result, they lauded those aspects of technology that worked

*"In Action": The many hours of drill were meant to prepare gun crews for battle surrounded by fire and death. Charles E. Stedman Sketchbook, courtesy of the Boston Athenaeum.*

in their favor, like iron plating and steam power, but cursed and feared the negative aspects of technological change like boiler explosions and torpedoes.[108]

During combat, every sailor had a specific task to perform at his station. Gun crews loaded, fired, and then reloaded their heavy guns and rifled cannons as fast as they could.[109] In order to keep the cannons fed, powder boys dodged their way from the magazine to the guns toting boxes of black powder and ammunition at times twice as large as themselves. Fire crews stamped out the blazes that erupted to keep the powder monkeys from being blown to bits as they made their way from the magazine to the stations. Coal heavers shoveled furiously in the boiler room to keep the ship at full steam and moving as swiftly as possible.

Controlling their emotions long enough to perform their duties represented the greatest challenge for sailors during combat. If men stopped working the guns swiftly, hesitated too long, or ceased working altogether, the Confederate batteries would never be silenced, the carnage would increase, and the ship might be sunk.[110] Combat preservation required sailors to work in concert and with precision, no matter what was happening around them, relying on the instincts they had acquired through the countless—and at the time seemingly meaningless—hours of drill.

Naval combat proved physically exhausting. The heat, the strenuous nature of the work, the pervasive smoke, and the raking din wore sailors out in short periods of time. Heat quickly sapped men's strength. To combat it, men stripped to the waist and perspired profusely. Sailors working at the guns perspired so much that they likened it to rain.[111] Moisture coursed so thick down men's bodies that one marine recalled that sailors wearing shoes usually "chuckled" when they walked.[112]

The smoke and the noise proved more difficult to stem. Thick, black smoke from guns, smokestacks, and burning parts of the ship blinded and gagged sailors. One man recalled that after a few minutes sailors became "black as demons."[113] Sailors complained that the dense smoke hung low over the decks, making it impossible to breathe.[114] The smoke was so thick and so dark that a sailor often could not see the man standing right next to him. "It was impossible to see anything," wrote one sailor. Smoke disrupted group cohesion since men lost visual contact with one another, making them more susceptible to panic.[115]

The noise generated by the firing of their own guns and the receipt of Confederate ordnance also made it almost impossible for Union sailors to hear. Bartholomew Diggins equated the roar with "two hundred guns and mortars of the largest caliber in full blast, double this by the explosion of the shells, then add to this the hissing and crashing through the air . . . and confine this in a half mile square." Only then, Diggins wrote, could a person "get some idea of the noise and uproar that has taken place."[116] At times, the din reached such levels that sailors' eardrums shattered. It was not uncommon to see men bleeding from the nose and ears from the impact of the noise.[117] Sailors would keep their mouths open while standing on their tiptoes in attempts to deaden the impact on their heads.[118]

As if the smoke and noise were not disorienting enough, the ship also offered an array of ghastly sights owing to its inability to absorb blood and guts. Unlike grass and earth, the wood and metal of a ship did not hide the carnage of battle—it plainly exhibited it. This compelled unwounded men to fight on blood-covered decks and amid gut-strewn guns, ropes, and ladders. Sailors routinely had to wage fights as they staggered and slipped across blood-soaked decks and moved among torn arms, legs, and headless torsos. "Imagine about one hundred men in such a small square, all wounded," wrote Patrick Meade, "some frightfully, some delirious from their wounds, some yelling, some groaning, some praying, more calling for their friends."[119]

The sights and smells were awful. Bartholomew Diggins wrote that "the decks and sides were smeared and bracked with blood, which ran in crooked streams to the scuppers, mangled portions of the human body were shoved in out-of-the-way places, or stuck to the sides of ropes and masts."[120] Willis J. Abbot wrote that men often fought surrounded by "lopped-off legs and arms, and bleeding, blackened bodies, scattered about by shells; while blood and brains actually dripped from the beams."[121] The presence of so much fresh blood mixed with burnt powder lent the ship, one sailor recalled, a "murderous smell."[122]

While the noise and the smoke made it difficult for sailors to perform their duties, the sounds of their friends and mess mates being dismembered produced a profound shock that compromised their ability to continue. This shock ate up much of the men's remaining resolve.[123] Bartholomew Diggins referred to this particular point—when sailors for the first time thought of giving up—as "this moment." This moment was the most critical point aboard a ship during battle. It was at this time that men began to look around and comprehend the full extent of the disorder, chaos, and death.[124] On the *Hartford*, Diggins recalled that when the moment of truth hit his crewmates, they seemed "lost" and "for a few moments it looked like everyone for himself."[125] "My youthfull emagination of hell," Diggins recounted, "did not equel the secne about us this moment."[126]

The noise, the smoke, the confusion, and the carnage had strained the senses of men to the breaking point. The sensory overload forced sailors to make a colossal series of adjustments in a very short period of time. All at once, Union sailors had to adjust to uncertainty, adjust to noise, adjust to confusion, adjust to danger, adjust to frustration, adjust to death, adjust to killing, and adjust to the reality that at any moment the ship could sink, catch fire, or explode.[127] It was no wonder that even though it appeared that the average time of combat exposure for sailors was shorter than for soldiers, almost to a man they claimed that every minute passed like an hour.[128]

Moreover, during combat, sailors seemed to run violently through a gamut of emotions—boredom, exultation, panic, anger, sorrow, and bewilderment. It was right about the time that the fighting became fast and furious and men began dying that sailors pondered for the first time the fact that they could die. As they did, they slid into a sort of emotional paralysis. This paralysis clouded the ability of sailors to ascertain what had just happened, what was going on at the moment, or what would happen next.[129]

A number of factors spurred Union sailors through. Working at one's particular duties was the most critical way men maintained their wits. Drill, so loathed and so resisted by sailors and so dull and repetitious at the time, enabled men to discharge battle duties even in life-threatening situations.[130] Drill schooled them to focus on their individual duties, to the exclusion of everything else. To stop working meant to start thinking. In battle, thinking became a liability.

Sailors' observations confirmed that when men stopped to think about what was going on all around them they panicked. William Van Cleef said that he felt extreme panic at certain points during combat. "But when we got good to work at them I did not mind it any more."[131] Stanley Campbell wrote that when he reflected on all that was going on in the middle of battle, he realized what a mistake he had made in joining the navy.[132] Bartholomew Diggins observed that the men who "found them selfs without occupation" often fell into "the greatest confusion."[133]

While working proved pivotal in maintaining sailors' wits, it was not the only motivating factor. Another important factor was the shared reality that they had little choice; they had nowhere else to go. Soldiers almost always had the opportunity to flee from a battlefield. They may not have done so owing to ideology, group cohesion, patriotism, or fear, but the fact remained that Union soldiers could run into the woods, fake death, or risk making an open break when the urge to preserve their lives overwhelmed them.

Fleeing was not an option for sailors. No matter how badly the battle went, if they were wounded, losing the fight, or tired, sailors quickly grasped the reality that if they gave up and the ship was vanquished, they would die. If they jumped ship they would drown. If they made it to shore, they would be shot.[134] Landsman Stanley Campbell crystallized the fundamental difference between land and sea fighting: "The worst of all was the fact that you could not run away when you were whipped. After escaping the peril from shot and shell, from the explosion from magazine or boilers, from consumption by fire or drowning by water—sevenfold the terrors of a battle on land—and knowing that you were thoroughly licked, you realized there was no place else to go. I decided, on several occasions, that if I went to war again, I would select the army instead of the navy upon the solid, bed-rock, copperfastened principle that I could run, or hide, when fighting ceased to be a virtue."[135]

Sailors, like soldiers, were sensitive about the issue of courage. While most men had not enlisted to prove their courage, the culture of Union sailors set forth acceptable ways of acting during combat.[136] Union sailors lived in a highly masculine culture that by any stretch of the imagination did not suffer cowards.[137] Sailors were supposed to be tough and collected. They did not have to exhibit the bravado and bloodlust of pirates, but they did have to prove themselves worthy members of the brotherhood of the sea and the coarse maritime culture from which they came.

Still, the definition of courage for sailors was different than it was for soldiers. For sailors, to be courageous did not mean taking some bold, heroic individual action without fear.[138] Men did not have to act dashing or take risks.[139] Instead, a sailor who clung to his post, without fanfare, under extreme exposure or while wounded, was considered to possess courage.[140] Leaving one's station in the middle of a fight, unless severely wounded, was a sign of cowardice.[141] In some ways, the different measure of courage for sailors forecast the new expression of personal valor for twentieth-century warfare. Heroism would come to be measured by how a man stood up in the path of a faceless enemy, where wounds were delivered by artillery instead of musketry. In this new environment, courage consisted of passive endurance rather than active intervention.[142]

Courageous tars were those who stood fast when heads, legs, and arms rolled around the deck. They remained fixed as splinters and shells whizzed overhead and exploded on the decks. Charles K. Mervine, a second-class boy on the *Powhatan*, watched in awe as tars battled the guns and elements around Charleston. "But amid it all their souls were undaunted and despair was a stranger to them," Mervine jotted in his daybook. "In a word they knew no fear, but toiled on in the discharge of their duty."[143]

Obviously, sailors felt fear during combat. However, it is clear that when the battle was on the line and the fighting fast and furious, most sailors stayed at their assigned stations.[144] Both the *Official Records* and the personal accounts reverberate with countless examples of Union sailors fighting at their posts, many while wounded or dying.[145] During combat on the *Cimarron*, Gunner's Mate John Merrett was in his hammock extremely ill, so ill that the gunboat was to take him to the hospital for extended care. Yet when the battle broke out, Merrett re-

*An example of how courageous sailors could be. James K. L. Duncan, ordinary seaman, is injured by the explosion of a burning cartridge that he was throwing overboard, during the engagement between the USS Fort Hindman and a Confederate battery near Harrisonburg, Louisiana, on 2 March 1864. He was awarded the Congressional Medal of Honor for this action. Courtesy of the U.S. Naval Historical Center.*

fused to brook inaction. He staggered to his post and fought through. Once the action ceased, he collapsed and could only be resuscitated by heavy stimulants.[146] During the *Kearsarge*'s successful chase of the raider *Alabama*, an exploding shell severely wounded Seaman William Gowin. Rather than let them render him assistance, Gowin ordered his crewmates to stay at the guns and keep fighting. Gowin then crawled bleeding on his hands and knees to the medical hatch while his gun mates fought on.[147]

"Cool" was the most common adjective used to describe courageous sailors.[148] "Men who cooly awaited the order of their officers" were deemed to be brave tars, wrote Charles Mervine.[149] A good example of cool courage was the type of behavior exhibited by the sailors on William Van Cleaf's gunboat. During the struggle for Island No. 10, in between loading and firing their guns, the gun crews did not take cover, look for incoming shells, or worry aloud. Instead, they played checkers.[150]

Although officers, in their after-battle reports published in the *Official Records*, and sailors, in their personal accounts, both consistently used the term "cool" to describe the admirable conduct of their crews, they did so for different purposes. Officers sought to convey the impression to Washington and their superiors that their crews performed in an ordered, well-drilled, and efficient manner. The conduct of the crews was a reflection on them. In almost every account, officers reported that "every crew did its duty," "showed no fear," and were "gallant." Absent from these reports were descriptions of fear, sadness, anger, and cowardice among sailors.[151]

For their part, sailors opted for the term "cool" because it reflected the values of their culture and society. Sailors were supposed to be indifferent to danger and to take a mocking attitude toward it. Whether they felt it or not, they were to be as surly and nonchalant about death and fear as they were about everything else aboard ship. On a deeper level, sailors were also trying to make sense of and elevate the deaths of mates whose lives had come to so horribly grotesque an end. Sailors sought to bestow dignity on the way their friends had fought and died, friends who otherwise had little or no legacy. Pride was extremely important to these men, especially in death.

Using "coolness" as a descriptive term for Union sailors was established early in the war when on 8 March 1862 the rebel ironclad *Merrimac* sent the wooden vessel the *Cumberland* and her stubborn crew to the bottom. One hundred twenty-one men, out of a crew of 376, died. The performance of the sailors on the *Cumberland* quickly reached mythical proportions.[152] The story of unflinching bravery also helped disguise the reality that a rebel vessel had made short work of a grand old ship of the navy.

The story of the *Cumberland*'s sailors achieved such fame because of the dogged determination with which the crew fought. Early in the battle, the *Merrimac* gored the *Cumberland*, creating such a large hole that the ship began to sink rapidly. According to eyewitness accounts, not a seaman on the *Cumberland* left his station as the ship made water. Instead, men continued to work the guns by leaping from deck to deck as the water rose. Thomas Selfridge, an officer on the *Cumberland*, remarked that even though the ship was simultaneously sinking and being blasted apart, his men continued with their duties, "cool, grim, silent and determined."[153] Sailors remained steadfast to their guns even when forced to the uppermost decks of the ship. Only when the crew found itself within minutes of submerging completely did the officers give the order, "Every man look out for himself," allowing sailors to leave their stations and save their lives.[154]

Some men jumped into the surging waters. Many did not. Hoping to land that one lucky shot and seized with what the *Cumberland*'s surgeon likened to "delirium," a number of sailors refused to leave their stations. Stripped to the waist, black as powder, and with handkerchiefs bound round their heads, a handful of sailors on the *Cumberland* continued to load and fire at will. They were like "demons," the surgeon recalled. One such demon had lost most of his appendages and had earlier refused any medical treatment. As the ship was about to go under he was purported to have shouted, "Back to your guns, boys! Give 'em hell!" He and the rest of those who remained went down with the ship.[155]

Part romance, part reality, the examples of courage set by the sailors on the *Cumberland* resonated in the imaginations of sailors, officers, and poets for the rest of the war. Memorialized in numerous poems, the crew of the *Cumberland* may have been the most remembered seamen of the war. Herman Melville attempted to portray what it meant to be a courageous sailor after the sinking of the *Cumberland*:

> What need to tell how she was fought—
> The sinking flaming gun—
>   The gunner leaping out the port—
>   Washed back, undone!
> Her dead unconquerably manned
>   The Cumberland.[156]

Yet the courageous example of the *Cumberland* may have been difficult for sailors to emulate not only because some of the tale smacked of mythmaking, but also because sailors did not see the quantity of death that soldiers did. Soldiers saw human and animal death up close and continuously as the war progressed. Sailors did not. They may have seen more grisly deaths, but sailors did not become accustomed to seeing men killed. It remained extremely difficult for them throughout the war to watch men die. One of the greatest tests of a sailor's constitution was not to fear dying. The worst psychological toll was exacted by watching other men die.[157]

Tars seemed to take every death hard, even when they did not like

*Sailors took every death hard. One of the most traumatic combat experiences for sailors was the sinking of the USS* Tecumseh *during the Battle of Mobile Bay. The* Tecumseh *was struck by a torpedo and sank almost instantly. The sketch is of sailors attempting to rescue the survivors of the sinking as the battle rages around them. Courtesy of the U.S. Naval Historical Center.*

or know the deceased. Coal Heaver Charles Poole wrote that "it seems very hard to have a ship mate taken from amongst us." Other sailors complained of intense "loneliness" when confronted with the death of a mate.[158] Deaths caused by combat affected them even more deeply. Marine Harrie Webster described the psychological trauma suffered by sailors on the *Manhattan* when it passed over the monitor *Tecumseh*, which had been struck by a torpedo and sunk: "The bubbling water round our bows . . . told us that we were passing directly over the struggling wretches fighting with death in the Tecumseh. The effect on our men was in some cases terrible. One of the firemen was crazed by the incident."[159]

Sailors knew this about themselves. When referring to a death aboard ship, they did not ask if someone had died. They would inquire quietly "if someone's number had come up" or say, "There aren't so many at mess today."[160] After Yeoman Isaac Bradbury had shot a rebel on the beach, he went into intense remorse. "I went up to the corpse and it was a terrible sight." He tried to comfort himself with immediate rationalizations. "I had to do this action for self defense," he confessed to a friend back home.[161] Even sailors like James Henneberry and John Swift, who saw dead combatants more regularly on the river campaign, never seemed to adjust to the sight of dead men.[162] Swift wrote poignantly of his examination of a dead soldier he found on a bank of the White River in Arkansas: "I stood & looked at him till I persuaded myself that he *could not* be dead & stooped & felt his heart but no movement, I even doubted then & took my knife & held the blade of it to his mouth, but it was useless; one touch of his face told me that, for it was as cold as death could make it. The man's face haunted me for days after & I could not rid of the remembrance."[163]

Sailors who mingled with soldiers expressed shock about how comfortable soldiers had become with death. After the Battle of Fort Fisher, sailors expressed horror as soldiers stepped on, sat on, and cooked among the dead who littered the beaches adjacent to the fort. This was not how sailors treated their fallen comrades. To their shock and amazement, Union sailors watched as grizzled veterans and recent recruits paid little heed to the fallen strewn all around them. It unsettled them to think that such a fate should befall any fellow combatant. Crew member Joseph Canning wrote in his journal that the sight of soldiers "eating, writing, and cursing in, among and over the ghastly dead" completely rankled the sailors.[164]

Sailors realized that, amid so much killing, something had died within soldiers. They also noted that soldiers paid little mind to civilian casualties and refugees, especially women, children, and the old.[165] This indifference troubled them. Sailors, not fully immersed in the war itself and immune from its intensifying, harder hand, recoiled at civilian casualties. George Bright reported that the sailors in his crew became incensed on hearing the news of children's deaths resulting from the Union shelling of Galveston. One sailor grew so upset that he dove off the ship and swam to shore to see for himself if children in Galveston had been killed in the attack.[166]

In Pensacola, Florida, sailors on the *Susquehanna* watched in horror as soldiers ransacked, terrorized, and killed babies, mothers, and the elderly. Particularly galling was the scene of soldiers dangling over the water and dunking a newborn baby while his mother watched, screaming. This and other incidents prompted Seaman John Eliot Parkman to marvel at the shocking indifference to death and suffering shown by his counterparts in the army. At least, he believed, sailors had survived the war with their humanity still intact. Writing to his mother, Parkman recalled: "Night before also one poor old man gentlemen not being quick enough, was burnt to death in one of them [sheds], to the intense relish of the soldiers . . . As rough and careless as sailors are, I'll take my oath not one of them would treat the women & children as these same dear, dirty volunteers—who gave up washing with their homes—seem to delight in doing."[167]

Post-battle scenes on ships were ghastly. The decks of ships were a twisted display of ship articles, wounded, and dead. Blood was everywhere. Sayres Nichols marveled that it ran so deep after a fight on the *Miami* that "the blood was over the soles of my boots all over the berth deck."[168] Sailors immediately attended to the wounded who were—due to the horrible nature of most wounds—in extreme agony. "The scene on the Quarter Deck after we got them all there," wrote James Henneberry, "was sickening in the extreme." Bartholomew Diggins, surveying the carnage on the *Hartford*, observed, "on the berth deck, the mess things, hastily laid aside, Mess chests, clothing, partitions, splinters, etc. were all fumbled together, almost covering the whole deck, while mingled with the debris were the killed and wounded." The wounded were often thrown together with the dead. Their cries, gasps, and slips into delirium rankled the unwounded sailors trying to free them.[169]

As unnerving as the sights and sounds were, sailors set about cleaning the ship because there was no other way to remove the horror from their decks. The "lucky" sailors, mainly carpenters, caulkers, and sailmakers, tended to the ship. They replaced shattered planks and decks, filled the loose seams and cracks in the ship, and mended sails and lines. Other sailors mopped up the blood that now lay in pools and streams all over the decks. Other sailors scraped brains and entrails from the decks and the ship's sides.

The less fortunate tars—the ones who could stomach the job—collected body parts. Men retrieved lost arms, legs, parts of chests, and heads and placed them in bags. Some of the dead were so disfigured that their identities were unrecognizable. Sailors often found clumps of bodies housed in sailor's dress.[170] Despite the carnage, "in a few hours," wrote one sailor, "the wreck of battle was all cleared away and the decks and sides were scrubbed and relieved of all stains of the conflict."[171]

Although holystoning might have washed the blood and guts from the decks, it was not as easy for a sailor to erase from memory the vivid images of what he had just witnessed. Unlike soldiers who could march away from the sites of their nightmares, sailors had to continue to live amid the reminders of the worst moments of their lives. Every time they saw a certain part of the deck or gun port where a mate had lost a life, they revisited the tragedy all over again. Many began to associate parts of the ship with death and dead comrades. Ships lost the clear veneer of sailors' romantic illusions and instead took on a sinister cast. After combat, sailors began to compare their ships to the only places that would ever proudly display so much blood: slaughterhouses or, to use a favored term, "slaughter pens."[172]

Sailors evidenced several patterns of behavior that seemed to be attempts to process psychologically their combat experiences. Following an engagement, some men would go into a sort of manic state, in which they talked incessantly about, but around, the bloodshed they had just witnessed. Charles Poole wrote that after the capture of the *Alabama* by the *Kearsarge*, the crew became notably more "talkative."[173] Others bore the strain of physical exertion, worry, and panic. Joseph Canning described most of the men as "haggard."[174] Persistent sleeplessness and increased anxiety were not uncommon the nights after combat.[175] E. W. Goble wrote to a friend that thoughts of death plagued him after battle. "I tell you Joe it was a sad thought and I passed the balance of the night in thought."[176]

Other sailors tried to downplay what they had just experienced by recharacterizing its nature. One popular practice was to count the dents in the iron plating caused by shot and shell and then rationalize that without iron to protect them things would have been worse. It is hard to see how sailors took comfort in this approach, even though they were correct; in many instances things could have been worse. Perhaps, by examining the dents made by shot and shell sailors tried to convince themselves that the ship and not their crewmates had suffered the worst of the damage.[177] It is difficult to tell.

One thing is certain. After combat, sailors did try to forget, recharacterize, and in many instances downplay their combat experiences. Many sailors attempted to ease their inner torment by applying harmless metaphors and images to the event. William Van Cleaf compared combat to baseball. E. W. Goble likened the action to a "dance."[178] Charles Mervine labeled the fierce fighting around Charleston as a "ball."[179] Not surprisingly, alcohol found its way into the post-combat adjustment. Although the navy officially prohibited its use, sailors, often with the blessing and encouragement of officers, consumed liquor immediately after battle in an attempt to repair themselves, calm down, or begin forgetting. John G. Morrison wrote that, after action ceased on the Yazoo River, "the main brace was now spliced and the excitement subsided a little."[180]

Sailors, however, did not want to forget the dead. They took great pains to give their fallen mates a proper farewell. The navy funeral represented the last bit of drill for the deceased and a way for those who remained to honor their memory. After the death of a sailor, his mess mates constructed a casket out of wood and placed their comrade in it. If no wood was available, a deceased sailor was sewn up in his hammock. Immediately thereafter, they draped the casket or hammock with the U.S. flag. Deceased hands lay in state for final review by the crew.[181]

The formal ceremony began with the boatswain piping a call for "all hands to bury the dead."[182] The ceremony was more military than religious in nature. Crew members gathered on one side of the body and officers on the other. The captain read the rites of burial over the body. After the burial rites, twelve marines in dress blues headed the procession carrying the body to its final resting place. If the ship was unable to touch land, the body was slipped into the ocean.[183] The mess mates of the deceased carried the body in procession, followed in order by boys, sailors, petty officers, and commissioned officers according to rank. The captain walked alone, last in the procession, and read the final blessing.

This stark reversal of rank represented a tacit acknowledgment that in death all sailors were equal. Death even superseded the captain's authority. At the close of the ceremony, the marines fired a three-round salute in order to ward off any devils hoping to slip into the man's heart at the moment of burial. As the crew returned to their stations, a bell tolled, commemorating the soul of the departed. It was a ceremony at once sad and stirring.[184] Alvah Hunter stated that during a funeral on his vessel "no eye was dry as we committed our young shipmate to the bosom of the deep." After such a funeral, wrote Milo Lacy, men wore "saddened expressions" and for the rest of the day "conversed in subdued voices."[185]

The intensity of feeling during and after funerals reflected the sadness and disillusionment many sailors experienced in light of the grim realities of naval combat in the Civil War. The impersonal, horrible nature of the deaths of sailors forever destroyed the romantic fantasies that many had nursed about what battle in the navy was going to be like. This sharp divergence between expectation and experience taught Union sailors a number of lessons, lessons they would not soon forget. The primary one was that combat—even when limited in scope—exacted both a physical and an emotional toll. Their traumas haunted sailors for days, weeks, and years after the experience, leaving disillusioned the many who had thought fighting at sea in the Civil War would be scar free.

# Epilogue

At the end of the war, most of the 51,000 sailors were mustered out of the Union navy. Before leaving the service, men received any payments owed and a free transport back to their port of origin. As they left the damp vessels they called home, they exchanged sad good-byes with mates and shook everyone's hand, some even the captain's. There were those who also bade good-bye to their ships. Sailors threw their belongings into their lucky bags, collected their pet monkeys and parrots, and trundled down the gang plank to dry land, as Seaman John Wirts wrote, often "amid cheer after cheer" from the sailors staying on.[1] Once more on familiar ground, sailors disappeared into the shadowy fringes from which they came.

Yet, as much as they had resisted, the navy and the war had changed them. While many had enlisted to avoid the war, not only had they suffered the monotony of naval life and the many hardships foisted on common people when they go to war, sailors managed to face the pivotal issues that had made the conflict so divisive and so bloody. Sailors had seen the new racial realities promised by emancipation by living, working, and fighting with former slaves. They had experienced firsthand the struggle with religion in a diverse crew and a navy increasingly suspicious of faith and more reliant on technology. Sailors had seen the face of modern combat.

Many left in an angry state of mind: angry about their treatment by the navy; angry about their pay, their lack of liberty, and their lack of prize money.[2] With all that they had faced and overcome, others were happy just to be out of the navy. The happiest sailors ever were aboard ship was when they were going home. "He now has no more weary lookouts in the rain, no more is he to be kicked about because he is a Landsman," wrote Landsman Milo Lacy, "and treated worse than a dog." Later, Lacy wrote, but he can "hold up his head and say that he is a free man once more, with none to say the contrary."[3]

Whatever their emotions upon mustering out might have been, their experiences had forever shaped them physically and psychologically. George Yost had been only sixteen years old when he shipped on the *Cairo* as a boy in 1862. In 1864, when he returned home to Missouri, some of his friends did not even recognize him. Only after forcefully protesting that it was he did some finally believe it was the same George. In his diary, he acknowledged the reason for his friends' confusion. "I may not have been the same as when I left," Yost confided. "So changed was I."[4]

In fact, one of the most telling accounts of the effect the Civil War had on its sailors was a story recounted by Ann Preston to her son Fowler about Charles Sweet, one of his acquaintances who had recently been mustered out of the navy. Charles had left the service because of the death of his father and had arrived home to take over the family's faltering general store in St. Joseph, Michigan. Unhappy with her son's choice to become a sailor and desiring to know what it was like to be a sailor, Ann snagged Charley on the street and began peppering him with motherly questions, such as how he had liked the navy and whether it was easier than the army, as everyone said.

Charley's answers were to the point. "He does not like the Navy," Ann told her son, "says it is a hard place said he would not take a great deal for what he has seen and learnt." When she asked about her son's prospects of getting his prize money, Sweet groused, "You may not see it." After a few more questions, Charley excused himself and pulled away in his rig. As he drove away, Mrs. Preston put a hard glance on Charley. She quizzically remarked to her son that Charley had returned to his "citizen clothes" except for one article. He was still wearing his blue sailor shirt.[5]

# Notes

PREFACE

1. Thomas O. Selfridge Jr., *Memoirs of Thomas O. Selfridge, Jr., Rear Admiral, U.S.N.*, with an introduction by Captain Dudley W. Knox (New York: G. P. Putnam's Sons, 1924), 82–83.

2. Cornelius Schoonmaker to Barnard Schoonmaker, 30 May 1865, Cornelius Schoonmaker Papers, Manuscripts, Library of Congress, Washington, D.C.

3. Joseph Fry to Wife, 28 November 1861, Joseph Fry Papers, Miscellaneous Manuscripts, New-York Historical Society, New York, N.Y.

4. *Cincinnati Daily Commercial*, 1 January 1862, in James M. Merrill, "Cairo, Illinois: Strategic Civil War River Port," *Journal of Illinois State History* 76 (Winter 1983): 243.

5. Anonymous, "Life on a Blockader," *Continental Monthly* 6 (July 1864): 49.

6. Some recently published works perpetuate the typical myths of sailors as happy wards of the service. See Dennis J. Ringle, *Life in Mr. Lincoln's Navy* (Annapolis: Naval Institute Press, 1998); Donald L. Canney, *Lincoln's Navy: The Ships, Men and Organization, 1861–65* (Annapolis: Naval Institute Press, 1998). For a more accurate, scholarly appraisal, see Robert M. Browning Jr., *From Cape Charles to Cape Fear: The North Atlantic Blockading Squadron during the Civil War* (Tuscaloosa: University of Alabama Press, 1993), and *Success Is All That Was Demanded: The South Atlantic Blockading Squadron during the Civil War* (Washington, D.C.: Brassey's, 2002).

7. Cornelius Cronin, *Recollection of Service in the U.S. Navy: Being Reminiscences as They Have Occurred to My Mind From the Commencement and Pending the Late War; while Serving on the U.S. Ships Sabine, Brooklyn, and Richmond* (n.p., 1894), 13.

8. The author acknowledges the contribution of Professor Iver Bernstein of Washington University in St. Louis in the formulation of these thoughts.

9. *Enlistment Returns, Changes, and Reports, 1846–1942, Weekly Returns of Enlistments at Naval Rendezvous, January 6, 1855–August 8, 1891*, vols. 17–43, Records of the Bureau of Naval Personnel, Record Group 24, National Archives Building, Washington, D.C.

10. See Joseph P. Reidy, "Black Jack: African American Sailors in the Civil War Navy," in *New Interpretations in Naval History: Selected Papers from the Twelfth Naval History Symposium*, ed. William B. Cogar (Annapolis: Naval Institute Press, 1997), 213.

CHAPTER 1

1. James M. McPherson, *What They Fought For, 1861–1865* (Baton Rouge: Louisiana State University Press, 1994), 5–7; James M. McPherson, *For Cause and Comrades: Why Men Fought in the Civil War* (New

York: Oxford University Press, 1997), 5–13; Gerald F. Linderman, *Embattled Courage: The Experience of Combat in the American Civil War* (New York: Free Press, 1987), 20–21; Reid Mitchell, *Civil War Soldiers: Their Expectations and Their Experiences* (New York: Viking Press, 1988), 20–23; Reid Mitchell, *The Vacant Chair: The Northern Soldier Leaves Home* (New York: Oxford University Press, 1993), 16–18.

2. Maris A. Vinovskis identifies six variables as the best predictors of enlistment in the army and navy: age, ethnicity, occupation, wealth, school attendance, and educational attainment. See Maris A. Vinovskis, "Have Social Historians Lost the Civil War? Some Preliminary Demographic Speculations," in Maris A. Vinovskis, ed., *Toward a Social History of the American Civil War* (Cambridge: Cambridge University Press, 1992), 16–19. Few have studied the characteristics of men who fought in the Civil War: see David F. Riggs, "Sailors of the U.S.S. Cairo: Anatomy of a Gunboat Crew," *Civil War History* 28 (September 1982): 273; Earl J. Hess, "The 12th Missouri Infantry: A Socio-Military Profile of a Union Regiment," *Missouri Historical Review* 76 (October 1981): 53–77; Emily J. Harris, "Sons and Soldiers: Deerfield, Massachusetts and the Civil War," *Civil War History* 30 (June 1984): 151–71; W. J. Rorabaugh, "Who Fought for the North in the Civil War? Concord, Massachusetts, Enlistments," *Journal of American History* 73 (December 1986): 695–701; George W. Creasey, *The City of Newburyport in the Civil War, from 1861 to 1865* (Boston: Griffith-Stillings Press, 1903).

3. Secretary of the Navy, *Report of the Secretary of the Navy, with an Appendix Containing Reports from Officers, December 1865* (Washington, D.C.: Government Printing Office, 1865), xiii; Robert M. Browning Jr., *From Cape Charles to Cape Fear: The North Atlantic Blockading Squadron during the Civil War* (Tuscaloosa: University of Alabama Press, 1993), 200–201.

4. Donald L. Canney, *Lincoln's Navy: The Ships, Men and Organization, 1861–65* (Annapolis: Naval Institute Press, 1998), 120.

5. Journal Entry, 23 September 1861, James E. Henneberry, Journal aboard U.S. Gunboat Essex, 23 September 1861–2 June 1863, James E. Henneberry Papers, Research Collections, Chicago Historical Society, Chicago, Ill. (hereafter "Henneberry Journal"); William N. Bock to Father, 15 January 1863, William N. Bock Papers, Illinois State Historical Library, Springfield, Ill.; William B. Avery, "Gun-Boat Service on the James River," in *Personal Narratives of the Events in the Rebellion, Being Papers Read before the Rhode Island Soldiers and Sailors Historical Society*, 3d ser., no. 3 (Providence: N. B. Williams, 1884), 37–38; Lester L. Swift, ed., "Letters from a Sailor on a Tinclad," *Civil War History* 10 (March 1961): 49; John D. Milligan, ed., "Navy Life on the Mississippi River," *Civil War Times Illustrated* 33 (May–June 1994): 66; Log Entries, 2 December 1861, 20, 24 December 1862, Log of Charles A. Poole, G. W. Blunt White Library, Mystic Seaport Museum, Mystic, Conn.

6. Dennis J. Ringle, *Life in Mr. Lincoln's Navy* (Annapolis: Naval Institute Press, 1998), 18.

7. John D. Harty to David D. Porter, 21 February 1864, David D. Porter Papers, Manuscripts, Huntington Library, San Marino, Calif.

8. Walter S. Thomas to David D. Porter, 31 December 1863, Porter Papers; Ringle, *Life in Mr. Lincoln's Navy*, 19.

9. Browning, *From Cape Charles to Cape Fear*, 202.

10. La Fayette C. Baker, *History of the United States Secret Service* (Philadelphia: L. C. Baker, 1867), 399.

11. S. R. Rantlett, R. S. Stewart, Archeble Pentz, Mr. Bell, Mr. Davis, and Mr. Kingsbury to Rear Admiral H. Paulding, 26 February 1864, Richard Worsam Meade II Collection, Documents of the USS North Carolina, Naval Historical Society Collection, New-York Historical Society, New York, N.Y.

12. Marcus Rediker, *Between the Devil and the Deep Blue Sea: Merchant Seamen, Pirates, and the Anglo-American Maritime World, 1700–1750* (Cambridge: Cambridge University Press, 1987), 14, 27, 43, 81, 224.

13. Jacob Sidles to Richard Worsam Meade II, 9 February 1864, Meade II Collection; T. Bailey to Gideon Welles, 16 December 1864, Box 356, Naval Recruiting (NR), Frauds in Enlistments at Brooklyn Navy Yard, Subject File, U.S. Navy, 1775–1910 (hereafter cited as "Navy Subject File"), Record Group 45, National Archives Building, Washington, D.C.; Statement of Manuel Thompson, Seaman, December 1864, Box 356, NR, Frauds in Enlistments at Brooklyn Navy Yard, Navy Subject File; Charles Green to Rear Admiral S. H. Stringham, December 1864, Box 356, NR, Frauds in Enlistments at Brooklyn Navy Yard, Navy Subject File.

14. Richard Worsam Meade II to Rear Admiral H. Paulding, 10 February 1864, Meade II Collection; Jacob Sidles to R. W. Meade II, 9 February 1864, Meade II Collection; Gideon Welles to Rear Admiral H. Paulding, 7 September 1864, Box 356, NR, Frauds in Enlistments at Brooklyn Navy Yard, Navy Subject File; Ringle, *Life in Mr. Lincoln's Navy*, 19–20; Browning, *From Cape Charles to Cape Fear*, 202.

15. Adam Mayers, "Stolen Soldiers," *Civil War Times Illustrated* 34 (June 1995): 56.

16. Secretary of the Navy, *Report of the Secretary of the Navy, 1865*, xiii.

17. James M. McPherson, *Battle Cry of Freedom: The Civil War Era* (New York: Oxford University Press, 1988), 605.

18. *An Act to Amend an Act Entitled "An Act for Enrolling and Calling the National Forces, and for Other Purposes," Approved March 3rd 1863*, 24 February 1864, 38th Cong., 1st sess., in *Public Laws of the United States of America, 1863–1864*, vol. 13 (Boston: Little, Brown, 1864), 6–11; William N. Still, "The Common Sailor: The Civil War's Uncommon Man; Part 1, Yankee Blue Jackets," *Civil War Times Illustrated* 23 (February 1985): 27.

19. John D. Harty to David Dixon Porter, 4 January 1864, Porter Papers; D. R. Jenkins to Gideon H. Welles, 28 January 1864, Gideon Welles Papers, Manuscripts, Huntington Library; Still, "The Common Sailor," 27.

20. Charles B. Hirsch, "Gunboat Personnel on the Western Waters," *Mid-America* 34 (April 1952): 77.

21. J. A. Winslow to Andrew H.

Foote, 14 October 1861, *Official Records of the Union and Confederate Navies in the War of the Rebellion*, ser. 1, 27 volumes (Washington, D.C.: Government Printing Office, 1894–1917) (hereafter cited as "ORN"), vol. 22: 392–93.

22. Horatio L. Wait, "The Blockading Service," in *Military Essays and Recollections: Papers Read before the Commandery of the State of Illinois, Military Order of the Loyal Legion of the United States*, vol. 1 (Chicago: A. C. McClurg, 1902), 213.

23. *An Act Authorizing Additional Enlistments in the Navy of the United States*, 5 August 1861, 37th Cong., 1st sess., in *The Statutes at Large, Treaties, and Proclamations of the United States of America, 1858 to 1863*, vol. 12 (Boston: Little, Brown, 1863), 315.

24. *An Act to Amend an Act Entitled "An Act for Enrolling and Calling the National Forces, and for Other Purposes,"* 6–11.

25. Linderman, *Embattled Courage*, 20–21; Michael C. C. Adams, *Fighting for Defeat: Union Military Failure in the East, 1861–1865* (Lincoln: University of Nebraska Press, 1992), viii.

26. Linderman, *Embattled Courage*, 21.

27. Willis J. Abbot, *Blue Jackets of '61: A History of the Navy in the War of Secession* (New York: Dodd, Mead, 1890), 152; Mary Jane Smith Demming to Sarah Anne Smith, 14 February 1863, Hibbard-Seaver Papers (1812–1938), Manuscripts, Massachusetts Historical Society, Boston, Mass.

28. Stephen F. Blanding, *Recollections of a Sailor Boy; or, The Cruise of the Gunboat Louisiana* (Providence: E. A. Johnson, 1886), 118–19, 139; Log Entry, 27 November 1862, Poole Log.

29. William N. Bock to Mother, 5 May 1864, Bock Papers; James M. Merrill, "Men, Monotony, and Mouldy Beans—Life on Board Civil War Blockaders," *American Neptune* 16 (January 1956): 50; Ann Preston to Fowler Preston, 30 April 1862, Preston Family Papers, Michigan Historical Collection, Bentley Historical Library, University of Michigan, Ann Arbor, Mich.; Joseph B. Osborne to Mary Osborne, 8 September 1864, Osborne Family Papers, Manuscripts, Library of Congress, Washington, D.C.

30. Jesse Lemisch, "Jack Tar in the Streets: Merchant Seamen in the Politics of Revolutionary America," *William and Mary Quarterly* 25 (July 1968): 377; Harold D. Langley, *Social Reform in the United States Navy, 1798–1862* (Urbana: University of Illinois Press, 1967), viii; Anonymous, "The Condition of the Sailor: Are Sailors Growing Worse and Worse?" *Sailor's Magazine* 34 (November 1861): 82–86; Peter Karsten, *The Naval Aristocracy: The Golden Age of Annapolis and the Emergence of Modern American Navalism* (New York: Free Press, 1972), 76–77; William Rounesville Alger, "Effect of Sea Life on Land Life," *Boatswain's Whistle*, 9 November 1864, 5, Americana Catalogue, Huntington Library.

31. James E. Valle, *Rocks and Shoals: Order and Discipline in the Old Navy, 1800–1861* (Annapolis: Naval Institute Press, 1980), 3, 4.

32. Secretary of the Navy, *Report of the Secretary of the Navy, 1865*, xxxiii.

33. The determination of the aver-

age age of sailor recruits is based on a sample of 4,570 sailors out of the 118,044 who enlisted during the war—4,033 from the Eastern rendezvous and 537 from the Western rendezvous (hereinafter cited as "Rendezvous Sample"). The Rendezvous Sample was collected by taking every twenty-fifth name from enlistment reports at every rendezvous where reports were collected or submitted from all naval rendezvous reports between April 1861 and April 1865, contained in *Enlistment Returns, Changes, and Reports, 1846–1942, Weekly Returns of Enlistments at Naval Rendezvous, January 6, 1855–August 8, 1891*, vols. 17–43, Records of the Bureau of Naval Personnel, Record Group 24, National Archives Building, Washington, D.C. (hereafter cited as "Rendezvous Reports").

34. Ringle, *Life in Mr. Lincoln's Navy*, 24; Rendezvous Sample, Rendezvous Reports.

35. Rendezvous Sample, Rendezvous Reports. Benjamin A. Gould, *Sanitary Memoirs of the War of the Rebellion: Investigations in the Military and Anthropological Statistics of American Soldiers* (Cambridge, Mass.: Riverside Press, 1869), 208–11; Bell I. Wiley, *The Life of Billy Yank: The Common Soldier of the Union* (Baton Rouge: Louisiana State University Press, 1978), 304; McPherson, *Battle Cry of Freedom*, 608.

36. Rendezvous Sample, Rendezvous Reports. Richard B. Stott, *Workers in the Metropolis: Class, Ethnicity, and Youth in Antebellum New York City* (Ithaca: Cornell University Press, 1990), 248. Marcus Rediker claims that sailors were the first group to form a distinct working-class consciousness; see Rediker, *Between the Devil and the Deep Blue Sea*, 8.

37. Gould, *Sanitary Memoirs of the War of the Rebellion*, 208–11.

38. Rendezvous Sample, Rendezvous Reports.

39. McPherson, *Battle Cry of Freedom*, 608.

40. Economic necessity as a factor in prompting men to join the navy seemed limited to the urban areas of the East. Recruits from the Western portion of the United States appeared to join the navy on a firmer employment footing than their Eastern counterparts. A sample of 537 sailors taken from all rendezvous reports west of Pennsylvania indicates that only 6 percent (5.95 percent) of Western sailors were unemployed when they enlisted. The sample was drawn from the 12,375 men who enlisted in the cities of Pennsylvania—not rejected for medical reasons—as recorded between November 1861 and April 1865 in Rendezvous Reports.

41. One could dismiss this as nothing more than men who had no listed specific skill or vocation, except for the fact that recruits were forced to list, with precision, any job, including skills, before the war. Consequently, if a man was a common laborer before the war, whether hauling bricks or carrying rocks, he wrote "common laborer." In other words, if a man wrote "none" under the heading occupation, then, based on the meticulous notations concerning jobs in the occupation category, it meant that he was, more than likely, idle or unemployed before the war; see Rendezvous Sample, Rendezvous Reports. Working on a more limited scale, David F. Riggs reaches a similar conclusion about

the large percentages of unemployed among sailors in the Union navy; see Riggs, "Sailors of the U.S.S. Cairo," 273.

42. James McPherson cites no separate category for those soldiers who enlisted unemployed; see McPherson, *Battle Cry of Freedom*, 608. Benjamin A. Gould, an actuary for the Sanitary Commission, also had no category for soldiers who responded "none" to the question of occupation; he did, however, have a category for miscellaneous occupations, such as hostler; see Gould, *Sanitary Memoirs of the War of the Rebellion*, 208–11.

43. Carter Goodrich and Sol Davidson, "The Wage-Earner in the Western Movement," Part 1, *Political Science Quarterly* 50 (June 1935): 161–85, and Part 2 (March 1936): 61–116; William L. Burton, *Melting Pot Soldiers: The Union's Ethnic Regiments* (New York: Fordham University Press, 1998), 55, 68.

44. James McPherson contends that 10 percent of soldier recruits could hope to jump classes as they grew older and gained experience; see McPherson, *Battle Cry of Freedom*, 608; see also Stephan Thernstrom, *The Other Bostonians: Poverty and Progress in the American Metropolis, 1880–1970* (Cambridge: Harvard University Press, 1973), 234.

45. Log Entries, 1 July, 14 October 1864, William Wainwright Log, G. W. Blunt White Library, Mystic Seaport Museum; William Keeler to Anna Keeler, 11 April 1863, in Robert W. Daly, ed., *Aboard the USS Florida, 1863–65: The Letters of Paymaster William Frederick Keeler, U.S. Navy, to His Wife, Anna* (Annapolis: Naval Institute Press, 1968), 18–19.

46. William Van Cleaf to Mother, 15, 16 February 1862, William Van Cleaf Papers, Special Collections and University Archives, Rutgers University, New Brunswick, N.J.

47. Anonymous, "Life on a Block-ader," *Continental Monthly* 6 (July 1864): 49.

48. Broadside titled "Here Is a Chance!" 17 July 1864, Smith-Spooner Collection, Manuscripts, Huntington Library.

49. Rediker, *Between the Devil and the Deep Blue Sea*, 155–56; Gary B. Nash, *The Urban Crucible: Social Change, Political Consciousness, and the Origins of the American Revolution* (Cambridge: Harvard University Press, 1979), 63–64. Nash contends that seamen and widows made up the bottom 30 percent of Boston's economic strata, labeling them "struggling, disease-prone, ill-paid." Many Union sailors lacked not only a marketable skill but also the education necessary for social mobility. According to a limited sample of 1,196 Union sailors collected by the Sanitary Commission, only three (.25 percent) had finished college, two had finished high school (.16 percent), and no one had attended a professional school. One hundred and fifty-three, close to 13 percent (12.8 percent), had never gone to any school, and 138 (11.5 percent) had only a slight education. The majority of sampled sailors possessed what the commission called a "limited common school" education. An amazing 69 percent of sailors possessed only a limited amount of elementary education. Although a sizable number of soldiers in the sample had a limited common school category, 45 percent of soldiers possessed what the Sanitary

Commission termed a "good common school" or "high school education." See Gould, *Sanitary Memoirs of the War of the Rebellion*, 569–73; Carl F. Kaestle, *Pillars of the Republic: Common Schools and American Society, 1780–1860* (New York: Hill and Wang, 1983), xi–xii.

50. Goodrich and Davidson, "The Wage-Earner in the Western Movement," Part 1 and Part 2; Langley, *Social Reform in the United States Navy*, viii; Karsten, *The Naval Aristocracy*, 77; Murray Kane, "Some Considerations on the Safety Valve Doctrine," *Mississippi Valley Historical Review* 23 (September 1936): 169–88; Fred Shannon, "A Post-mortem on the Safety-Valve Labor Theory," *Agricultural History* 19 (January 1945): 31–37.

51. Wiley, *The Life of Billy Yank*, 38; Log Entries, 21 October 1862, 7 November 1862, Milo Lacy Log, Manuscripts, Naval Historical Center Library, Washington Navy Yard, Washington, D.C.; Autobiography Entry, 19 June 1862, "The Autobiography of Tim Finn, 1854–1896," Manuscripts, Center for American History, University of Texas, Austin, Tex.; George Geer to Wife, 26 March 1862, in William Marvel, ed., *The Monitor Chronicles: One Sailor's Account* (New York: Simon and Schuster, 2000), 42; Rendezvous Sample, Rendezvous Reports.

52. Rorabaugh, "Who Fought for the North in the Civil War?" 700. For a look at the fears expressed by skilled workers, journeymen, and apprentices, see Steven J. Ross, *Workers on the Edge: Work, Leisure, and Politics in Industrializing Cincinnati, 1788–1890* (New York: Columbia University Press, 1985); Daniel J. Walkowitz, *Worker*

*City, Company Town: Iron and Cotton-Workers in Troy and Cohoes, New York, 1855–1884* (Urbana: University of Illinois Press, 1978); W. J. Rorabaugh, *The Craft Apprentice: From Franklin to the Machine Age in America* (New York: Oxford University Press, 1986).

53. Rendezvous Sample, Rendezvous Reports. Richard B. Stott contends that after 1840 most American workers were immigrants and by the 1850s the waves of immigrants had "remade" the American working class into the immigrant working class; see Stott, *Workers in the Metropolis*, 4. See also Robert Ernst, *Immigrant Life in New York City, 1825–1863* (New York: King's Crown Press, 1949), viii.

54. Francis R. Minton, ed., *Journal of Patrick Meade, Jr.* (Medford, Mass.: n.p., 1984), 3.

55. Burton, *Melting Pot Soldiers*, 55, 68.

56. Frederick Harrod, *Manning the New Navy: The Development of a Modern Naval Enlisted Force, 1899–1940* (Westport, Conn.: Greenwood Press, 1978), 15–18; *An Act for the Regulation of Seamen on Board the Public and Private Vessels of the United States*, 12th Cong., 2d sess., 3 March 1813, in *Annals of the Congress of the United States: The Debates and Proceedings in the Congress of the United States* (Washington, D.C.: Gales and Seaton, 1853), appendix, 1339–41; Browning, *From Cape Charles to Cape Fear*, 202; U.S. Congress, House of Representatives, *Report of the Secretary of the Navy Transmitting the Instructions Issued to the Officers of the Several Departments for the Enlistment of Seamen for the United States Navy*, House Exec. Doc. No. 7, 37th Cong., 1st sess., 13 July 1861 (ser. 1114),

1–4; Dale T. Knobel, *Paddy and the Republic: Ethnicity and Nationality in Antebellum America* (Middletown, Conn.: Wesleyan University Press, 1986), 138–39, 171–74, 177.

57. Rendezvous Sample, Rendezvous Reports.

58. The percentages and numbers of foreign-born soldiers are based on the following sources: Gould, *Sanitary Memoirs of the War of the Rebellion*, 27–28; William F. Fox, *Regimental Losses in the American Civil War, 1861–1865* (Albany, N.Y.: Joseph McDonough, 1898), 62–63; Ella Lonn, *Foreigners in the Union Army and Navy* (Baton Rouge: Louisiana State University Press, 1951), 90–110, 146, 578, 663–72; Wiley, *The Life of Billy Yank*, 307; McPherson, *Battle Cry of Freedom*, 607; Diary Entry, 6 June 1863, in Howard K. Beale, ed., *Diary of Gideon Welles: Secretary of the Navy under Lincoln and Johnson*, 2 vols. (New York: W. W. Norton, 1960), 1:324.

59. Harrod, *Manning the New Navy*, 14–16.

60. Still, "The Common Sailor," 27.

61. Rendezvous Sample, Rendezvous Reports; Log Entries, 25 May, 15 November 1863, Poole Log; Diary Entry, 2 July 1863, Fayette Clapp Diary, 1862–1863, Western Historical Manuscript Collection, Ellis Library, University of Missouri, Columbia, Mo.; Alvah F. Hunter, *A Year on a Monitor and the Destruction of Fort Sumter*, ed. Craig L. Symonds (Columbia: University of South Carolina Press, 1987), 41; Henry Clay to Nellie Demarest, 22 September 1864, Abraham Demarest Papers, Special Collections and University Archives, Rutgers University.

62. Gustavus Vasa Fox to Samuel Lee, 8 April 1864, ORN, 9:589; Karsten, *The Naval Aristocracy*, 214.

63. John Swift to Mother, 6 March 1865, in Swift, "Letters from a Sailor on a Tinclad," 57–58, 61; John P. Brogan, "A Winter's Cruise during the Civil War," 26, 28, 30, John P. Brogan Journal, William Pendleton Palmer Collection, Manuscripts, Western Reserve Historical Society, Cleveland, Ohio.

64. Rendezvous Sample, Rendezvous Reports. Wiley, *The Life of Billy Yank*, 308.

65. The percentages of foreign-born sailors are from the Rendezvous Sample, Rendezvous Reports. These percentages are consistent with the limited research done in the past on the ethnicity of Union sailors. Based on the ships' muster rolls she examined, Ella Lonn concluded that while foreign influence varied in the Union navy, anywhere between one-fourth to one-half of crews were foreign-born; see Lonn, *Foreigners in the Union Army and Navy*, 637–38, 640. In a more recent study limited to the composition of the crew of the USS *Cairo*, David F. Riggs concludes that one-third of the crew was foreign-born; see Riggs, "Sailors of the U.S.S. Cairo," 269.

66. Rendezvous Sample, Rendezvous Reports.

67. George Geer to Wife, 29 May 1862, 16 November 1862, in Marvel, *The Monitor Chronicles*, 91, 207.

68. Log Entry, 12 February 1864, Poole Log; William Keeler to Anna Keeler, 20 July 1863, in Daly, *Aboard the USS Florida*, 70.

69. Burton, *Melting Pot Soldiers*, 55.

70. William E. Hinch to Brothers,

25 December 1864, William E. Hinch Papers, Manuscripts, Historical Society of Pennsylvania, Philadelphia, Pa.

71. Charles O. Paullin, *Paullin's History of Naval Administration, 1775–1911* (Annapolis: Naval Institute Press, 1968), 303.

72. Robert Bennet Forbes, *The Voyage of the Jamestown on Her Errand of Mercy* (Boston: Eastburn Press, 1847).

73. An 1839 directive from Acting Secretary of the Navy Isaac Chauncey instructed that recruiting stations "not . . . enter a greater proportion of free colored persons than 5 percent of the whole number of white persons entered . . . weekly or monthly, and in no instance and under no circumstances to enter a slave." See Acting Secretary of the Navy Isaac Chauncey to John Downs, Commander of the Boston Naval Office, 19 April 1839, in Herbert Aptheker, "The Negro in the Union Navy," *Journal of Negro History* 32 (April 1947): 173 n. 15. The navy seems to have followed this guideline until the Civil War; see Secretary of the Navy A. P. Upshur to Speaker of the House, 10 August 1842, in House Exec. Doc. No. 282, 27th Cong., 2d sess. (ser. 405).

74. Andrew H. Foote to Leonard Paulding, 17 September 1861, ORN, 22:337.

75. Still, "The Common Sailor," 28; Gideon Welles to Louis M. Goldsborough, 25 September 1861, ORN, 6:252; McPherson, *Battle Cry of Freedom*, 564. The Militia Bill of July 1862 authorized the enlistment of slaves in the army. Formal organization of black regiments began in August 1862.

76. Aptheker, "The Negro in the Union Navy," 179.

77. David L. Valuska, *The African American in the Union Navy, 1861–1865* (New York: Garland, 1993), 9.

78. Joseph P. Reidy, "Black Jack: African American Sailors in the Civil War Navy," in William B. Cogar, ed., *New Interpretations in Naval History: Selected Papers from the Twelfth Naval History Symposium* (Annapolis: Naval Institute Press, 1997), 213; Ringle, *Life in Mr. Lincoln's Navy*, 14; Browning, *From Cape Charles to Cape Fear*, 204.

79. Journal Entry, 23 September 1861, Henneberry Journal; Milligan, "Navy Life on the Mississippi River," 16, 66; William N. Bock to Father, 15 January 1863, Bock Papers; Avery, "Gun-Boat Service on the James River," 37–38; Mitchell, *Civil War Soldiers*, 20–23; Mitchell, *The Vacant Chair*, 16–18.

80. McPherson, *For Cause and Comrades*, 5–13.

81. Linderman, *Embattled Courage*, 20–21.

82. Secretary of the Navy, *Report of the Secretary of the Navy, 1866*, 34.

83. Lemisch, "Jack Tar in the Streets," 377; Jesse Lemisch, *Jack Tar vs. John Bull: The Role of New York's Seamen in Precipitating the Revolution* (New York: Garland Press, 1997), 8–9.

84. Joseph McDonald, "How I Saw the Monitor-Merrimac Fight," *New England Magazine* 36 (July 1907): 548.

85. Browning, *From Cape Charles to Cape Fear*, 202; James M. Merrill, *The Rebel Shore: The Story of Union Sea Power in the Civil War* (Boston: Little, Brown, 1957), 61.

86. Still, "The Common Sailor," 27–28.

87. Log Entry, 20 December 1862, Poole Log.

88. Journal Entry, 23 September 1861, Henneberry Journal; Milligan, "Navy Life on the Mississippi River," 16, 66.

89. William E. Hinch to Brothers, 25 December 1864, Hinch Papers.

90. Log Entry, 18 August 1862, Poole Log.

91. Joseph Osborne to Mary Osborne, 27 October 1864, 5 January 1865, Osborne Family Papers; Log Entry, 25 November 1862, Wainwright Log; William Marvel, *The Alabama and the Kearsarge: The Sailor's Civil War* (Chapel Hill: University of North Carolina Press, 1996), 206–12; Merrill, *The Rebel Shore*, 61.

92. Samuel J. Bartlett to Brother, 16 March 1863, in L. Moody Simms Jr., ed., "A Union Volunteer with the Mississippi Ram Fleet," *Lincoln Herald* 70 (Winter 1968): 189–92, 191.

93. Log Entry, 1 February 1864, Poole Log.

94. Rowland Stafford True, "Life aboard a Gunboat," *Civil War Times Illustrated* 9 (February 1971): 39; Edward A. Pierson to Auntie, 25 April 1862, Edward A. Pierson Papers, New Jersey Historical Society, Newark, N.J.

95. John Swift to Mother, 2 July 1863, in Swift, "Letters from a Sailor on a Tinclad," 49; William N. Bock to Mother, 5 May 1864, Bock Papers.

96. Joseph B. Osborne to Mary Osborne, 27 October 1864, Osborne Family Papers.

97. George Geer to Wife, 6 January 1863, in Marvel, *The Monitor Chronicles*, 232; Frederic Sherman to Father, 22 September 1862, Frederic Sherman Letters, Southern Historical Collection, Wilson Library, University of North Carolina, Chapel Hill, N.C.

98. Hirsch, "Gunboat Personnel on the Western Waters," 83.

99. Diary Entry, 15 February 1862, The Civil War Diary of John G. Morrison, 1861–1865, Naval Historical Foundation Collection, Washington Navy Yard, Washington, D.C.

100. William Van Cleaf to Mother, 12, 16 February, 14 March, 29 May 1862, Van Cleaf Papers.

101. Gideon Welles to Captain Charles H. Davis, 8 August 1862, Box 356, NR, 1861–65, Transfer of Enlisted Men from Army to the Navy, Navy Subject File; Ringle, *Life in Mr. Lincoln's Navy*, 22–23; Browning, *From Cape Charles to Cape Fear*, 202–6.

102. C. G. Leland, "The Soldier and the Civilian," *Continental Monthly* 2 (July–December 1862): 282.

103. Gideon Welles to Captain Charles H. Davis, 8 August 1862, Box 356, NR, Regulations Governing Enlistments, Navy Subject File.

104. Diary Entry, 26 August 1864, in Beale, *Diary of Gideon Welles*, 2:121.

105. Gustavus Vasa Fox to Mr. Sedgewick, 14 August 1862, Gustavus Vasa Fox Papers, Manuscripts, New-York Historical Society.

106. Diary Entry, 26 August 1864, in Beale, *Diary of Gideon Welles*, 2:121.

107. Walter S. Thomas to David D. Porter, 31 December 1863, Porter Papers.

108. Broadside titled "Serve Your Country without Conscription," 8 December 1863, and broadside titled "The Conscript Bill!" n.d., Box 356, NR, 1861–65, Recruiting Posters, Navy Subject File.

109. Log Entry, 1 September 1864, Wainwright Log.

110. Joseph Osborne to Mary Os-

borne, 27 October 1864, 5 January 1865, Osborne Family Papers.

111. Log Entry, 1 September 1864, Wainwright Log; Browning, *From Cape Charles to Cape Fear*, 202; George Geer to Wife, 15 July 1862, in Marvel, *The Monitor Chronicles*, 127; Log Entry, 2 September 1862, Lacy Log.

112. Wiley, *The Life of Billy Yank*, 37–38; Emerson D. Fite, *Social and Industrial Conditions in the North during the Civil War* (1910; reprint, New York: Frederick Ungar, 1963), 183.

113. The custom of awarding prize money had originated in the British Royal Navy. The Union navy adopted the practice as part of its blockade policy. Robert W. Daly, "Pay and Prize Money in the Old Navy, 1776–1899," *U.S. Naval Institute Proceedings* 74 (August 1948): 967.

114. "The Conscript Bill!" Navy Subject File; William Van Cleaf to Mother, 15, 16 February 1862, Van Cleaf Papers; Charles J. Hill to William Thoms, 3 December 1863, William F. Thoms Papers, Letters from Seamen, New York Nautical School, 1853–1864, Manuscripts, New-York Historical Society; George Arnold to Brother, 29 December 1863, in Arthur M. Schlesinger Jr., ed., "A Blue Bluejacket's Letters Home, 1863–1864," *New England Quarterly* 1 (October 1928): 559; Edward Blue to Frank H. Stickney, 19 May 1864, Frank L. Stickney Papers, Naval Historical Foundation Collection, Library of Congress; Log Entry, 23 November 1862, Wainwright Log; Joseph T. Collins to Mother and Father, 19 January 1863, James B. and Joseph T. Collins Papers, Manuscripts, New-York Historical Society; C. R. P.

Rodgers to Gideon Welles, 9 January 1865, ORN, 3:406; D. H. Sumner to Abraham Lincoln, 23 February 1865, ORN, 3:82; Samuel F. Du Pont to Gustavus Vasa Fox, 7 July 1862, ORN, 13:173.

115. Autobiography Entry, 9 May 1861, "The Autobiography of Tim Finn"; William H. Anderson, "Blockade Life," in *War Papers Read before the Commandery of the State of Maine, Military Order of the Loyal Legion of the United States* (Portland: Lefavor-Tower, 1898), 3; Log Entry, 21 October 1862, Lacy Log; Cornelius Cronin, *Recollection of Service in the U.S. Navy: Being Reminiscences as They Have Occurred to My Mind from the Commencement and pending the Late War; while Serving on the U.S. Ships Sabine, Brooklyn, and Richmond* (n.p., 1894), 3; Log Entries, 1 July, 14 October 1864, Wainwright Log; John Truesdale, "Bluecoats Afloat," in *The Bluecoats, and How They Lived, Fought and Died for the Union* (Philadelphia: Jones Brothers, 1867), 464; Edward Everett, "Address of Mr. Everett at the Opening of the Fair," *Boatswain's Whistle*, 12 November 1864, 26, Americana Catalogue, Huntington Library; Wait, "The Blockading Service," 227; Ann Preston to Fowler Preston, 30 April 1862, Preston Family Papers; Fowler Preston to Ann Preston, 13 May 1862, Preston Family Papers; Wallace Preston to Ann Preston, 6 July 1864, Preston Family Papers.

116. General Order of Gideon Welles, 23 December 1861, Box 356, NR, 1861–65, Regulations Regarding Enlistments, Navy Subject File. This practice had been common among tra-

ditional maritime wage arrangements; see Rediker, *Between the Devil and the Deep Blue Sea*, 125–26.

117. Browning, *From Cape Charles to Cape Fear*, 206.

118. George Geer to Wife, 18 March 1862, in Marvel, *The Monitor Chronicles*, 39; Log Entry, 2 September 1862, Lacy Log; John Henry Taylor to Wife and Children, 5 January 1862, in Alice P. Mortensen and Edwin H. Mortensen, eds., *The Family of John Henry Taylor, Jr.: Featuring Family Letters Written during and after the Civil War* (Baltimore: Gateway Press, 1995), 3–4.

119. Gideon Welles reported that in New York and Philadelphia a large number of recent immigrants "sought employment on our public vessels as landsmen under the general depression of business"; see *Report of the Secretary of the Navy Transmitting the Instructions Issued to the Officers of the Several Departments for the Enlistment of Seamen for the United States Navy*, 1–4.

120. Andrew H. Foote to Gideon Welles, 30 September 1861, ORN, 22:355.

121. John D. Harty to David D. Porter, 21 February 1864, Porter Papers.

122. Rorabaugh, "Who Fought for the North in the Civil War?" 697; George Geer to Wife, 24 May 1862, in Marvel, *The Monitor Chronicles*, 87.

123. The name did not originate with the war but from the Royal Navy. Officers and civilians had used the term to caricature the personality and behavior of the hard characters who joined on as British seamen; see John Laffin, *Jack Tar: The Story of the British Sailor* (London: Cassel, 1969), 88–95; Journal Entry, 5 February 1862,

Anonymous, Journal aboard USS Ino, February 5, 1862–June 3, 1862, G. W. Blunt White Library, Mystic Seaport Museum; George Bright to Father, 25 October 1863, George Adams Bright Collection, Manuscripts, Huntington Library; Journal Entry, 15 May 1862, Carsten DeWitt Journal, G. W. Blunt White Library, Mystic Seaport Museum; Ludwell H. Johnson, *Red River Campaign: Politics and Cotton in the Civil War* (Baltimore: Johns Hopkins University Press, 1958), 101–3; Everett, "Address of Mr. Everett at the Opening of the Fair," 26; George Bright to Father, 27 November 1864, Bright Collection; William Keeler to Anna Keeler, 20 July 1863, in Daly, *Aboard the USS Florida*, 70–71.

124. Diary Entries, 13, 25 April 1863, in Charles A. Post, "A Diary on the Blockade in 1863," *United States Naval Institute Proceedings* 44 (March 1918): 2349, 2359; Joseph Fry to Wife, 28 November 1861, Joseph Fry Papers, Manuscripts, New-York Historical Society.

125. Ringle, *Life in Mr. Lincoln's Navy*, 29–31.

126. Gould, *Sanitary Memoirs of the War of the Rebellion*, 132–43, 286–91.

127. Rendezvous Sample, Rendezvous Reports; "Descriptive List of Enlisted Men on Gunboat USS Reindeer," Smith-Spooner Collection; George Geer to Wife, 24 May 1862, in Marvel, *The Monitor Chronicles*, 87.

128. See William H. Goetzmann, "The Mountain Man as Jacksonian Man," *American Quarterly* 15 (Fall 1963): 403–4.

129. Stott, *Workers in the Metropolis*, 248; Sean Wilentz, *Chants Demo-*

cratic: New York City and the Rise of the American Working Class, 1788–1850 (New York: Oxford University Press, 1984), 53–60; Rediker, *Between the Devil and the Deep Blue Sea*, 8; Harrod, *Manning the New Navy*, 17–18. Yet, the group may be broader in scope than just economic. Charles Sellers has written about a "subsistence culture" directly opposed to the market revolution and its repressive middle-class values, a culture that embraced equality, masculinity, charity, alcohol, and sexual freedom; see Sellers, *The Market Revolution*, 6, 9–19, 237–60, 444. Also see W. J. Rorabaugh, *The Alcoholic Republic: An American Tradition* (New York: Oxford University Press, 1979), xi.

130. George Bright to Father, 25 October 1863, Bright Collection; William Keeler to Anna Keeler, 11 April 1863, in Daly, *Aboard the USS Florida*, 17–19; Theodore Lyman to Kate Hamlin, 21 October 1864, Lyman Family Papers, Manuscripts, New-York Historical Society. Amy S. Greenberg contends that as Northern society became more domesticated, feminized, and harnessed, certain types of men sought out enclaves where they could reaffirm and exercise their values; see Greenberg, *Cause for Alarm: The Volunteer Fire Department in the Nineteenth-Century City* (Princeton: Princeton University Press, 1998), 6–9, 56, 80–91.

131. Michael Barton, *Goodmen: The Character of Civil War Soldiers* (University Park: Pennsylvania State University Press, 1981), 2–4; Earl J. Hess, *Liberty, Virtue, and Progress: The Northerners and Their War for Union* (New York: New York Uni-

versity Press, 1988), 1; Mitchell, *The Vacant Chair*, 25, 31, 57, 102.

132. Andrew H. Foote to Henry H. Halleck, 25 February 1862, ORN, 22:632; James Birtwistle to Dr. William F. Thoms, 8 November 1862, Thoms Papers; I. E. Vail, *Three Years on the Blockade: A Naval Experience* (New York: Abbey Press, 1902), 156; George E. Clark, *Seven Years of a Sailor's Life* (Boston: Adams, 1867), 170–71.

133. Francis A. Roe to Captain Henry W. Morris, 30 April 1862, ORN, 18:204; David D. Porter to Acting Master A. S. Bowen, 19 August 1863, ORN, 25:374.

134. David D. Porter to Andrew H. Foote, 16 May 1863, ORN, 24:677–78; Hirsch, "Gunboat Personnel on the Western Waters," 85.

135. Browning, *From Cape Charles to Cape Fear*, 201–2; True, "Life aboard a Gunboat," 37; *Report of the Secretary of the Navy Transmitting the Instructions Issued to the Officers of the Several Departments for the Enlistment of Seamen for the United States Navy*, 2; William Keeler to Anna Keeler, 11 April 1863, in Daly, *Aboard the USS Florida*, 18–19.

136. Andrew H. Foote to D. A. Raxford, 30 September 1861, ORN, 22:353; Andrew Hull Foote to Gideon Welles, 22 January 1862, ORN, 22:515; Charles Ellet Jr. to Edwin M. Stanton, 26 April 1862, ORN, 23:75; Order of the Secretary of the Navy to Commodore Wilkes, 31 July 1862, ORN, 7:606; George McClellan to Commodore Wilkes, 1 August 1862, ORN, 7:611; Captain Armstrong Explanatory Statement, 24 April 1861, ORN, 4:50; Gideon Welles to John Rodgers,

20 September 1864, ORN, 3:219; John Dahlgren to Assistant Secretary of the Navy, 18 October 1863, ORN, 15:51.

137. David D. Porter to Andrew H. Foote, 16 May 1863, ORN, 24:678.

138. Karsten, *The Naval Aristocracy*, 52, 84.

139. Diary Entry, n.d. [15 September 1861], Diary of John B. Wirts, Cruise of the Lancaster in the North and South Pacific from May 12, 1859, to October 15, 1861, Special Collections, University of California at Los Angeles, Los Angeles, Calif.

140. Vail, *Three Years on the Blockade*, 156; Francis B. Butts, "Reminiscences of Gunboat Service on the Nansemond," in *Personal Narratives of the Events in the War of Rebellion, Being Papers Read Before Rhode Island Soldiers and Sailors Historical Society*, 3d ser. (Providence: N. B. Williams, 1884), 7; Log Entries, 1 July, 1 September, 14 October, 3 November 1864, Wainwright Log.

141. James Birtwistle to Dr. William F. Thoms, 8 November 1862, Thoms Papers; Diary Entry, 2 March 1864, in Lawrence Van Alstyne, *Diary of an Enlisted Man* (New Haven, Conn.: Tuttle, Morehouse and Taylor, 1910), 276.

142. Clark, *Seven Years of a Sailor's Life*, 170–71; William Van Cleaf to Mother, 5 September 1862, Van Cleaf Papers; Memorandum Book Entry, 17 March 1864, Alexander R. Miller Memorandum Book of the U.S. Steamers DeKalb and Lafayette, 1861–64, Louisiana and Lower Mississippi Valley Collections, Hill Memorial Library, Louisiana State University, Baton Rouge, La.; William Bock to Father, 19 April 1864, Bock Papers; William Keeler to Anna Keeler, 4 February 1864, in Daly, *Aboard the USS Florida*,

144; Edward T. Barker to Mother, 3, 19 March 1862, Barker-Edes-Noyes Collection, Manuscripts, Massachusetts Historical Society; Journal Entry, 3 May 1863, Journal of Thomas Lyons, Journal Kept on Board U.S. Steam Gunboat Carondolet and U.S.S. Lafayette, 8 January 1863–20 January 1863, Manuscripts, Library of Congress; Ludwell Johnson, *Red River Campaign*, 101–3; Jonathan A. Duble to Charles H. Davis, 18 June 1862, ORN, 23:180; Journal Entry, 28 February 1862, DeWitt Journal; Swift, "Letters from a Sailor on a Tinclad," 57; Avery, "Gun-Boat Service on the James River," 37–38.

143. Log Entry, 26 August 1863, Lacy Log.

144. Lemisch, "Jack Tar in the Streets," 377.

145. Journal Entry, 1 November 1865, Journal of Donald C. McLaren, July 25, 1865, to October 24, 1867, P. H. W. Smith Collection, Manuscripts, New Jersey Historical Society; Diary Entry, 15 September 1861, Wirts Diary; George R. Vance to Father, 29 December 1861, Samuel C. Vance Papers, Indiana Historical Society, Indianapolis, Ind.; Secretary of the Navy, *Report of the Secretary of the Navy, with an Appendix Containing Reports from Officers, December 1866* (Washington, D.C.: Government Printing Office, 1866), 34; Rorabaugh, *The Alcoholic Republic*, 144.

146. Log Entries, 1 July, 14 October 1864, Wainwright Log; William F. Keeler to Anna Keeler, 3 November 1863, in Daly, *Aboard the USS Florida*, 108–9.

147. Log Entries, 1 July, 14 October 1864, Wainwright Log; Diary Entry, n.d. [September–October 1861], Wirts Diary; Alger, "Effect of Sea Life on

Land Life," 5; Diary Entry, 23 February 1862, Morrison Diary.

148. Barton, *Goodmen*, 3–4; Bell I. Wiley, "Johnny Reb and Billy Yank Compared," *American History Illustrated* 3 (April 1968): 4–9, 44–47; William R. Taylor, *Cavalier and Yankee: The Old South and the American National Character* (1961; reprint, Garden City, N.Y.: Doubleday Books, 1963), xxi.

149. Wilentz, *Chants Democratic*, 53–60.

150. Alger, "Effect of Sea Life on Land Life," 5; Charles Rockwell, *Sketches of Foreign Travel and Life at Sea* (Boston: Tappan and Dennet, 1842), 2:389.

151. Francis A. Roe, *Naval Duties and Discipline, with the Policy and Principles of Naval Organization* (New York: D. Van Nostrand, 1865), 138.

152. William F. Hutchinson, "Life on the Texan Blockade," in *Personal Narratives of Events in the War of Rebellion, Being Papers Read before the Rhode Island Soldiers and Sailors Historical Society*, 3d ser. (Providence: N. B. Williams, 1883), 23; Log Entry, 12 January 1864, Poole Log.

153. Log Entries, 25 May 1863, 12 January 1864, Poole Log; Hutchinson, "Life on the Texan Blockade," 23; Diary Entry, 1 April 1865, Frank Judd Diary, Historical Society of Pennsylvania.

154. Minton, *Journal of Patrick Meade*, 18; Log Entry, 18 February 1864, in Kent Packard, ed., "Jottings by the Way: A Sailor's Log—1862 to 1864," Part 2, *Pennsylvania Magazine of History and Biography* 71 (July 1947): 262.

155. Log Entries, 9 December 1863, 21 January 1864, in Packard, "Jottings

by the Way," Part 2, 249, 256; Diary Entry, 28 November 1862, Diary of George R. Yost, Illinois State Historical Library.

156. Master E. B. Hussey to Commander J. M. B. Clitz, 27 March 1864, Box 284, Naval Justice, 1860–1870, Folder 1, Minor Delinquencies and Cases Where There Is No Record That a Court Martial Was Held, Navy Subject File; Court of Enquiry on the Fernandina, 3 May 1862, Box 284, Naval Justice, 1860–1870, Navy Subject File; A. Farenholt, "And There Were Giants in Those Days," 8, Box 298, Naval Living Conditions, Navy Subject File.

157. John Harty to Andrew H. Foote, 21 May 1862, in James M. Merrill, "Cairo, Illinois: Strategic Civil War River Port," *Journal of Illinois History* 76 (Winter 1983): 638.

158. Still, "The Common Sailor," 35; Diary Entry, 7 March 1863, Charles A. Hart Diary, History and Genealogy, Connecticut State Library, Hartford, Conn.; Diary Entry, 1 December 1861, in Charles W. Wills, *Army Life of an Illinois Soldier: Including a Day-by-Day Record of Sherman's March to the Sea*, comp. Mary E. Kellogg (Carbondale: Southern Illinois University Press, 1996), 46.

159. Clark, *Seven Years of a Sailor's Life*, 246–47; Log Entries, 9 December 1863, 21 January 1864, in Packard, "Jottings by the Way," Part 2, 249, 256.

160. Roe, *Naval Duties and Discipline*, 138.

161. Rediker, *Between the Devil and the Deep Blue Sea*, 146–49; Alger, "Effect of Sea Life on Land Life," 5; William Keeler to Anna Keeler, 29 September 1863, in Daly, *Aboard the USS Florida*, 98; Diary Entry, 16 February 1865, Judd Diary; Paul A. Gilje, "The

Meaning of Freedom for Waterfront Workers," in *Devising Liberty: Preserving and Creating Freedom in the New American Republic*, ed. David Thomas Konig (Stanford: Stanford University Press, 1995), 115.

162. Joseph B. Osborne to Mary Osborne, 16 October 1864, Osborne Family Papers; Roe, *Naval Duties and Discipline*, 139; Alger, "Effect of Sea Life on Land Life," 5.

163. Log Entry, 16 June 1864, in Packard, "Jottings by the Way," Part 2, 267–68; George Geer to Wife, 13 September 1862, in Marvel, *The Monitor Chronicles*, 184.

164. William Van Cleaf to Mother, 5 September 1862, Van Cleaf Papers; Memorandum Book Entry, 17 March 1864, Miller Memorandum Book; William Bock to Father, 19 April 1864, Bock Papers; William Keeler to Anna Keeler, 4 February 1864, in Daly, *Aboard the USS Florida*, 144; Edward T. Barker to Mother, 3, 19 March 1862, Barker-Edes-Noyes Collection; Journal Entry, 3 May 1863, Lyons Journal.

165. William Keeler to Anna Keeler, 4 February 1864, in Daly, *Aboard the USS Florida*, 144–45; Edward T. Barker to Mother, 3, 19 March 1862, Barker-Edes-Noyes Collection; Journal Entry, 3 May 1863, Lyons Journal; Ludwell Johnson, *Red River Campaign*, 101–3.

166. William Van Cleaf to Mother, 14 March 1862, 5 September 1862, Van Cleaf Papers; Memorandum Book Entries, 31 October 1862, 17 March 1864, Miller Memorandum Book; William Bock to Father, 19 April 1864, Bock Papers; Journal Entry, 17 August 1863, Henneberry Journal; Frederic Sherman to Mother, 7 March 1863, Sherman Letters; Autobiography

Entry, 9 May 1861, "The Autobiography of Tim Finn"; Journal Entry, 28 February 1862, DeWitt Journal; Still, "The Common Sailor," 31.

167. Alger, "Effect of Sea Life on Land Life," 5.

168. Diary Entry, n.d. [September–October 1861], Wirts Diary.

169. Roe, *Naval Duties and Discipline*, 139.

170. Alger, "Effect of Sea Life on Land Life," 5.

171. Log Entry, 16 June 1864, in Packard, "Jottings by the Way," Part 2, 267–68.

172. John W. Dempsey to Sister, 14 December 1863, Miscellaneous Manuscripts, 1856–1864, Massachusetts Historical Society.

173. Freeman Foster to Father, 15 May 1862, Freeman Foster Papers, Louisiana and Lower Mississippi Valley Collections, Louisiana State University; Memorandum Book Entries, 28 June 1862, 21 May 1863, Miller Memorandum Book; Journal Entries, 30 November 1862, 18 April 1864, Henneberry Journal.

174. George Geer to Wife, 16 April, 18 July 1862, in Marvel, *The Monitor Chronicles*, 54, 133.

175. John H. Taylor to Wife and Children, 18 April 1862, in Mortensen and Mortensen, *The Family of John Henry Taylor*, 22–23.

176. Secretary of the Navy, *Report of the Secretary of the Navy, 1866*, 34.

CHAPTER 2
1. Secretary of the Navy to Hannibal Hamlin, 30 March 1864, in U.S. Congress, Senate, *Transfer of Seamen from the Army*, Senate Exec. Doc. No. 33, 38th Cong., 1st sess. (ser. 1176), 4.

2. Autobiography Entry, 15 May

1861, "The Autobiography of Tim Finn, 1854–1896," Center for American History, University of Texas, Austin, Tex.; Stephen F. Blanding, *Recollections of a Sailor Boy; or, The Cruise of the Gunboat Louisiana* (Providence: E. A. Johnson, 1886), 9; Peter Karsten, *The Naval Aristocracy: The Golden Age of Annapolis and the Emergence of Modern American Navalism* (New York: Free Press, 1972), 51.

3. U.S. Congress, House of Representatives, *Report of the Secretary of the Navy Transmitting the Instructions Issued to the Officers of the Several Departments for the Enlistment of Seamen for the United States Navy*, House Exec. Doc. No. 7, 37th Cong., 1st sess., 13 July 1861 (ser. 1114), 1–2; Secretary of the Navy, *Report of the Secretary of the Navy, with an Appendix Containing Reports from Officers, December 1862* (Washington, D.C.: Government Printing Office, 1862), 24; Secretary of the Navy, *Report of the Secretary of the Navy, with an Appendix Containing Reports from Officers, December 1863* (Washington, D.C.: Government Printing Office, 1863), xxv–xxvi; D. R. Jenkins to Gideon Welles, 28 January 1864, Gideon Welles Papers, Manuscripts, Huntington Library, San Marino, Calif.

4. Secretary of the Navy, *Report of the Secretary of the Navy, with an Appendix Containing Reports from Officers, December 1865* (Washington, D.C.: Government Printing Office, 1865), xiii. Using a sample of 4,570 sailors out of the total 118,044 men who enlisted at United States Navy Rendezvous between April 1861 and April 1865, I found that only 22 percent listed their prewar occupation

as "sailor," "seaman," "waterman," "mariner," or "boatman." The sample was collected by taking the name and descriptive information of every twenty-fifth recruit appearing in enlistment returns between April 1861 and April 1865 (hereafter cited as the "Rendezvous Sample"), in *Enlistment Returns, Changes, and Reports, 1846–1942, Weekly Returns of Enlistments at Naval Rendezvous, January 6, 1855–August 8, 1891*, vols. 17–43, Record Group 24, Records of the Bureau of Naval Personnel, National Archives Building, Washington, D.C. (hereafter cited as "Rendezvous Reports").

5. John D. Milligan, *Gunboats down the Mississippi* (Annapolis: Naval Institute Press, 1965), 9, 25–26.

6. Letterbook Entry, 5 February 1862, Letterbook of Edward Tobey Barker, Barker-Edes-Noyes Collection, Massachusetts Historical Society, Boston, Mass.

7. Blanding, *Recollections of a Sailor Boy*, 9–25; George E. Clark, *Seven Years of a Sailor's Life* (Boston: Adams, 1867), 170–71; United States Navy, *Regulations for the Government of the United States Navy 1865* (Washington, D.C.: Government Printing Office, 1865), 179.

8. Aubrey Henry Polser, "The Administration of the United States Navy, 1861–1865" (Ph.D. diss., University of Nebraska, 1975), 152–53; Dennis J. Ringle, *Life in Mr. Lincoln's Navy* (Annapolis: Naval Institute Press, 1998), 26–28.

9. Autobiography Entry, 15 May 1861, "The Autobiography of Tim Finn."

10. Alvah F. Hunter, *A Year on a Monitor and the Destruction of Fort*

*Sumter*, ed. Craig L. Symonds (Columbia: University of South Carolina Press, 1987), 8.

11. William Still, "The Common Sailor: The Civil War's Uncommon Man; Part 1, Yankee Blue Jackets," *Civil War Times Illustrated* 23 (February 1985): 30.

12. Blanding, *Recollections of a Sailor Boy*, 34–36; Rowland Stafford True, "Life aboard a Gunboat," *Civil War Times Illustrated* 9 (February 1971): 37; John D. Milligan, ed., "Navy Life on the Mississippi River," *Civil War Times Illustrated* 33 (May–June 1994): 66; Petition from Crew of U.S.S. Princeton, n.d., Cosam T. Bartlett Papers, James S. Schoff Civil War Collection, William L. Clements Library, University of Michigan, Ann Arbor, Mich.

13. Milligan, "Navy Life on the Mississippi River," 66.

14. Autobiography Entry, 15 May 1861, "The Autobiography of Tim Finn"; Log Entry, 17 March 1862, Charles Poole Log, G. W. Blunt White Library, Mystic Seaport Museum, Mystic, Conn.; Log Entry, 14 November 1863, in Kent Packard, ed., "Jottings by the Way: A Sailor's Log—1862 to 1864," Part 2, *Pennsylvania Magazine of History and Biography* 71 (July 1947): 242.

15. True, "Life aboard a Gunboat," 37.

16. Journal Entry, 5 February 1862, Anonymous, Journal aboard USS Ino, February 5, 1862–June 3, 1862, G. W. Blunt White Library, Mystic Seaport Museum (hereafter "Ino Journal"); Cornelius M. Schoonmaker to Barnard Schoonmaker, 27 July 1864, Cornelius Schoonmaker Papers, Manuscripts, Library of Congress, Washington, D.C.

17. Journal Entry, 5 February 1862, Ino Journal; Diary Entry, 21 February 1862, The Civil War Diary of John G. Morrison, 1861–1865, Naval Historical Foundation Collection, Washington Navy Yard, Washington, D.C.

18. Journal Entry, 5 February 1862, Ino Journal.

19. Autobiography Entry, 18 May 1861, "The Autobiography of Tim Finn."

20. Marcus Rediker, *Between the Devil and the Deep Blue Sea: Merchant Seamen, Pirates, and the Anglo-American Maritime World, 1700-1750* (Cambridge: Cambridge University Press, 1987), 11; Louis A. Zurcher Jr., "The Sailor aboard Ship: A Study of Role Behavior in a Total Institution," *Social Forces* 43 (March 1965): 393–95.

21. Journal Entry, 22 February 1865, Journal of Samuel Pollock, Illinois State Historical Library, Springfield, Ill.; George Bright to John Bright, 13 December 1862, George Adams Bright Collection, Manuscripts, Huntington Library.

22. William Marvel, *The Alabama and the Kearsarge: The Sailor's Civil War* (Chapel Hill: University of North Carolina Press, 1996), 148–49; Samuel W. Powell, "Blockading Memories of the Gulf Squadron," *Magazine of History with Notes and Queries* 8 (July 1908): 4.

23. Diseases were not spread through the air by vapors—called miasma—as most people believed at the time. When men previously unexposed to those diseases came into close contact with the bacteria, they were highly susceptible. See James M. McPherson, *Battle Cry of Freedom: The Civil War Era* (New York: Oxford University Press, 1988), 486–87.

24. Symmes Browne to Fannie Bassett, 27 July 1862, in John D. Milligan, ed., *From the Fresh-Water Navy: 1861–64; the Letters of Acting Master's Mate Henry R. Browne and Acting Ensign Symmes E. Browne* (Annapolis: Naval Institute Press, 1970), 111.

25. Journal Entry, 1 August 1864, William Mason Bright Journal, Bright Collection.

26. Ringle, *Life in Mr. Lincoln's Navy*, 39.

27. John Swift to Rosie Whiteside, 2 July 1864, in Lester L. Swift, ed., "Letters from a Sailor on a Tinclad," *Civil War History* 10 (March 1961): 59.

28. True, "Life aboard a Gunboat," 38.

29. Log Entries, 14 November 1863, 15 January 1864, in Packard, "Jottings by the Way," Part 2, 242, 255–56; Joseph T. Collins to Mother and Father, 10 December 1862, James B. and Joseph T. Collins Papers, Manuscripts, New-York Historical Society, New York, N.Y.

30. Diary Entry, 7 March 1863, Charles A. Hart Diary, History and Genealogy, Connecticut State Library, Hartford, Conn.

31. Symmes Browne to Fannie Bassett, 27 July 1862, in Milligan, *From the Fresh-Water Navy*, 111.

32. Edward Everett, "Address of Mr. Everett at the Opening of the Fair," *Boatswain's Whistle*, 9 November 1864, 26, Americana Catalogue, Huntington Library.

33. William J. Clark to Mother, 25 May 1863, William J. Clark Papers, Historical Society of Pennsylvania, Philadelphia, Pa.

34. Clark, *Seven Years of a Sailor's Life*, 171; Karsten, *The Naval Aristocracy*, 81; Powell, "Blockading Memo-

ries of the Gulf Squadron," 8; W. Jeffrey Bolster, *Black Jacks: African American Seamen in the Age of Sail* (Cambridge: Harvard University Press, 1997), 88.

35. Alban C. Stimers to Wife, 25 March 1862, Alban C. Stimers Papers, Manuscripts, New-York Historical Society.

36. Everett, "Address of Mr. Everett at the Opening of the Fair," 26.

37. Marvel, *The Alabama and the Kearsarge*, 149.

38. Hunter, *A Year on a Monitor and the Destruction of Fort Sumter*, 64, 100; C. W. Fleyne to William Thoms, 21 August 1864, William F. Thoms Papers, Letters from Seamen, 1853–1864, New York Nautical School, New-York Historical Society; Thomas Copernicus Wright to Jane Wright, 1 October 1864, Civil War Papers — Union, Civil War Collection, Missouri Historical Society, St. Louis, Mo.

39. Powell, "Blockading Memories of the Gulf Squadron," 8–11.

40. Petition from the Crew of the U.S.S. Springer to Gideon Welles, 25 April 1865, Box 298, Naval Living Conditions, Subject File, U.S. Navy, 1775–1910 (hereafter cited as "Navy Subject File"), Record Group 45, National Archives Building, Washington, D.C.; Greg Dening, *Mr. Bligh's Bad Language: Passion, Power, and Theatre on the Bounty* (Cambridge: Cambridge University Press, 1992), 19.

41. Karsten, *The Naval Aristocracy*, 81.

42. Hunter, *A Year on a Monitor and the Destruction of Fort Sumter*, 13; Ringle, *Life in Mr. Lincoln's Navy*, 34–35.

43. Frederick M. Clarke to David D. Porter, 23 July 1863, David D. Porter

Papers, Manuscripts, Huntington Library.

44. Milligan, *Gunboats down the Mississippi*, 100–101.

45. Joseph B. Osborne to Elias Osborne, 17 November 1864, Osborne Family Papers, Manuscripts, Library of Congress.

46. Robert M. Browning Jr., *From Cape Charles to Cape Fear: The North Atlantic Blockading Squadron during the Civil War* (Tuscaloosa: University of Alabama Press, 1993), 209–10.

47. Asa Beetham to Emma Beetham, 31 July 1861, Asa Beetham Papers, Manuscripts, Library of Congress; Edward Tobey Barker to Mother, 5 October 1862, Barker Letterbook, Barker-Edes-Noyes Papers.

48. Milligan, "Navy Life on the Mississippi River," 67.

49. Thomas Turner to L. M. Goldsborough, 28 August 1862, Thomas Turner Letterbook, Manuscripts and Archives, New York Public Library, New York, N.Y.

50. Log Entries, 9 January, 18 January 1864, Poole Log.

51. Oceolo Smith to Mother, 27 March 1864, Miles C. Smith Papers, Special Collections and University Archives, Rutgers University, New Brunswick, N.J.; Asa Beetham to Emma Beetham, 14 July 1862, Beetham Papers; Joseph Osborne to Louise Landau, 2 October 1864, Osborne Family Papers; Henry Clay Van Gieson to Nellie Van Gieson, 22 May 1864, Civil War Letters Received of Ellen Van Gieson from Brothers Henry Clay Van Gieson and Augustus Van Gieson, Abraham G. Demarest Papers, Special Collections and University Archives, Rutgers University.

52. Hunter, *A Year on a Monitor and the Destruction of Fort Sumter*, 64, 104; Frederick M. Clarke to David D. Porter, 23 July 1863, Porter Papers; Clark, *Seven Years of a Sailor's Life*, 170; Alan Booth, ed., *Human Crowding* (Blacksburg: Virginia Polytechnic Institute and State University, 1975), v.

53. Thomas Turner to Gideon Welles, 27 August 1862, Turner Letterbook.

54. Joseph L. Brigham to Father, 16, 24 June 1861, Joseph Brigham Papers, Manuscripts, Massachusetts Historical Society.

55. Hunter, *A Year on a Monitor and the Destruction of Fort Sumter*, 64; Bartholomew Diggins, "Recollections of the War Cruise of the U.S. Flag Ship Hartford, January 8, 1862, to December 24, 1864," 164, Manuscripts and Archives, New York Public Library.

56. E. W. Goble to Joseph B. Boyd, 14 January 1862, Manuscripts, Joseph B. Boyd Papers, Manuscripts, Cincinnati Historical Society, Cincinnati, Ohio; Log Entry, 27 July 1864, William Wainwright Log, G. W. Blunt White Library, Mystic Seaport Museum.

57. Log Entries, 31 July 1862, 30 November 1863, Poole Log; Diary Entries, 12 February, 26 March 1865, Edwin R. Benedict Diary, 1864–65, Special Collections, Woodruff Library, Emory University, Atlanta, Ga.; Log Entry, 27 July 1864, Wainwright Log; E. W. Goble to Joseph B. Boyd, 14 January 1862, Boyd Papers; Joseph Osborne to Louise Landau, 30 October 1863, in James M. Merrill, "Men, Monotony, and Mouldy Beans—Life on Board Civil War Blockaders," *American Neptune* 16 (January 1956): 55.

58. Autobiography Entry, 9 May 1861, "The Autobiography of Tim Finn"; Andrew Hull Foote to L. O.

Cottle, 7 March 1863, in Polser, "The Administration of the United States Navy, 1861–1865," 156.

59. U.S. Navy, *Regulations for the Government of the United States Navy 1865, 1864*, 179.

60. Special Order of Commodore Rowan, South Atlantic, 20 April 1864, *Official Records of the Union and Confederate Navies in the War of the Rebellion*, ser. 1, 27 vols. (Washington, D.C.: Government Printing Office, 1894–1917) (hereafter cited as "ORN"), 15:406–7.

61. D. R. Jenkins to Gideon Welles, 28 January 1864, Welles Papers; Polser, "The Administration of the United States Navy, 1861–1865," 157.

62. Ringle, *Life in Mr. Lincoln's Navy*, 41.

63. Bolster, *Black Jacks*, 79.

64. D. R. Jenkins to Gideon Welles, 28 January 1864, Welles Papers; Polser, "The Administration of the United States Navy, 1861–1865," 157.

65. Ringle, *Life in Mr. Lincoln's Navy*, 47, 92.

66. Donald L. Canney, *Lincoln's Navy: The Ships, Men, and Organization, 1861–65* (Annapolis: Naval Institute Press, 1998), 120.

67. C. W. Fleyne to William Thoms, 21 August 1864, Thoms Papers.

68. George E. Arnold to Cousin, 28 November 1863, 15 May 1864, in Arthur M. Schlesinger Jr., ed., "A Blue Bluejacket's Letters Home, 1863–1864," *New England Quarterly* 1 (October 1928): 557, 565; Lawrence C. Buhl, "Mariners and Machines: Resistance to Technological Change in the American Navy, 1865–1869," *Journal of American History* 61 (March 1974): 703–4.

69. Milligan, "Navy Life on the Mississippi River," 66.

70. Hunter, *A Year on a Monitor and the Destruction of Fort Sumter*, 9, 21.

71. Milligan, "Navy Life on the Mississippi River," 69.

72. Blanding, *Recollections of a Sailor Boy*, 52; Autobiography Entry, 18 May 1861, "The Autobiography of Tim Finn."

73. Memorandum Book Entries, 4 November 1861, 7 January 1862, Hugh Burns Memorandum Book, Manuscripts, Huntington Library; Blanding, *Recollections of a Sailor Boy*, 52; Autobiography Entry, 15 May 1861, "The Autobiography of Tim Finn"; James E. Valle, *Rocks and Shoals: Order and Discipline in the Old Navy, 1800–1861* (Annapolis: Naval Institute Press, 1980), 15.

74. William F. Hutchinson, "Life on the Texan Blockade," in *Personal Narratives of Events in the War of Rebellion, Being Papers Read before the Rhode Island Soldiers and Sailors Historical Society*, 3d ser., no. 1 (Providence: N. B. Williams, 1883), 23.

75. Clark, *Seven Years of a Sailor's Life*, 171.

76. Zurcher, "The Sailor aboard Ship," 395–96.

77. Clark, *Seven Years of a Sailor's Life*, 251–52.

78. Diary Entry, n.d. [15 September 1861], John B. Wirts Diary, Cruise of the Lancaster in the North and South Pacific from May 12, 1859, to October 15, 1861, Special Collections, University of California, Los Angeles, Los Angeles, Calif.

79. George Bright to Mother, 8 October 1864, Bright Collection.

80. James B. Collins to Mother, 11 September 1862, Collins Papers.

81. Joseph Osborne to Brother,

18 September 1864, in Merrill, "Men, Monotony, and Mouldy Beans," 51.

82. I. E. Vail, *Three Years on the Blockade: A Naval Experience* (New York: Abbey Press, 1902), 18.

83. Log Entry, 8 December 1862, Poole Log; Diary Entry, 20 December 1864, Benedict Diary; Margaret S. Creighton, *Rites and Passages: The Experience of American Whaling, 1830–1870* (Cambridge: Cambridge University Press, 1995), 59.

84. Autobiography Entry, 24 May 1861, "The Autobiography of Tim Finn."

85. Autobiography Entry, 24 May 1861, "The Autobiography of Tim Finn"; Lawrence Van Alstyne, *Diary of an Enlisted Man* (New Haven: Tuttle, Morehouse and Taylor, 1910), 68.

86. Hunter, *A Year on a Monitor and the Destruction of Fort Sumter*, 28; Frederic Sherman to Mother, 12 October 1862, Frederic Sherman Letters, Southern Historical Collection, Wilson Library, University of North Carolina.

87. Zurcher, "The Sailor aboard Ship," 395.

88. Diary Entry, n.d. [15 September 1861], Wirts Diary; John P. Brogan, "A Winter's Cruise during the Civil War," 2, William Pendleton Palmer Collection, Manuscripts, Western Reserve Historical Society, Cleveland, Ohio.

89. Journal Entries, 17 July, 24 July, 20 August, 25 August, 7 September 1864, William Mason Bright Journal, Bright Collection; Karsten, *The Naval Aristocracy*, 81; Zurcher, "The Sailor aboard Ship," 395.

90. George Bright to Mother, 8 October 1864, Bright Collection; Creighton, *Rites and Passages*, 59–60.

91. Paul L. Berkman, "Life aboard an Armed-Guard Ship," *American Journal of Sociology* 51 (November 1946): 384.

92. Secretary of the Navy to Hannibal Hamlin, 30 March 1864, in U.S. Congress, Senate, *Transfer of Seamen from the Army*, 4. See also Gideon Welles to Abraham Lincoln, 25 March 1864, ORN, 15:382.

93. Dening, *Mr. Bligh's Bad Language*, 57.

94. Berkman, "Life aboard an Armed-Guard Ship," 385.

95. C. Hilton Turney, "Log of a Long Voyage—Based upon the Notes of Charles Alexander Schetky," Part 1, 28, Charles Alexander Schetky Papers, Historical Society of Pennsylvania; U.S. Navy, *The Bluejackets' Manual* (Annapolis: Naval Institute Press, 1938), 597.

96. James Edwin Campbell, "The Mississippi Squadron," *Ohio Archaeological and Historical Society Quarterly* 34 (January 1925): 58.

97. Log Entry, 23 June 1863, in Kent Packard, ed., "Jottings by the Way: A Sailor's Log—1862 to 1864," Part 1 *Pennsylvania Magazine of History and Biography* 71 (April 1947): 131; Alan Villiers, *The Way of a Ship* (New York: Charles Scribner's Sons, 1953), 80.

98. Richard Henry Dana Jr., *Two Years before the Mast* (1840; reprint, New York: New World Press, 1980), 16–17.

99. Journal Entry, 5 February 1862, Ino Journal.

100. Ibid.; Zurcher, "The Sailor aboard Ship," 395.

101. Charles A. Post, "A Diary on the Blockade in 1863," *United States Naval Institute Proceedings* 44 (March 1918): 2349.

102. Powell, "Blockading Memories of the Gulf Squadron," 4.

103. Journal Entry, 5 February 1862, Ino Journal.

104. True, "Life aboard a Gunboat," 37; Clark, *Seven Years of a Sailor's Life*, 221.

105. Cornelius Schoonmaker to Barnard Schoonmaker, 6 June 1861, Schoonmaker Papers.

106. John Rodgers to Dear Sir, 30 June 1861, in Milligan, *Gunboats down the Mississippi*, 9; Oceolo Smith to Mother, 23, 27 December 1864, Smith Papers.

107. William Van Cleaf to Mother, 29 May 1862, William Van Cleaf Papers, Special Collections and University Archives, Rutgers University; Cosam T. Bartlett to Friend, 21 September 1862, Bartlett Papers; Nimrod B. McPherson to Ulysses S. Grant, 4 August 1863, Original Letters and Reports Concerning the Opening of the Mississippi River in the Civil War, Bixby Collection, Missouri Historical Society; James Glazier to Charles Glazier, 3 January 1864, James Glazier Collection, Manuscripts, Huntington Library.

108. Diggins, "Recollections of the War Cruise of the U.S. Flag Ship Hartford," 59–60.

109. Turney, "Log of a Long Voyage," 30.

110. Dana, *Two Years before the Mast*, 17.

111. Calvin G. Hutchinson to Hill, 18 July 1864, Calvin G. Hutchinson Papers, Manuscripts, Huntington Library; "Internal Regulations of the USS San Jacinto," Richard Worsam Meade II Collection, Naval Historical Society Collection, New-York Historical Society.

112. Turney, "Log of a Long Voyage," 34; Journal Entry, 1 September 1864, William Mason Bright Journal, Bright Collection; Log Entry, 9 March 1864, Wainwright Log; Log Entry, 30 March 1863, Poole Log; Diggins, "Recollections of the War Cruise of the U.S. Flag Ship Hartford," 56.

113. William B. Avery, "Gun-Boat Service on the James River," in *Personal Narratives of the Events in the War of Rebellion, Being Papers Read before the Rhode Island Soldiers and Sailors Historical Society*, 3d ser., no. 3 (Providence: N. B. Williams, 1884), 37–38.

114. Charles L. Green to S. H. Stringham, 3 July 1861, Charles L. Green Letterbook, Manuscripts, Huntington Library; Commander Selim E. Woodworth to Gustavus Vasa Fox, 3 March 1863, ORN, 24:454; Browning, *From Cape Charles to Cape Fear*, 201.

115. Harry Browne to Symmes Browne, 1 December 1861, in Milligan, *From the Fresh-Water Navy*, 6; Diggins, "Recollections of the War Cruise of the U.S. Flag Ship Hartford," 56; R. B. Forbes to Gustavus Vasa Fox, 2 April 1862, Gustavus Vasa Fox Papers, Manuscripts, New-York Historical Society; Charles L. Green to J. G. Pendergrast, 15 June 1861, Charles L. Green Letterbook.

116. Clark, *Seven Years of a Sailor's Life*, 171; Browning, *From Cape Charles to Cape Fear*, 205.

117. Brogan, "A Winter's Cruise during the Civil War," 2; Autobiography Entry, 18 May 1861, "The Autobiography of Tim Finn."

118. Log Entry, 25 May 1863, Poole Log.

119. Still, "The Common Sailor," 29; Journal Entry, 6 March 1862, Harry A. Simmons, "Journal of a Cruise in the U.S. Schooner Sophronia Attached

to the Bomb Flotilla," 30 December 1861–31 July 1862, James S. Schoff Civil War Collection, William L. Clements Library, University of Michigan, Ann Arbor, Mich.

120. C. H. Davis, *Life of Charles Henry Davis* (Boston, 1899), 236.

121. Charles O. Paullin, *Paullin's History of Naval Administration, 1775–1911* (Annapolis: Naval Institute Press, 1968), 303; Lieutenant Murphy to Acting Ensign Butler, 7 January 1864, Meade II Collection; Richard Worsam Meade III to Pierre Girard, 18 October 1864, Richard Worsam Meade III Collection, Naval Historical Society Collection, New-York Historical Society; Richard Worsam Meade II to Rear Admiral H. Paulding, 10 February 1864, Meade II Collection; Gideon Welles to Samuel F. Du Pont, 11 October 1861, ORN, 12:213; Gideon Welles to Samuel F. Du Pont, 25 November 1861, ORN, 12:328; Captain John Pope to Flag Officer William Mervine, 15 September 1861, ORN, 16:676; David G. Farragut to Gideon Welles, 12 February 1862, ORN, 18:27; Extract of Journal of F. A. Roe, 13 August 1862, ORN, 19:771; B. F. Isherwood to Gideon Welles, 12 August 1863, ORN, 20:456; Commander Selim E. Woodworth to Gustavus Vasa Fox, 3 March 1863, ORN, 24:454; Gideon Welles to Captain T. T. Craven, 11 October 1861, ORN, 4:713; Gideon Welles to L. M. Goldsborough, 25 November 1861, ORN, 4:454; Opinion of John D. Rodgers to Samuel L. Phillips, Naval Court Martial Regarding Loss of U.S. Steamer Satellite, ORN, 5:341; Gideon Welles to L. M. Goldsborough, 11 October 1861, ORN, 6:308.

122. Richard Worsam Meade III to Pierre Girard, 18 October 1864,

Meade III Collection; Browning, *From Cape Charles to Cape Fear*, 205.

123. Francis A. Roe, *Naval Duties and Discipline, with the Policy and Principles of Naval Organization* (New York: D. Van Nostrand, 1865), 26–27.

124. Rendezvous Sample, Rendezvous Reports.

125. Charles L. Green to J. G. Pendergrast, 15 June 1861, Charles L. Green Letterbook.

126. Edward Barrett, *Gunnery Instructions Simplified for the Volunteer Officers of the U.S. Navy* (New York: D. Van Nostrand, 1863), 17.

127. Henry R. Browne to Symmes E. Browne, 1 December 1861, in Milligan, *From the Fresh-Water Navy*, 6.

128. Powell, "Blockading Memories of the Gulf Squadron," 7.

129. Journal Entry, 5 February 1862, Ino Journal.

130. Milligan, "Navy Life on the Mississippi," 68.

131. Clark, *Seven Years of a Sailor's Life*, 171.

132. Valle, *Rocks and Shoals*, 15.

133. Blanding, *Recollections of a Sailor Boy*, 52; Autobiography Entries, 15, 18 May 1861, "The Autobiography of Tim Finn."

134. Reuben E. Stivers, *Privateers and Volunteers: The Men and Women of Our Reserve Naval Forces, 1766 to 1866* (Annapolis: Naval Institute Press, 1975), 223; Samuel F. Du Pont to Gustavus Vasa Fox, 10 January 1863, in Robert Means Thompson and Richard Wainwright, eds., *Confidential Correspondence of Gustavus Vasa Fox, Assistant Secretary of the Navy, 1861–1865*, 2 vols. (New York: De Vinne Press, 1918–19), 1:174–75; Polser, "The Administration of the United States Navy, 1861–1865," 31–34; David D.

Porter to Gideon Welles, 28 June 1864, ORN, 26:444–45; Gideon Welles to Commander Wilkes, 7 August 1862, ORN, 7:634; John A. Dahlgren to Gideon Welles, 14 December 1863, ORN, 15:175; Andrew H. Foote to Lieutenant Paulding, 30 September 1861, ORN, 22:353.

135. Valle, *Rocks and Shoals*, 16; Campbell, "The Mississippi Squadron," 60; David D. Porter to Gideon Welles, 16 May 1863, ORN, 24:676–77; Samuel P. Lee to Gideon Welles, 30 January 1865, ORN, 27:31–33.

136. Secretary of the Navy, *Report of the Secretary of the Navy, with an Appendix Containing Reports from Officers, December 1861* (Washington, D.C.: Government Printing Office, 1861), 8–9.

137. Edmund Curtis Ellis to Mother, 5 January 1865, Edmund Curtis Ellis Papers, Missouri Historical Society.

138. William Van Cleaf to Brother, 4 May 1862, Van Cleaf Papers; Journal Entry, 26 November 1862, George Bright Journal, Bright Collection.

139. Freeman Foster to Father, 3 April 1862, Freeman Foster Papers, Louisiana and Lower Mississippi Valley Collections, Hill Memorial Library, Louisiana State University, Baton Rouge, La.

140. Clark, *Seven Years of a Sailor's Life*, 201.

141. Barrett, *Gunnery Instructions Simplified for the Volunteer Officers of the U.S. Navy*, 64; John W. Grattan, *Under the Blue Pennant; or, Notes of a Naval Officer, 1863–1865*, ed. Robert J. Schneller (New York: Wiley, 1999), 61.

142. Secretary of the Navy, *Report of the Secretary of the Navy, December 1861*, 8–9.

143. James B. Collins to Mother and Father, 10 December 1862, Collins Papers.

144. Log Entry, 8 December 1863, in Packard, "Jottings by the Way," Part 2, 248–49; Erving Goffman, *Asylums* (New York: Doubleday, 1961), xiii; Zurcher, "The Sailor aboard Ship," 391; William N. Still Jr., ed., *The Confederate Navy: The Ships, Men, and Organization, 1861–1865* (Annapolis: Naval Institute Press, 1997), 175.

145. Diary Entry, 8 May 1862, Morrison Diary; "Proceeding of the San Jacinto, 1864–65," U.S.S. San Jacinto Letterbook, Meade II Collection; George Geer to Wife, 20 May 1862, in William Marvel, ed., *The Monitor Chronicles: One Sailor's Account* (New York: Simon and Schuster, 2000), 84–85.

146. Diary Entry, 11 June 1862, Morrison Diary; Milligan, "Navy Life on the Mississippi River," 69.

147. Ringle, *Life in Mr. Lincoln's Navy*, 45.

148. John Swift to Rosie Whiteside, May 1864, in Swift, "Letters from a Sailor on a Tinclad," 51; Diary Entry, 13 October 1862, Diary of George R. Yost, Illinois State Historical Library.

149. Merrill, "Men, Monotony, and Mouldy Beans," 50; Joseph Watson, "Life on Board a Blockader: Being Reminiscences of a Paymaster in the U.S. Navy, 1863," 379, 381, Rare Books, Huntington Library.

150. Cosam T. Bartlett to Unknown Newspaper, October 1862, Bartlett Papers.

151. Charles Nordhoff, "Two Weeks at Port Royal," *Harper's New Monthly Magazine* 27 (June 1863): 111.

152. Anonymous, "Life on a Blockader," *Continental Monthly* 6 (July 1864): 50.

153. Ringle, *Life in Mr. Lincoln's Navy*, 73–74.

154. A. W. Farenholt, "And There Were Giants in Those Days," 10, Box 298, Naval Living Conditions, Navy Subject File.

155. U. P. Levy, *Manual of Internal Rules and Regulations for Men-of-War* (New York: D. Van Nostrand, 1862), 9.

156. Log Entry, 17 October 1863, Poole Log; Diary Entry, 22 December 1861, George R. Durand Diaries, Manuscripts, New-York Historical Society; Symmes Browne to Fannie Bassett, 12 April 1864, in Milligan, *From the Fresh-Water Navy*, 259; Journal Entry, 13 July 1863, James E. Henneberry, Journal aboard U.S. Gunboat Essex, 23 September 1861–2 June 1863, James E. Henneberry Papers, Research Collections, Chicago Historical Society, Chicago, Ill.; William P. Mack and Royal W. Connell, *Naval Ceremonies, Customs, and Traditions*, 5th ed. (Annapolis: Naval Institute Press, 1980), 174–84.

157. True, "Life aboard a Gunboat," 38.

158. Edward T. Barker to Mother, 25 June 1862, Barker-Edes-Noyes Papers; David D. Porter's General Order No. 1, 10 March 1862, Selim E. Woodworth Papers, Manuscripts, Huntington Library.

159. Frederic Sherman to Mother, 19 August 1862, Sherman Letters; George R. Vance to Samuel Vance, 5 May 1863, Samuel C. Vance Papers, Indiana Historical Society, Indianapolis, Ind.

160. True, "Life aboard a Gunboat," 37; Log Entry, 15 January 1864, in Packard, "Jottings by the Way," Part 2, 255–56.

161. John Swift to Rosie Whiteside, May 1864, in Swift, "Letters from a Sailor on a Tinclad," 52; Log Entries, 17, 18 March 1862, Poole Log.

162. John Swift to Rosie Whiteside, 6 March 1865, in Swift, "Letters from a Sailor on a Tinclad," 61.

163. Horatio L. Wait, "The Blockading Service," in *Military Essays and Recollections, Papers Read before the Commandery of the State of Illinois, Military Order of the Loyal Legion of the United States* (Chicago: A. C. McClurg, 1902), 1:214; Barrett, *Gunnery Instructions Simplified for the Volunteer Officers of the U.S. Navy*, 17.

164. Memorandum Book Entry, 5 October 1863, Alexander R. Miller Memorandum Book of the U.S. Steamers DeKalb and Lafayette, 1861–64, Louisiana and Lower Mississippi Valley Collections, Hill Memorial Library, Louisiana State University.

165. Ringle, *Life in Mr. Lincoln's Navy*, 58.

166. U.S.S. Malvern, "Regulations for Crew, 1863," Manuscripts, Library of Congress; Log Entry, 24 November 1863, Poole Log.

167. James A. Barnes and Elinor Barnes, eds., *Naval Surgeon Blockading the South, 1862–1866: The Diary of Samuel Pellman Boyer* (Bloomington: Indiana University Press, 1963), 99; John Swift to Mother, 6 March 1865, in Swift, "Letters from a Sailor on a Tinclad," 61; Milligan, *Gunboats down the Mississippi*, 13, 171.

168. Log Entry, 30 March 1863, Poole Log; Diary Entry, 25 September 1862, Yost Diary.

169. Diary Entry, 27 February 1863, Hart Diary.

170. E. W. Goble to Joseph B. Boyd,

14 January 1862, Boyd Papers; Memorandum Book Entry, 5 October 1863, Miller Memorandum Book.

171. Anonymous, "Life on a Blockader," 50.

172. Edmund Curtis Ellis to Mother, 1 February 1865, Ellis Papers.

173. Merrill, "Men, Monotony, and Mouldy Beans," 49; Watson, "Life on Board a Blockader," 379; Log Entry, 21 April 1862, Poole Logs; Diary Entry, 18 April 1863, Fayette Clapp Diary, 1862–1862, Western Historical Manuscript Collection, Ellis Library, University of Missouri, Columbia, Mo.; Anonymous, "Life on a Blockader," 50.

174. Diggins, "Recollections of the War Cruise of the U.S. Flag Ship Hartford," 56.

175. Log Entry, 30 March 1863, Poole Log; Log Entry, 9 March 1864, Wainwright Log.

176. Powell, "Blockading Memories of the Gulf Squadron," 2; Samuel Hale to Joseph Green, 1 October 1863, Joseph F. Green Papers, Naval Historical Foundation Collection, Library of Congress; Paddy Griffith, *Battle Tactics of the Civil War* (New Haven: Yale University Press, 1987), 91, 105; Rediker, *Between the Devil and the Deep Blue Sea*, 174; Diary Entries, 19 February, 18 March 1865, Benedict Diary.

177. John Swift to Rosie Whiteside, May 1864, in Swift, "Letters from a Sailor on a Tinclad," 51; Marvel, *The Alabama and the Kearsarge*, 86; U.S. Navy, Department of the Mississippi, *Internal Rules and Regulations for Vessels of the Mississippi Fleet in the Mississippi River and Tributaries* (Cincinnati: Rickey and Carroll, 1862–63), 6; Log Entry, 30 November 1863, Wainwright Log; Vail, *Three Years on the Blockade*, 32; Journal Entries, 21,

27 August 1864, William Mason Bright Journal, Bright Collection; Joseph Osborne to Elias Osborne, 17 November 1864, Osborne Family Papers; Log Entry, 31 July 1862, Poole Logs; Diary Entries, 12 February, 26 March 1865, Benedict Diary.

178. James Glazier to Annie G. Monroe, 26 March 1863, Glazier Collection.

179. Marvel, *The Alabama and the Kearsarge*, 149; C. W. Fleyne to William Thoms, 21 August 1864, Thoms Papers.

180. George Bright to John Bright, 8 July 1862, Bright Collection.

181. Marvel, *The Alabama and the Kearsarge*, 86, 149.

182. Turney, "Log of a Long Voyage," 34; Log Entry, 24 March 1863, Poole Log; Journal Entry, 5 February 1862, Ino Journal.

183. James Glazier to Annie G. Monroe, 26 March 1863, Glazier Collection.

184. Diary Entry, 8 December 1862, Yost Diary; Sam Ettinger to James Collins, June 1862, Collins Papers; Anonymous, "Life on a Blockader," 49.

185. George E. Arnold to Brother, 29 December 1863, in Schlesinger, "A Blue Bluejacket's Letters Home," 558; E. W. Goble to Joseph B. Boyd, 14 January 1862, Boyd Papers; Diary Entry, 24 January 1864, Yost Diary.

CHAPTER 3

1. James M. Merrill, "Men, Monotony, and Mouldy Beans—Life on Board Civil War Blockaders," *American Neptune* 16 (January 1956): 50–51.

2. Thomas Turner to George E. Belknap, 27 September 1862, Thomas Turner Letterbook, Manuscripts and Archives, New York Public Library, New York, N.Y.; Isaac Bradbury to

W. B. Smith, 11 February 1864, Isaac Bradbury Papers, Manuscripts, New-York Historical Society, New York, N.Y.; James Russell Soley, *The Navy in the Civil War: The Blockade and the Cruisers* (New York: Charles Scribner's Sons, 1883), 93–94.

3. Isaac Bradbury to W. B. Smith, 11 February 1864, Bradbury Papers.

4. Gus Van Gieson to Ellen Van Gieson, 9 October 1864, Civil War Letters Received of Ellen Van Gieson from Brothers Henry Clay Van Gieson and Augustus Van Gieson, April 1864–July 1864, Abraham G. Demarest Papers, Special Collections and University Archives, Rutgers University, New Brunswick, N.J.; Diary Entry, November 1864, Frank Judd Diary, Historical Society of Pennsylvania, Philadelphia, Pa.; Log Entry, 5 August 1863, Charles A. Poole Log, G. W. Blunt White Library, Mystic Seaport Museum, Mystic, Conn.; Francis P. B. Sands, "Lest We Forget: Memories of Service Afloat from 1862 to 1866," *Military Order of the Loyal Legion of the United States: Commandery of the District of Columbia*, War Papers 73 (Washington, D.C.: Companion, 1908), 5; Ann Preston to Fowler Preston, 30 April 1862, Preston Family Papers, Michigan Historical Collection, Bentley Historical Library, University of Michigan, Ann Arbor, Mich.

5. Frederic Sherman to Mother, 12 October 1862, Frederic Sherman Letters, Southern Historical Collection, Wilson Library, University of North Carolina, Chapel Hill, N.C.

6. James B. Collins to Mother, 11 September 1862, James B. Collins and Joseph T. Collins Papers, Manuscripts, New-York Historical Society.

7. Diary Entry, 8 November 1861, Diary of Edward Saltonstall, October 1861–April 1862, Edward Saltonstall Papers, Manuscripts, New-York Historical Society.

8. James Thayer to William F. Thoms, 31 October 1861, William F. Thoms Papers, Letters from Seamen, 1853–1864, New York Nautical School, Manuscripts, New-York Historical Society; Frederic Sherman to Mother, 19 August 1862, Sherman Letters; Journal Entry, May 1863, Journal of Francis S. McKey, 1863–1866, Beinecke Library, Yale University, New Haven, Conn.; Oceolo Smith to Mother, 27 March 1864, Oceolo Smith Letters, Miles C. Smith Papers, Special Collections and University Archives, Rutgers University; Henry T. Rommel, 5 April 1863, Henry T. Rommel Papers, Books, Manuscripts, and Special Collections, Perkins Library, Duke University, Durham, N.C.

9. Charles A. Post, "A Diary on the Blockade in 1863," *United States Naval Institute Proceedings* 44 (March 1918): 2348; William F. Keeler to Anna Keeler, 11 April 1863, in Robert W. Daly, ed., *Aboard the USS Florida, 1863–65: The Letters of Paymaster William Frederick Keeler, U.S. Navy, to His Wife, Anna* (Annapolis: Naval Institute Press, 1968), 20–21.

10. Merrill, "Men, Monotony, and Mouldy Beans," 49.

11. I. E. Vail, *Three Years on the Blockade: A Naval Experience* (New York: Abbey Press, 1902), 33.

12. Autobiography Entry, 1 September 1861, "The Autobiography of Tim Finn, 1854–1896," Manuscripts, Center for American History, University of Texas, Austin, Tex.; Virginia Jean Laas,

"Sleepless Sentinels: The North Atlantic Blockading Squadron, 1862–1864," *Civil War History* 31 (March 1985): 29.

13. Daniel Carrison, *The Navy from Wood to Steel, 1860–1890* (New York: Franklin Watts, 1965), 27–28; Kent Packard, ed., "Jottings by the Way: A Sailor's Log—1862 to 1864," Part 1, *Pennsylvania Magazine of History and Biography* 71 (April 1947): 151; Reuben E. Stivers, *Privateers and Volunteers: The Men and Women of Our Reserve Naval Forces, 1766 to 1866* (Annapolis: Naval Institute Press, 1975), 127–30; James A. Barnes and Elinor Barnes, eds., *Naval Surgeon Blockading the South, 1862–1866: The Diary of Samuel Pellman Boyer* (Bloomington: Indiana University Press, 1963), xvii.

14. Francis B. Butts, "A Cruise along the Blockade," in *Personal Narratives of Events in the War of Rebellion, Being Papers Read before the Rhode Island Soldiers and Sailors Historical Society*, 2d ser., no. 12 (Providence: N. B. Williams, 1881), 14.

15. Augustus Van Gieson to Nellie Van Gieson, 9 October 1864, Demarest Papers.

16. Vail, *Three Years on the Blockade*, 33; Merrill, "Men, Monotony, and Mouldy Beans," 49.

17. Anonymous, "Life on a Blockader," *Continental Monthly* 6 (July 1864): 52.

18. Post, "A Diary on the Blockade in 1863," 2567.

19. William F. Keeler to Anna Keeler, 9 August 1863, in Daly, *Aboard the USS Florida*, 78.

20. Robert M. Browning Jr., *From Cape Charles to Cape Fear: The North Atlantic Blockading Squadron during the Civil War* (Tuscaloosa: University of Alabama Press, 1993), 258; Robert M. Browning Jr., *Success Is All That Was Demanded: The South Atlantic Blockading Squadron during the Civil War* (Washington, D.C.: Brassey's, 2002); John P. Brogan, "A Winter's Cruise during the Civil War," 20–21, 24–25, William Pendleton Palmer Collection, Manuscripts, Western Reserve Historical Society, Cleveland, Ohio.

21. Isaac Bradbury to W. B. Smith, 11 February 1864, Bradbury Papers; William F. Keeler to Anna Keeler, 9 August 1863, in Daly, *Aboard the USS Florida*, 78.

22. Francis A. Roe to Samuel P. Lee, 4 February 1864, in *Official Records of the Union and Confederate Navies in the War of the Rebellion*, ser. 1, 27 vols. (Washington, D.C.: Government Printing Office, 1894–1917) (hereafter cited as "ORN"), 9:422–23.

23. Isaac Bradbury to W. B. Smith, 11 February 1864, Bradbury Papers.

24. Journal Entry, 22 April 1862, in William C. Holton, "Cruise of the U.S. Flag-Ship Hartford, 1862–1863," ed. B. S. Osbon, *Magazine of History Notes and Queries* 22 (extra no. 87, 1922): 131, 136; Samuel F. Du Pont to Gustavus Vasa Fox, 6 December 1861, in Robert Means Thompson and Richard Wainwright, eds., *Confidential Correspondence of Gustavus Vasa Fox, Assistant Secretary of the Navy, 1861–1865*, 2 vols. (New York: De Vinne Press, 1918–19), 1:77; Samuel F. Du Pont to Gustavus Vasa Fox, 10 February 1862, ibid., 104.

25. James B. Collins to Father and Mother, 13 October 1862, Collins Papers.

26. T. M. Coan to Nattie Coan, 9 May 1864, Titus Munson Coan

Papers, Manuscripts, New-York Historical Society; Calvin G. Hutchinson to Wife, 6 June 1863, Calvin G. Hutchinson Papers, Manuscripts, Huntington Library, San Marino, Calif.; Post, "A Diary on the Blockade in 1863," 2579.

27. Dawson Carr, *Gray Phantoms of the Cape Fear: Running the Civil War Blockade* (Winston-Salem: John F. Blair, 1998), 22; Browning, *From Cape Charles to Cape Fear*, 251.

28. Sands, "Lest We Forget," 6.

29. James M. Merrill, *The Rebel Shore: The Story of Union Sea Power in the Civil War* (Boston: Little, Brown, 1957), 66.

30. William Keeler to Anna Keeler, 15 April 1863, in Daly, *Aboard the USS Florida*, 20.

31. T. M. Coan to Nattie Coan, 9 May 1864, Coan Papers.

32. Stephen F. Blanding, *Recollections of a Sailor Boy; or, The Cruise of the Gunboat Louisiana* (Providence: E. A. Johnson, 1886), 99–100; William H. Anderson, "Blockade Life," in *War Papers Read before the Commandery of the State of Maine, Military Order of the Loyal Legion of the United States*, 3 vols. (Portland: Lefavor-Tower, 1898), 2:4; Log Entry, 13 January 1863, Milo Lacy Log, Manuscripts, Naval Historical Center Library, Washington Navy Yard, Washington, D.C.

33. Frederic Stanhope Hill, *Twenty Years at Sea; or, Leaves from My Old Log Books* (Boston: Houghton, Mifflin, 1893), 195–204; Cornelius Cronin, *Recollections of Service in the United States Navy: Being Reminiscences as They Have Occurred to My Mind from the Commencement and pending the*

Late War; while Serving on the Ships *Sabine, Brooklyn, and Richmond* (n.p., 1894), 3.

34. Browning, *From Cape Charles to Cape Fear*, 258–59.

35. Ibid., 259–60.

36. William F. Keeler to Anna Keeler, 12 June 1863, in Daly, *Aboard the USS Florida*, 45.

37. Post, "A Diary on the Blockade in 1863," 2580.

38. Ibid., 2574, 2580–82.

39. Journal Entry, 28 November 1864, Joseph C. Canning Journal, Manuscripts and Archives, New York Public Library.

40. Anonymous, "Life on a Blockader," 53.

41. There has been a great deal of historical discussion concerning the effectiveness of the Union blockade. James Russell Soley declared the blockade to be effective based on the number of vessels seized on the blockade (1,149) and the number burned or destroyed (355); he also gauged that effectiveness in light of the conditions dealt with by Union vessels: thousands of miles of shoreline; the close proximity of neutral ports; and the presence of steam power on blockade runners. See Soley, *The Blockade and the Cruisers*, 43–46. Frank Owsley reaches the opposite conclusion by focusing on how many blockade runners escaped the blockade cordon. Owsley presents a detailed, periodic examination of the blockade on both the Atlantic and Gulf coasts and found over 7,500 violations of the blockade by blockade runners. Owsley contends that the rate of capture in 1861–62 was only one vessel in ten. Only in early 1865, Owsley argues, did the blockade

become "effective" when the capture ratio rose to one out of two. See Frank Owsley, *King Cotton Diplomacy: Foreign Relations of the Confederate States of America* (Chicago: University of Chicago Press, 1931), 240, 257–62. See also Marcus W. Price, "Ships That Tested the Blockade of Carolina Ports, 1861–1865," *American Neptune* 8 (July 1948): 24–39, 27; Robert Erwin Johnson, "Investment by Sea: The Civil War Blockade," *American Neptune* 32 (March 1972): 45–57; William N. Still Jr., "A Naval Sieve: The Union Blockade in the Civil War," *Naval War College Review* 36 (May–June 1983): 38–45; Steven R. Wise, *Lifeline of the Confederacy: Blockade Running during the Civil War* (Columbia: University of South Carolina Press, 1988), 221; David G. Surdam, "The Union Navy's Blockade Reconsidered," *Naval War College Review* 51 (Autumn 1998): 85–107.

42. Merrill, *The Rebel Shore*, 66.

43. Samuel W. Powell, "Blockading Memories of the Gulf Squadron," *Magazine of History with Notes and Queries* 8 (July 1908): 5.

44. Journal Entry, 21 September 1861, Ralph Chandler Journal, Journal on the Vandalia, 1860–61, Porter R. Chandler Papers, Manuscripts, New-York Historical Society.

45. Post, "A Diary on the Blockade in 1863," 2348; William F. Keeler to Anna Keeler, 15 April 1863, in Daly, *Aboard the USS Florida*, 20–21.

46. Sands, "Lest We Forget," 8.

47. Anonymous, "Life on a Blockader," 53.

48. T. M. Coan to Nattie Coan, 9 May 1864, Coan Papers; Journal Entry, 21 September 1861, Chandler

Journal; Post, "A Diary on the Blockade in 1863," 2348, 2569.

49. Post, "A Diary on the Blockade in 1863," 2569.

50. Anderson, "Blockade Life," 1; Sands, "Lest We Forget," 12; Edward Blue to Frank H. Stickney, 19 May 1864, Frank L. Stickney Papers, Naval Historical Foundation Collection, Library of Congress, Washington, D.C.

51. Temple to Henry Augustus Wise, 30 October 1863, Henry Augustus Wise Papers, Naval Historical Society Collection, New-York Historical Society; Elisha Hansen to Edward Hansen, 7 June 1864, Elisha Hansen Letters, Naval War Correspondence, Manuscripts, Naval Historical Center Library.

52. Post, "A Diary on the Blockade in 1863," 2348.

53. Henry T. Rommel to Father and Mother, 4 April 1863, Rommel Papers.

54. Charles Post to Father, 12 April 1863, in Post, "A Diary on the Blockade in 1863," 2348; Charles Post to Father, 6 June 1863, ibid., 2578; Log Entry, 18 January 1863, Lacy Log.

55. Post, "A Diary on the Blockade in 1863," 2580.

56. Isaac Bradbury to W. B. Smith, 11 February 1864, Bradbury Papers; Edward Everett, "Address of Mr. Everett at the Opening of the Fair," *Boatswain's Whistle*, 12 November 1864, 26, Americana Catalogue, Huntington Library.

57. Post, "A Diary on the Blockade in 1863," 2348.

58. Journal Entry, 23 October 1861, Canning Journal; Henry Clay Taylor to Father, 5 April 1863, Henry Clay Taylor Papers, Naval Historical Foundation Collection, Library of Congress; Mer-

rill, *The Rebel Shore*, 63; Richard S. West Jr., *Mr. Lincoln's Navy* (New York: Longmans, Green, 1957), 61.

59. James B. Collins to Mother, 11 September 1862, Collins Papers; Diary Entry, 16 January 1864, in Barnes and Barnes, *Naval Surgeon Blockading the South*, 261–62.

60. Anderson, "Blockade Life," 3; Log Entry, 23 November 1862, William Wainwright Log, G. W. Blunt White Library, Mystic Seaport Museum; West, *Mr. Lincoln's Navy*, 61.

61. Robert W. Daly, "Pay and Prize Money in the Old Navy, 1776–1899," *United States Naval Institute Proceedings* 74 (August 1948): 967.

62. Broadside titled "The Conscription Bill! How to Avoid It!! $50,000,000 Prizes!" n.d., Recruiting Posters, Box 356, Naval Recruiting, Regulations and Enlistments, Subject File, U.S. Navy, 1775–1910 (hereafter cited as "Navy Subject File"), Record Group 45, National Archives Building, Washington, D.C.; William Van Cleaf to Mother, 15 February 1862, William Van Cleaf Papers, Special Collections and University Archives, Rutgers University; Charles J. Hill to William Thoms, 3 December 1863, Thoms Papers; Autobiography Entry, 18 May 1862, "The Autobiography of Tim Finn"; Wallace Preston to Ann Preston, 6 July 1864, Preston Family Papers; Ann Preston to Fowler Preston, 30 April 1862, Preston Family Papers.

63. Calvin G. Hutchinson to Wife, 6 June 1863, Hutchinson Papers.

64. Log Entries, 21, 23, 25 October, 1, 15 December 1862, Lacy Log; Charles J. Hill to William Thoms, 3 December 1863, Thoms Papers; Anonymous, "Life on a Blockader," 47;

Cronin, *Recollections of Service in the United States Navy*, 3.

65. William F. Keeler to Anna Keeler, 24 October 1863, in Daly, *Aboard the USS Florida*, 105.

66. Anonymous, "Life on a Blockader," 51.

67. Post, "A Diary on the Blockade in 1863," 2581.

68. Ibid., 2578; Horatio L. Wait, "The Blockading Service," in *Military Essays and Recollections, Papers Read before the Commandery of the State of Illinois, Military Order of the Loyal Legion of the United States* (Chicago: A. C. McClurg, 1891), 1:227; William Still, "The Common Sailor: The Civil War's Uncommon Man; Part 1, Yankee Blue Jackets," *Civil War Times Illustrated* 23 (February 1985): 29.

69. General Order No. 41, 9 November 1864, ORN, 11:37–38; P. G. Watmough, W. E. Dennison, Samuel Hall to David D. Porter, 18 November 1864, ORN, 11:38; Horatio L. Wait, "The Blockade of the Confederacy," *Century Magazine* 34 (May–October 1898): 919; Anderson, "Blockade Life," 4; Powell, "Blockading Memories of the Gulf Squadron," 5.

70. The law passed on 17 July 1862 directed that "when one or more vessels of the navy shall be within *signal distance* of another making a prize, all shall share in the prize." See *An Act for the Better Government of the Navy of the United States*, 37th Cong., 2d sess., 17 July 1862, in *The Statutes at Large, Treaties, and Proclamations of the United States of America, 1859 to 1863*, vol. 12 (Boston: Little, Brown, 1863), 607.

71. Browning, *From Cape Charles to Cape Fear*, 259.

72. Anderson, "Blockade Life," 4; Powell, "Blockading Memories of the Gulf Squadron," 5.

73. P. G. Watmough to Judge P. Sprague, 1 November 1864, ORN, 11:32–33; Blanding, *Recollections of a Sailor Boy*, 99–100; Diary Entry, 9 June 1863, in Barnes and Barnes, *Naval Surgeon Blockading the South*, 128.

74. Vail, *Three Years on the Blockade*, 118.

75. David G. Farragut to Gideon Welles, 25 June 1864, ORN, 21:350–51; Anderson, "Blockade Life," 4; Madeline Russell Robinton, *An Introduction to the Papers of the New York Prize Court, 1861–1865* (New York: Columbia University Press, 1945), 131–32, 146–47; Sands, "Lest We Forget," 8; Diary Entry, 19 February 1862, Diary of John Simpson while on U.S.S. *Richmond* and *Brooklyn*, William Pendleton Palmer Collection, Manuscripts, Western Reserve Historical Society, Cleveland, Ohio; Journal Entry, 11 July 1863, Henry M. Bonney Journal, Journal of Remarks on Board the U.S.S. DeSoto, 1863, Manuscripts, Butler Library, Columbia University, New York, N.Y.; Cronin, *Recollections of Service in the United States Navy*, 3.

76. Anderson, "Blockade Life," 4.

77. Statement of the Crew of the U.S.S. William Anderson, 16 March 1864, Discipline and Minor Delinquencies, F to N, Box 287, Naval Justice, Navy Subject File; Sands, "Lest We Forget," 8; John Van Nest to Mother, 8 July 1864, Van Nest Papers, Manuscripts, New-York Historical Society.

78. In his report of 7 December 1863, Secretary of the Navy Gideon Welles raised the unsettled issue of awarding bounties, instead of prize money, for the destruction of enemy vessels and blockade runners. Welles advocated that the bounties be divided among the crew and officers the same way as prize money. See Barnes and Barnes, *Naval Surgeon Blockading the South*, 235.

79. Edward Blue to Frank H. Stickney, 19 May 1864, Stickney Papers; Carrison, *The Navy from Wood to Steel*, 35.

80. *An Act for the Better Government of the Navy of the United States*, 607.

81. Browning, *From Cape Charles to Cape Fear*, 261.

82. Marcus Rediker, *Between the Devil and the Deep Blue Sea: Merchant Seamen, Pirates, and the Anglo-American Maritime World, 1700–1750* (Cambridge: Cambridge University Press, 1987), 264.

83. William Keeler to Anna Keeler, 2 March 1864, in Daly, *Aboard the USS Florida*, 148; Diary Entry, 30 May 1863, Simpson Diary; J. C. Barrow to Captain J. P. Courtney, 16 September 1863, U.S. Naval Papers, Book, Manuscript, and Special Collections, Perkins Library, Duke University.

84. Isaac Bradbury to W. B. Smith, 11 February 1864, Bradbury Papers.

85. William F. Keeler to Anna Keeler, 4 February 1864, in Daly, *Aboard the USS Florida*, 143–45.

86. Everett, "Address of Mr. Everett at the Opening of the Fair," 26.

87. Journal Entry, 21 September 1861, Chandler Journal; Post, "A Diary on the Blockade in 1863," 2348.

88. Log Entries, 1 July, 14 October 1864, Wainwright Log. The general custom provided that the navy pension fund receive one-half of the proceeds, with the other one-half divided among the officers and crew. See Wait, "The

Blockading Service," 227. Congress amended this formula on 17 July 1862, ordering that prize money after said date be shared according to rates of pay; see *An Act for the Better Government of the Navy of the United States*, 606–7.

89. Autobiography Entry, 9 July 1862, "The Autobiography of Tim Finn."

90. Robinton, *An Introduction to the Papers of the New York Prize Court, 1861–1865*, 108.

91. Joseph T. Collins to Mother and Father, 19 January 1863, Collins Papers.

92. George Arnold to Cousin, 29 December 1863, in Arthur M. Schlesinger Jr., ed., "A Blue Bluejacket's Letters Home, 1863–1864," *New England Quarterly* 1 (October 1928): 559.

93. John Truesdale, "Bluecoats Afloat," in *The Bluecoats, and How They Lived, Fought and Died for the Union* (Philadelphia: Jones Brothers, 1867), 464; Log Entry, 23 November 1862, Wainwright Log; C. R. P. Rodgers to Gideon Welles, 9 January 1865, ORN, 3:406; D. H. Sumner to Abraham Lincoln, 23 February 1865, ORN, 3:82; Samuel F. Du Pont to Gustavus Vasa Fox, 7 July 1862, ORN, 13:173.

94. Oceolo Smith to Mother, 23 December 1864, Smith Papers.

95. Frederick Law Olmsted, *A Journey in the Back Country* (1860; reprint, Williamstown, Mass.: Corner House Publishers, 1972), 287.

96. Charles Rockwell, *Sketches of Foreign Travel and Life at Sea*, 2 vols. (Boston: Tappan and Dennet, 1842), 2:386; Greg Dening, *Mr. Bligh's Bad Language: Passion, Power, and Theatre on the Bounty* (Cambridge: Cambridge University Press, 1992), 105.

97. Judith Fingard, *Jack in Port: Sailortowns in Eastern Canada* (Toronto: University of Toronto Press, 1982), 74, 96–97, 126–39; Elmo Paul Hohman, *History of American Merchant Seamen* (Hamden, Conn.: Shoe String Press, 1956), 8. Hohman contends that American merchant seamen suffered from a "vacation psychology," which explains their intense social reactions once shoreside. The reactions were partially based on the memory of the privations and limitations of the voyage just concluded and the dreadful prospect of another one in the offing.

98. Blanding, *Recollections of a Sailor Boy*, 257–59; Wallace Preston to Ann Preston, 11 October 1864, Preston Family Papers; Merrill, "Men, Monotony, and Mouldy Beans," 49; Order of John A. Dahlgren, 24 October 1863, ORN, 15:70; S. C. Rowan to Gideon Welles, 18 March 1864, ORN, 15:370; James Shedden Palmer to Thorton Alexander Jenkins, 3 December 1864, David G. Farragut Papers, Manuscripts, Huntington Library.

99. Oceolo Smith to Mother, 23 December 1864, Smith Papers.

100. Vail, *Three Years on the Blockade*, 68; Still, "The Common Sailor," 35; William A. Parker to Samuel P. Lee, 17 February 1863, ORN, 8:533; Samuel F. Du Pont to Henry Winter Davis, 8 July 1862, in Craig L. Symonds, ed., *Charleston Blockade: The Journals of John B. Marchand, U.S. Navy, 1861–1862* (Newport, R.I.: Naval War College, 1976), 244–45.

101. Journal Entry, 17 August 1863, McKey Journal; Diary Entry, 23 February 1863, Charles A. Hart Diary, History and Genealogy, Connecticut State Library, Hartford, Conn.

102. Wait, "The Blockading Service," 223.

103. Vail, *Three Years on the Blockade*, 37.

104. Log Entry, 27 November 1862, Poole Log; Merrill, "Men, Monotony, and Mouldy Beans," 49.

105. Merrill, "Men, Monotony, and Mouldy Beans," 50–51; Edward Blue to Frank H. Stickney, 19 May 1864, Stickney Papers; Journal Entry, 10 December 1861, Canning Journal; Anderson, "Blockade Life," 1; A. Noel Blakeman, "Some Personal Reminiscences of the Naval Service," in *Personal Recollections of the War of the Rebellion; Addresses before the Commandery of the State of New York, Military Order of the Loyal Legion of the United States*, 2d ser., 4 vols. (New York: Knickerbocker Press, 1897), 2:236; Vail, *Three Years on the Blockade*, 32; George E. Buker, *Blockaders, Refugees, and Contrabands: Civil War on Florida's Gulf Coast, 1861–1865* (Tuscaloosa: University of Alabama Press, 1993), 24–27.

106. John Van Nest to Mother, 8 July 1864, Van Nest Papers; Joseph Fry to Wife, 28 November 1861, Joseph Fry Papers, Manuscripts, New-York Historical Society.

107. Joseph Osborne to Louise Landau, 2 October 1864, in Merrill, "Men, Monotony, and Mouldy Beans," 50; Diary Entry, 8 November 1864, Diary of Edwin R. Benedict, 1864–65, Special Collections, Woodruff Library, Emory University, Atlanta, Ga.; Cosam T. Bartlett to Friend, 21 September 1862, Cosam T. Bartlett Papers, James S. Schoff Civil War Collection, William Clements Library, University of Michigan; Cronin, *Recollections of Service in the United States Navy*, 11.

108. Diary Entry, 21 February 1865, Benedict Diary; Elisha Hansen to Edward Hansen, 7 June 1864, Hansen Letters; Post, "A Diary on the Blockade in 1863," 2346.

109. Frederic Sherman to Brother, 16 December 1862, Sherman Letters.

110. Journal Entry, 5 February 1862, Anonymous, Journal of the USS Ino, February 5, 1862–June 3, 1862, G. W. Blunt White Library, Mystic Seaport Museum; Joseph Osborne to Mary Osborne, 25 March 1865, Osborne Family Papers; Bartholomew Diggins, "Recollections of the War Cruise of the U.S. Flag Ship Hartford, January 8, 1862, to December 24, 1864," 244, Manuscripts and Archives, New York Public Library; Joseph Osborne to Mary Osborne, 25 March 1865, Osborne Family Papers; Joseph Watson, "Life on Board a Blockader: Being Reminiscences of a Paymaster in the U.S. Navy, 1863," 379, Rare Books, Huntington Library; Frederic Sherman to Mother, 12 October 1862, Sherman Letters.

111. Diggins, "Recollections of the War Cruise of the U.S. Flag Ship Hartford," 244.

112. William C. Miller to Brother Thoms, 14 December 1861, Thoms Papers.

113. Blanding, *Recollections of a Sailor Boy*, 218; Dennis J. Ringle, *Life in Mr. Lincoln's Navy* (Annapolis: Naval Institute Press, 1998), 83–84; Frederic Sherman to Mother, 12 October 1862, Sherman Letters.

114. William Keeler to Anna Keeler, 28 March 1863, in Daly, *Aboard the USS Florida*, 11.

115. Mary Osborne to Joseph B. Osborne, 8 September 1864, Osborne Family Papers.

116. George Bright to John Bright,

17 September 1862, Bright Collection, Manuscripts, Huntington Library; Diggins, "Recollections of the War Cruise of the U.S. Flag Ship Hartford," 244; William F. Hutchinson, "Life on the Texan Blockade," in *Soldiers and Sailors Historical Society of Rhode Island, Personal Narratives of Events in the War of Rebellion Being Papers Read before the Rhode Island Soldiers and Sailors Historical Society*, 3d ser. (Providence: N. B. Williams, 1883), 23–24; Diary Entry, 13 May 1859, Diary of John B. Wirts, Cruise of the Lancaster in the North and South Pacific from May 12, 1859, to October 15, 1861, Special Collections, University Library, The University of California at Los Angeles; Diary Entry, 8 November 1861, Diary of Edward Saltonstall; Joseph Osborne to Louise Landau, 2 October 1864, Osborne Family Papers; Diary Entries, 3, 5 March 1865, Benedict Diary; Frederic Sherman to Mother, 12 October 1862, Sherman Letters; George Geer to Wife, 29 May 1862, in Marvel, *The Monitor Chronicles*, 89.

117. William Rounesville Alger, "Effect of Sea Life on Land Life," *Boatswain's Whistle*, 9 November 1864, 5, Americana Catalogue, Huntington Library.

118. Log Entry, 31 July 1862, Poole Log; Joseph Osborne to Mary Osborne, 16 October 1864, Osborne Family Papers; Joseph Osborne to Louise Landau, 2 October 1864, Osborne Family Papers.

119. William C. Miller to Brother William Thoms, 14 December 1861, Thoms Papers; Log Entry, 27 November 1862, Lacy Log.

120. Joseph Osborne to Louise Landau, 30 October 1863, in Merrill, "Men, Monotony, and Mouldy Beans," 55; Log Entries, 31 July 1862, 30 November 1863, Poole Log; Diary Entries, 12 February, 26 March 1865, Benedict Diary; Log Entry, 27 July 1864, Wainwright Log; Browning, *From Cape Charles to Cape Fear*, 212.

121. Log Entry, 21 March 1863, Log of H. G. Thayer aboard the Brazileira, 46–48, 83, Manuscripts, Library of Congress; Merrill, "Men, Monotony, and Mouldy Beans," 55.

122. Journal Entry, 15 May 1862, Carsten DeWitt Journal, G. W. Blunt White Library, Mystic Seaport Museum.

123. This description of the types of tattoos sported by Union sailors is based upon an impressionistic analysis of 4,570 sailors collected by taking every twenty-fifth name from enlistment reports at every rendezvous where reports were collected or submitted from all naval rendezvous reports between April 1861 and April 1865, contained in *Enlistment Returns, Changes, and Reports, 1846–1942, Weekly Returns of Enlistments at Naval Rendezvous, January 6, 1855–August 8, 1891*, vols. 17–43, Records of the Bureau of Naval Personnel, Record Group 24, National Archives Building; "Descriptive List of Enlisted Men on Gunboat USS Reindeer," Smith-Spooner Papers, Manuscripts, Huntington Library.

124. Vail, *Three Years on the Blockade*, 65.

125. Diggins, "Recollections of the War Cruise of the U.S. Flag Ship Hartford," 244; Frieda Fromm-Reichmann, "Psychiatric Aspects of Anxiety," in Maurice R. Stein, Arthur J. Vidich, and David Manning White, eds., *Identity*

and *Anxiety: Survival of the Person in Mass Society* (Glencoe, Ill.: Free Press, 1960), 134–35.

126. Diary Entry, 12 February 1865, Benedict Diary.

127. Log Entry, 30 November 1863, Poole Log.

128. Diary Entry, n.d. [15 September 1861], Wirts Diary.

129. Diary Entry, n.d. [15 September 1861], Wirts Diary; James Birtwistle to Dr. William F. Thoms, 8 November 1862, Thoms Papers; Vail, *Three Years on the Blockade*, 156; Cosam T. Bartlett to Unknown Newspaper, October 1862, Bartlett Papers; Cosam T. Bartlett to Friend, 21 September 1862, Bartlett Papers.

130. Diary Entry, n.d. [15 September 1861], Wirts Diary; Log Entry, 2 December 1863, Poole Log; Cosam T. Bartlett to Unknown Newspaper, October 1862, Bartlett Papers; Cosam T. Bartlett to Friend, 21 September 1862, Bartlett Papers; Paul L. Berkman, "Life aboard an Armed-Guard Ship," *American Journal of Sociology* 51 (November 1946): 380.

131. Alfred Thayer Mahan, "The Minor Trials of Blockade Duty," *Harper's Magazine*, 26 October 1907, 1556.

132. Everett, "Address of Mr. Everett at the Opening of the Fair," 26.

133. Rear Admiral John Dahlgren to Gideon Welles, 17 August 1864, ORN, 15:635.

134. Blanding, *Recollections of a Sailor Boy*, 130; Everett, "Address of Mr. Everett at the Opening of the Fair," 26.

135. Anonymous, "Life on a Blockader," 50.

136. Watson, "Life on Board a Blockader," 379.

137. Oceolo Smith to Mother, 27 March, 27 December 1864, Smith Papers; Blakeman, "Some Personal Reminiscences of the Naval Service," 236; James Thayer to William F. Thoms, 31 October 1861, Thoms Papers; Diary Entry, November 1864, Judd Diary; Diary Entry, 6 December 1864, Benedict Diary; Anonymous, "Life on a Blockader," 50.

138. Sebastian Brant published *Das Narrenschiff* in 1494. British monk Alexander Barclay adapted and translated the work in 1509 under the title of *The Shyp of Fools of the Worlde*. As the title suggests, Brant's ship was manned by fools of various types, and the device was used as a satire on the vices and follies of the times. The purpose of the ship was to colonize the world with those fools who survive the journey. Brant attacks six follies in particular: (1) vicious or criminal offenses (including adultery, licentiousness, and blasphemy); (2) insolence (including scorning of God and the wise); (3) riotousness; (4) sloth; (5) presumptuousness (contempt of the Holy Writ); (6) mere perversities, foibles, and peccadilloes (including creating disturbances during church services, dancing, and working on holy days). See Edwin H. Zeydel, *Sebastian Brant* (New York: Twayne Publishers, 1967), 77, 83; Jean Christophe-Agnew, *Worlds Apart: The Market and Theater in Anglo-American Thought, 1550–1750* (Cambridge: Cambridge University Press, 1986), 63.

139. Anonymous, "Life on a Blockader," 50; Ringle, *Life in Mr. Lincoln's Navy*, 50.

140. Merrill, "Men, Monotony, and Mouldy Beans," 49; Journal Entry, 3 May 1863, George Bright Journal,

Bright Collection; Franklin E. Smith to Family, 26 December 1861, in Merrill, "Men, Monotony, and Mouldy Beans," 49; Post, "A Diary on the Blockade in 1863," 2569–70.

141. Rollo May, *The Meaning of Anxiety* (New York: W. W. Norton, 1977), 191–93; William Whelan to Gideon Welles, 5 August 1863, ORN, 14:418–19; F. Stanly to D. B. Ridgely, 19 February 1865, ORN, 16:240; Phillip S. Wales to Acting Lieutenant Edgar Broadhead, 30 January 1862, ORN, 17:79.

142. Log Entry, 24 September 1864, Wainwright Log; John Van Nest to Mother, 8 July 1864, Van Nest Papers.

143. John D. Milligan, ed., *From the Fresh-Water Navy: 1861–64; the Letters of Acting Master's Mate Henry R. Browne and Acting Ensign Symmes E. Browne* (Annapolis: Naval Institute Press, 1970), xix.

144. Log Entry, 13 August 1863, in Packard, "Jottings by the Way," Part 1, 140.

145. Samuel F. Du Pont to Henry Winter Davis, 8 July 1862, in Symonds, *Charleston Blockade*, 244–45.

146. William A. Parker to Samuel P. Lee, 17 February 1863, ORN, 8:533.

147. Charles Nordhoff, "Two Weeks at Port Royal," *Harper's New Monthly Magazine* 27 (June 1863): 110.

148. Powell, "Blockading Memories of the Gulf Squadron," 9.

149. Mahan, "Minor Trials of Blockade Duty," 1556.

150. Post, "A Diary on the Blockade in 1863," 2569.

151. Herman Melville, *White-Jacket; or, The World in a Man-of-War* (1850; reprint, New York: Quality Paperback Book Club, 1996), 277.

152. Cosam T. Bartlett to Friend, 21 September 1862, Bartlett Papers; T. M. Coan to Hattie Coan, 15 June 1864, Coan Papers.

153. Nordhoff, "Two Weeks at Port Royal," 110.

154. Mahan, "Minor Trials of Blockade Duty," 1556.

155. Francis Minton, ed., *Journal of Patrick Meade, Jr.* (Medford, Mass.: n.p., 1984), 4.

156. Blakeman, "Some Personal Reminiscences of the Naval Service," 237.

157. William Marvel, *The Alabama and the Kearsarge: The Sailor's Civil War* (Chapel Hill: University of North Carolina Press, 1996), 240.

158. Log Entry, 12 May 1864, Poole Log.

159. Log Entry, 19 August 1863, Lacy Log.

160. Log Entries, 1 March, 4 July 1864, Wainwright Log.

161. Log Entries, 9 December 1863, 21 January, 12 February 1864, in Kent Packard, ed., "Jottings by the Way: A Sailor's Log—1862 to 1864," Part 2, *Pennsylvania Magazine of History and Biography* 71 (July 1947): 249, 256, 260; Merrill, *The Rebel Shore*, 69.

162. Schlesinger, "A Blue Bluejacket's Letters Home, 1863–1864," 562.

163. Still, "The Common Sailor," 35.

164. Quoted in Peter Karsten, *The Naval Aristocracy: The Golden Age of Annapolis and the Emergence of a Modern American Navalism* (New York: Free Press, 1972), 51.

165. Merrill, *The Rebel Shore*, 69.

166. Fromm-Reichmann, "Psychiatric Aspects of Anxiety," 134–35. W. J. Rorabaugh contends that sailors' displacement to a ship generated feelings of societal isolation and anxiety,

which the sailors and others in similar circumstances—such as rivermen, lumberjacks, and soldiers—tried to drive away by resorting to and then later depending on alcohol; see W. J. Rorabaugh, *The Alcoholic Republic: An American Tradition* (New York: Oxford University Press, 1979), 144.

167. Log Entries, 23, 24 September, 12, 19 October 1864, Wainwright Log; Oceolo Smith to Mother, 23 December 1864, Smith Papers.

168. John Van Nest to Mother, 8 July 1864, Van Nest Papers.

169. Gussie Van Gieson to Nellie Van Gieson, 24 July 1864, Demarest Papers.

170. William Miller to Brother Thoms, 14 December 1861, Thoms Papers.

171. Hunter, *A Year on a Monitor and the Destruction of Fort Sumter*, 104.

172. Ibid.

173. Phillipson to Gideon Welles, 11 February 1862, in Merrill, "Men, Monotony, and Mouldy Beans," 51; C. F. Mayer to Henry Wise, 15 August 1863, Wise Papers.

174. Log Entry, 1 September 1864, in Packard, "Jottings by the Way," Part 2, 270; Acting Ensign William J. Eldredge to Gideon Welles, 24 August 1864, ORN, 17:748; Secretary of the Navy, *Report of the Secretary of the Navy, with an Appendix Containing Reports from Officers, December 1862* (Washington, D.C.: Government Printing Office, 1862), 899.

175. Log Entry, 23 September 1864, Wainwright Log.

176. Log Entry, 2 November 1864, in Packard, "Jottings by the Way," Part 2, 275; Diary Entry, 2 March 1864, in Lawrence Van Alstyne, *Diary of an Enlisted Man* (New Haven, Conn.: Tuttle, Morehouse, and Taylor, 1910), 276.

177. William F. Keeler to Anna Keeler, 7 August 1864, in Daly, *Aboard the USS Florida*, 190.

178. Wait, "The Blockading Service," 227, 250; Log Entry, 19 October 1864, Wainwright Log.

179. Percival Drayton to Hamilton, 16 March 1863, in Merrill, "Men, Monotony, and Mouldy Beans," 50; Everett, "Address of Mr. Everett at the Opening of the Fair," 26.

CHAPTER 4

1. Phillip S. Paludan, *Victims: A True Story of the Civil War* (Knoxville: University of Tennessee Press, 1980), x.

2. H. Allen Gosnell, *Guns on the Western Waters: The Story of the River Gunboats in the Civil War* (Baton Rouge: Louisiana State University Press, 1949), 13–17.

3. John D. Milligan, *Gunboats down the Mississippi* (Annapolis: Naval Institute Press, 1960), 14–15.

4. Gosnell, *Guns on the Western Waters*, 17.

5. Secretary of the Navy, *Report of the Secretary of the Navy, with an Appendix Containing Reports from Officers, December 1863* (Washington, D.C.: Government Printing Office, 1863), ix.

6. William N. Still, "The Common Sailor: The Civil War's Uncommon Man; Part 1, Yankee Blue Jackets," *Civil War Times Illustrated* 23 (February 1985): 26.

7. Commander J. P. Sanford to Andrew Hull Foote, 12 February 1862, *Official Records of the Union and Confederate Navies in the War of the Rebellion*, ser. 1, 27 vols. (Washington, D.C.: Government Printing Office,

1894–1917) (hereafter cited as "ORN"), 22:580.

8. Charles B. Hirsch, "Gunboat Personnel on the Western Waters," *Mid-America* 34 (April 1952): 75–76, 78.

9. Milligan, *Gunboats down the Mississippi*, 14–15.

10. Memorandum Book Entry, n.d., John T. Hawkins Memorandum Book, 93, Manuscripts and Archives, New York Public Library, New York, N.Y.

11. John Rodgers to Gideon Welles, 8 June 1861, ORN, 22:283.

12. Seth Ledyard Phelps to Colonel Cook, 13 August 1863, Seth Ledyard Phelps Papers, Missouri Historical Society, St. Louis, Mo.

13. John Swift to Rosie Whiteside, May 1864, in Lester L. Swift, ed., "Letters from a Sailor on a Tinclad," *Civil War History* 10 (March 1961): 53.

14. John D. Milligan, ed., "Navy Life on the Mississippi River," *Civil War Times Illustrated* 33 (May–June 1994): 68.

15. De Witt C. Morse to Cousin, 28 February 1864, in Jeffrey L. Patrick, ed., "A Fighting Sailor on the Western Rivers: The Civil War Letters of 'Gunboat,'" *Journal of Mississippi History* 58 (September 1996): 259.

16. W. W. Barry to Editor of the Evening Standard, New Bedford Massachusetts, 10 January 1864, William Wesley Barry Papers, Manuscripts, New-York Historical Society, New York, N.Y.

17. Frederic E. Davis to Parents, 6 May 1862, Frederic E. Davis Papers, 1860–1863, Special Collections, Robert W. Woodruff Library, Emory University, Atlanta, Georgia.

18. John Rodgers to S. L. Phelps, 15 July 1861, Phelps Papers; S. L.

Phelps to John Rodgers, 24 July 1861, Phelps Papers; Diary Entry, 16 September 1862, Diary of George R. Yost, Illinois State Historical Library, Springfield, Ill. Congress acquiesced and on 30 September 1862 legislation transferred the "Western Flotilla" to the navy and renamed it the "Mississippi Squadron"; see Milligan, *Gunboats down the Mississippi*, 93.

19. Over a two-month period in 1863, 1,105 Confederate prisoners from Rock Island and Camp Douglas in Illinois enlisted in the navy. Based on a sample of 537 sailors who enlisted at all Western rendezvous during the war, Confederate prisoners represented almost 12 percent (11.5 percent) of the total number of recruits in the West, see vol. 30, Rendezvous Report No. 679, November 28, 1863, to January 1, 1864; vol. 31, Rendezvous Report No. 68, January 2, 1864, to February 28, 1864; vol. 32, Rendezvous Report No. 149, March 5, 1864, to April 16, 1864, in *Enlistment Returns, Changes, and Reports, 1846–1942, Weekly Returns of Enlistments at Rendezvous, January 6, 1855–August 8, 1891*, Records of the Bureau of Naval Personnel, Record Group 24, National Archives Building, Washington, D.C.

20. James M. Merrill, "Cairo, Illinois: Strategic Civil War River Port," *Journal of Illinois State History* 76 (Winter 1983): 247, 251.

21. David D. Porter to Andrew H. Foote, 16 May 1863, in Merrill, "Cairo, Illinois," 252.

22. Andrew H. Foote to Gustavus Vasa Fox, 27 January 1862, in Robert Means Thompson and Richard Wainwright, eds., *Confidential Correspondence of Gustavus Vasa Fox, Assistant*

*Secretary of the Navy, 1861–1865*, 2 vols. (New York: De Vinne Press, 1918–19), 2:34.

23. Charles B. Boynton, *History of the Navy during the Rebellion*, 2 vols. (New York: D. Appleton, 1869–70), 1:525, 531; Andrew Hull Foote to Gideon Welles, 11 February 1862, ORN, 22:550; Andrew Hull Foote to Edwin M. Stanton, 11 February 1862, ORN, 22:579; Henry A. Wise to Andrew Hull Foote, 16 February 1862, ORN, 22:613; Andrew Hull Foote to Brigadier General M. C. Meigs, 28 February 1862, ORN, 22:642.

24. Hirsch, "Gunboat Personnel on the Western Waters," 79–82, 83. See Charles W. Wills, *Army Life of an Illinois Soldier: Including a Day-by-Day Record of Sherman's March to the Sea*, comp. Mary E. Kellogg (Carbondale: Southern Illinois University Press, 1996).

25. Ulysses S. Grant to Captain J. C. Kelton, 6 January 1862, *Official Records of the Union and Confederate Armies in the War of the Rebellion*, ser. 1, 128 vols. (Washington, D.C.: Government Printing Office, 1880–1898) (hereafter cited as "OR"), 7:534.

26. General Order No. 34, 8 February 1863, ORN, 24:324–25; David D. Porter to U. S. Grant, 8 February 1863, ORN, 24:325.

27. Still, "The Common Sailor," 27.

28. Hirsch, "Gunboat Personnel on the Western Waters," 82–84; William Van Cleaf to Mother, 16 February 1862, 29 May 1862, William Van Cleaf Papers, Special Collections and University Archives, Rutgers University, New Brunswick, N.J.; Nimrod B. McPherson to Ulysses S. Grant, 4 August 1863, Original Letters and Reports Concerning the Opening of the Mis-sissippi River in the Civil War, Bixby Collection, Missouri Historical Society.

29. Herbert Saunders to Mother, 20 January 1864, in Ronald K. Huch, ed., "The Civil War Letters of Herbert Saunders," *Register of the Kentucky Historical Society* 69 (March 1971): 17–18.

30. Andrew H. Foote to Gideon Welles, 24 February 1862, ORN, 22:632; Hirsch, "Gunboat Personnel on the Western Waters," 85; Merrill, "Cairo, Illinois," 252.

31. Theodore R. Parker, "The Federal Gunboat Flotilla on the Western Rivers during Its Administration by the War Department to October 1, 1862" (Ph.D. diss., University of Pittsburgh, 1939), 123–30.

32. Myron J. Smith Jr., "The U.S. Gunboat Carondolet, 1861–1865" (M.A. thesis, Shippensburg State University, 1969), 74; David D. Porter to Andrew H. Foote, 16 May 1863, ORN, 24:677–78.

33. Seth Ledyard Phelps to John D. Rodgers, 24 July 1861, Phelps Papers.

34. John Rodgers to Dear Sir, 30 June 1861, in Milligan, *Gunboats down the Mississippi*, 9.

35. Merrill, "Cairo, Illinois," 243.

36. Frederic E. Davis to Father, 22 April 1862, Davis Papers; Frederic E. Davis to Parents, 6 May 1862, Davis Papers; Diary Entry, 12 November 1863, David Low Huntington Diary, David Low Huntington Papers, Manuscripts, Huntington Library, San Marino, Calif.

37. Diary Entry, 21 February 1862, Civil War Diary of John G. Morrison, 1861–1865, Naval Historical Foundation Collection, Washington Navy Yard, Washington, D.C.; George R. Vance to Mother, 26 February 1863, Samuel C. Vance Papers, Indiana Historical Society, Indianapolis, Ind.

38. Merrill, "Cairo, Illinois," 252.

39. William Van Cleaf to Mother, 14 March 1862, Van Cleaf Papers.

40. Merrill, "Cairo, Illinois," 252.

41. Log Entry, 19 June 1865, Steam Room Log Book of the *USS Dictator*, April 1, 1865, to July 1, 1865, Naval Historical Society Collection, The New-York Historical Society.

42. Log Entries, 1–13 April 1865, ibid.

43. Journal Entry, 21 October 1862, James E. Henneberry, Journal aboard U.S. Gunboat Essex, 23 September 1861–2 June 1863, James E. Henneberry Papers, Research Collections, Chicago Historical Society, Chicago, Ill. (hereafter cited as "Henneberry Journal"); L. Moody Simms Jr., ed., "A Union Volunteer with the Mississippi Ram Fleet," *Lincoln Herald* 70 (Winter 1968): 190.

44. Smith, "The U.S. Gunboat Carondolet," 71–73.

45. David D. Porter to Gideon Welles, 16 May 1863, ORN, 24:676–77; James Edwin Campbell, "The Mississippi Squadron," *Ohio Archaeological and Historical Quarterly* 34 (January 1956): 60; Barry to Editor of Evening Standard, 10 January 1864, Barry Papers.

46. Henry R. Browne to Symmes E. Browne, 1 December 1861, in John D. Milligan, ed., *From the Fresh-Water Navy: 1861–1864; the Letters of Acting Master's Mate Henry R. Browne and Acting Ensign Symmes E. Browne* (Annapolis: Naval Institute Press, 1970), 6.

47. Barry to Editor of Evening Standard, 10 January 1864, Barry Papers.

48. Freeman Foster to Father, 2 April 1862, Freeman Foster Papers, Louisiana and Lower Mississippi Val-ley Collections, Hill Memorial Library, Louisiana State University, Baton Rouge, La.

49. E. W. Goble to Joseph B. Boyd, 14 January 1862, Joseph B. Boyd Papers, Manuscripts, Cincinnati His-torical Society, Cincinnati, Ohio.

50. Diary Entry, 9 March 1863, Yost Diary; Seth L. Phelps to Andrew H. Foote, 2 October 1861, ORN, 22:356–57.

51. John D. Milligan, ed., "Gunboat War at Vicksburg," *American Heritage* 29 (August–September 1978): 65.

52. Barry to Editor of Evening Stan-dard, 10 January 1864, Barry Papers.

53. Diary Entry, 9 March 1863, Yost Diary.

54. Diary Entry, 23 March 1862, Morrison Diary.

55. Diary Entry, 9 March 1863, Yost Diary; John Swift to Rosie Whiteside, May 1864, in Swift, "Letters from a Sailor on a Tinclad," 52–53; Journal Entry, 15 December 1861, Henneberry Journal.

56. Charles Spooner to Le Roy Fitch, 30 July 1864, Smith-Spooner Collection, Manuscripts, Huntington Library.

57. Frederic E. Davis to Parents, 8, 15 July 1862, Davis Papers; Diary Entry, 12 May 1864, Robert A. Tyson Diary, Louisiana and Lower Mississippi Val-ley Collections, Hill Memorial Library, Louisiana State University.

58. Bartholomew Diggins, "Recol-lections of the War Cruise of the U.S. Flag Ship Hartford, January 8, 1862, to December 24, 1864," 64, Manu-scripts and Archives, New York Public Library.

59. Freeman Foster to Father, 3 April 1862, Foster Papers.

60. The explanation of hog chains is from the descriptive panels located

at the USS *Cairo*, Vicksburg National Military Park, Vicksburg, Mississippi.

61. Freeman Foster to Father, 2, 3 April 1862, Foster Papers.

62. George R. Vance to Mother, 26 March 1863, Vance Papers.

63. Department of the Navy, Naval History Division, *Riverine Warfare: The United States Navy's Operations on Inland Waters* (Washington, D.C.: Government Printing Office, 1967), 33.

64. Eliot Callender, "What a Boy Saw on the Mississippi," in *Military Essays and Recollections, Papers Read Before the Commandery of the State of Illinois, Military Order of the Loyal Legion of the United States*, vol. 1 (Chicago: A. C. McClurg and Company, 1891), 51–52.

65. Ibid., 51–52; Virgil Carrington Jones, *The Civil War at Sea*, 3 vols. (New York: Holt, Rinehart, and Winston, 1962), 1:213.

66. Andrew H. Foote to Gideon Welles, 23 April 1862, ORN, 23:11.

67. Diggins, "Recollections of the War Cruise of the U.S. Flag Ship Hartford," 64, 68; S. L. Phelps to Andrew H. Foote, 20 October 1861, ORN, 22:374–75.

68. Milligan, *Gunboats down the Mississippi*, 63–68; James Thayer to William Thoms, 31 October 1861, William F. Thoms Papers, Letters from Seamen, 1853–1864, New York Nautical School, Manuscripts, New-York Historical Society; Journal Entries, 18, 19 January, 28 February 1863, Henneberry Journal; Diary Entries, 11, 12, 24, 31 December 1862, Yost Diary; Memorandum Book Entry, 13 July 1863, Alexander R. Miller Memorandum Book of the U.S. Steamers DeKalb and Lafayette, 1861–1864, Louisiana and Lower Mississippi Valley Collections,

Hill Memorial Library, Louisiana State University; E. W. Goble to Joseph B. Boyd, 11 February 1862, Boyd Papers; Samuel J. Bartlett to Mary Bartlett, 16 January 1863, in Simms, "A Union Volunteer with the Mississippi Ram Fleet," 190; Department of the Navy, *Riverine Warfare*, 32; John Cronan to David D. Porter, 4 August 1863, Porter Papers.

69. Diary Entry, 7 April 1862, in Wills, *Diary of an Illinois Soldier*, 79.

70. Milligan, "Gunboat War at Vicksburg," 65.

71. Milligan, *Gunboats down the Mississippi*, 49.

72. Andrew Hull Foote to Lieutenant Leonard Paulding, 17 September 1861, ORN, 22:337; Merrill, "Cairo, Illinois," 252–54; Charles C. Brewer, "African American Sailors and the Unvexing of the Mississippi River," *Prologue* 30 (Winter 1998): 279.

73. Lt. Comm. Le Roy Fitch to Mayor and Citizens of Henderson and Vicinity, 9 June 1864, ORN, 26:384–85.

74. "Autobiography of Emily Caroline Douglas," 128, Emily Caroline Douglas Papers, Louisiana and Lower Mississippi Valley Collections, Hill Memorial Library, Louisiana State University.

75. Callender, "What a Boy Saw on the Mississippi," 67; William Van Cleaf to Mother, 3 May 1862, Van Cleaf Papers; W. H. Price to Friend, 8 October 1862, W. H. Price Papers, Manuscripts, Illinois State Historical Library.

76. Callender, "What a Boy Saw on the Mississippi," 52.

77. Diary Entry, 6 May 1863, Morrison Diary.

78. De Witt C. Morse to Cousin, 20 July 1864, in Patrick, "A Fighting

Sailor on the Western Rivers," 273; Wallace Shugg, "The Gunboats are the Devil," Wallace Shugg Papers, Naval Historical Foundation Collection, Washington Navy Yard.

79. Diary Entry, 7 April 1862, in Wills, *Diary of an Illinois Soldier*, 79.

80. Journal Entry, 17 December 1862, Henneberry Journal.

81. Diary Entry, 2 February 1863, Yost Diary.

82. Frederic E. Davis to Father, 16 July 1862, Davis Papers; Diary Entry, 17 February 1863, Yost Diary; Master George W. Brown to David D. Porter, 8 February 1863, ORN, 24:323; Guy R. Everson, ed., "Service Afield and Afloat: A Reminiscence of the Civil War," *Indiana Magazine of History* 89 (March 1993): 49; Diary Entry, 9 May 1863, Morrison Diary; Sylvanus T. Harrison to Mother, 17 April 1864, Harrison Family Papers, Manuscripts, State Historical Society of Wisconsin, Madison, Wis.; George Harris to Aunt, 20 December 1864, George Harris Letters, Southern Historical Collection, Wilson Library, University of North Carolina, Chapel Hill, N.C.

83. Symmes Browne to Fannie Bassett, 13 May 1864, 29 May 1864, in Milligan, *From the Fresh-Water Navy*, 278, 286; John Swift to Rosie Whiteside, 8 June 1864, in Swift, "Letters from a Sailor on a Tinclad," 55–56; True, "Life aboard a Gunboat," 41.

84. Edward Morgan to David D. Porter, 2 September 1863, Porter Papers.

85. Lt. Comm. Le Roy Fitch to David D. Porter, 2 April 1863, ORN, 24:62.

86. Milligan, "Navy Life on the Mississippi River," 71.

87. Frederic E. Davis to Father,

16 July 1862, Davis Papers; Diary Entry, 30 August 1862, Yost Diary; John Swift to Mother, 8 June 1864, in Swift, "Letters from a Sailor on a Tinclad," 55–56; Memorandum Book Entry, 24 December 1862, Miller Memorandum Book; Symmes Browne to Fannie Bassett, 13 May 1864, 29 May 1864, in Milligan, *From the Fresh-Water Navy*, 278, 286; Diary Entry, 5 April 1863, Fayette Clapp Diary, 1862–1863, Western Historical Manuscript Collection, Ellis Library, University of Missouri, Columbia, Mo.

88. Stephen F. Blanding, *Recollections of a Sailor Boy; or, The Cruise of the Gunboat Louisiana* (Providence: E. A. Johnson, 1886), 257–59.

89. S. Teackle Wallis, "The Guerrillas: A Southern War Song" (1864), in Paludan, *Victims*, 84.

90. Diary Entries, 30 August, 7 September 1862, Yost Diary.

91. Frederic E. Davis to Father, 16 July 1862, Davis Papers; Milligan, "Gunboat War at Vicksburg," 65.

92. Daniel Ullman to Lt. Col. George B. Drake, 27 November 1864, ORN, 26:745; James A. Winslow to Charles H. Davis, 25 June 1862, ORN, 23:181; Charles H. Davis to Col. G. N. Fitch, 14 June 1862, ORN, 23:163; Frank Drake to Sister, 27 September 1864, Ralzemond A. Parker Papers, Manuscripts, Clarke Historical Library, Central Michigan University, Mount Pleasant, Mich.

93. Michael Fellman, *Inside War: The Guerrilla Conflict in Missouri during the American Civil War* (New York: Oxford University Press, 1989), 164.

94. David D. Porter to Gideon Welles, 14 March 1863, ORN, 24:472; Log Entries, 23, 26 July 1862, Abstract of Log of U.S.S. Carondolet,

26 May 1862–29 November 1862, ORN, 23:683–88; Log Entry, 29 November 1862, Abstract of Log of USS Mamora, 21 October 1862–29 December 1862, ORN, 23:688; Log Entry, 31 December 1862, Abstract of Log of U.S.S. Conestoga, 23 December 1862–31 December 1862, ORN, 23:694.

95. Diary Entry, 30 August 1862, Yost Diary; Frederic E. Davis to Parents, 27 August 1862, Davis Papers.

96. Diary Entry, 10 December 1862, Yost Diary.

97. David D. Porter to Lt. Comm. Joshua Bishop, 19 December 1862, ORN, 23:640.

98. Diary Entry, 30 August 1862, Yost Diary; Frederic E. Davis to Father, 26 September 1862, Davis Papers; Paludan, *Victims*, 94–95.

99. De Witt C. Morse to Cousin, 12 April 1864, in Patrick, "A Fighting Sailor on the Western Rivers," 264.

100. John Swift to Rosie Whiteside, 6 June 1863, in Swift, "Letters from a Sailor on a Tinclad," 50.

101. Diary Entries, 9, 14 February 1862, in Wills, *Diary of an Illinois Soldier*, 60–61, 62.

102. Diary Entry, 2 July 1863, Clapp Diary.

103. Acting Master Joseph C. Coyle to Lt. Comm. Le Roy Fitch, 29 May 1864, ORN, 26:332–33.

104. Le Roy Fitch to David D. Porter, 2 April 1863, ORN, 24:62.

105. De Witt C. Morse to Cousin, 12 April 1864, in Patrick, "A Fighting Sailor on the Western Rivers," 264.

106. General Order No. 4, 18 October 1862, ORN, 23:421. See also Mark Grimsley, *The Hard Hand of War: Union Military Policy toward Civilians, 1861–1865* (Cambridge: Cambridge University Press, 1995), 111–19.

107. General Order No. 4, 18 October 1862, ORN, 23:421.

108. Diary Entry, 5 April 1863, Clapp Diary.

109. Diary Entry, 30 August 1862, Yost Diary; Memorandum Book Entries, 24 December 1862, 11 April 1864, Miller Memorandum Book; Log Entry, 30 March 1863, Milo Lacy Log, Manuscripts, Naval Historical Center Library, Washington Navy Yard; Journal Entry, 23 December 1862, Frederic E. Davis Journal, Davis Papers.

110. Lt. Comm. Le Roy Fitch to David D. Porter, 5 November 1863, ORN, 23:309–11.

111. Lt. Comm. Richard Meade Jr. to David D. Porter, 21 October 1862, ORN, 23:431; David D. Porter to Gideon Welles, 27 October 1862, ORN, 23:451; Lt. Comm. Le Roy Fitch to David D. Porter, 6 April 1863, ORN, 24:71; Diary Entry, 8 December 1863, Morrison Diary.

112. Lt. Comm. James P. Foster to David D. Porter, 8 June 1864, ORN, 26:373.

113. Memorandum Book Entry, 4 December 1863, Miller Memorandum Book.

114. In fact, army instructions told soldiers that they need not give guerrillas the protections afforded prisoners of war; see *Instructions for the Government of Armies of the United States in the Field*, Article 82, General Order No. 100 (1863), in Paludan, *Victims*, 56.

115. Diary Entries, 6, 30 January 1863, Yost Diary.

116. C. Hilton Turney, ed., "Log of a Long Voyage: Based on the Notes of Charles Alexander Schetky," 17, Charles Alexander Schetky Papers, Historical Society of Pennsylvania, Philadelphia, Pa.

117. John Swift to Rosie Whiteside, 6 September 1863, in Swift, "Letters from a Sailor on a Tinclad," 50.

118. William Van Cleaf to Mother, 22 June 1862, Van Cleaf Papers; Extract of *Mobile Daily Tribune*, 2 July 1862, in ORN, 23:204.

119. Merrill, "Cairo, Illinois," 252; Journal Entry, 17 August 1863, Henneberry Journal; William Van Cleaf to Mother, 5 September 1862, Van Cleaf Papers.

120. David D. Porter to Col. Alfred W. Ellet, 26 March 1863, ORN, 24:514.

121. Merrill, "Cairo, Illinois," 252–53.

122. Milligan, "Gunboat War at Vicksburg," 63; Memorandum Book Entries, 3 May 1863, 17 March 1864, Miller Memorandum Book; Journal Entry, 5 March 1863, Journal of Thomas Lyons, Journal Kept on Board U.S. Steam Gunboat Carondolet and U.S.S. Lafayette, 8 January 1863–20 January 1863, Manuscripts, Library of Congress, Washington, D.C.

123. Diary Entry, 5 April 1862, Morrison Diary.

124. Log Entries, 17, 29 March 1863, Lacy Log; Memorandum Book Entry, 3 May 1863, Miller Memorandum Book.

125. William N. Bock to Father, 19 April 1864, William Bock Papers, Illinois State Historical Library.

126. James A. Greer to David D. Porter, 14 September 1863, Bixby Collection; George Hentig to David D. Porter, 23 February 1863, ORN, 24:432; De Witt C. Morse to Archibald Beal, 30 April 1864, in Patrick, "A Fighting Sailor on the Western Rivers," 267; Diary Entry, 5 November 1862, Yost Diary.

127. De Witt C. Morse to Archibald

Beal, 30 April 1864, in Patrick, "A Fighting Sailor on the Western Rivers," 267.

128. David D. Porter to Thomas H. Yeatman, 11 November 1863, ORN, 26:349–50; De Witt C. Morse to Cousin, 12 April 1864, in Patrick, "A Fighting Sailor on the Western Rivers," 264.

129. David D. Porter to Lt. Comm. James A. Greer, 6 October 1863, ORN, 25:449–50; Frank Drake to Sister, 19 July 1864, Parker Papers.

130. Everson, "Service Afield and Afloat," 53.

131. Warren D. Crandall, "An Ambuscade," Civil War Collection, Missouri Historical Society.

132. Memorandum Book Entry, 18 March 1864, Miller Memorandum Book; William Leahey to David D. Porter, 10 August 1863, Porter Papers; Diary Entry, 26 July 1862, Yost Diary; Journal Entry, 10 March 1863, Davis Journal, Davis Papers.

133. William Bock to Father, 19 March 1864, Bock Papers.

134. David D. Porter to Gideon Welles, 2 November 1862, ORN, 23:387–88.

135. Milligan, "Gunboat War at Vicksburg," 64–65; Diary Entry, 5 November 1862, Yost Diary; Herbert Saunders to Mother, 10 April 1864, in Huch, "The Civil War Letters of Herbert Saunders," 25; Everson, "Service Afield and Afloat," 53.

136. Memorandum Book Entries, 18 March 1864, 9, 10, 11, 13 April 1864, Miller Memorandum Book; James A. Winslow to Gideon Welles, 16 September 1862, ORN, 23:353; Testimony of Captain Thomas O. Selfridge, 14 March 1865, in U.S. Congress, *Report of the Joint Committee on the Conduct of*

the War at the Second Session, Thirty-Eighth Congress (Washington, D.C.: Government Printing Office, 1865), 297.

137. James A. Winslow to Gideon Welles, 16 September 1862, ORN, 23:358; Thomas O. Selfridge to Lt. Comm. James P. Foster, 19 February 1864, ORN, 25:747; Lt. Comm. Le Roy Fitch to David D. Porter, 2 April 1863, ORN, 24:62–65; Le Roy Fitch to David D. Porter, 25 April 1863, ORN, 24:87–88; Extract of Private Journal of Officer aboard the Cincinnati, 24 March 1863, ORN, 24:496.

138. Testimony of Nathaniel P. Banks, 14 December 1864, in U.S. Congress, Report of the Joint Committee on the Conduct of the War, 18; Testimony of Major D. C. Houston, 12 January 1865, ibid., 74; Testimony of Brigadier General William Dwight, 16 February 1865, ibid., 224–25.

139. Statement of Wellington W. Withenbury, 18 March 1865, ibid., 303.

140. Testimony of John M. Martin, 9 March 1865, ibid., 288; Statement of Wellington W. Withenbury, 9 March 1865, ibid., 284.

141. Testimony of Colonel James G. Wilson, 12 January 1865, ibid., 81.

142. Thomas O. Selfridge Jr., Memoirs of Thomas O. Selfridge, Jr., Rear Admiral, U.S.N. (New York: G. P. Putnam's Sons, 1924), 96–97.

143. Testimony of Colonel James G. Wilson, 12 January 1865, in U.S. Congress, Report of the Joint Committee on the Conduct of the War, 82; Testimony of Major D. C. Houston, 12 January 1865, ibid., 74.

144. Captain D. N. Welch to Colonel S. B. Holabird, 19 March 1864, OR, 34, part 2: 655.

145. Testimony of Colonel James G. Wilson, 12 January 1865, in U.S. Congress, Report of the Joint Committee on the Conduct of the War, 81.

146. David D. Porter to U. S. Grant, 14 February 1863, ORN, 24:341; Diary Entries, 25, 26, 27 March 1865, in Walter Rankins, ed., Diary of a Union Soldier, 1864–1865 (Frankfort, Ky.: Roberts Printing Company, 1952), 22.

147. Everson, "Service Afield and Afloat," 53; Journal Entry, 12 March 1863, Davis Journal, Davis Papers.

148. Diary Entry, 10 May 1864, Tyson Diary; Testimony of Colonel James G. Wilson, 12 January 1865, in U.S. Congress, Report of the Joint Committee on the Conduct of the War, 82–83; Nathaniel P. Banks to David D. Porter, 11 May 1864, ORN, 26:140–41.

149. Commander Robert Townsend to David D. Porter, 24 April 1864, ORN, 26:250.

150. Milligan, "Gunboat War at Vicksburg," 65.

151. Ibid.; Memorandum Book Entries, 8–13 April 1864, Miller Memorandum Book.

152. Milligan, "Gunboat War at Vicksburg," 65; Diary Entry, 5 November 1862, Yost Diary.

153. William N. Bock to Mother, 5 May 1864, Bock Papers; Lieutenant J. A. Greer to Lieutenant J. V. Johnston, 27 June 1864, Box 286, Naval Justice, Discipline and Minor Delinquencies, Individual Cases, J–L, Subject File, U.S. Navy, 1775–1910, Record Group 45, National Archives Building.

154. De Witt C. Morse to Archibald Beal, 30 April 1864, in Patrick, "A Fighting Sailor on the Western Rivers," 267.

155. Ludwell H. Johnson, Red River

Campaign: Politics and Cotton in the Civil War (Baltimore: Johns Hopkins University Press, 1958), 102, 287–88.

156. Gosnell, *Guns on the Western Waters*, 246–47.

157. William N. Bock to Father, 10 November 1864, Bock Papers.

158. Johnson, *Red River Campaign*, 101–3, 262–63, 287. In 1863, however, the U.S. Supreme Court ruled that prize law did not apply to inland seizures, see *Prize Cases* 67 U.S. (2 Black) 635 (1863).

159. Frederic E. Davis to Father, 16 July 1862, Davis Papers.

CHAPTER 5

1. Officers and sailors used the phrase "all hands drunk and rioting" to describe the behavior of Union sailors; see Diary Entries, 30 May 1863, 4 September 1864, Diary of John Simpson while on U.S.S. *Richmond* and *Brooklyn*, William Pendleton Palmer Papers, Manuscripts, Western Reserve Historical Society, Cleveland, Ohio. The title of this chapter also comes from an article done about the drunken and riotous conduct of merchant mariners by Allan Arnold; see his "All Hands Drunk and Rioting: Disobedience in the Merchant Marine," in Timothy J. Runyan, ed., *Ships, Seafaring and Society: Essays in Maritime History* (Detroit: Wayne State University Press, 1987), 227–37.

2. William Rounesville Alger, "Effect of Sea Life on Land Life," *Boatswain's Whistle*, 9 November 1864, 5, Americana Catalogue, Huntington Library, San Marino, Calif.; Robert M. Browning Jr., *From Cape Charles to Cape Fear: The North Atlantic Blockading Squadron during the Civil War*

(Tuscaloosa: University of Alabama Press, 1993), 211–16.

3. Concerning historians who view culture as a medium for managing economic and social upheavals, including class conflict, the rise of the market, and institutional assimilation, see Charles G. Sellers, *The Market Revolution: Jacksonian America, 1815–1846* (New York: Oxford University Press, 1991), 444; Michael T. Gilmore, *American Romanticism and the Marketplace* (Chicago: University of Chicago Press, 1985); Donald G. Matthews, "The Second Great Awakening as an Organizing Process, 1780–1830: An Hypothesis," *American Quarterly* 21 (Spring 1969): 23–43; William G. McLoughlin, *Revivals, Awakenings, and Reform: An Essay on Religion and Social Change in America, 1607–1977* (Chicago: University of Chicago Press, 1978).

4. Yet, aside from work by Rediker and Bolster, there has been little scholarly research seeking to uncover the sources and meanings of sailor culture. See Marcus Rediker, *Between the Devil and the Deep Blue Sea: Merchant Seamen, Pirates, and the Anglo-American Maritime World, 1700–1750* (Cambridge: Cambridge University Press, 1987); W. Jeffery Bolster, *Black Jacks: African American Seamen in the Age of Sail* (Cambridge: Harvard University Press, 1997).

5. The only discipline that has made a concerted effort to uncover the cultural lives of sailors is sociology, which in the last forty years has done an admirable—albeit jargon-filled—job of investigating the cultural lives of sailors. See Louis A. Zurcher Jr., "The Sailor aboard Ship: A Study of Role Behavior in a Total Institution," *Social*

*Forces* 43 (March 1965): 393; Paul L. Berkman, "Life aboard an Armed-Guard Ship," *American Journal of Sociology* 51 (November 1946): 384.

6. Greg Dening, *Mr. Bligh's Bad Language: Passion, Power, and Theatre on the Bounty* (Cambridge: Cambridge University Press, 1992), 55–56.

7. John P. Brogan, "A Winter's Cruise during the Civil War," 17, William Pendleton Palmer Collection, Manuscripts, Western Reserve Historical Society; Zurcher, "The Sailor aboard Ship," 395; Samuel W. Powell, "Blockading Memories of the Gulf Squadron," *Magazine of History* 8 (July 1908): 4; Journal Entry, 5 February 1862, Anonymous, Journal of the USS Ino, February 5, 1862–June 3, 1862, G. W. Blunt White Library, Mystic Seaport Museum, Mystic, Conn.

8. Peter Karsten, *The Naval Aristocracy: The Golden Age of Annapolis and the Emergence of a Modern American Navalism* (New York: Free Press, 1972), 84; Dening, *Mr. Bligh's Bad Language*, 155–56.

9. James E. Valle, *Rocks and Shoals: Order and Discipline in the Old Navy, 1800–1861* (Annapolis: Naval Institute Press, 1980), 185; Dening, *Mr. Bligh's Bad Language*, 150–51; Harold D. Langley, *Social Reform in the United States Navy, 1798–1862* (Urbana: University of Illinois Press, 1967), viii–ix.

10. Charles Rockwell, *Sketches of Foreign Travel and Life at Sea*, 2 vols. (Boston: Tappan and Dennet, 1842), 2:399.

11. Frederick Law Olmsted, *A Journey in the Back Country* (1860; reprint Williamstown, Mass.: Corner House Publishers, 1972), 287.

12. Log Entry, 2 December 1863, Log of Charles A. Poole, G. W. Blunt White Library, Mystic Seaport Museum; Log Entry, 27 November 1863, William Wainwright Log, G. W. Blunt White Library, Mystic Seaport Museum; Memorandum Book Entry, 16 June 1862, Hugh Burns Memorandum Book, Manuscripts, Huntington Library; James M. Merrill, "Men, Monotony, and Mouldy Beans—Life on Board Civil War Blockaders," *American Neptune* 16 (January 1956): 53; Valle, *Rocks and Shoals*, 18.

13. William N. Still, "The Common Sailor: The Civil War's Uncommon Man; Part 1, Yankee Blue Jackets," *Civil War Times Illustrated* 23 (February 1985): 33.

14. George E. Clark, *Seven Years of a Sailor's Life* (Boston: Adams, 1867), 214.

15. Journal Entries, 18, 22, 24 April 1863, Journal aboard U.S. Gunboat Essex, 23 September 1861–2 June 1863, James E. Henneberry Papers, Research Collections, Chicago Historical Society, Chicago, Ill. (hereafter cited as "Henneberry Journal"); Symmes Browne to Fannie Bassett, 27 March 1864, in John D. Milligan, ed., *From the Fresh-Water Navy: 1861–64; the Letters of Acting Master's Mate Henry R. Browne and Acting Ensign Symmes E. Browne* (Annapolis: Naval Institute Press, 1970), 255.

16. Clark, *Seven Years of a Sailor's Life*, 214.

17. George Bright to Father, 17 November 1861, George Adams Bright Collection, Manuscripts, Huntington Library; Diary Entries, 3, 5 March 1865, Edwin R. Benedict Diary, 1864–65, Special Collections, Woodruff Library,

Emory University, Atlanta, Ga.; Log Entry, 2 December 1863, Poole Log.

18. I. E. Vail, *Three Years on the Blockade: A Naval Experience* (New York: Abbey Press, 1902), 32.

19. Paul A. Gilje, "The Meaning of Freedom for Waterfront Workers," in David Thomas Konig, ed., *Devising Liberty: Preserving and Creating Freedom in the New American Republic* (Stanford: Stanford University Press, 1995), 121.

20. Joseph Green to Gideon Welles, 21 October 1861, Joseph F. Green Papers, Naval Historical Foundation Collection, Library of Congress, Washington, D.C.; Thomas Turner to G. P. Pendergast, 18 August 1862, Thomas Turner Letterbook, August 19, 1862–July 6, 1863, Manuscripts and Archives, New York Public Library, New York, N.Y.; Journal Entry, 30 May 1862, Carsten B. DeWitt Journal, G. W. Blunt White Library, Mystic Seaport Museum; Copy of a Report of Lieutenant S. Mach to Commander Corbin, 20 October 1864, Cornelius Schoonmaker Papers, Manuscripts, Library of Congress.

21. Still, "The Common Sailor," 39; James M. McPherson, *Ordeal By Fire: The Civil War and Reconstruction* (New York: McGraw-Hill, 1982), 467–68.

22. Constance Lathrop, "Grog: Its Origins in the United States Navy," *United States Naval Institute Proceedings* 61 (March 1935): 377–80.

23. "Splicing the main brace" refers to the detail of sailors charged with repairing the main cable that secured the main mast on a ship. The term became synonymous with any difficult task completed by the crew; see William P. Mack and Royal W. Connell, *Naval Ceremonies, Customs, and Traditions*, 5th ed. (Annapolis: Naval Institute Press, 1980), 283.

24. Stephen F. Blanding, *Recollections of a Sailor Boy; or, Cruise of the Gunboat Louisiana* (Providence: E. A. Johnson, 1886), 60–61; Fowler Preston to Mother, 13 May 1862, Preston Family Papers, Michigan Historical Collection, Bentley Historical Library, University of Michigan, Ann Arbor, Mich.; John Henry Taylor Jr. to Wife and Children, 27 January 1862, in Alice P. Mortensen and Edwin H. Mortensen, eds., *The Family of John Henry Taylor, Jr.: Featuring Family Letters Written during and after the Civil War* (Baltimore: Gateway Press, 1995), 10–11.

25. Log Entry, 21 July 1863, in Kent Packard, ed., "Jottings by the Way: A Sailor's Log—1862 to 1864," Part 1 *Pennsylvania Magazine of History and Biography* 71 (April 1947): 136; George Geer to Wife, 24 August 1862, in William Marvel, ed., *The Monitor Chronicles: One Sailor's Account* (New York: Simon and Schuster, 2000), 169; John Laffin, *Jack Tar: The Story of the British Sailor* (London: Cassel, 1969), 88–95; Merrill, "Men, Monotony, and Mouldy Beans," 56.

26. Dening, *Mr. Bligh's Bad Language*, 120.

27. Blanding, *Recollections of a Sailor Boy*, 60; Charles Wilkes to Gideon Welles, 15 August 1862, *Official Records of the Union and Confederate Navies in the War of the Rebellion*, ser. 1, 27 vols. (Washington, D.C.: Government Printing Office, 1894–1917) (hereafter cited as "ORN"), 7:651–52.

28. Journal Entry, 28 September 1861, Joseph C. Canning Journal, Cruise of the U.S.S. Cambridge, September 1861–July 1864, Manu-

scripts and Archives, New York Public Library.

29. Henry R. Browne to Sadie Bassett, 23 December 1861, in Milligan, *From the Fresh-Water Navy*, 11.

30. Unknown Sailor to Zeily, 25 December 1861, Manuscripts, Civil War Collection, Missouri Historical Society, St. Louis, Mo.; Jonathan A. Duble to Charles H. Davis, 18 June 1862, ORN, 23:180.

31. Dennis J. Ringle, *Life in Mr. Lincoln's Navy* (Annapolis: Naval Institute Press, 1998), 72–73; John Dahlgren to J. O. Bradford, 26 July 1863, ORN, 14:398; Merrill, "Men, Monotony, and Mouldy Beans," 56–57.

32. Cosam T. Bartlett to Unknown Newspaper, October 1862, James S. Schoff Civil War Collection, William L. Clements Library, University of Michigan, Ann Arbor, Mich.; Laffin, *Jack Tar*, 88–89.

33. W. J. Rorabaugh, *The Alcoholic Republic: An American Tradition* (New York: Oxford University Press, 1979), 144.

34. William F. Keeler to Anna Keeler, 3 November 1863, in Robert W. Daly, ed., *Aboard the USS Florida, 1863–65: The Letters of Paymaster William Frederick Keeler, U.S. Navy, To His Wife, Anna* (Annapolis: Naval Institute Press, 1968), 108–9.

35. Log Entry, 18 July 1864, Wainwright Log; Marvel, *The Monitor Chronicles*, 53.

36. Browning, *From Cape Charles to Cape Fear*, 211–12.

37. George Geer to Wife, 31 July 1862, in Marvel, *The Monitor Chronicles*, 146.

38. Log Entries, 1 March, 4 July 1864, Wainwright Log; Diary Entry, 9 January 1865, Benedict Diary.

39. Diary Entry, 30 May 1863, Simpson Diary.

40. Diary Entry, 7 September 1862, in James A. Barnes and Elinor Barnes, eds., *Naval Surgeon Blockading the South, 1862–1866: The Diary of Samuel Pellman Boyer* (Bloomington: Indiana University Press, 1963), 15.

41. William Whelan to John Dahlgren, 4 August 1863, ORN, 14:418.

42. W. L. Hudson to Gideon Welles, 27 May 1861, Box 286, 1860–1870, Naval Justice ("NJ"), Discipline and Minor Delinquencies, Individual Cases, H–I, Subject File, U.S. Navy, 1775–1910 (hereafter cited as "Navy Subject File"), Record Group 45, National Archives Building, Washington, D.C.; Log Entry, 17 April 1863, Milo Lacy Log, Manuscripts, Naval Historical Foundation Center Library, Washington Navy Yard, Washington, D.C.; Charles Kember to Dr. William F. Thoms, 4 August 1861, William F. Thoms Papers, Letters from Seamen, New York Nautical School, 1853–1864, Manuscripts, New-York Historical Society; Log Entry, 18 July 1864, Wainwright Log.

43. Wade to Ringgold, 10 November 1861, in Merrill, "Men, Monotony, and Mouldy Beans," 57.

44. George Bright to Father, 25 October 1863, Bright Collection.

45. William F. Keeler to Anna Keeler, 1 August 1863, in Daly, *Aboard the USS Florida*, 74–75; William F. Keeler to Anna Keeler, 4 February 1864, ibid., 143–45.

46. Diary Entry, 30 May 1863, Simpson Diary; John J. Almy to Gideon Welles, 19 November 1863, ORN, 9:315–16; Statement of Crew of British Steamer Emilie, 5 August 1862, ORN, 13:181–82.

47. George Bright to Father, 25 October 1863, Bright Collection.

48. Valle, *Rocks and Shoals*, 18; Herbert Saunders to Father, 25 March 1864, in Ronald K. Huch, ed., "The Civil War Letters of Herbert Saunders," *Register of the Kentucky Historical Society* 69 (March 1971): 21.

49. Frederic E. Davis to Father, 22 April 1862, Frederic E. Davis Papers, Special Collections, Woodruff Library, Emory University; Diary Entry, 24 May 1862, The Civil War Diary of John G. Morrison, 1861–1865, Naval Historical Foundation Collection, Washington Navy Yard; John Harty to Andrew Hull Foote, 21 May 1862, in James M. Merrill, "Cairo, Illinois: Strategic Civil War River Port," *Journal of Illinois History* 76 (Winter 1983): 638; Log Entry, 10 February 1864, in Kent Packard, ed., "Jottings by the Way: A Sailor's Log — 1862 to 1864," Part 2, *Pennsylvania Magazine of History and Biography* 71 (July 1947): 259–60.

50. Jonathan A. Duble to Charles H. Davis, 18 June 1862, ORN, 23:168.

51. Senator James Grimes to Gustavus Vasa Fox, 28 May 1862, in Robert Means Thompson and Richard Wainwright, eds., *Confidential Correspondence of Gustavus Vasa Fox, Assistant Secretary of the Navy, 1861–1865*, 2 vols. (New York: De Vinne Press, 1918–19), 2:304; John C. Rives, ed., *The Congressional Globe: Containing the Debates and Proceedings of the Second Session of the Thirty-seventh Congress* (Washington, D.C.: Congressional Globe Office, 1862), 2707–8, 3082, 3261; Langley, *Social Reform in the United States Navy*, 262–67; General Order of Gideon Welles, 17 July 1862, ORN, 7:584.

52. *An Act for the Better Government of the Navy of the United States*, 37th Cong., 2d sess., 17 July 1862, in *The Statutes at Large, Treaties, and Proclamations of the United States of America, 1859 to 1863*, vol. 12 (Boston: Little, Brown, 1863), 602.

53. Diary Entry, 12 September 1862, George R. Yost Diary, Illinois State Historical Library, Springfield, Ill.

54. Franklin Smith to Daughter, 28 August 1862, in Merrill, "Men, Monotony, and Mouldy Beans," 56.

55. George Geer to Wife, 31 July 1862, in Marvel, *The Monitor Chronicles*, 146.

56. Samuel Du Pont to J. F. Nickles, 23 August 1862, ORN, 13:275–76.

57. George Geer to Wife, 24 September 1862, in Marvel, *The Monitor Chronicles*, 188.

58. Diary Entry, 1 October 1862, Simpson Diary.

59. George Geer to Wife, 31 July 1862, in Marvel, *The Monitor Chronicles*, 146; Charles Wilkes to Gideon Welles, 15 August 1862, ORN, 7:651–52; Cosam T. Bartlett to Unknown Newspaper, October 1862, Bartlett Papers.

60. Ringle, *Life in Mr. Lincoln's Navy*, 71; Virgil Carrington Jones, *The Civil War at Sea*, 3 vols. (New York: Holt, Rinehart, and Winston, 1961), 2:180.

61. James Eggo, "Jack Ratlin's Lament," in Amos Burton, *A Journal of the Cruise of the U.S. Ship Susquehanna* (New York: Edward O. Jenkins, 1863), 136–37.

62. Ringle, *Life in Mr. Lincoln's Navy*, 71; Jones, *The Civil War at Sea*, 2: 180; Jim Dan Hill, *The Civil War Sketchbook of Charles Ellery Sted-*

man, *Surgeon, United States Navy* (San Rafael, Calif.: Presidio Press, 1976), 186.

63. George Geer to Wife, 3 August 1862, in Marvel, *The Monitor Chronicles*, 149.

64. Still, "The Common Sailor," 35; Extract of Journal on U.S.S. Richmond, 31 August 1862, ORN, 19:754.

65. Blanding, *Recollections of a Sailor Boy*, 61; Cornelius Schoonmaker to Mother, 11 January 1863, Schoonmaker Papers.

66. Diary Entry, 24 May 1862, Morrison Diary; Merrill, "Men, Monotony, and Mouldy Beans," 57; Ringle, *Life in Mr. Lincoln's Navy*, 71–72; Log Entry, 28 April 1863, Lacy Log.

67. Journal Entry, 15 May 1862, DeWitt Journal; George Geer to Wife, 13 September 1862, in Marvel, *The Monitor Chronicles*, 184; Diary Entry, 7 September 1862, in Barnes and Barnes, *Naval Surgeon Blockading the South*, 15.

68. Journal Entry, 23 March 1864, Journal of Samuel Pollock, 13 October 1863–17 March 1865, Illinois State Historical Library.

69. Log Entry, 14 October 1862, in Packard, "Jottings by the Way," Part 1, 124; Diary Entry, 30 May 1863, Simpson Diary; J. W. A. Nicholson to Captain Rodgers, 17 June 1862, ORN, 13:109.

70. Still, "The Common Sailor," 35.

71. Sellers, *The Market Revolution*, 259; Rorabaugh, *The Alcoholic Republic*, 150–52, 163, 169, 249.

72. Blanding, *Recollections of a Sailor Boy*, 61; Ringle, *Life in Mr. Lincoln's Navy*, 70–73; Rorabaugh, *The Alcoholic Republic*, 144; Cornelius Schoonmaker to Mother, 11 January 1863, Schoonmaker Papers; Log

Entry, 1 September 1862, in Burton, *A Journal of the Cruise of the U.S. Ship Susquehanna*, 136.

73. Valle, *Rocks and Shoals*, 16.

74. Theodore Lyman to Kate Hamlin, 4 February 1865, Lyman Family Papers, Manuscripts, New-York Historical Society; Bartholomew Diggins, "Recollections of the War Cruise of the U.S. Flag Ship Hartford, January 8, 1862, to December 24, 1864," 59–60, Manuscripts and Archives, New York Public Library; Log Entry, 31 July 1863, Lacy Log.

75. George Bright to Father, 25 October 1863, Bright Collection.

76. Joseph L. Brigham to Mother, 11 July 1861, Joseph Lincoln Brigham Papers, Manuscripts, Massachusetts Historical Society, Boston, Mass.; James J. Heslin, ed., "Two New Yorkers in the Union Navy: Narrative Based on Letters of the Collins Brothers," *New-York Historical Society Quarterly* 43 (April 1959): 184; Log Entry, 1 July 1864, Wainwright Log; George Geer to Wife, 24 September 1862, in Marvel, *The Monitor Chronicles*, 188. The communicative device of "grumbling" was not invented by Union sailors. The practice had been universal among British tars as well; see Laffin, *Jack Tar*, 19.

77. Log Entry, 1 July 1864, Wainwright Log; George Henry Preble to John A. Dahlgren, 19 December 1864, ORN, 16:91.

78. William F. Hutchinson, "Life on the Texan Blockade," in *Personal Narratives of Events in the War of Rebellion, Being Papers Read before the Rhode Island Soldiers and Sailors Historical Society*, 3d ser. (Providence: N. B. Williams, 1883), 23; Log Entry, 12 January 1864, Poole

Log; Diary Entry, 1 April 1865, Frank Judd Diary, Historical Society of Pennsylvania, Philadelphia, Pa.; Blanding, *Recollections of a Sailor Boy*, 31.

79. John D. Milligan, ed., "Navy Life on the Mississippi River," *Civil War Times Illustrated* 33 (May–June 1994): 66.

80. Log Entry, 12 January 1864, Poole Log; Log Entry, 27 October 1862, Lacy Log.

81. Paul Fussell, *Wartime: Understanding and Behavior in the Second World War* (New York: Oxford University Press, 1989), 80–91.

82. Diary Entry, 24 March 1863, Simpson Diary.

83. Francis A. Roe, *Naval Duties and Discipline, with the Policy and Principles of Naval Organization* (New York: D. Van Nostrand, 1865), 138; Rockwell, *Sketches of Foreign Travel and Life at Sea*, 2:399.

84. Adolphus Dixon to Captain G. J. Van Brunt, 4 July 1862, Box 286, NJ, 1860–1870, Discipline and Minor Delinquencies, Individual Cases, J–L, Navy Subject File; Gilje, "The Meaning of Freedom for Waterfront Workers," 121–22.

85. Thomas Smith to Joseph F. Green, 28 September 1863, Joseph F. Green Papers; Acting Master Samuel Hale to Joseph F. Green, 9 April 1864, Joseph F. Green Papers; Edward Barrett, *Gunnery Instructions Simplified for the Volunteer Officers of the U.S. Navy* (New York: D. Van Nostrand, 1863), 64.

86. James A. Greer to David D. Porter, 14 September 1864, Box 284, NJ, 1860–1870, Minor Delinquencies and Cases Where There Is No Record That a Court Martial Was Held, Navy

Subject File; Richard Ellis to Mother, 5 January 1865, Edmund Curtis Ellis Papers, Manuscripts, Missouri Historical Society.

87. Journal Entry, 5 March 1863, Journal of Thomas Lyons, Journal Kept on Board U.S. Steam Gunboat Carondolet and U.S.S. Lafayette, 8 January 1863–20 January 1863, Naval Historical Foundation Collection, Library of Congress.

88. Log Entry, 1 March 1863, Poole Log; Journal Entry, 5 March 1863, Lyons Journal.

89. Ensign John R. Peacock to Lieutenant J. W. Graves, 15 December 1864, Box 284, NJ, 1860–1870, Minor Delinquencies and Cases Where There Is No Record That a Court Martial Was Held, Folder 1, Navy Subject File; Lieutenant Alfred Hopkins to Lt. Comm. H. K. Davenport, 5 August 1862, Box 284, NJ, 1860–1870, Minor Delinquencies and Cases Where There Is No Record That a Court Martial Was Held, Folder 1, Navy Subject File; Ensign F. M. Montell to John A. Dahlgren, 21 January 1864, Box 284, NJ, 1860–1870, Minor Delinquencies and Cases Where There Is No Record That a Court Martial Was Held, Folder 1, Navy Subject File.

90. Thomas Smith to Joseph F. Green, 28 September 1863, Joseph F. Green Papers.

91. Karsten, *The Naval Aristocracy*, 52, 84.

92. Diary Entries, 26 March 1863, 4 February 1864, Simpson Diary; Lieutenant H. De Haven Manley to Joseph F. Green, 28 March 1863, Joseph F. Green Papers; Ensign John R. Peacock to Lieutenant J. W. Graves, 15 December 1864, Box 284, NJ, 1860–1870, Minor Delinquencies and Cases

Where There Is No Record That a Court Martial Was Held, Folder 1, Navy Subject File; Master E. B. Hussey to J. W. Clitz, 27 March 1864, Box 284, NJ, 1860–1870, Minor Delinquencies and Cases Where There Is No Record That a Court Martial Was Held, Folder 1, Navy Subject File; Log Entry, 31 July 1862, Lacy Log.

93. E. W. Goble to Joseph B. Boyd, 19 April 1863, Joseph B. Boyd Papers, Manuscripts, Cincinnati Historical Society, Cincinnati, Ohio.

94. Thomas McNeil to William Thoms, 5 November 1862, Thoms Papers; William C. Miller to Brother Thoms, 14 December 1861, Thoms Papers; Log Entry, 31 July 1862, Lacy Log; Diary Entry, 12 September 1862, Yost Diary; Journal Entry, 28 February 1862, DeWitt Journal; Log Entry, 31 October 1863, in Packard, "Jottings by the Way," Part 1, 151; General Order No. 6, 17 December 1861, ORN, 22:467; Charles H. Davis to Lieutenant Bogart, 13 July 1862, ORN, 23:256–57; *An Act for the Better Government of the Navy of the United States*, 602; Adolphus Dixon to Captain G. J. Van Brunt, 4 July 1862, Box 286, NJ, 1860–1870, Discipline and Minor Delinquencies, Individual Cases, J–L, Navy Subject File; Ensign F. M. Montell to John A. Dahlgren, 21 January 1864, Box 284, NJ, 1860–1870, Minor Delinquencies and Cases Where There Is No Record That a Court Martial Was Held, Folder 1, Navy Subject File; Lieutenant Alfred Hopkins to Lt. Comm. H. K. Davenport, 5 August 1862, Box 284, NJ, 1860–1870, Minor Delinquencies and Cases Where There Is No Record That a Court Martial Was Held, Folder 1, Navy Subject File.

95. Fussell, *Wartime*, 94.

96. Rediker, *Between the Devil and the Deep Blue Sea*, 166, 273; Journal Entry, 31 October 1863, in Packard, "Jottings by the Way," Part 1, 151; Reuben E. Stivers, *Privateers and Volunteers: The Men and Women of Our Reserve Naval Forces, 1766 to 1866* (Annapolis: Naval Institute Press, 1975), 352–53.

97. William Marvel, *The Alabama and the Kearsarge: The Sailor's Civil War* (Chapel Hill: University of North Carolina Press, 1996), 44; Diary Entry, 30 May 1862, DeWitt Journal.

98. Dening, *Mr. Bligh's Bad Language*, 78–79.

99. A. W. Farenholt, "And There Were Giants in those Days," 9, Box 298, Naval Living Conditions, Customs, etc. ("NL"), Navy Subject File; Gilje, "The Meaning of Freedom for Waterfront Workers," 125.

100. Journal Entries, 8 April 1863, 4 September 1864, Henneberry Journal; Journal Entry, 28 February 1862, DeWitt Journal; Log Entry, 5 April 1862, Poole Log; John Swift to Rosie Whiteside, May 1864, in Lester L. Swift, ed., "Letters from a Sailor on a Tinclad," 10 *Civil War History* (March 1961): 52.

101. Diary Entry, n.d. [15 September 1861], John B. Wirts Diary, Cruise of the Lancaster in the North and South Pacific from May 12, 1859, to October 15, 1861, Special Collections, University Library, University of California at Los Angeles, Los Angeles, Calif.; Marvel, *The Alabama and the Kearsarge*, 44.

102. Diary Entry, 19 April 1865, Judd Diary; Dening, *Mr. Bligh's Bad Language*, 78–79; Diary Entry, n.d.

[September–October 1861], Wirts Diary; Diary Entry, 23 December 1864, Benedict Diary.

103. Log Entry, 5 April 1862, Poole Log.

104. Rediker, *Between the Devil and the Deep Blue Sea*, 186–89; Henning Henningsen, *Crossing the Equator: Sailors' Baptism and Other Initiation Rites* (Copenhagen: Munksgaard, 1961), 88, 84, 245, 266.

105. Rediker, *Between the Devil and the Deep Blue Sea*, 188–89.

106. Joseph B. Osborne to Louise Landau, 1 January 1865, Osborne Family Papers, Manuscripts, Library of Congress; Diary Entry, 23 December 1864, Benedict Diary; Rediker, *Between the Devil and the Deep Blue Sea*, 187.

107. Log Entry, 5 April 1862, Poole Log; Journal Entry, 4 September 1864, Henneberry Journal.

108. Oceolo Smith to Mother, 23, 27 December 1864, Miles C. Smith Papers, Special Collections and University Archives, Rutgers University, New Brunswick, N.J.; Stivers, *Volunteers and Privateers*, 223; Samuel F. Du Pont to Gustavus Vasa Fox, 10 January 1863, in Means and Wainwright, *The Confidential Correspondence of Gustavus Vasa Fox*, 1:174–75; Aubrey Henry Polser, "The Administration of the United States Navy, 1861–1865" (Ph.D. diss., University of Nebraska, 1975), 31–34; David D. Porter to Gideon Welles, 28 June 1864, ORN, 26:444–45.

109. Valle, *Rocks and Shoals*, 108, 120, 123; Order of Acting Master James Taylor, 20 July 1863, ORN, 5:308; Abstract Log of U.S.S. Augusta Dinsmore, ORN, 21:90; George Bright to John Bright, 17 September 1862, Bright Collection; Diary Entry, 8 November 1861,

Diary of Edward Saltonstall, Edward Hallem Saltonstall Papers, Manuscripts, New-York Historical Society; Diggins, "Recollections of the War Cruise of the U.S. Flag Ship Hartford," 244; Joseph Osborne to Louise Landau, 2 October 1864, Osborne Family Papers; William Van Cleaf to Brother, 4 May 1862, William Van Cleaf Papers, Special Collections and University Archives, Rutgers University; Richard Ellis to Mother, 5 January 1865, Ellis Papers; Webb Garrison, *Mutiny in the Civil War* (Shippensburg, Pa.: White Mane Publishing, 2001).

Sailor behavior had been a problem for the navy in the Home Squadron's blockade of the Mexican coast during the Mexican War. Discipline and morale deteriorated to such dangerous levels under the tedium of the Mexican blockade that the navy hanged Seaman Samuel Jackson for mutiny aboard the sloop *St. Mary's*; see K. Jack Bauer, *Surfboats and Horse Marines: U.S. Naval Operations in the Mexican War, 1846–1848* (Annapolis: Naval Institute Press, 1969), 42.

110. Karsten, *The Naval Aristocracy*, 84.

111. Diggins, "Recollections of the War Cruise of the U.S. Flag Ship Hartford," 168; William Van Cleaf to Brother, 4 May 1862, Van Cleaf Papers; Oceolo Smith to Mother, 23 December 1864, Smith Papers.

112. Cosam T. Bartlett to Friend, 21 September 1862, Bartlett Papers; Statement of Seaman William Brown, 24 December 1864, Box 286, NJ, 1860–1870, Discipline and Minor Delinquencies, Individual Cases, M–N, Navy Subject File; William Hunter to Captain G. J. Brunt, 25 July 1862, Box 286, NJ, 1860–1870, Discipline and Minor

Delinquencies, Individual Cases, F–G, Navy Subject File; Petition of Seaman John Palmer, Heinrig Brown, A. H. Stiles, Henry Johnson, P. Shuster, Anthony West, Edwin Booth, C. Weaver, Charles Squires, Thomas Fahey Larias, John Van Houston to Sir, 25 April 1865, Box 298, NL, Navy Subject File; Autobiography Entry, 18 January 1862, "The Autobiography of Tim Finn, 1854–1896," Manuscripts, Center for American History, University of Texas, Austin, Tex.

113. Richard W. Meade III to David D. Porter, 30 October 1862, Letterbooks on U.S.S. Louisville, Marblehead, Chocura, Richard Worsam Meade III Collection, Naval Historical Society Collection, New-York Historical Society; Order of John A. Dahlgren, 24 October 1863, ORN, 15:70; Richard W. Meade III to John Dahlgren, 9 December 1863, Meade III Collection; S. C. Rowan to Gideon Welles, 18 March 1864, ORN, 15:370.

114. Diary Entries, 15 July 1861, 1 August 1861, Wirts Diary.

115. George Geer to Wife, 18 July 1862, in Marvel, *The Monitor Chronicles*, 132; John H. Taylor, Jr. to Wife, Mother, and Children, 13 October 1862, in Mortensen and Mortensen, *The Family of John Henry Taylor*, 71; Fowler Preston to Mother, 13 May 1862, Preston Family Papers, Michigan Historical Collection, Bentley Historical Library, University of Michigan, Ann Arbor, Mich.

116. Charles L. Green to Gideon Welles, 17 May 1862, Charles L. Green Letterbook, Manuscripts, Huntington Library; Diary Entry, 23 May 1865, Judd Diary.

117. *An Act for the Better Government of the Navy of the United States*, 602; Order of John A. Dahlgren, 24 October 1863, ORN, 15:70; James Shedden Palmer to Thorton Alexander Jenkins, 3 December 1864, David G. Farragut Papers, Manuscripts, Huntington Library; Richard W. Meade III to David D. Porter, 30 October 1862, Meade III Collection.

118. S. C. Rowan to Gideon Welles, 18 March 1864, ORN, 15:370.

119. Jacob Cochran to Dr. Thoms, 27 July 1862, Thoms Papers; Oceolo Smith to Mother, 23 December 1864, Smith Papers; Samuel Vance to George R. Vance, 6 August 1863, Samuel C. Vance Papers, Manuscripts, Indiana Historical Society, Indianapolis, Ind.

120. S. C. Rowan to Gideon Welles, 18 March 1864, ORN, 15:370; Richard W. Meade III to John A. Dahlgren, 9 December 1863, Meade III Collection.

121. The Ship's Company of the Hartford to the Editor of the New York Herald, *New York Herald*, Sunday, 16 August 1863.

122. William N. Bock to Father, 5 February 1864, William N. Bock Papers, Manuscripts, Illinois State Historical Library; Oceolo Smith to Mother, 23 December 1864, Smith Papers.

123. Browning, *From Cape Charles to Cape Fear*, 209–10; William Van Cleaf to Brother, 4 May 1862, Van Cleaf Papers; Oceolo Smith to Mother, 23 December 1864, Smith Papers.

124. George Geer to Wife, 18 June 1862, in Marvel, *The Monitor Chronicles*, 99–100.

125. Journal Entry, 1 January 1862, Henneberry Journal.

126. H. K. Davenport to L. M. Goldsborough, 15 July 1862, Box 284, NJ, 1860–1870, Minor Delinquen-

cies and Cases Where There Is No Record That a Court Martial Was Held, Folder 1, Navy Subject File; Valle, *Rocks and Shoals*, 15; Memorandum Book Entry, 18 March 1864, Alexander R. Miller, Memorandum Book of the U.S. Steamers DeKalb and Lafayette, 1861–64, Louisiana and Lower Mississippi Valley Collections, Hill Memorial Library, Louisiana State University, Baton Rouge, La.; James B. Collins to Mother and Father, 9 April 1863, Papers of James B. and Joseph T. Collins, Manuscripts, New-York Historical Society; William N. Bock to Father, 5 February 1864, Bock Papers; James Glazier to Charles Glazier, 3 January 1864, James Glazier Collection, Manuscripts, Huntington Library; Marvel, *The Alabama and the Kearsarge*, 212; Joseph T. Collins to Mother and Father, 25 January 1863, Collins Papers; Diary Entries, 8, 30 May 1863, Simpson Diary; Journal Entry, 3 September 1864, Journal of Benjamin Heath Jr., February 19, 1864–April 19, 1865, Special Collections and University Archives, Rutgers University.

127. The Ship's Company of the Hartford to the Editor of the New York Herald, *New York Herald*, Sunday, 16 August 1863; Anti Shoddy to the Editor of the New York Herald, *New York Herald*, Sunday, 26 January 1862.

128. Edward W. Hammond, "A Personal Reminiscence by Edward Hammond Boatswain, U.S. Navy, of an Incident on Board the U.S. Ship St. Mary's in Valparaiso Harbor 1865," 4–5, 13–15, Box 284, NJ, Discipline and Minor Delinquencies, 1855–1870, Navy Subject File; Journal Entry, 1 January 1862, Henneberry Journal; Commander Daniel Ammen to

Gideon Welles, 5 June 1864, ORN, 3:28–30; Affidavit of Daniel Ammen, 19 May 1864, ORN, 3:32; Affidavit of Edward L. Tinklepaugh, 16 May 1864, ORN, 3:33–36; Gideon Welles to Commander Ammen, William B. Johnston, B. A. Bedlack, T. G. Bell, E. R. Phelps, George F. Woodward, E. H. Abel, 15 August 1864, ORN, 3:36–37; Valle, *Rocks and Shoals*, 109; Christopher McKee, "Fantasies of Mutiny and Murder: A Suggested Psycho-History of Seamen in the U.S. Navy, 1798–1815," *Armed Forces and Society* 4 (February 1978): 297; John D. Milligan, *Gunboats down the Mississippi* (Annapolis: Naval Institute Press, 1965), xix; Samuel F. Du Pont to Henry Winter Davis, 8 July 1862, in Craig L. Symonds, ed., *Charleston Blockade: The Journals of John B. Marchand, U.S. Navy, 1861–1862* (Newport, R.I.: Naval War College, 1976), 244–45.

129. Diary Entry, 9 April 1863, Morrison Diary; Merrill, "Cairo, Illinois," 253; Journal Entry, 3 March 1863, Henneberry Journal; Richard Worsam Meade III to John Dahlgren, 20 October 1863, Meade III Collection.

130. Journal Entry, 3 March 1863, Henneberry Journal.

131. Merrill, "Cairo, Illinois," 251–52.

132. Rediker, *Between the Devil and the Deep Blue Sea*, 97, 99, 106, 140, 291.

133. Valle, *Rocks and Shoals*, 127.

134. Major S. Hoffman to Commander H. K. Davenport, 2 December 1862, ORN, 8:250; Amos P. Foster to Commander H. K. Davenport, 5 December 1862, ORN, 8:251; H. H. Lockwood to S. P. Lee, 27 October 1862, ORN, 8:150; Diary Entry, 8 February 1863, Fayette Clapp Diary, 1862–

1863, Western Historical Manuscript Collection, Ellis Library, University of Missouri, Columbia, Mo.; H. K. Davenport to S. P. Lee, 2 December 1862, ORN, 8:238; Major-General J. G. Foster to Commander H. K. Davenport, 28 November 1862, ORN, 8:238; Commander H. K. Davenport to Major-General Foster, 28 November 1862, ORN, 8:238; Major-General Foster to H. K. Davenport, 29 November 1862, ORN, 8:238.

135. Diary Entry, 12 January 1863, Clapp Diary; Still, "The Common Sailor," 26.

136. Diggins, "Recollections of the War Cruise of the U.S. Flag Ship Hartford," 165; Thomas Turner to Commander G. P. Pendergast, 18 August 1862, Turner Letterbook.

137. William N. Bock to Mother, 6 December 1864, Bock Papers; Journal Entry, 1 January 1862, Henneberry Journal; Diggins, "Recollections of the War Cruise of the U.S. Flag Ship Hartford," 164–66.

138. Diary Entry, 8 May 1863, Simpson Diary.

139. Journal Entry, 4 April 1862, Canning Journal; Diggins, "Recollections of the War Cruise of the U.S. Flag Ship Hartford," 164–66; Hammond, "Incident on Board the U.S. Ship St. Mary's," 9, 13–16.

140. Report of Lieutenant Commander George Brown, 5 April 1862, Box 286, NJ, Discipline and Minor Delinquencies, Fernandina, U.S. Bark, Mutiny on Board, Navy Subject File; Journal Entry, 4 April 1862, Canning Journal; Valle, *Rocks and Shoals*, 126–127.

141. Diggins, "Recollections of the War Cruise of the U.S. Flag Ship Hartford," 164–66.

142. Valle, *Rocks and Shoals*, 126–127.

143. Samuel P. Lee to Gideon Welles, 29 October 1862, ORN, 8:169–70.

144. Diary Entries, 12 January, 8 February 1863, Clapp Diary; David D. Porter to U. S. Grant, 8 February 1863, ORN, 24:325.

CHAPTER 6

1. James M. McPherson, *For Cause and Comrades: Why Men Fought in the Civil War* (New York: Oxford University Press, 1997), 63.

2. Journal Entry, 8 September 1861, in Amos Burton, *A Journal of the Cruise of the U.S. Ship Susquehanna* (New York: Edward O. Jenkins, 1863), 75–76; James M. Merrill, "Men, Monotony, and Mouldy Beans—Life on Board Civil War Blockaders," *American Neptune* 16 (January 1956): 54.

3. There exists no detailed analysis of the problem of religion and the Union sailor in the Civil War. Those works that address the subject do so only superficially and take the general position that Union sailors benefited from divine services administered by a navy that sincerely cared about the plight of their souls. This likely reflects the more modern approach taken by the navy with regard to its sailors and a lack of inquiry into sources left by sailors and chaplains; see Robert M. Browning Jr., *From Cape Charles to Cape Fear: The North Atlantic Blockading Squadron during the Civil War* (Tuscaloosa: The University of Alabama Press, 1993), 211; William N. Still, "The Common Sailor: The Civil War's Uncommon Man; Part 1, Yankee Blue Jackets," *Civil War Times Illustrated* 23 (February 1985): 32–33; Dennis J.

Ringle, *Life in Mr. Lincoln's Navy* (Annapolis: Naval Institute Press, 1998), 88–89.

4. James McPherson contends that Father William Thomas Cummings coined the phrase in a field sermon on Bataan in 1942; see McPherson, *For Cause and Comrades*, 63, 204 n. 3; see Frances C. Steckel, "Morale and Men: A Study of the American Soldier in World War II" (Ph.D. diss., Temple University, 1990), 311.

5. Samuel A. Stouffer et al., *The American Soldier: Combat and Its Aftermath*, 2 vols. (Princeton: Princeton University Press, 1949), 2:178.

6. Ibid., 186–87.

7. James McPherson contends that, as was the case for a soldier in World War II, religion served "the important function of increasing his resources for enduring the conflict-ridden situation of combat stress." Even if a man only became an "Army Christian," it still made him a better soldier; see McPherson, *For Cause and Comrades*, 76. Earl J. Hess reaches the same conclusion; see Earl J. Hess, *The Union Soldier in Combat: Enduring the Ordeal of Combat* (Lawrence: University Press of Kansas, 1997), 194; Warren B. Armstrong, *For Courageous Fighting and Confident Dying: Union Chaplains in the Civil War* (Lawrence: University Press of Kansas, 1998), x; Gerald Linderman, *Embattled Courage: The Experience of Combat in the American Civil War* (New York: Free Press, 1987), 102–7.

8. Lemuel Moss, *Annals of the United States Christian Commission* (Philadelphia: J. B. Lippincott, 1868), 42; Gardiner H. Shattuck Jr., *A Shield and a Hiding Place: The Religious Life of the Civil War Armies* (Macon,

Ga.: Mercer University Press, 1987), 22; McPherson, *For Cause and Comrades*, 63; Charles J. Stille, *History of the United States Sanitary Commission: Being the General Report of Its Work during the War of Rebellion* (Philadelphia: J. B. Lippincott, 1866), 20–21.

9. Theresa Rose McDevitt, "Fighting for the Soul of America: A History of the United States Christian Commission" (Ph.D. diss., Kent State University, 1997), 97.

10. Marcus Rediker provides an excellent starting point for analyzing the origins of sailor irreligiosity in the Anglo-American merchant marine; see Marcus Rediker, *Between the Devil and the Deep Blue Sea: Merchant Seamen, Pirates, and the Anglo-American Maritime World, 1700–1750* (Cambridge: Cambridge University Press, 1987), 167–68, 173–77. Charles Rockwell, *Sketches of Foreign Travel and Life at Sea*, 2 vols. (Boston: Tappan and Dennet, 1842), 2:293; Richard Henry Dana Jr., *Two Years before the Mast: A Personal Narrative of a Life at Sea* (1840; reprint, New York: World Publishing Company, 1946); Harold D. Langley, *Social Reform in the United States Navy, 1798–1862* (Urbana: University of Illinois Press, 1967), 43–67. For works of fiction, based on fact, that illustrate the irreligiosity of sailors, see Daniel Defoe, *Robinson Crusoe* (1719; reprint, New York: New American Library, 1960); Herman Melville, *White-Jacket; or, The World in a Man-of-War* (1850; reprint, New York: Quality Paperback Book Club, 1996).

11. Mary Osborne to Joseph B. Osborne, 8 September 1864, Osborne Family Papers, Manuscripts, Library of Congress, Washington, D.C.

12. Log Entry, 7 December 1862, Milo Lacy Log, Manuscripts, Naval Historical Center Library, Washington Navy Yard, Washington, D.C.; Francis R. Minton, ed., *Journal of Patrick Meade, Jr.* (Medford, Mass.: n.p., 1984), 4; Reuben E. Stivers, *Privateers and Volunteers: The Men and Women of Our Reserve Naval Forces, 1766 to 1866* (Annapolis: Naval Institute Press, 1975), 353–54.

13. C. W. Fleyne to Dr. William F. Thoms, 21 August 1864, William F. Thoms Papers, Letters from Seamen, New York Nautical School, 1853–1864, Manuscripts, New-York Historical Society, New York, N.Y.; New York Bible Society, *Thirty-ninth Annual Report of the New York Bible Society: Auxiliary of the American Bible Society* (New York: New York Bible Society, 1863), 34.

14. Edward P. Smith, *Incidents of the United States Christian Commission* (Philadelphia: J. B. Lippincott, 1871), 469.

15. Clifford M. Drury, *The History of the Chaplain Corps, United States Navy*, vol. 1, *1789–1939* (Washington, D.C.: Government Printing Office, 1949), 101; Joseph Stockbridge to Navy Department, 18 May 1863, Officers' Letters, Official Correspondence, U.S. Navy, 1853–1884 (hereafter cited as "Official Navy Correspondence"), Manuscripts, Huntington Library, San Marino, Calif.

16. Langley, *Social Reform in the United States Navy*, 279–80.

17. Willard L. Sperry, ed., *Religion in the Post-war World*, vol. 2, *Religion of Soldier and Sailor* (Cambridge: Harvard University Press, 1945), 49–52; Marcus Rediker asserts that strong notions of irreligiosity and skepticism had their roots in sailor plebeian culture and anticlericalism; see Rediker, *Between the Devil and the Deep Blue Sea*, 173–79.

18. Minton, *Journal of Patrick Meade*, 4; William Rounesville Alger, "Effect of Sea Life on Land Life," *Boatswain's Whistle*, 9 November 1864, 5, Americana Catalogue, Huntington Library.

19. Frederic E. Davis to Parents, 29 May 1862, Frederic E. Davis Papers, Special Collections, Woodruff Library, Emory University, Atlanta, Ga.; Frederic E. Davis to Mother, 3 August 1862, Davis Papers.

20. Diary Entry, 23 February 1862, Civil War Diary of John G. Morrison, 1861–1865, Naval Historical Foundation Collection, Washington Navy Yard, Washington, D.C.; Log Entry, 16 August 1863, Lacy Log.

21. Drury, *The History of the Chaplain Corps*, 100.

22. Descriptions of tattoos are from physical descriptions of men contained in rendezvous reports between 1861 and 1865, recorded in *Enlistment Returns, Changes, and Reports, 1846–1942, Weekly Returns of Enlistments at Naval Rendezvous, January 6, 1855–August 8, 1891*, vols. 17–43, Records of the Bureau of Naval Personnel, Record Group 24, National Archives Building, Washington, D.C. (hereafter cited as "Rendezvous Reports"). See also George Geer to Wife, 24 May 1862, in William Marvel, ed., *The Monitor Chronicles: One Sailor's Account* (New York: Simon and Schuster, 2000), 87; William P. Mack and Royal W. Connell, *Naval Ceremonies, Customs, and Traditions*, 5th ed. (Annapolis: Naval Institute Press, 1980), 288.

23. John Swift to Rosie Whiteside,

3 December 1863, in Lester L. Swift, ed., "Letters from a Sailor on a Tinclad," *Civil War History* 10 (March 1961): 50.

24. Peter Karsten, *The Naval Aristocracy: The Golden Age of Annapolis and the Emergence of a Modern American Navalism* (New York: Free Press, 1972), 73; Merrill, "Men, Monotony, and Mouldy Beans," 49–51; Browning, *From Cape Charles to Cape Fear*, 209–10; Alger, "Effect of Sea Life on Land Life," 5; Joseph Collins to Mother and Father, 10 December 1862, James B. and Joseph T. Collins Papers, Manuscripts, New-York Historical Society; George E. Clark, *Seven Years of a Sailor's Life* (Boston: Adams, 1867), 171.

25. Alger, "Effect of Sea Life on Land Life," 5.

26. Ibid., 5.

27. Joseph Osborne to Mary Osborne, 16 October 1864, Osborne Family Papers.

28. William C. Miller to Brother William Thoms, 14 December 1861, Thoms Papers.

29. Rediker, *Between the Devil and the Deep Blue Sea*, 173.

30. Nancy F. Cott, *The Bonds of Womanhood: "Women's Sphere" in New England, 1780–1835* (New Haven: Yale University Press, 1977), 126–59.

31. Mary Osborne to Joseph B. Osborne, 8 September 1864, Osborne Family Papers.

32. Thomas Copernicus Wright to Jane Wright, 30 September 1864, Civil War Papers—Union, Civil War Collection, Manuscripts, Missouri Historical Society, St. Louis, Mo.

33. Alger, "Effect of Sea Life on Land Life," 5.

34. Rediker, *Between the Devil and the Deep Blue Sea*, 169.

35. James Birtwistle to Dr. William F. Thoms, 8 November 1862, Thoms Papers; I. E. Vail, *Three Years on the Blockade: A Naval Experience* (New York: Abbey Press, 1902), 156; Clark, *Seven Years of a Sailor's Life*, 170–71; New York Bible Society, *Thirty-ninth Annual Report of the New York Bible Society*, 34; Frederic E. Davis to Parents, 31 May 1862, Davis Papers.

36. Stivers, *Privateers and Volunteers*, 354.

37. Smith, *Incidents of the United States Christian Commission*, 453–55; New York Bible Society, *Thirty Ninth Annual Report of the New York Bible Society*, 34.

38. Adolphus Dixon to Captain G. J. Van Brunt, 4 July 1862, Box 286, Naval Justice ("NJ"), 1860–1870, Discipline and Minor Delinquencies, Individual Cases, J–L, Subject File, United States Navy, 1775–1910 (hereafter cited as "Navy Subject File"), Record Group 45, National Archives Building, Washington, D.C.; Ensign F. M. Montell to John A. Dahlgren, 21 January 1864, Box 284, NJ, 1860–1870, Minor Delinquencies and Cases Where There Is No Record That a Court Martial Was Held, Folder 1, Navy Subject File; Lieutenant Alfred Hopkins to Lt. Comm. H. K. Davenport, 5 August 1862, Box 284, NJ, 1860–1870, Minor Delinquencies and Cases Where There Is No Record That a Court Martial Was Held, Folder 1, Navy Subject File.

39. Minton, *Journal of Patrick Meade*, 4; Thomas McNeil to William Thoms, 5 November 1862, Thoms Papers; William C. Miller to Brother Thoms, 14 December 1861, Thoms

Papers; Diary Entry, 12 September 1862, George R. Yost Diary, Illinois State Historical Library, Springfield, Ill.; Log Entry, 31 October 1863, in Kent Packard, ed., "Jottings by the Way: A Sailor's Log—1862 to 1864," Part 1, *Pennsylvania Magazine of History and Biography* 71 (April 1947): 151; Stivers, *Privateers and Volunteers*, 353–54.

40. Rediker, *Between the Devil and the Deep Blue Sea*, 167.

41. *An Act for the Better Government of the Navy of the United States*, 17 July 1862, 37th Cong., 2d sess., in *The Statutes at Large, Treaties, and Proclamations of the United States of America, 1859 to 1863*, vol. 12 (Boston: Little, Brown, 1863), 602.

42. Rediker, *Between the Devil and the Deep Blue Sea*, 167.

43. General Order No. 158 of Rear-Admiral David D. Porter, 18 January 1864, in *Official Records of the Union and Confederate Navies in the War of the Rebellion*, ser. 1, 27 vols. (Washington, D.C.: Government Printing Office, 1894–1917) (hereafter cited as "ORN"), 25:701; Browning, *From Cape Charles to Cape Fear*, 212; Journal Entry, 25 June 1863, Thomas Lyons Journal, Journal Kept on Board U.S. Steam Gun Boat Carondolet and U.S.S. Lafayette, January 8, 1863–January 20, 1863, Naval Historical Foundation Collection, Library of Congress; Still, "The Common Sailor," 34–36; Journal Entry, 1 November 1865, Journal of Chaplain Donald C. McLaren, July 25, 1865, to October 24, 1867, P. H. W. Smith Collection, Manuscripts, New Jersey Historical Society, Newark, N.J.; Sperry, *Religion in the Post-war World*, 59–60; Frederic E. Davis to Parents, 31 May 1862, Davis Papers.

44. James E. Valle, *Rocks and Shoals: Order and Discipline in the Old Navy, 1800–1861* (Annapolis: Naval Institute Press, 1980), 15.

45. James Birtwistle to William F. Thoms, 8 November 1862, Thoms Papers; Andrew H. Foote to Henry H. Halleck, 25 February 1862, ORN, 22:632; Francis B. Butts, "Reminiscences of Gunboat Service on the Nansemond," in *Personal Narratives of the Events in the War of Rebellion, Being Papers Read before the Rhode Island Soldiers and Sailors Historical Society*, 3d ser. (Providence: N. B. Williams, 1884), 7; Diary Entry, n.d. [15 September 1861], Diary of John B. Wirts, Cruise of the Lancaster in the North and South Pacific from May 12, 1859, to October 15, 1861, Special Collections, University of California at Los Angeles, Los Angeles, Calif.; Valle, *Rocks and Shoals*, 15–16.

46. Joseph B. Osborne to Louise Landau, 3 October 1864, in Merrill, "Men, Monotony, and Mouldy Beans," 57.

47. George Geer to Wife, 13 June 1862, in Marvel, *The Monitor Chronicles*, 96; Anonymous, "Life on a Blockader," *Continental Monthly* 6 (July 1864): 50; Ringle, *Life in Mr. Lincoln's Navy*, 50; Franklin E. Smith to Family, 26 December 1861, in Merrill, "Men, Monotony, and Mouldy Beans," 49; Diary Entries, 2 July 1863, 29 August 1863, Fayette Clapp Diary, 1862–1863, Western Historical Manuscript Collection, Ellis Library, University of Missouri, Columbia, Mo.

48. Thomas McNeil to William F. Thoms, 5 November 1862, Thoms Papers; Stivers, *Privateers and Volunteers*, 354.

49. Drury, *The History of the Chaplain Corps*, 1–2.

50. U.S. Congress, House of Representatives, *Chaplains in Congress and in the Army and Navy*, House Report No. 124, 33d Cong., 1st sess., 27 March 1854 (ser. 743), 7–8.

51. Drury, *The History of the Chaplain Corps*, 94.

52. Still, "The Common Sailor," 25.

53. Drury, *The History of the Chaplain Corps*, 95. Charts Showing Numbers of Chaplains, Vessels, and Men in the United States Navy, 1861–1865, 1906, 12 July 1924, Box 360, Naval Personnel, Miscellaneous Material, Chaplains in the Navy, 1855, Navy Subject File; Anonymous, "Only Three Chaplains in the Navy in Sea Going Vessels," *Sailor's Magazine* 35 (January 1863): 134–35; Anonymous, "Naval Chaplains," *Sailor's Magazine* 35 (February 1863): 161–62.

54. "Second Annual Report of the U.S. Christian Commission for the Army and Navy," April 1864, in U.S. Christian Commission, *United States Christian Commission for the Army and Navy: Work and Incidents* (Philadelphia: U.S. Christian Commission, 1862–65), 231 (hereafter cited as *Work and Incidents*); Moss, *Annals of the U.S. Christian Commission*, 337.

55. "Third Annual Report of the U.S. Christian Commission for the Army and Navy," January 1865, Mississippi Squadron, in U.S. Christian Commission, *Work and Incidents*, 101.

56. Bell I. Wiley, "'Holy Joes' of the Sixties: A Study of Civil War Chaplains," *Huntington Library Quarterly* 16 (May 1953): 290–91; Anonymous, "Religious Instruction in the Army," *Princeton Review* 35 (July 1863): 386–99.

57. Journal Entry, 8 September 1861, George Adams Bright Journal, George Adams Bright Collection, Manuscripts, Huntington Library.

58. Gustavus Vasa Fox to George S. Blake, 30 September 1862, in Robert M. Thompson and Richard Wainwright, eds., *Confidential Correspondence of Gustavus Vasa Fox, Assistant Secretary of the Navy, 1861–1865*, 2 vols. (New York: De Vinne Press, 1918–19), 2:389.

59. Armstrong, *For Courageous Fighting and Confident Dying*, 44.

60. Rollin Quimby, "The Chaplains' Predicament," *Civil War History* 8 (March 1962): 26; George Fredrickson, "The Coming of the Lord: The Northern Protestant Clergy and the Civil War Crisis," in Randall M. Miller, Harry S. Stout, and Charles Reagan Wilson, *Religion and the American Civil War*, (New York: Oxford University Press, 1998), 110–30.

61. Rockwell, *Sketches of Foreign Travel and Life at Sea*, 2:392.

62. Journal Entry, 24 October 1865, McLaren Journal; William J. Clark to Mother, 28 January 1862, William J. Clark Papers, Historical Society of Pennsylvania, Philadelphia, Pennsylvania.

63. New York Bible Society, *Thirty Ninth Report of the New York Bible Society*, 34; *An Act to Increase and Regulate Pay of the Navy of the United States*, 1 June 1860, 36th Cong., 1st sess., in *Statutes at Large*, 12:24.

64. Drury, *The History of the Chaplain Corps*, 108.

65. Rediker, *Between the Devil and the Deep Blue Sea*, 174.

66. Joseph Stockbridge to Navy Department, 18 May 1863, Official Navy Correspondence.

67. Ibid.

68. Thomas G. Salter to Gideon Welles, 18 July 1864, Gideon Welles Papers, Manuscripts, Huntington Library.

69. United States Navy, *Regulations for the Government of the United States Navy, 1865* (Washington, D.C.: Government Printing Office, 1865), 102.

70. Karsten, *The Naval Aristocracy*, 73.

71. Dorothy Denneen Volo and James M. Volo, *Daily Life in Civil War America* (Westport, Conn.: Greenwood Press, 1998), 39–40.

72. Denominational figures are from tables originally published in the *Christian Almanac* and appended to U.S. Congress, House of Representatives, *Chaplains in Congress and in the Army and Navy*, 5, 9–10.

73. A Chart Showing Religious Affiliations of United States Navy Chaplains from 1778 to September 1939, in Drury, *The History of the Chaplain Corps*, 255.

74. Drury, *The History of the Chaplain Corps*, 100. According to Drury, there were no Jewish chaplains in the navy during the Civil War.

75. Based on a sample of 4,570 sailors out of the total 118,044 men who enlisted at U.S. Navy Rendezvous between 15 April 1861 and 22 April 1865, in the Rendezvous Reports, 45 percent of all Union sailors were foreign-born.

76. Thomas G. Salter to the Secretary of the Navy, 26 April 1854, Letters of the Brazil Squadron, Official Navy Correspondence; Commander Samuel Mercer to Secretary of the Navy, 25 April 1854, Letters of the Brazil Squadron, Official Navy Correspondence.

77. Joseph Stockbridge to Honorable Hannibal Hamlin, 20 March 1861, in Drury, *The History of the Chaplain Corps*, 98 n. 18.

78. *An Act to Increase and Regulate Pay of the Navy of the United States*, 24.

79. Joseph Stockbridge to Navy Department, 18 May 1863, Official Navy Correspondence.

80. Drury, *The History of the Chaplain Corps*, 101; Charles O. Paullin, *Paullin's History of Naval Administration, 1775–1911* (Annapolis: Naval Institute Press, 1968), 303; New York Bible Society, *Thirty-ninth Report of the New York Bible Society*, 34; Karsten, *The Naval Aristocracy*, 73–74.

81. Drury, *The History of the Chaplain Corps*, 69, 100–101; Karsten, *The Naval Aristocracy*, 73.

82. Karsten, *The Naval Aristocracy*, 87–88.

83. Still, "The Common Sailor," 32; Rowland Stafford True, "Life aboard a Gunboat," *Civil War Times Illustrated* 9 (February 1971): 37; Log Entry, 18 March 1862, Charles A. Poole Log, G. W. Blunt White Library, Mystic Seaport Museum, Mystic, Conn.; Diary Entry, 1 February 1863, Clapp Diary.

84. Karsten, *The Naval Aristocracy*, 87–88; Stivers, *Privateers and Volunteers*, 354; William Keeler to Ann Keeler, 14 July 1864, in Robert W. Daly, ed., *Aboard the USS Florida, 1863–65: The Letters of Paymaster William Frederick Keeler, U.S. Navy, to his Wife, Anna* (Annapolis, Md.: Naval Institute Press, 1968), 185–86.

85. Journal Entry, 8 September 1861, in Burton, *A Journal of the Cruise of the U.S. Ship Susquehanna*, 75.

86. Stivers, *Privateers and Volunteers*, 354–55.

87. John D. Milligan, ed., "Navy Life

on the Mississippi River," *Civil War Times Illustrated* 33 (May–June 1994): 67–70; Diary Entry, 1 February 1863, Clapp Diary; Diary Entry, 18 March 1862, Poole Log; Diary Entry, 16 April 1865, Frank S. Judd Diary, Historical Society of Pennsylvania; Symmes E. Browne to Fannie E. Bassett, 27 April 1862, in John D. Milligan, ed., *From the Fresh-Water Navy: 1861–64; the Letters of Acting Master's Mate Henry R. Browne and Acting Ensign Symmes E. Browne* (Annapolis: Naval Institute Press, 1970), 69; Journal Entry, 8 September 1861, in Burton, *A Journal of the Cruise of the U.S. Ship Susquehanna*, 75.

88. Still, "The Common Sailor," 32.

89. Charles C. Coffin, *My Days and Nights on the Battlefield* (Boston: Estes and Lauriat, 1887), 255; William F. Hutchinson, "Life on the Texan Blockade," in *Personal Narratives of Events in the War of Rebellion, Being Papers Read before the Rhode Island Soldiers and Sailors Historical Society,* 3d ser. (Providence: N. B. Williams, 1883), 12; Journal Entry, 23 November 1862, Journal aboard the U.S. Gunship Essex, 23 September 1861–2 June 1863, James E. Henneberry Papers, Research Collections, Chicago Historical Society, Chicago, Ill. (hereafter cited as "Henneberry Journal").

90. Diary Entry, 1 February 1863, Clapp Diary; Diary Entry, 8 March 1863, in James A. Barnes and Elinor Barnes, eds., *Naval Surgeon Blockading the South, 1862–1866: The Diary of Samuel Pellman Boyer* (Bloomington: Indiana University Press, 1963), 77. In all likelihood, captains and Episcopal chaplains used the Book of Common Prayer of 1789 (First American Prayer Book); see Chester S. Zinni Jr., *A Concise History of the Book of Common Prayer: 1549 to 1979* (New York: Nomis Publications, 1981), 31.

91. Log Entry, 24 July 1864, William Wainwright Log, G. W. Blunt White Library, Mystic Seaport Museum; Edward A. Pierson to Mother, 12 March 1862, Edward A. Pierson Papers, New Jersey Historical Society; Clark, *Seven Years of a Sailor's Life,* 190; Journal Entry, 10 February 1866, McLaren Journal.

92. Joseph Watson, "Life on Board a Blockader: Being the Reminiscences of a Paymaster in the U.S. Navy, 1863," 379–80, Rare Books, Huntington Library.

93. Reid Mitchell, *The Vacant Chair: The Northern Soldier Leaves Home* (New York: Oxford University Press, 1993), 73–74.

94. Log Entry, 24 July 1864, Wainwright Log; Clark, *Seven Years of a Sailor's Life,* 250–51.

95. John D. Rodgers to Dear Sir, 30 June 1861, in John D. Milligan, *Gunboats down the Mississippi* (Annapolis: Naval Institute Press, 1960), 9.

96. Journal Entry, 22 June 1862, George A. Bright Journal, Bright Collection.

97. Drury, *The History of the Chaplain Corps,* 71.

98. Watson, "Life on Board a Blockader," 380.

99. Ibid.

100. Diary Entry, 24 December 1864, Diary of Calvin G. Hutchinson, Calvin G. Hutchinson Papers, Manuscripts, Huntington Library.

101. John D. Rodgers to Dear Sir, 30 June 1861, in Milligan, *Gunboats down the Mississippi,* 9.

102. Karsten, *The Naval Aristocracy,* 74.

103. Ibid., 84.

104. Journal Entry, 13 October 1861, in Burton, *A Journal of the Cruise of the U.S. Ship Susquehanna*, 82; Diary Entry, 10 January 1864, George Durand Diaries, Manuscripts, New-York Historical Society.

105. Rockwell, *Sketches of Foreign Life and Travel at Sea*, 2:394.

106. Journal Entry, 16 February 1862, Harry A. Simmons, "Journal of the Cruise in the U.S. Schooner Sophronia Attached to the Bomb Flotilla," 30 December 1861–31 July 1862, James S. Schoff Collection, William L. Clements Library, University of Michigan; Log Entry, 3 July 1864, Wainwright Log.

107. Diary Entry, 17 September 1865, McLaren Diary.

108. Edward A. Pierson to Mother, 12 March 1862, Pierson Papers.

109. Karsten, *The Naval Aristocracy*, 87–88.

110. Log Entry, 5 April 1863, Lacy Log; Watson, "Life on Board a Blockader," 380.

111. Log Entry, 13 December 1863, Wainwright Log.

112. Log Entry, 13 March 1864, in Kent Packard, "Jottings by the Way: A Sailor's Log—1862 to 1864," Part 2, *Pennsylvania Magazine of History and Biography* 71 (July 1947): 265; Log Entry, 26 November 1863, Wainwright Log; Journal Entry, 24 August 1861, in Burton, *A Journal of the Cruise of the U.S. Ship Susquehanna*, 67.

113. Merrill, "Men, Monotony, and Mouldy Beans," 54.

114. Journal Entry, 23 November 1862, Henneberry Journal.

115. Joseph Stockbridge to Navy Department, 18 May 1863, Official Navy Correspondence; Log Entry, 10 May 1863, Poole Log; Log Entry, 3 May 1863, Wainwright Log.

116. Diary Entry, 18 March 1865, Edwin R. Benedict Diary, 1864–65, Special Collections, Woodruff Library, Emory University, Atlanta, Ga.; Diary Entry, 4 October 1863, in Barnes and Barnes, *Naval Surgeon Blockading the South*, 167.

117. Journal Entry, 23 November 1862, Henneberry Journal.

118. Diary Entry, 12 October 1862, Yost Diary; Log Entries, 3 May, 26 November, 25 December 1863, Wainwright Log; Log Entry, 10 May 1863, Poole Log; Joseph B. Osborne to Louise Landau, 17 October 1864, Osborne Family Papers.

119. Diary Entry, 4 January 1863, Morrison Diary.

120. Diary Entry, 4 October 1863, in Barnes and Barnes, *Naval Surgeon Blockading the South*, 168; John Henry Taylor to Wife and Children, 27 January, 16 November 1862, in Alicia P. Mortensen and Edwin H. Mortensen, eds., *The Family of John Henry Taylor, Jr.: Featuring Family Letters Written during and after the Civil War* (Baltimore: Gateway Press, 1995), 10–11, 80–81.

121. Robert H. Abzug, *Cosmos Crumbling: American Reform and the Religious Imagination* (New York: Oxford University Press, 1994), 111–12.

122. Log Entry, 14 April 1862, Poole Log; Journal Entry, 1 February 1863, Lyons Journal.

123. Diary Entry, 10 January 1864, Durand Diaries; Log Entry, 6 November 1864, in Kent Packard, ed., "Jottings by the Way: A Sailor's Log—1862 to 1864," Part 2, *Pennsylvania Magazine of History and Biography* 71 (July 1947): 276.

124. Log Entry, 6 November 1864, in Packard, "Jottings by the Way," Part 2, 276.

125. Joseph Stockbridge to Navy Department, 18 May 1863, Official Navy Correspondence; Diary Entry, 10 January 1864, Durand Diaries.

126. Diary Entry, 7 March 1865, Benedict Diary; George Geer to Wife, 20 May 1862, in Marvel, *The Monitor Chronicles*, 78; Journal Entry, 8 September 1861, in Burton, *A Journal of the Cruise of the U.S. Ship Susquehanna*, 75.

127. John Swift to Rosie Whiteside, 3 December 1863, in Swift, "Letters from a Sailor on a Tinclad," 50.

128. Mitchell, *The Vacant Chair*, 73.

129. Log Entries, 29 November 1863, 24 July 1864, Wainwright Log; Log Entry, 14 April 1862, Poole Log.

130. Joseph B. Osborne to Louise Landau, 17 October 1864, Osborne Family Papers; Joseph Stockbridge to Navy Department, 18 May 1863, Official Navy Correspondence.

131. Diary Entry, 19 February 1865, Benedict Diary.

132. Log Entry, 14 April 1862, Poole Log.

133. Joseph Stockbridge to Navy Department, 18 May 1863, Official Navy Correspondence.

134. Ibid.; *An Act for the Better Government of the Navy of the United States*, 23 April 1800, in Drury, *The History of the Chaplain Corps*, 100–101.

135. *An Act for the Better Government of the Navy of the United States*, 602.

136. U.S. Congress, House of Representatives, *Chaplains in Congress and in the Army and Navy*, 5.

137. Isaac Toucey to Captain William S. Hudson, 20 February 1860, Box 298, Naval Living Conditions, Customs, etc., 1860–1939, Navy Subject File.

138. Abraham Lincoln to Arnold Fischel, 14 December 1861, and Abraham Lincoln to Archbishop John J. Hughes, 21 October 1861, in Roy P. Basler, ed., *The Collected Works of Abraham Lincoln*, 9 vols. (New Brunswick, N.J.: Rutgers University Press, 1953), 4:69; 5:559–60.

139. Smith, *Incidents of the United States Christian Commission*, 168–69.

140. Diary Entry, 3 December 1865, McLaren Diary.

141. W. Jeffrey Bolster, *Black Jacks: African American Seamen in the Age of Sail* (Cambridge: Harvard University Press, 1997), 123–25. Even though black sailors shared Christian denominations with white sailors, many whites viewed the black practice of Christianity as a different sort of religion, "black religion." This characterization of black Christianity as a separate form of worship also fit neatly into racial attitudes favoring segregation. See Mitchell, *The Vacant Chair*, 59; Reid Mitchell, *Civil War Soldiers: Their Expectations and Their Experiences* (New York: Viking Press, 1988), 119–20; U.S. Navy, Department of the Mississippi, *Internal Rules and Regulations for Vessels of the Mississippi Fleet in the Mississippi River and its Tributaries* (Cincinnati: Rickey and Carroll, 1862–63), 7–13.

142. Journal Entry, 15 June 1863, Lyons Journal.

143. Journal Entry, 17 November 1862, Henneberry Journal; Diary Entry, 30 May 1863, Durand Diaries.

144. Mack and Connell, *Naval Ceremonies, Customs, and Traditions,*

174, 180; James Glazier to Parents, 31 July 1863, James Glazier Collection, Manuscripts, Huntington Library.

145. Log Entry, 26 August 1863, Wainwright Log.

146. Robert McClure to Dr. William F. Thoms, 28 November 1861, and Thomas McNeil to Dr. William F. Thoms, 5 November 1862, Thoms Papers; Joseph Stockbridge to Navy Department, 18 May 1863, Official Navy Correspondence; Chaplain Report, U.S.S. *Lancaster*, Bay of Panama, 27 October 1862, Miscellaneous Letters, Official Navy Correspondence; Log Entries, 9 November, 7 December 1862, Lacy Log; New York Bible Society, *Thirty-ninth Report of the New York Bible Society*, 34.

147. Smith, *Incidents of the United States Christian Commission*, 469.

148. Drury, *The History of the Chaplain Corps*, 101; Joseph Stockbridge to Navy Department, 18 May 1863, Official Navy Correspondence.

149. Drury, *The History of the Chaplain Corps*, 101; Joseph Stockbridge to Navy Department, 18 May 1863, Official Navy Correspondence; New York Bible Society, *Thirty Ninth Report of the New York Bible Society*, 34.

150. Journal Entry, 23 November 1862, Henneberry Journal.

151. Log Entry, 13 March 1864, Wainwright Log.

152. Drury, *The History of the Chaplain Corps*, 101–2; Joseph Stockbridge to Navy Department, 18 May 1863, Official Navy Correspondence.

153. Moss, *Annals of the United States Christian Commission*, 327.

154. Log Entries, 13 March, 3 July, 24 July, 18 September 1864, Wainwright Log; Joseph Stockbridge to

Navy Department, 18 May 1863, Official Navy Correspondence; Drury, *The History of the Chaplain Corps*, 100–101.

155. Log Entry, 29 November 1863, Wainwright Log.

156. Edmund C. Bittinger to Navy Department, 10 March 1862, in Drury, *History of the Chaplain Corps*, 100.

157. Basler, *Collected Works of Abraham Lincoln*, 5:498 n. 1. An account dated 13 November 1862 in the *New York Tribune*, recorded that "Messrs. Fred. Winston, David Hoodley, Foster, Booth, and another gentleman, representing religious bodies in New York City, called upon the President and the heads of departments today to urge upon him the propriety of enforcing a better observance of the Sabbath in the army. The interviews are represented as agreeable and satisfactory."

158. *Order for Sabbath Observance*, General Order, 15 November 1862, in Basler, *Collected Works of Abraham Lincoln*, 5:497–98.

159. Joseph Stockbridge to Navy Department, 18 May 1863, Official Navy Correspondence.

160. Ibid.

161. Joseph B. Osborne to Louise Landau, 17 October 1864, Osborne Family Papers; Journal Entry, 8 September 1861, in Burton, *A Journal of the Cruise of the U.S. Ship Susquehanna*, 75.

162. Joseph Stockbridge to Navy Department, 18 May 1863, Official Navy Correspondence.

163. The constitutionality of the government's providing chaplains for the military is far from settled; see Israel Drazin and Cecil B. Currey, *For God and Country: The History*

of a *Constitutional Challenge to the Army Chaplaincy* (New York: Ktav Publishing House, 1995).

164. U.S. Congress, House of Representatives, *Chaplains in Congress and in the Army and Navy*, 7–8; Stivers, *Privateers and Volunteers*, 353.

165. Still, "The Common Sailor," 32; James Thayer to William F. Thoms, 31 October 1861, Thoms Papers; Log Entry, 2 November 1864, in Packard, "Jottings by the Way," Part 2, 275; Arthur M. Schlesinger, ed., "A Blue Bluejacket's Letters Home, 1863–1864," *New England Quarterly* 1 (October 1928): 562; Merrill, "Men, Monotony, and Mouldy Beans," 51.

166. Joseph Stockbridge to Navy Department, 18 May 1863, Official Navy Correspondence.

167. Joseph Osborne to Louise Landau, 2 October 1864, in Merrill, "Men, Monotony, and Mouldy Beans," 50; Stivers, *Privateers and Volunteers*, 345; Merrill, "Men, Monotony, and Mouldy Beans," 51; Log Entry, 23 September 1864, Wainwright Log; Log Entry, 25 October 1864, in Packard, "Jottings by the Way," Part 2, 275; Diary Entry, 2 March 1864, in Lawrence Van Alstyne, *Diary of an Enlisted Man* (New Haven: Tuttle, Morehouse, and Taylor, 1910), 276.

168. "The History of the Christian Commission," in William C. Wilkinson, *A Free Lance in the Field of Life and Letters* (New York: Albert Mason, 1874), 270–71.

169. Valle, *Rocks and Shoals*, 18; General Order, Navy Department, 17 July 1862, ORN, 7:584.

170. Langley, *Social Reform in the United States Navy*, viii, 67; Drury, *The History of the Chaplain Corps*, 97; *Annual Reports of the Protestant Epis-*

copal Church Missionary Society for Seamen, *1851–1891* (New York: White and Ross, 1965), 7–47.

171. Langley, *Social Reform in the United States Navy*, viii, 67; see General Order of Gideon Welles, 17 July 1862, ORN, 7:584.

172. Robert H. Bremner, "The Impact of the Civil War on Philanthropy and Social Welfare," *Civil War History* 12 (December 1966): 301.

173. McDevitt, "Fighting for the Soul of America," 9; U.S. Christian Commission, *Work and Incidents*, 83.

174. Bremner, "The Impact of the Civil War on Philanthropy and Social Welfare," 301.

175. McDevitt, "Fighting for the Soul of America," 152.

176. George M. Fredrickson, *The Inner Civil War: Northern Intellectuals and the Crisis of Union* (New York: Harper and Row, 1965), 107.

177. Drury, *The History of the Chaplain Corps*, 97; Diary Entry, 28 August 1864, Samuel Pollock Diary, Samuel Pollock Papers, Illinois State Historical Library.

178. U.S. Christian Commission, *Work and Incidents*, 101, 115, 121, 163–64, 231.

179. Drury, *The History of the Chaplain Corps*, 97; Moss, *Annals of the United States Christian Commission*, 687; U.S. Christian Commission, *Work and Incidents*, 120–21; McDevitt, "Fighting for the Soul of America," 151 n. 166; Ringle, *Life in Mr. Lincoln's Navy*, 89.

180. Stivers, *Privateers and Volunteers*, 354; Moss, *Annals of the United States Christian Commission*, 707.

181. U.S. Christian Commission, *Principles and Position of the United States Christian Commission* (San

Francisco: Towne and Bacon, 1864), 1. Reid Mitchell contends that links to home and the family were central to soldiers' understanding and surviving the Civil War; see Mitchell, *The Vacant Chair*, xiii.

182. McDevitt, "Fighting for the Soul of America," 195; U.S. Christian Commission, *Work and Incidents*, 72; Reverend H. Loomis, *Christian Work among Soldiers* (Yokohama, Japan: Fukuin, 1908), 10.

183. Still, "The Common Sailor," 34; U.S. Christian Commission, *Work and Incidents*, 189, 71–72, 83; Smith, *Incidents of the United States Christian Commission*, 298, 444.

184. U.S. Christian Commission, *Work and Incidents*, 71–72.

185. Gideon Welles to George H. Stuart, 16 December 1861, in U.S. Christian Commission, *Work and Incidents*, 107. President Lincoln also seemed to view the commission as a double-edged sword. George Stuart invited the president to speak at its first meeting of the year on 12 February 1863 in Washington, D.C. The president, calling the matter "not *very* important," still felt the matter of his appearance weighty enough that he asked the cabinet whether he should attend. Only one cabinet member, Secretary of the Treasury Salmon P. Chase, recommended that the president attend. He did not. See Abraham Lincoln to Alexander Reed, 22 February 1863, and Abraham Lincoln to William H. Seward, 18 February 1863, Basler, *Collected Works of Abraham Lincoln*, 6:114–15, 110.

186. U.S. Christian Commission, *Principles and Position of the United States Christian Commission*, 10.

187. John Eliot Parkman to Eliza-beth Parkman, 11 December 1864, John Eliot Parkman Papers, vol. 1, Massachusetts Historical Society, Boston, Mass.; Fredrickson, *The Inner Civil War*, 107.

188. U.S. Christian Commission, *Principles and Position of the United States Christian Commission*, 10–13.

189. Bell I. Wiley, *The Life of Billy Yank: The Common Soldier of the Union* (Baton Rouge: Louisiana State University Press, 1971), 269.

190. U.S. Christian Commission, *Work and Incidents*, 101.

191. Ibid., 151.

192. Smith, *Incidents of the United States Christian Commission*, 454.

193. Fredrickson, *The Inner Civil War*, 107.

194. John Eliot Parkman to Eliza-beth Parkman, 11 December 1864, Parkman Papers.

195. Ibid.

196. McDevitt, "Fighting for the Soul of America," 157.

197. John Swift to Rosie Whiteside, 2 June 1864, in Swift, "Letters from a Sailor on a Tinclad," 55.

198. Diary Entry, 23 May 1865, Judd Diary; John Swift to Rosie Whiteside, 2 June 1864, in Swift, "Letters from a Sailor on Tinclad," 55; George A. Bright to John Bright, 17 November 1861, Bright Collection.

199. Wilkinson, *A Free Lance*, 288–91.

200. Fredrickson, *The Inner Civil War*, 107; Journal Entry, 24 July 1864, Journal of Levi Hayden, vol. 1, May 27, 1864–January 31, 1879, Levi Hayden Papers, Manuscripts and Archives, New York Public Library.

201. Journal Entry, 16 October 1864, Hayden Journal; U.S. Christian Commission, *Hymn-Book for the Army*

*and Navy* (Cincinnati: U.S. Christian Commission, n.d.), 14–16.

202. Ibid., 15–16.

203. Smith, *Incidents of the United States Christian Commission*, 453–54.

204. Ibid., 454–55.

205. John Swift to Rosie Whiteside, 2 June 1864, in Swift, "Letters from a Sailor on a Tinclad," 55.

206. Drury, *The History of the Chaplain Corps*, 97.

207. Journal Entry, 24 July 1864, Hayden Journal.

208. Still, "The Common Sailor," 32; Ringle, *Life in Mr. Lincoln's Navy*, 139.

209. U.S. Christian Commission, *Work and Incidents*, 120–21.

210. Moss, *Annals of the United States Christian Commission*, 327.

211. Drury, *The History of the Chaplain Corps*, 101; Chaplain Report, U.S.S. *Lancaster*, 27 October 1862, Official Navy Correspondence; Journal Entry, 1 November 1865, McLaren Journal; Charles Kember to Dr. William F. Thoms, 4 August 1861, Thoms Papers.

212. U.S. Christian Commission, *Work and Incidents*, 101.

213. Stivers, *Privateers and Volunteers*, 353.

214. James Moorhead, *American Apocalypse: Yankee Protestants and the Civil War, 1860–1869* (New Haven: Yale University Press, 1978), 65–69; Wiley, "'Holy Joes' of the Sixties," 287; Stephen E. Woodworth, *While God Is Marching On: The Religious World of Civil War Soldiers* (Lawrence: University Press of Kansas, 2001).

CHAPTER 7

1. Joseph T. Glatthaar, *Forged in Battle: The Civil War Alliance of Black Soldiers and White Officers* (New York: Free Press, 1990), 198–99.

2. Steven Ramold incorrectly contends that "the sharing of a common maritime experience, along with a tradition of African American service in the navy, tended to minimize friction between white and black sailors." He also maintains that they suffered no segregation. See Steven J. Ramold, *Slaves, Sailors, Citizens: African Americans in the Union Navy* (DeKalb: Northern Illinois University Press, 2002), 5, 97, 100, 112, 114.

3. Harold D. Langley, *Social Reform in the United States Navy, 1798–1862* (Urbana: University of Illinois Press, 1967), viii; Eric Lott, *Love and Theft: Blackface Minstrelsy and the American Working Class* (New York: Oxford University Press, 1995), 68.

4. W. Jeffery Bolster, *Black Jacks: African American Seamen in the Age of Sail* (Cambridge: Harvard University Press, 1997), 70. For comparisons between a sailor's life at sea and a slave's life on the plantation, see Richard B. Morris, *Government and Labor in Early America* (New York: Columbia University Press, 1946), 230, 247, 256, 262, 274; Robert McColley, *Slavery and Jeffersonian Virginia* (Urbana: University of Illinois Press, 1964), 103; and Frederick Law Olmsted, *The Cotton Kingdom: A Traveller's Observations on Cotton and Slavery in the American Slave States*, ed. Arthur M. Schlesinger (1860; reprint, New York: Alfred A. Knopf, 1953), 453. For a history of black maritime workers along the North Carolina coast and the dynamic relationship between race and the maritime South, see David S. Cecelski, *The Waterman's Song: Slavery and Freedom in Maritime North Carolina* (Chapel Hill: University of North Carolina Press, 2001).

5. David R. Roediger, *The Wages of Whiteness: Race and the Making of the American Working Class* (New York: Verso Press, 1991), 68; Greg Dening, *Mr. Bligh's Bad Language: Passion, Power, and Theatre on the Bounty* (Cambridge: Cambridge University Press, 1992), 154–55.

6. Langley, *Social Reform in the United States Navy*, viii.

7. Olmsted, *The Cotton Kingdom*, 380, 452–56; Herman Melville, *White-Jacket; or, The World in a Man-of-War* (1850; reprint, New York: Quality Paperback Book Club, 1996).

8. Richard Henry Dana Jr., *Two Years before the Mast: A Personal Narrative of a Life at Sea* (1840; reprint, New York: World Publishing Company, 1946), 121.

9. An 1839 directive from Acting Secretary of the Navy Isaac Chauncey instructed recruiting officers "not to enter a greater proportion of free colored persons than five percent of the whole number of white persons entered by him weekly or monthly, and in no instance and under no circumstances to enter a slave." See Acting Secretary of the Navy Isaac Chauncey to John Downs, Commander of the Boston Naval Office, 19 April 1839, in Herbert Aptheker, "The Negro in the Union Navy," *Journal of Negro History* 32 (April 1947): 173 n. 15. The navy seems to have followed this guideline hereafter; see Secretary of the Navy A. P. Upshur to Speaker of the House, 10 August 1842, in House Exec. Doc. No. 282, 27th Cong., 2d sess. (ser. 405), vol. 5.

10. James M. McPherson, *Ordeal by Fire: The Civil War and Reconstruction* (New York: McGraw-Hill, 1992), 347; James M. McPherson, *The Negro's Civil War: How American Negroes Felt and Acted during the War for the Union* (New York: Pantheon Books, 1965), 19–23.

11. Jesse Lemisch, "Jack Tar in the Streets: Merchant Seamen in the Politics of Revolutionary America," *William and Mary Quarterly* 25 (July 1968): 380. As late as 1897, the U.S. Supreme Court declared that "seamen are treated by Congress, as well as the Parliament of Great Britain, as deficient in that full and intelligent responsibility for their acts which is accredited to ordinary adults." See Elmo Paul Hohman, *Seamen Ashore: A Study of the United Seamen's Service and of Merchant Seamen in Port*, with a foreword by William S. Newell and E. S. Land (New Haven: Yale University Press, 1952), 214. For a description of the character failings of sailors, see Charles Rockwell, *Sketches of Foreign Travel and Life at Sea*, 2 vols. (Boston: Tappan and Dennet, 1842), 2:388–93; and William Rounesville Alger, "Effect of Sea Life on Land Life," *Boatswain's Whistle*, 9 November 1864, 5, Americana Catalogue, Huntington Library, San Marino, Calif.

12. Gaddis Smith, "Black Seamen and the Federal Courts, 1789–1860," in Timothy J. Runyan, ed., *Ships, Seafaring, and Society: Essays in Maritime History* (Detroit: Wayne State University Press, 1987), 321; Bolster, *Black Jacks*, 218.

13. Margaret S. Creighton, *Rites and Passages: The Experience of American Whaling, 1830–1870* (Cambridge: Cambridge University Press, 1995), 59.

14. W. Jeffrey Bolster, "To Feel Like a Man: Black Seamen in Northern States, 1800–1860," *Journal of American History* 76 (March 1990): 1194.

15. David L. Valuska, *The African American in the Union Navy, 1861–1865* (New York: Garland, 1993), 19–20.

16. O. S. Glisson to Silas H. Stringham, 15, 17 July 1861, *Official Records of the Union and Confederate Navies in the War of the Rebellion*, ser. 1, 27 vols. (Washington, D.C.: Government Printing Office, 1894–1917) (hereafter cited as "ORN"), 6:8–9; Silas H. Stringham to Gideon Welles, 18 July 1861, ORN, 6:8–9; S. H. Stringham to Gideon Welles, 14 August 1861, ORN, 6:80–81; J. W. Livingston to Silas H. Stringham, 15 August 1861, ORN, 6:85–86; O. S. Glisson to Silas H. Stringham, 20 August 1861, ORN, 6:95; O. S. Glisson to Silas H. Stringham, 22 August 1861, ORN, 6:107; Samuel Lockwood to Silas H. Stringham, 26 August 1861, ORN, 6:113–14; Aptheker, "The Negro in the Union Navy," 174–75; Diary Entries, 14, 24 December 1862, George R. Yost Diary, Illinois State Historical Library, Springfield, Ill.

17. Valuska, *The African American in the Union Navy*, 19–21.

18. George A. Prentiss to S. F. Du Pont, 12 June 1862, ORN, 13:92–93; S. F. Du Pont to George Balch, 21 August 1862, ORN, 13:270; S. F. Du Pont to Gustavus Vasa Fox, 22 December 1862, ORN, 13:485–86.

19. James Barker Farr, "Black Odyssey: The Seafaring Traditions of Afro-Americans" (Ph.D. diss., University of California, Santa Barbara, 1975), 131–32.

20. John D. Milligan, ed., "Gunboat War at Vicksburg," *American Heritage* 29 (August–September 1978): 65.

21. I. E. Vail, *Three Years on the Blockade: A Naval Experience* (New York: Abbey Press, 1902), 91–92.

22. Gideon Welles to Louis M. Goldsborough, 25 September 1861, ORN, 6:252; William N. Still, "The Common Sailor: The Civil War's Uncommon Man; Part 1, Yankee Blue Jackets," *Civil War Times Illustrated* 23 (February 1985): 28.

23. James Birtwistle to Dr. William F. Thoms, 8 November 1862, William F. Thoms Papers, Letters from Seamen, 1853–1864, New York Nautical School, Manuscripts, New-York Historical Society, New York, N.Y.; Vail, *Three Years on the Blockade*, 156; George E. Clark, *Seven Years of a Sailor's Life* (Boston: Adams, 1867), 170–71.

24. U.S. Navy, Department of the Mississippi, *Internal Rules and Regulations for Vessels of the Mississippi Fleet in the Mississippi River and Tributaries* (Cincinnati: Rickey and Carroll, 1862–63), 13; Bartholomew Diggins, "Recollections of the War Cruise of the U.S. Flag Ship Hartford, January 8, 1862, to December 24, 1864," 149, Manuscripts and Archives, New York Public Library, New York, N.Y.

25. Vail, *Three Years on the Blockade*, 91–93.

26. Lieutenant Joseph P. Couthouy to Friend, 15 April 1862, in Michael Harris Goodman, "The Black Tar: Negro Seamen in the Union Navy" (Ph.D. diss., University of Nottingham, 1975), 225.

27. Louis S. Gerteis, *From Contraband to Freedman: Federal Policy toward Southern Blacks, 1861–1865* (Westport, Conn.: Greenwood Press, 1973), 193–94.

28. Journal Entry, 23 November 1862, Journal aboard U.S. Gunship

Essex, 23 September 1861–2 June 1863, James E. Henneberry Papers, Research Collections, Chicago Historical Society, Chicago, Ill. (hereafter cited as "Henneberry Journal"); Silas H. Stringham to Gideon Welles, 18 July 1861, ORN, 6:8–9.

29. Clark, *Seven Years of a Sailor's Life*, 212; J. B. Marchard to S. F. Du Pont, 26 May 1862, ORN, 13:36.

30. Diggins, "Recollections of the War Cruise of the U.S. Flag Ship Hartford," 149–150; Freeman Foster to Father, 15 May 1862, Freeman Foster Papers, Louisiana and Lower Mississippi Valley Collections, Hill Memorial Library, Louisiana State University, Baton Rouge, La.; Memorandum Book Entries, 28, 29 May 1863, 7, 8, 11 June 1863, Alexander R. Miller Memorandum Book aboard the U.S. Steamers DeKalb and Lafayette, 1861–1864, Louisiana and Lower Mississippi Valley Collections, Hill Memorial Library, Louisiana State University; William Van Cleaf to Mother, 14 April 1862, William Van Cleaf Papers, Special Collections and University Archives, Rutgers University, New Brunswick, N.J.; Diary Entries, 3, 14 June 1863, Fayette Clapp Diary, 1862–1863, Western Historical Manuscript Collection, Ellis Library, University of Missouri, Columbia, Mo.; George Geer to Wife, 9 June 1862, in William Marvel, ed., *The Monitor Chronicles: One Sailor's Account* (New York: Simon and Schuster, 2000), 93–95; Log Entries, 18 May, 4 June 1863, Milo Lacy Log, Manuscripts, Naval Historical Center Library, Washington Navy Yard, Washington, D.C.

31. J. C. Chaplin to L. M. Goldsborough, Endorsement of L. M.

Goldsborough, 27 October 1861, ORN, 6:363–64; S. P. Lee to Gideon Welles, 5 October 1862, ORN, 8:118–19; Thomas J. Woodward to Charles W. Flusser, 19 November 1862, ORN, 8:217–18.

32. Journal Entry, 17 June 1863, Thomas Lyons Journal, Journal Kept on Board U.S. Steam Gunboat Carondolet and U.S.S. Lafayette, January 8, 1863–January 20, 1863, Naval Historical Foundation Collection, Library of Congress, Washington, D.C.; Memorandum Book Entries, 11, 19, 22 June 1863, Miller Memorandum Book.

33. Valuska, *The African American in the Union Navy*, 86–87.

34. Leon Litwack, *North of Slavery: The Negro in the Free States, 1790–1860* (Chicago: University of Chicago Press, 1961), viii–ix, 99.

35. John Swift to Rosie Whiteside, 3 December 1863, in Lester L. Swift, ed., "Letters from a Sailor on a Tinclad," *Civil War History* 10 (March 1961): 50; Journal Entry, 11 April 1864, Henneberry Journal.

36. Rowland Stafford True, "Life aboard a Gunboat," *Civil War Times Illustrated* 9 (February 1971): 38. The term "romanticized racism" is discussed in George M. Fredrickson, *The Black Image in the White Mind: The Debate on Afro-American Character and Destiny, 1817–1914* (Hanover, N.H.: Wesleyan University Press, 1987), 102.

37. Diary Entry, 23 April 1863, Charles A. Hart Diary, History and Genealogy, Connecticut State Library, Hartford, Conn.

38. William H. Price to Friend, 2 May 1864, W. H. Price Papers, Illinois State Historical Library.

39. Silas H. Stringham to Gideon

Welles, 18 July 1861, ORN, 6:8–9; S. F. Du Pont to Brigadier General Saxton, 2 November 1862, ORN, 13:426.

40. William B. Gould IV, "Lincoln, Labor, and the Black Military: The Legacy Provided," Speech before the Military Order of the Loyal Legion of the United States in Honor of President Lincoln, 11 February 1995, 1; Diary Entries, 23 January, 10 February 1863, in James A. Barnes and Elinor Barnes, eds., *Naval Surgeon Blockading the South, 1862–1866: The Diary of Samuel Pellman Boyer* (Bloomington: Indiana University Press, 1963), 50, 66; Journal Entry, 4 June 1863, Service on a Ferry-Boat of Joint Army and Navy Work, 1861–1863, 17, Calvin G. Hutchinson Papers, Manuscripts, Huntington Library.

41. Diary Entry, 3 June 1863, Clapp Diary; Charles C. Brewer, "African American Sailors and the Unvexing of the Mississippi River," *Prologue* 30 (Winter 1998): 279; J. B. Marchard to S. F. Du Pont, 5 June 1862, ORN, 13:77; John H. Taylor Jr. to Wife, Mother, and Children, 10 July 1862, in Alice P. Mortensen and Edwin H. Mortensen, eds., *The Family of John Henry Taylor, Jr.: Featuring Family Letters Written during and after the Civil War* (Baltimore: Gateway Press, 1995), 47–48.

42. Thomas M. Buchanan to William N. McKean, 6 January 1862, Box 360, Naval Personnel, Miscellaneous Material, Miscellaneous Material Relative to Survivors and Destitute Civilians and Refugees, Materials Relative to Contrabands, Subject File, U.S. Navy, 1775–1910 (hereafter cited as "Navy Subject File"), Record Group 45, National Archives Building, Washington, D.C.

43. Log Entry, 18 April 1863, in Kent Packard, ed., "Jottings by the Way: A Sailor's Log—1862 to 1864," Part 1, *Pennsylvania Magazine of History and Biography* 71 (April 1947): 129.

44. Journal Entry, 18 April 1864, Henneberry Journal.

45. Freeman Foster to Father, 15 May 1862, Foster Papers; Diary Entry, 10 February 1863, Yost Diary; Edward Morgan to David D. Porter, 2 September 1863, David D. Porter Papers, Manuscripts, Huntington Library; William N. Bock to Father, 19 April 1864, William N. Bock Papers, Manuscripts, Illinois State Historical Library; O. S. Glisson to Silas H. Stringham, 17 July 1861, ORN, 6:9; M. Woodhull to Charles Wilkes, 19 August 1862, ORN, 7:658.

46. Journal Entry, 4 June 1863, Service on a Ferry-Boat of Joint Army and Navy Work, Hutchinson Papers.

47. James M. McPherson, *For Cause and Comrades: Why Men Fought in the Civil War* (New York: Oxford University Press, 1997), 126–30.

48. O. S. Glisson to L. M. Goldsborough, 22 July 1862, ORN, 7:588–89.

49. William H. Price to Friend, 8 October 1862, Price Papers; Memorandum Book Entries, 2, 3, 4, 5 February 1864, Miller Memorandum Book; True, "Life aboard a Gunboat," 38; William N. Bock to George Bock, 17 February 1864, Bock Papers; Diary Entries, 1 January, 2 February 1863, in Barnes and Barnes, *Naval Surgeon Blockading the South*, 50, 66.

50. U.S. Navy, *Internal Rules and Regulations for Vessels of the Mississippi Fleet*, 13; Vail, *Three Years on the Blockade*, 91–92.

51. U.S. Navy, *Internal Rules and Regulations for Vessels of the Mississippi Fleet*, 13; Diggins, "Recollections

of the War Cruise of the U.S. Flag Ship Hartford," 149; Reuben E. Stivers, *Privateers and Volunteers: The Men and Women of Our Reserve Naval Forces, 1766 to 1866* (Annapolis: Naval Institute Press, 1975), 349–50.

52. Clark, *Seven Years of a Sailor's Life*, 212.

53. John Swift to Rosie Whiteside, 3 December 1863, in Swift, "Letters from a Sailor on a Tinclad," 50; True, "Life aboard a Gunboat," 38.

54. Clark, *Seven Years of a Sailor's Life*, 212.

55. Ibid., 213.

56. Gould, "Lincoln, Labor and the Black Military," 8.

57. Clark, *Seven Years of a Sailor's Life*, 212–13; Log Entry, 16 April 1862, Charles A. Poole Log, G. W. Blunt White Library, Mystic Seaport Museum, Mystic, Conn.; Log Entries, 29 October 1862, 31 May 1863, Lacy Log.

58. Diary Entries, 23 January, 10 February 1863, in Barnes and Barnes, *Naval Surgeon Blockading the South*, 50, 51; Log Entry, 1 January 1863, Log of the U.S. Bark Brazileira, June 7, 1862–August 18, 1863, H. G. Thayer Papers, Manuscripts, 3, 7, Library of Congress, (hereafter cited as "Thayer Log").

59. William Marvel, *The Alabama and the Kearsarge: The Sailor's Civil War* (Chapel Hill: University of North Carolina Press, 1996), 42.

60. True, "Life aboard a Gunboat," 38.

61. Lieutenant Louis Kempff to Friend Herman, 9 August 1861, Louis Kempff Papers, Illinois State Historical Library.

62. This conclusion directly contradicts Benjamin Quarles's assertion that only a "minimum" of segregation and discrimination was leveled at black sailors. See Benjamin Quarles, *The Negro in the Civil War* (Boston: Little, Brown, 1953), 229.

63. Order of the Secretary of the Navy to Flag-Officers of the Blockade Service, 30 April 1862, ORN, 7:294.

64. Fredrickson, *The Black Image in the White Mind*, 102.

65. Bolster, *Black Jacks*, 77.

66. Memorandum Book Entries, 2, 3, 4, 5 February 1864, Miller Memorandum Book; True, "Life aboard a Gunboat," 38; Post Script, Commodore Thatcher to Commodore H. H. Bell, 8 December 1863, ORN, 20:712; Jeanette B. Secret, *Iverson Granderson: First Class "Colored" Boy, Union Navy (1863–1865)* (Bowie, Md.: Heritage Books, 1998), 16.

67. William N. Bock to George Bock, 17 February 1864, Bock Papers; Diary Entries, 1 January, 2 February 1863, in Barnes and Barnes, *Naval Surgeon Blockading the South*, 50, 66.

68. Frederick S. Harrod, *Manning the New Navy: The Development of a Modern Naval Enlisted Force, 1899–1940* (Westport, Conn.: Greenwood Press, 1978), 11; Langley, *Social Reform in the United States Navy*, 93; Journal Entry, 24 October 1861, in Amos Burton, *A Journal of the Cruise of the U.S. Ship Susquehanna* (New York: Edward O. Jenkins, 1863), 84.

69. James E. Valle, *Rocks and Shoals: Order and Discipline in the Old Navy, 1800–1861* (Annapolis: Naval Institute Press, 1980), 19–20. After the Civil War, the navy abandoned its policy of an integrated navy. See Frederick S. Harrod, "Jim Crow in the Navy (1798–1941)," *Proceedings of the United States Naval Institute* 105

(September 1979): 46–53; Frederick S. Harrod, "Integration of the Navy (1941–1978)," *Proceedings of the United States Naval Institute* 105 (October 1979): 40–47; Quarles, *The Negro in the Civil War*, 230.

70. Memorandum Book Entries, 2, 3, 4, 5 February 1864, Miller Memorandum Book.

71. True, "Life aboard a Gunboat," 38; Benedict Donohue to Father, 2 December 1862, Benedict Donohue Papers, Manuscripts, Naval Historical Center Library, Washington Navy Yard; Harrod, *Manning the New Navy*, 10–11.

72. Valuska, *The African American in the Union Navy*, 32; Farr, "Black Odyssey," 135, 137.

73. Bolster, *Black Jacks*, 218–19.

74. Andrew Hull Foote to Lieutenant Leonard Paulding, 17 September 1861, ORN, 22:337; James M. Merrill, "Cairo, Illinois: Strategic Civil War River Port," *Journal of Illinois State History* 76 (Winter 1983): 252–54.

75. David D. Porter to Joshua Bishop, 3 August 1863, ORN, 25:338. Andrew H. Foote to Henry H. Halleck, 25 February 1862, ORN, 22:632.

76. V. Jacques Voegeli, *Free but Not Equal* (Chicago: University of Chicago Press, 1967), 1, 4; Valuska, *The African American in the Union Navy*, 48; see also Thomas C. Buchanan, "The Slave Mississippi: African American Steamboat Workers, Networks of Resistance, and the Commercial World of the Western Rivers, 1811–1880" (Ph.D. dissertation, Carnegie Mellon University, 1998).

77. Order of the Secretary of the Navy to Flag-Officers of the Blockade Service, 30 April 1862, ORN, 7:294; Instructions from the Secretary of the Navy to Flag-Officers Regarding Enlistment of Contrabands, 30 April 1862, ORN, 23:80–81.

78. U.S. Navy, *Internal Rules and Regulations for Vessels of the Mississippi Fleet*, 7; True, "Life aboard a Gunboat," 38.

79. U.S. Navy, *Internal Rules and Regulations for Vessels of the Mississippi Fleet*, 7.

80. True, "Life aboard a Gunboat," 38.

81. Farr, "Black Odyssey," 135.

82. Ibid., 135; Goodman, "The Black Tar," 244.

83. Valle, *Rocks and Shoals*, 19–20.

84. Journal Entry, 6 August 1862, Henneberry Journal.

85. Louis A. Zurcher Jr., "The Sailor aboard Ship: A Study of Role Behavior in a Total Institution," *Social Forces* 43 (March 1965): 390.

86. The grog ration was so important that after its official abolition in September 1862, the navy still paid sailors, white and black, daily grog money, which compensated sailors in currency what the navy had deprived them in social and cultural wages, about three dollars per month. See U.S. Navy, *Internal Rules and Regulations for Vessels of the Mississippi Fleet*, 13; Stephen F. Blanding, *Recollections of a Sailor Boy; or, The Cruise of the Gunboat Louisiana* (Providence: E. A. Johnson, 1886), 60.

87. Diary Entry, 29 December 1861, George Durand Diaries, Manuscripts, New-York Historical Society; U.S. Navy, *Internal Rules and Regulations for Vessels of the Mississippi Fleet*, 13.

88. U.S. Navy, *Internal Rules and Regulations for Vessels of the Mississippi Fleet*, 13; David D. Porter to

Gideon Welles, 26 October 1862, ORN, 23:449; Samuel Du Pont to Gideon Welles, 10 June 1863, ORN, 14:251; Stivers, *Privateers and Volunteers*, 349–50.

89. David D. Porter to Gustavus Vasa Fox, 16 January 1863, in Robert Means Thompson and Richard Wainwright, eds., *Confidential Correspondence of Gustavus Vasa Fox, Assistant Secretary of the Navy, 1861–1865*, 2 vols. (New York: De Vinne Press, 1918–19), 2:153–56.

90. Significant numbers of both whites and blacks thought the Civil War was or should be a "white man's war." See Valuska, *The African American in the Union Navy*, 26–27; Bell I. Wiley, *The Life of Billy Yank: The Common Soldier of the Union* (Baton Rouge: Louisiana State University Press, 1971), 119–21.

91. Valuska, *The African American in the Union Navy*, 87–88.

92. William H. Price to Friend, 8 October 1862, Price Papers.

93. David D. Porter, after he was placed in command of the North Atlantic Blockade Squadron in 1864, tried to stem the practice of using blacks as lookouts. Porter believed that they were "not fit to be entrusted with such important duty." David D. Porter to W. A. Parker, 24 November 1864, ORN, 11:90–91; Zurcher, "The Sailor aboard Ship," 397.

94. Diary Entry, 1 January 1862, Durand Diaries.

95. Valuska, *The African American in the Union Navy*, 94–96; Aptheker, "The Negro in the Union Navy," 191; Quarles, *The Negro in the Civil War*, 231–32; Dennis Denmark Nelson, "The Integration of the Negro into the United States Navy, 1776–1947" (M.A. thesis, Howard University, 1948), 20; Vail, *Three Years on the Blockade*, 91–92.

96. Milligan, "Gunboat War at Vicksburg," 65; Freeman Foster to Father, 15 May 1862, Foster Papers; Journal Entry, 24 October 1861, in Burton, *A Journal of the Cruise of the U.S. Ship Susquehanna*, 84.

97. William N. Bock to Father, 2 March 1864, Bock Papers; Diary Entry, 15 January 1862, Durand Diaries; Albert S. Barker, *Everyday Life in the Navy* (Boston: Gorham Press, 1928), 31; Aptheker, "The Negro in the Union Navy," 190; Dennis J. Ringle, *Life in Mr. Lincoln's Navy* (Annapolis: Naval Institute Press, 1998), 13.

98. Robert M. Browning Jr., *From Cape Charles to Cape Fear: The North Atlantic Blockading Squadron during the Civil War* (Tuscaloosa: University of Alabama Press, 1993), 205.

99. Aptheker, "The Negro in the Union Navy," 190–97; General L. Thomas to William H. Stanton, 4 April 1863, ibid., 192.

100. David D. Porter to Andrew Hull Foote, 3 January 1863, ORN, 23:603; Symmes Browne to Fannie Bassett, 27 July 1862, in John D. Milligan, ed., *From the Fresh-Water Navy: 1861–64; the Letters of Acting Master's Mate Henry R. Browne and Acting Ensign Symmes E. Browne* (Annapolis: Naval Institute Press, 1970), 110.

101. James V. Johnson to David D. Porter, 18 August 1863, Bixby Collection, Missouri Historical Society, St. Louis, Mo.; Harrod, *Manning the New Navy*, 10–11; Quarles, *The Negro in the Civil War*, 230; Merrill, "Cairo, Illinois," 251; George B. Balch

to Samuel F. Du Pont, 24 July 1862, ORN, 13:208–9; Percival Drayton to A. G. Clary, 26 May 1862, ORN, 13:43; T. H. Eastman to Foxhall A. Parker, 18 March 1865, ORN, 5:535–36; Goodman, "The Black Tar," 438.

102. Joseph P. Reidy, "Black Jack: African American Sailors in the Civil War Navy," in William B. Cogar, ed., *New Interpretations in Naval History: Selected Papers from the Twelfth Naval History Symposium* (Annapolis: Naval Institute Press, 1997), 213.

103. Circular from the Secretary of the Navy Regarding Rating of Contrabands Employed in U.S. Navy, 18 December 1862, ORN, 5:201.

104. Steven J. Ramold contends that the experience of black sailors proved different and better than that of black soldiers owing to integration, equal pay, and benefits, at least from an institutional standpoint; see Ramold, *Slaves, Sailors, Citizens*, 81–82.

105. See 1864 Pay Schedule in Ringle, *Life in Mr. Lincoln's Navy*, 95; Goodman, "The Black Tar," 252, 257–58; Ramold, *Slaves, Sailors, Citizens*, 67–68, 75.

106. Jacob Cochran to Dr. William Thoms, 27 July 1862, Thoms Papers; Samuel P. Lee to Gideon Welles, 15 December 1862, in Valuska, *The African American in the Union Navy*, 36.

107. See compendium of offenses and punishments kept by Seaman Harry Stanley in Leon Basile, ed., "Harry Stanley's Mess Book: Offenses and Punishments aboard the Ethan Allen," *Civil War History* 23 (March 1977): 69–79; Ringle, *Life in Mr. Lincoln's Navy*, 104.

108. Statement of Seaman William Brown, 24 December 1864, Box 286,

Naval Justice ("NJ"), 1860–1870, Discipline and Minor Delinquencies, Individual Cases, M–N, Navy Subject File; William H. Price to Friend, 8 October 1862, Price Papers.

109. Letterbook Entry, "Memoranda for Senior Officers," 26 January 1862, Charles L. Green Letterbook, Manuscripts, Huntington Library; Statement of Seaman William Brown, 24 December 1864, Box 286, NJ, 1860–1870, Discipline and Minor Delinquencies, Individual Cases, M–N, Navy Subject File.

110. Creighton, *Rites and Passages*, 59; W. J. Rorabaugh, *The Alcoholic Republic: An American Tradition* (New York: Oxford University Press, 1979), 144; Rockwell, *Sketches of Foreign Travel and Life at Sea*, 2:388–93; Roediger, *The Wages of Whiteness*, 13–15.

111. Alvah F. Hunter, *A Year on a Monitor and the Destruction of Fort Sumter*, ed. Craig L. Symonds (Columbia: University of South Carolina Press, 1987), 41.

112. Diary Entries, 15, 16 September 1861, John B. Wirts Diary, Cruise of the Lancaster in the North and South Pacific from May 12, 1859, to October 15, 1861, Special Collections, University of California at Los Angeles; Valuska, *The African American in the Union Navy*, 94.

113. Emerson D. Fite, *Social and Industrial Conditions in the North during the Civil War* (1910; reprint, New York: Frederick Ungar, 1963), 189–90.

114. William Van Cleaf to Brother, 4 May 1862, Van Cleaf Papers; Anonymous, "Life on a Blockader," *Continental Monthly* 6 (July 1864): 50.

115. Letterbook Entry, "Memoranda for Senior Officers," 26 January

1862, Charles L. Green Letterbook; Log Entries, 17 January, 19 July 1864, Poole Log; Log Entries, 20 August, 26 September 1863, Lacy Log.

116. George E. Arnold to Cousin, 15 May 1864, in Arthur M. Schlesinger, ed., "A Blue Bluejacket's Letters Home, 1863–1864," *New England Quarterly* 1 (October 1928): 565.

117. James Eggo, "Jack Ratlin's Lament," in Burton, *A Journal of the Cruise of the U.S. Ship Susquehanna*, 136–37.

118. The navy officially announced the Emancipation Proclamation on 14 January 1863; see General Order No. 4, in Thomas Truxton Moebs, ed., *America's Naval Heritage: A Catalog of Early Imprints from the Navy Department Library* (Washington: Department of the Navy, 2000), 114; McPherson, *For Cause and Comrades*, 123.

119. Joseph Gregory Jr. to William F. Thoms and Family, 25 October 1862, Thoms Papers; Diary Entry, 14 June 1863, Clapp Diary.

120. William H. Price to Friend, 8 October 1862, Price Papers; Diary Entry, 14 June 1863, Clapp Diary.

121. Journal Entry, 1 January 1863, Henneberry Journal.

122. Joseph T. Collins to Mother and Father, 25 January 1863, Letters of James B. and Joseph T. Collins, Manuscripts, New-York Historical Society.

123. Hunter, *A Year on a Monitor and the Destruction of Fort Sumter*, 41; Francis R. Minton, ed., *Journal of Patrick Meade, Jr.* (Medford, Mass.: n.p., 1984), 4.

124. Joseph Osborne to Elias Osborne, 16 November 1864, Osborne Family Papers, Manuscripts, Library of Congress.

125. Edward W. Hammond, "A Personal Reminiscence by Edward Hammond Boatswain, U.S. Navy, of an Incident on Board the U.S. Ship St. Mary's in Valparaiso Harbor 1865," 5, 9, Box 284, 1855–1870, NJ, Discipline and Minor Delinquencies, Attempt by Crew Members to Run the USS St. Mary's into the Mole, Navy Subject File.

126. William Van Cleaf to Mother, 14 April 1862, Van Cleaf Papers.

127. George E. Arnold to Cousin, 15 May 1864, in Schlesinger, "A Blue Bluejacket's Letters Home, 1863–1864," 565; William N. Bock to Father, 19 April 1864, Bock Papers.

128. William N. Bock to Father, 17 February 1864, Bock Papers; Journal Entry, 17 June 1863, Lyons Journal; Valuska, *The African American in the Union Navy*, 87–88.

129. Diggins, "Recollections of the War Cruise of the U.S. Flag Ship Hartford," 149–50.

130. John Swift to Rosie Whiteside, 3 December 1863, in Swift, "Letters from a Sailor on a Tinclad," 50.

131. William C. Holton, "Cruise of the U.S. Flag-Ship Hartford, 1862–1863," ed. B. S. Osbon, *Magazine of History with Notes and Queries* 22 (September–October 1922): 166.

132. Benedict Donohue to Father, 2 December 1862, Donohue Papers; Log Entry, 11 May 1863, Lacy Log.

133. Diggins, "Recollections of the War Cruise of the U.S. Flag Ship Hartford," 149–50.

134. James B. Collins to Father and Mother, 16 January 1863, Collins Papers; Diggins, "Recollections of the War Cruise of the U.S. Flag Ship Hartford," 149–50; Journal Entry, 17 June 1863, Lyons Journal; James Glazier to

Parents, 14 July 1863, James Glazier Collection, Manuscripts, Huntington Library.

135. George E. Arnold to Cousin, 15 May 1864, in Schlesinger, "A Blue Bluejacket's Letters Home, 1863–1864," 565; Diary Entry, 9 March 1863, in Barnes and Barnes, *Naval Surgeon Blockading the South*, 78.

136. William H. Price to Friend, 8 October 1862, Price Papers; Diggins, "Recollections of the War Cruise of the U.S. Flag Ship Hartford," 149–50; James Glazier to Parents, 14 July 1863, Glazier Collection; U.S. Navy, *Internal Rules and Regulations for Vessels of the Mississippi Fleet*, 13; Journal Entry, 15 June 1863, Lyons Journal; Diary Entry, 30 May 1863, George Durand Diary, U.S. Steamer Mohawk, South Atlantic Blockading Squadron, June 23, 1862–August 16, 1863, George Durand Diaries, Manuscripts, New-York Historical Society; Journal Entry, 17 November 1862, Henneberry Journal.

137. Diary Entry, 25 December 1864, Diary of Samuel Pollock, Samuel Pollock Papers, Illinois State Historical Library; Diary Entry, n.d., Oscar C. Lewis Diary, Oscar C. Lewis Papers, Manuscripts, New-York Historical Society; James Glazier to Parents, 14 July 1863, Glazier Collection.

138. Log Entry, 1 January 1863, Thayer Log, 3.

139. Log Entry, 2 November 1864, in Kent Packard, ed., "Jottings by the Way: A Sailor's Log—1862 to 1864," Part 2, *Pennsylvania Magazine of History and Biography* 71 (July 1947): 275.

140. James M. Merrill, "Men, Monotony, and Mouldy Beans—Life on Board Civil War Blockaders," *American Neptune* 16 (January 1956): 53.

141. Still, "The Common Sailor," 33; Joseph Osborne to Louise Landau, 22 October 1864, in Merrill, "Men, Monotony, and Mouldy Beans," 53; "Shipboard Life in the Civil War," in *Civil War Naval Chronology, 1861–1865*, 6 vols. (Washington, D.C.: Government Printing Office, 1966), 6:106–7; Log Entry, 12 June 1862, Poole Log; Vail, *Three Years on the Blockade*, 91–92.

142. Litwack, *North of Slavery*, 99.

143. Lott, *Love and Theft*, 6. Louis S. Gerteis contends that minstrel productions provide strong evidence of a shared culture between blacks and whites and that Lott's interpretation limits one's ability to see beyond late-twentieth-century perceptions of nineteenth-century views about race; see Louis S. Gerteis, "Blackface Minstrelsy and the Construction of Race in Nineteenth-Century America," in David W. Blight and Brooks D. Simpson, eds., *Union and Emancipation: Essays on Politics and Race in the Civil War Era* (Kent, Ohio: Kent State University Press, 1997), 79–104.

144. Log Entry, 1 January 1863, Thayer Log, 6–7.

145. Log Entry, 26 January 1863, Thayer Log, 16–17.

146. Log Entry, 17 March 1863, Thayer Log, 44.

147. Still, "The Common Sailor," 33.

148. True, "Life aboard a Gunboat," 38; John Swift to Rosie Whiteside, 3 December 1863, in Swift, "Letters from a Sailor on a Tinclad," 50; Journal Entry, 6 August 1862, Henneberry Journal; Louis Kempff to Friend Herman, 9 August 1861, Kempff Papers. For a vivid analysis of the role of social

control in the forms of charivari and lynching in the South as applied to blacks, see Bertram Wyatt-Brown, *Southern Honor: Ethics and Behavior in the Old South* (New York: Oxford University Press, 1982), 435–61.

149. Diary Entry, 18 May 1865, in William B. Gould, ed., *Diary of a Contraband: The Civil War Passage of a Black Sailor* (Stanford: Stanford University Press, 2002), 188.

150. True, "Life aboard a Gunboat," 38.

151. William N. Bock to Father, 17 February 1864, Bock Papers; Journal Entry, 3 March 1863, Henneberry Journal; True, "Life aboard a Gunboat," 38.

152. Racial violence by white sailors was not confined to the decks of ships. See Edward M. Kellogg to David Kellogg, April 26–May 7, 1863, Edward M. Kellogg Papers, Manuscripts, Huntington Library; Diary Entry, 23 April 1863, Hart Diary.

153. Edward Pierson to Mother, 7 January 1863, Edward A. Pierson Papers, Manuscripts, New Jersey Historical Society, Newark, N.J.

154. Journal Entry, 17 June 1863, Lyons Journal; Hunter, *A Year on a Monitor and the Destruction of Fort Sumter*, 41.

155. George Geer to Wife, 24 May 1862, in Marvel, *The Monitor Chronicles*, 88–89; C. Moses Lee to Joseph Titcomb, 23 May 1862, Joseph Titcomb Letterbook, Joseph Titcomb Papers, James S. Schoff Civil War Collection, William L. Clements Library, University of Michigan; Log Entry, 16 March 1864, in Packard, "Jottings by the Way," Part 2, 265.

156. James B. Collins to Mother and Father, 19 January 1863, Collins Papers.

157. James B. Collins to Father and Mother, 16 January 1863, Collins Papers.

158. Ibid.; J. G. Wells to David D. Porter, 25 June 1863, in Merrill, "Cairo, Illinois," 251.

159. James B. Collins to Father and Mother, 12 January 1863, Collins Papers; Joseph Collins to Mother and Father, 25 January 1863, Collins Papers.

160. H. H. Bell to Gideon Welles, 25 November 1863, in Valuska, *The African American in the Union Navy*, 71.

161. Journal Entry, 6 June 1864, Benjamin Heath Jr. Journal, 19 February 1864–19 April 1865, Special Collections and University Archives, Rutgers University.

162. Diggins, "Recollections of the War Cruise of the U.S. Flag Ship Hartford," 149–51.

163. Still, "The Common Sailor," 28.

164. Francis Gifford to Parents, 10 January 1864, Gifford Papers, Southern Historical Collection, University of North Carolina, Chapel Hill, N.C.

165. James B. Collins to Mother and Father, 12 January 1863, Collins Papers; Joseph T. Collins to Mother and Father, 25 January 1863, Collins Papers.

166. Wiley, *The Life of Billy Yank*, 121; C. P. Weaver, ed., *Thank God My Regiment an African One: The Civil War Diary of Nathan W. Daniels* (Baton Rouge: Louisiana State University Press, 1998).

167. Log Entry, 23 May 1863, Thayer Log, 80; Still, "The Common Sailor," 33.

168. Hammond, "The Incident aboard the U.S. Ship St. Mary's," 3–6.

169. Ibid., 13–16.

170. Wiley, *The Life of Billy Yank*, 119–23; McPherson, *For Cause and Comrades*, 126–28.

171. Bell Wiley contends that there were several instances of Union soldiers killing or wounding black soldiers. He asserts, however, that such instances were the exception, not the rule; see Wiley, *The Life of Billy Yank*, 121. Joseph T. Glatthaar concludes that the violence exacted on black soldiers by white ones may have been more extensive than once thought. He finds that "there was considerable hatred between black units and 'unprincipled white ones,'" which they seemed to encounter everywhere." Certain high-ranking officers proposed, in response to the pervasiveness of the problem, the policy of confining black soldiers to camp at all times. See Glatthaar, *Forged in Battle*, 198–99.

172. Valuska, *The African American in the Union Navy*, 86.

173. J. P. Bergam to Dudley Mann, 14 August 1862, *Official Records of the Union and Confederate Navies in the War of Rebellion*, ser. 2, 3 vols. (Washington, D.C.: Government Printing Office, 1922–27), 3:512; Iver Bernstein, *The New York City Draft Riots: Their Significance for American Society and Politics in the Age of the Civil War* (New York: Oxford University Press, 1990), 9–10.

CHAPTER 8

1. The chapter title is a quotation from Seaman Bartholomew Diggins's account of the Battle of Mobile Bay, 5 August 1864; see Bartholomew Diggins, "Recollections of the War Cruise of the U.S. Flag Ship Hartford, January 8, 1862, to December 24, 1864," 88, Manuscripts and Archives, New York Public Library, New York, N.Y. The origin of the analysis of the human component in war is John Keegan, *The*

*Face of Battle* (New York: Viking Press, 1976). For the historiography of combat in the Civil War, see Marvin R. Cain, "A Face of Battle Needed: An Assessment of Men and Motives in Civil War Historiography," *Civil War History* 28 (March 1982): 5–27.

2. James M. Merrill, *The Rebel Shore: The Story of Union Sea Power in the Civil War* (Boston: Little, Brown, 1957), 61; John Swift to Mother, 2 July 1863, in Lester L. Swift, ed., "Letters from a Sailor on a Tinclad," *Civil War History* 10 (March 1961): 49; Joseph B. Osborne to Mary Osborne, 27 October 1864, Osborne Family Papers, Manuscripts, Library of Congress, Washington, D.C.

3. Gunpowder, shot, and shell accounted for 3,226 of these casualties, 1,164 of whom died. Steam explosions scalded 456 tars, killing 342. Three hundred and eight sailors drowned during combat. See Secretary of the Navy, *Report of the Secretary of the Navy, with an Appendix Containing Reports from Officers, December 1866* (Washington, D.C.: Government Printing Office, 1866), 41.

4. Dennis J. Ringle, *Life in Mr. Lincoln's Navy* (Annapolis: Naval Institute Press, 1998), 126–27; Secretary of the Navy, *Report of the Secretary of the Navy, with an Appendix Containing Reports from Officers, December 1864* (Washington, D.C.: Government Printing Office, 1864), 463; William F. Fox, *Regimental Losses in the American Civil War, 1861–1865* (Albany, N.Y.: Joseph McDonough, 1898), 537–39.

5. Keegan, *The Face of Battle*, 28, 39, 40, 47, 73.

6. William N. Bock to Mother, 5 May 1864, William N. Bock Papers, Illinois State Historical Library,

Springfield, Ill.; James M. Merrill, "Men, Monotony, and Mouldy Beans—Life on Board Civil War Blockaders," *American Neptune* 16 (January 1956): 50; William Van Cleaf to Mother, 14 March 1862, William Van Cleaf Papers, Special Collections and University Archives, Rutgers University, New Brunswick, N.J.; Swift, "Letters from a Sailor on a Tinclad," 55; Joseph B. Osborne to Mary Osborne, 27 October 1864, Osborne Family Papers.

7. William H. Price to Friend, 8 October 1862, W. H. Price Papers, Illinois State Historical Library; Earl J. Hess, "The Northern Response to the Ironclad: A Prospect for the Study of Military Technology," *Civil War History* 31 (June 1985): 140; William Keeler to Anna Keeler, 13 March 1862, 23 July 1862, 30 July 1862, 12 May 1862, in Robert W. Daly, ed., *Aboard the USS Monitor, 1862: The Letters of Acting Paymaster William Frederick Keeler, U.S. Navy, to his Wife, Anna* (Annapolis: Naval Institute Press, 1964), 47, 191, 198, 132; Grenville M. Weeks, "The Last Cruise of the Monitor," *Atlantic Monthly* 11 (March 1863): 367; Anonymous, "The Age of Iron," *Harper's New Monthly Magazine* 27 (July 1863): 285–86.

8. William Van Cleaf to Mother, 10 May 1862, Van Cleaf Papers; George Bright to Father, 16 January 1865, Bright Correspondence, George Adams Bright Collection, Manuscripts, Huntington Library, San Marino, Calif.; William J. Clark to Mother, 14, 25 July 1863, William J. Clark Papers, Manuscripts, Historical Society of Pennsylvania, Philadelphia, Pa.; E. W. Goble to Joseph B. Boyd, 14 January 1862, Joseph B. Boyd Papers, Cincin-nati Historical Society Library, Cincinnati, Ohio; De Witt C. Morse to Cousin, 28 February 1864, in Jeffrey L. Patrick, ed., "A Fighting Sailor on the Western Rivers: The Civil War Letters of 'Gunboat,'" *Journal of Mississippi History* 58 (September 1996): 259; Guy R. Everson, ed., "Service Afield and Afloat: A Reminiscence of the Civil War," *Indiana Magazine of History* 89 (March 1993): 49.

9. Journal Entries, September–October 1861, 24 May 1863, Journal aboard U.S. Gunboat Essex, 23 September 1861–2 June 1863, James E. Henneberry Papers, Research Collections, Chicago Historical Society, Chicago, Ill. (hereafter cited as "Henneberry Journal"); Sayres O. Nichols to Eliza Dunn Nichols, 19 April 1864, in Roy F. Nichols, ed., "Fighting in North Carolina Waters," *North Carolina Historical Review* 40 (Winter 1963): 79.

10. John T. Hawkins Memorandum Book, 93, Manuscripts and Archives, New York Public Library.

11. Maurice F. Maury to William Ballard Preston, 22 October 1861, *Official Records of the Union and Confederate Navies in the War of the Rebellion*, ser. 2, 3 vols. (Washington, D.C.: Government Printing Office, 1921–27) (hereafter cited as "ORN 2"), 2:100–104; Fox, *Regimental Losses in the American Civil War*, 537–39; Richard A. Gabriel and Karen S. Metz, *History of Military Medicine* (New York: Greenwood Press, 1992), 118–21.

12. John Rodgers to Gideon Welles, 8 June 1861, *Official Records of the Union and Confederate Navies in the War of the Rebellion*, ser. 1, 27 vols. (Washington, D.C.: Government Printing Office, 1894–1917) (hereafter cited as "ORN"), 22:283; S. L. Phelps to

Colonel John Cook, 13 August 1861, Seth Ledyard Phelps Papers, Missouri Historical Society, St. Louis, Mo.; Lance C. Buhl, "Mariners and Machines: Resistance to Technological Change in the American Navy, 1865–1869," *Journal of American History* 61 (March 1974): 707.

13. Earl J. Hess, *The Union Soldier in Combat: Enduring the Ordeal of Combat* (Lawrence: University Press of Kansas, 1997), 194; Gerald Linderman, *Embattled Courage: The Experience of Combat in the American Civil War* (New York: Free Press, 1987), 135. However, Hess contends that sailors embraced monitors, the use of technology, and iron as signs of moral superiority; see Hess, "The Northern Response to the Ironclad," 129–31, 140–41.

14. Alvah F. Hunter, *A Year on a Monitor and the Destruction of Fort Sumter*, ed. Craig L. Symonds (Columbia: University of South Carolina Press, 1987), 26; Diary Entry, 31 December 1862, Civil War Diary of John G. Morrison, 1861–1865, Naval Historical Foundation Collection, Washington Navy Yard, Washington, D.C.

15. Cornelius Schoonmaker to Brother, 11 January 1863, Cornelius Schoonmaker Papers, Naval Historical Foundation Collection, Library of Congress.

16. James Alden to Henry Augustus Wise, 7 May 1862, Henry Augustus Wise Papers, Naval Historical Society Collection, New-York Historical Society; Diggins, "Recollections of the War Cruise of the U.S. Flag Ship Hartford," 79–80; Diary Entry, 11 August 1862, George R. Yost Diary, Illinois State Historical Library.

17. Diggins, "Recollections of the War Cruise of the U.S. Flag Ship Hartford," 76–78; Journal Entry, 22 July 1862, Henneberry Journal; Diary Entry, 27 February 1863, Charles A. Hart Diary, History and Genealogy, Connecticut State Library, Hartford Conn.; Diary Entry, 26 August 1862, Yost Diary; Ivan Musicant, *Divided Waters: The Naval History of the Civil War* (New York: HarperCollins, 1995), 312; James Alden to Henry Augustus Wise, 7 May 1862, Wise Papers; Log Entries, 11, 14 March 1863, Milo Lacy Log, Manuscripts, Naval Historical Center Library, Washington Navy Yard.

18. Diary Entry, 24 April 1862, Diary of John Simpson while on U.S.S. *Richmond* and *Brooklyn*, William Pendleton Palmer Collection, Manuscripts, Western Reserve Historical Society, Cleveland, Ohio; Diggins, "Recollections of the War Cruise of the U.S. Flag Ship Hartford," 77; George Bright to Father, 12, 24 February 1863, Bright Collection; Francis R. Minton, ed., *Journal of Patrick Meade Jr.* (Medford, Mass.: n.p., 1984), 35.

19. Diggins, "Recollections of the War Cruise of the U.S. Flag Ship Hartford," 79–80.

20. George Bright to Father, 24 February 1863, Bright Collection.

21. Log Entry, 21 April 1862, Abstract of Log of U.S. Schooner Sarah Bruen, ORN, 18:418; Log Entries, 21, 22 April 1862, Abstract of Log of U.S. Schooner Racer, ORN, 18:418–19; David G. Farragut to Gideon Welles, 2 July 1862, ORN, 18:608–9; Thomas Craven to David G. Farragut, 30 June 1862, ORN, 18:600; David G. Farragut to Gideon Welles, 12 August 1864, ORN, 21:415–19; L. A. Kimberly to

P. Drayton, 8 April 1864, ORN, 21:428–29; W. Radford to David D. Porter, 16 January 1865, ORN, 11:461.

22. Diary Entries, 8 May, 15 July 1862, Morrison Diary; Journal Entry, 5 August 1864, "The Journal of Private Charles Brother, USMC," in Department of the Navy, *Civil War Naval Chronology*, 6 vols. (Washington, D.C.: Government Printing Office, 1966), 6:80.

23. Diary Entry, 8 May 1862, Morrison Diary.

24. Journal Entry, 14 December 1862, Henneberry Journal; Everson, "Service Afield and Afloat," 45; De Witt C. Morse to Cousin, 30 May 1864, in Patrick, "A Fighting Sailor on the Western Rivers," 270.

25. William Van Cleaf to Brother, 23 May 1862, Van Cleaf Papers; Edward Blue to Frank H. Stickney, 19 May 1864, Frank L. Stickney Papers, 1863–1875, Naval Historical Foundation Collection, Library of Congress; E. W. Goble to Joseph B. Boyd, 19 April 1863, Boyd Papers.

26. Diary Entry, 1 May 1863, Fayette Clapp Diary, 1862–1863, Western Historical Manuscript Collection, Ellis Library, University of Missouri, Columbia, Mo.

27. E. W. Goble to Joseph B. Boyd, 19 April 1863, Boyd Papers.

28. Journal Entry, 24 December 1864, Calvin G. Hutchinson Journal, Part 2, The Fort Fisher, Wilmington, and Richmond Captures, Calvin G. Hutchinson Papers, Manuscripts, Huntington Library; Diggins, "Recollections of the War Cruise of the U.S. Flag Ship Hartford," 80–82; Diary Entry, 24 April 1862, Simpson Diary.

29. E. W. Goble to Joseph B. Boyd, 19 April 1863, Boyd Papers.

30. Diggins, "Recollections of the War Cruise of the U.S. Flag Ship Hartford," 76; Joseph McDonald, "How I Saw the Monitor-Merrimac Fight," *New England Magazine* 36 (July 1907): 551.

31. Diggins, "Recollections of the War Cruise of the U.S. Flag Ship Hartford," 76; Diary Entry, 24 April 1862, Simpson Diary.

32. Diggins, "Recollections of the War Cruise of the U.S. Flag Ship Hartford," 78; Gideon Welles to John A. Dahlgren, 5 August 1863, ORN, 14:418.

33. William Van Cleaf to Mother, 27 March 1862, Van Cleaf Papers; Francis B. Butts, "The Loss of the Monitor," 746, Frank H. Pierce Papers, Manuscripts, New York Public Library.

34. Log Entry, 14 March 1863, Lacy Log; John D. Milligan, ed., "Navy Life on the Mississippi River," *Civil War Times Illustrated* 33 (May–June 1994): 70.

35. E. W. Goble to Joseph B. Boyd, 19 April 1863, Boyd Papers.

36. Diggins, "Recollections of the War Cruise of the U.S. Flag Ship Hartford," 82.

37. Peter Karsten, *The Naval Aristocracy: The Golden Age of Annapolis and the Emergence of a Modern American Navalism* (New York: Free Press, 1972), 84, 87–88.

38. Diggins, "Recollections of the War Cruise of the U.S. Flag Ship Hartford," 160.

39. Journal Entry, 6 February 1862, Henneberry Journal.

40. Diary Entries, 30 April, 1 May 1862, Clapp Diary.

41. Diary Entry, 13 February 1863, Clapp Diary.

42. E. W. Goble to Joseph B. Boyd, 19 April 1863, Boyd Papers.

43. Diary Entry, 1 May 1863, Clapp Diary; Diary Entry, 17 March 1862, Morrison Diary.

44. Journal Entry, 13 August 1864, Samuel Pollock Journal, Samuel Pollock Papers, Manuscripts, Illinois State Historical Library.

45. John Swift to Rosie Whiteside, May 1864, in Swift, "Letters from a Sailor on a Tinclad," 55.

46. Diary Entry, 17 March 1862, Morrison Diary.

47. T. M. Coan to Sister, 10 October 1864, Titus Munson Coan Papers, September–October 1864, Manuscripts, New-York Historical Society; William Van Cleaf to Mother, 10 May 1862, Van Cleaf Papers.

48. Cornelius Cronin, *Recollections of Service in the United States Navy: Being Reminiscences as They Have Occurred to My Mind from the Commencement and pending the Late War; while Serving on the Ships Sabine, Brooklyn, and Richmond* (n.p., 1894), 4; Secretary of the Navy, *Report of the Secretary of the Navy, December 1864*, 463.

49. A. H. Foote to Gideon Welles, 7 February 1862, ORN, 22:538; David G. Farragut to Gideon Welles, 20 April 1862, ORN, 18:135–36; David G. Farragut to Gideon Welles, 2 July 1862, ORN, 18:609; R. Wainwright to David G. Farragut, 29 June 1862, ORN, 18:615.

50. Diary Entry, 16 April 1863, Morrison Diary; De Witt C. Morse to Cousin, 30 May 1864, in Patrick, "A Fighting Sailor on the Western Rivers," 270.

51. Diary Entry, 27 December 1862, Clapp Diary.

52. Journal Entry, 5 August 1861,

George Bright Journals, Journal of the Cruise in the U.S. Steamer South Carolina, May 24, 1861, to April 4, 1862, Bright Collection; George M. Bache to David D. Porter, 27 May 1863, ORN, 25:38–39.

53. Journal Entry, 7 February 1862, Henneberry Journal.

54. James Edwin Campbell, "Recent Addresses of James Edwin Campbell: The Mississippi Squadron," *Ohio Archaeological and Historical Quarterly* 34 (January 1925): 62 (hereafter cited as "The Mississippi Squadron").

55. Ringle, *Life in Mr. Lincoln's Navy*, 133.

56. Diary Entry, 16 April 1863, Morrison Diary.

57. Campbell, "The Mississippi Squadron," 62.

58. Walter F. Beyer and Oscar F. Keydel, *Acts of Bravery: Deeds of Extraordinary American Heroism, from the Personal Records and Reminiscences of Courageous Americans Who Risked Everything for their Comrades and Country* (1903; reprint, Stamford, Conn.: Longmeadow Press, 1994), 21–22; Diary Entry, 16 April 1863, Morrison Diary; Cronin, *Recollections of Service in the United States Navy*, 4–5.

59. Charles J. Hill to William Thoms, 3 December 1863, William F. Thoms Papers, Letters from Seamen, 1853–1864, New York Nautical School, Manuscripts, New-York Historical Society.

60. Theodorus Bailey to J. L. Davis, 20 April 1862, ORN, 18:137; James W. Shirk to David D. Porter, 27 May 1863, ORN, 25:28; Beyer and Keydel, *Acts of Bravery*, 25–28.

61. E. W. Goble to Joseph B. Boyd, 19 April 1863, Boyd Papers; Diggins,

"Recollections of the War Cruise of the U.S. Flag Ship Hartford," 64, 66; Journal Entry, 6 February 1862, Henneberry Journal; Albert Bigelow Paine, *A Sailor of Fortune: Personal Memoirs of Captain B. S. Osbon* (New York: McClure, Phillips, 1906), 196; R. Wainwright to David G. Farragut, 30 April 1862, ORN, 18:168.

62. Journal Entry, 28 May 1863, Henneberry Journal.

63. Lord Moran, *The Anatomy of Courage* (Boston: Houghton, Mifflin, 1967), 20–21.

64. Diary Entry, 16 April 1863, Morrison Diary.

65. Milligan, "Navy Life on the Mississippi River," 68; Samuel Du Pont to Henry Winter Davis, 8 April 1863, in Hess, "The Northern Response to the Ironclad," 132.

66. Asa Beetham to Emma Beetham, 23 February 1864, Asa Beetham Papers, Manuscripts, Library of Congress; Joseph T. Collins to Mother and Father, 25 January 1863, James B. and Joseph T. Collins Papers, Manuscripts, New-York Historical Society; E. W. Goble to Joseph B. Boyd, 23 January 1862, Boyd Papers.

67. Hunter, *A Year on a Monitor and the Destruction of Fort Sumter*, 60.

68. Cronin, *Recollections of Service in the United States Navy*, 4–5; Beyer and Keydel, *Acts of Bravery*, 21–22; William Van Cleaf to Mother, 31 August 1862, Van Cleaf Papers; Hunter, *A Year on a Monitor and the Destruction of Fort Sumter*, 51.

69. Diary Entry, 12 May 1865, Charles L. Green Letterbook, Manuscripts, Huntington Library; Cronin, *Recollections of Service in the United States Navy*, 4–5; Log Entry, 14 March 1863, Lacy Log.

70. W. G. Saltonstall to R. T. Renshaw, 20 April 1863, ORN, 8:692; Assistant Surgeon Philip H. Barton to William H. Macomb, 2 November 1864, ORN, 11:16–17; Surgeon Albert C. Gorgas to William Rogers Taylor, 25 December 1864, ORN, 11:322; James W. Shirk to David D. Porter, 27 May 1863, ORN, 25:28; Beyer and Keydel, *Acts of Bravery*, 25–28.

71. William J. Clark to Mother, 14 July 1863, Clark Papers.

72. George Cornelius, "What Did Farragut See?" *Naval History* 8 (August 1994): 17.

73. Campbell, "The Mississippi Squadron," 62; William J. Clark to Mother, 14 July 1863, Clark Papers; Edward T. Barker to Mother, 6, 7 August 1864, Barker-Edes-Noyes Papers, Manuscripts, Massachusetts Historical Society, Boston, Mass.

74. Edward T. Barker to Mother, 6 August 1864, Barker-Edes-Noyes Papers.

75. Journal Entry, 5 August 1864, Brother Journal, in Department of the Navy, *Civil War Naval Chronology*, 6:83.

76. Diggins, "Recollections of the War Cruise of the U.S. Flag Ship Hartford," 156; T. M. Coan to Sister, 10 October 1864, Coan Papers.

77. Willis J. Abbot, *Blue Jackets of '61: A History of the Navy in the War of Secession* (New York: Dodd, Mead, 1890), 133.

78. Journal Entry, 6 February 1862, Henneberry Journal.

79. James B. Collins to Mother and Father, 13 October 1862, Collins Papers.

80. William Van Cleaf to Mother,

14 July 1862, Van Cleaf Papers; Journal Entry, 13 August 1864, Pollock Journal; Minton, *The Journal of Patrick Meade*, 38.

81. T. M. Coan to Sister, 10 October 1864, Coan Papers.

82. Ibid.

83. Hunter, *A Year on a Monitor and the Destruction of Fort Sumter*, 53.

84. Sayres O. Nichols to Eliza Dunn Nichols, 19 April 1864, in Nichols, "Fighting in North Carolina Waters," 79.

85. John D. Milligan, ed., "Gunboat War at Vicksburg," *American Heritage* 29 (August–September 1978): 67.

86. The feeling was also prevalent among soldiers; see Hess, *The Union Soldier in Combat*, 97.

87. David G. Farragut to Gideon Welles, 12 August 1864, ORN, 21:415.

88. Charles C. Coffin, *My Days and Nights on the Battlefield* (Boston: Estes and Lauriat, 1887), 261–62.

89. Samuel J. Bartlett to Mary Bartlett, 16 January, 16 March 1863, in L. Moody Simms Jr., ed., "A Union Volunteer with the Mississippi Ram Fleet," *Lincoln Herald* 70 (Winter 1968): 190–91.

90. William Van Cleaf to Mother, 15 May 1862, Van Cleaf Papers; A. M. Williams to Robert C. Newton, 21 June 1862, ORN, 23:205.

91. Joseph C. Alcom to Warren D. Crandall, 7 September 1899, Civil War Collection, Missouri Historical Society; A. W. Muldaur to Francis A. Roe, 5 May 1864, ORN, 9:765; John L. Worden to S. F. Du Pont, 3 March 1863, ORN, 13:700.

92. Autobiography Entry, 5 February 1862, "The Autobiography of Tim Finn, 1854–1896," Manuscripts, Center for American History, University of Texas, Austin, Tex.; Sylvester Doss to W. D. Crandall, 8 October 1894, Civil War Collection, Manuscripts, Missouri Historical Society; Journal Entry, 6 February 1862, Henneberry Journal; Diary Entry, 20 April 1863, Clapp Diary; William White to Joseph M. Willson, 29 March 1863, Joseph M. Willson Papers, Illinois State Historical Library; Memorandum Book Entry, 6 February 1862, Alexander R. Miller Memorandum Book aboard the U.S. Steamers DeKalb and Lafayette, 1861–1864, Louisiana and Lower Mississippi Valley Collections, Hill Memorial Library, Louisiana State University, Baton Rouge, La.; A. H. Foote to Gideon Welles, 7 February 1862, ORN, 22:538; Egbert Thompson to A. H. Foote, 17 February 1862, 27:592–93.

93. Extract of the Journal of the U.S.S. Richmond, 15 July 1862, ORN, 19:747; David G. Farragut to Gideon Welles, 2 July 1862, ORN, 18:608–10; Log of the Ram Lancaster No. 3, 1862, 15 July 1862, ORN, 23:244–45.

94. Symmes Browne to Fannie Bassett, 9, 10 February 1862, in John D. Milligan, ed., *From the Fresh-Water Navy: 1861–64; the Letters of Acting Master's Mate Henry R. Browne and Acting Ensign Symmes E. Browne* (Annapolis: Naval Institute Press, 1970), 26–27; Symmes Browne to Cornelia C. Gunn, 9 August 1862, ibid., 96–98; Campbell, "The Mississippi Squadron," 62.

95. Ringle, *Life in Mr. Lincoln's Navy*, 127–29.

96. Joseph T. Collins to Father and Mother, 23 December 1862, Collins Papers; William Van Cleaf to Mother, 27 March 1862, Van Cleaf Papers; Journal Entry, 28 February 1863, Henneberry Journal; E. W. Goble to Joseph B.

Boyd, 19 April 1863, Boyd Papers; Diary Entry, 11 December 1862, Morrison Diary.

97. Department of the Navy, *Civil War Naval Chronology*, 2:105.

98. Ringle, *Life in Mr. Lincoln's Navy*, 127–29; Journal Entry, 28 February 1863, Henneberry Journal; Fox, *Regimental Losses in the American Civil War*, 537; Journal Entries, 29 May, 1, 8 June 1864, Levi Hayden Journal, May 27, 1864–January 31, 1879, Levi Hayden Papers, Manuscripts and Archives, New York Public Library.

99. Diary Entry, 12 December 1862, Yost Diary; Memorandum Book Entry, 13 July 1863, Miller Memorandum Book.

100. George Bright to Father, 18 March 1863, Bright Collection.

101. David G. Farragut to Gideon Welles, 12 August 1864, ORN, 21:415; John Cronan to David D. Porter, 4 August 1863, David D. Porter Papers, Huntington Library; Journal Entries, 5, 6 May, 18 June 1864, Journal of Benjamin Heath Jr., February 19, 1864– April 19, 1865, Special Collections and University Archives, Rutgers University; Edward Blue to Frank H. Stickney, 19 May 1864, Frank L. Stickney Papers, Naval Historical Foundation Collection, Library of Congress; Samuel J. Bartlett to Mary Bartlett, 16 January 1863, in Simms, "A Union Volunteer with the Mississippi Ram Fleet," 190.

102. Hunter, *A Year on a Monitor and the Destruction of Fort Sumter*, 143–44.

103. Journal Entries, January– February 1863, Henneberry Journal; E. W. Goble to Joseph B. Boyd, 11 February 1862, Boyd Papers; Hunter, *A Year on a Monitor and the Destruction of Fort Sumter*, 59, 69, 136.

104. Calvin G. Hutchinson to William M. Hill, 23 February 1865, Calvin G. Hutchinson Correspondence, Hutchinson Papers; T. M. Coan to Hattie Coan, 14 December 1864, Coan Papers.

105. Journal Entry, 28 February 1863, Henneberry Journal; Calvin G. Hutchinson to William M. Hill, 19 May 1864, Hutchinson Papers.

106. Calvin G. Hutchinson to William M. Hill, 19 May 1864, Hutchinson Papers.

107. Thomas T. Craven to Gideon Welles, 31 October 1861, ORN, 4:743; William A. Abbot to Gideon Welles, 9 January 1862, ORN, 6:517.

108. Herman Melville, "A Utilitarian View of the *Monitor*'s Fight" in *Battle-Pieces and Aspects of the War* (1866; reprint, Gainesville, Fla.: Scholars' Facsimiles and Reprints, 1960); David A. Mindell, *War, Technology, and Experience aboard the USS Monitor* (Baltimore: Johns Hopkins University Press, 2000); C. G. Hutchinson to William M. Hill, 19 May 1864, Hutchinson Papers; Journal Entry, 6 May 1864, Heath Journal; William H. McNeill, *The Pursuit of Power: Technology, Armed Force, and Society since A.D. 1000* (Chicago: University of Chicago Press, 1982), 382.

109. Diary Entry, 15 July 1862, Morrison Diary.

110. Percival Drayton to Henry Augustus Wise, 12 November 1863, Wise Papers.

111. Daly, *Aboard the USS Monitor*, 35.

112. Harrie Webster, "An August Morning with Farragut at Mobile," in *Civil War Naval Chronology*, 6:94.

113. Paine, *A Sailor of Fortune*, 236–37.

114. Diary Entry, 24 April 1862, Simpson Diary; Charles J. Hill to William Thoms, 3 May 1862, Thoms Papers.

115. Diggins, "Recollections of the War Cruise of the U.S. Flag Ship Hartford," 84; Maurice F. Maury to William Ballard Preston, 22 October 1861, ORN 2, 2:100–104; Cronin, *Recollections of Service in the United States Navy*, 4–5; Minton, *The Journal of Patrick Meade*, 38.

116. Diggins, "Recollections of the War Cruise of the U.S. Flag Ship Hartford," 85–86; Minton, *The Journal of Patrick Meade*, 37–38.

117. Daniel Carrison, *The Navy from Wood to Steel, 1860–1890* (New York: Franklin Watts, 1965), 71.

118. Ringle, *Life in Mr. Lincoln's Navy*, 132; Diary Entry, 22 July 1862, Morrison Diary.

119. Minton, *The Journal of Patrick Meade*, 36; McDonald, "How I Saw the Monitor-Merrimac Fight," 650.

120. Diggins, "Recollections of the War Cruise of the U.S. Flag Ship Hartford," 156, 264; Journal Entry, 13 August 1864, Pollock Journal; Abbot, *Blue Jackets of '61*, 133.

121. Abbot, *Blue Jackets of '61*, 133; Diggins, "Recollections of the War Cruise of the U.S. Flag Ship Hartford," 282; Diary Entry, 2 June 1864, Diary of Amos W. Bellows on Board the Diana (Ram Fleet), March 1863–January 1865, Warren D. Crandall Collection, Manuscripts, Missouri Historical Society; Journal Entry, 5 August 1864, Brother Journal, in Department of the Navy, *Civil War Naval Chronology*, 6:83.

122. Diggins, "Recollections of the War Cruise of the U.S. Flag Ship Hartford," 84–88.

123. Moran, *The Anatomy of Courage*, xii, 22.

124. Charles J. Hill to William Thoms, 3 May 1862, Thoms Papers; Diary Entry, 24 April 1862, Simpson Diary.

125. Diggins, "Recollections of the War Cruise of the U.S. Flag Ship Hartford," 88, 90.

126. Ibid., 88.

127. Samuel A. Stouffer et al., *The American Soldier: Combat and Its Aftermath*, 2 vols. (Princeton: Princeton University Press, 1949), 2:77–83.

128. E. W. Goble to Joseph B. Boyd, 19 April 1863, Boyd Papers; William Van Cleaf to Mother, 15 May 1862, Van Cleaf Papers; Journal Entry, 5 August 1861, George Bright Journals, Bright Collection; Diary Entry, 22 July 1862, Morrison Diary; "Announcement of National Reunion of Ex-Soldiers and Sailors Association of Franklin County, Ohio," 6 July 1883, Symmes Browne Papers, Manuscripts, Ohio Historical Society, Columbus, Ohio.

129. Keegan, *The Face of Battle*, 47.

130. McNeill, *The Pursuit of Power*, 125–39, 245–46, 254–55.

131. William Van Cleaf to Mother, 23 May 1862, Van Cleaf Papers.

132. Campbell, "The Mississippi Squadron," 62.

133. Diggins, "Recollections of the War Cruise of the U.S. Flag Ship Hartford," 88, 90.

134. Carrison, *The Navy from Wood to Steel*, 71; William Van Cleaf to Mother, 22 June 1862, Van Cleaf Papers; Diary Entry, 19 June 1862, Morrison Diary.

135. Campbell, "The Mississippi Squadron," 62; E. F. Green to Father, 23 July 1864, Otis F. Green Family

Papers, Manuscripts, Ohio Historical Society.

136. Abbot, *Blue Jackets of '61*, 152; Log Entry, 27 November 1862, Charles A. Poole Log, G. W. Blunt White Library, Mystic Seaport Museum, Mystic, Conn.

137. Abbot, *Blue Jackets of '61*, 133.

138. Gerald Linderman and Earl J. Hess both define courage for soldiers as heroic action taken without fear; see Linderman, *Embattled Courage*, 8–17, and Hess, *The Union Soldier in Combat*, 96.

139. William Van Cleaf to Mother, 31 August 1862, Van Cleaf Papers; Milligan, "Navy Life on the Mississippi," 72.

140. James C. Stephens, "Combat between the Merrimac and the Monitor," 11, James C. Stephens Papers, Western Historical Manuscript Collection, Ellis Library, University of Missouri; Journal Entry, 13 August 1864, Pollock Journal; William Van Cleaf to Mother, 31 August 1862, Van Cleaf Papers; Memorandum Book Entries, 2 May, 10 June 1863, Miller Memorandum Book; John Swift to Rosie Whiteside, 6 March 1865, in Swift, "Letters from a Sailor on a Tinclad," 61.

141. William Van Cleaf to Mother, 31 August 1862, Van Cleaf Papers; Milligan, "Navy Life on the Mississippi River," 72.

142. Linderman, *Embattled Courage*, 150–51.

143. Log Entry, 18 July 1863, in Kent Packard, ed., "Jottings by the Way: A Sailor's Log—1862 to 1864," Part 1, *Pennsylvania Magazine of History and Biography* 71 (April 1947): 134.

144. Eliot Callender, "What a Boy Saw on the Mississippi," in *Military*

*Essays and Recollections, Papers Read before the Commandery of the State of Illinois, Military Order of the Loyal Legion of the United States*, vol. 1 (Chicago: A. C. McClurg, 1891), 52; Hess, *The Union Soldier in Combat*, 75.

145. See, for example, Journal Entry, 20 September 1863, Henneberry Journal; David D. Porter to John H. Dorman, 27 January 1888, John H. Dorman Papers, Manuscripts, Ohio Historical Society; J. McLeod Murphy to John H. Dorman, 17 August 1864, Dorman Papers; plus the sources cited in nn. 146 and 147.

146. M. Woodhull to Commodore Wilkes, 1 August 1862, ORN, 7:607–8.

147. James S. Thorton to Gideon Welles, 21 June 1864, ORN, 3:61.

148. G. J. Van Brunt to Gideon Welles, 10 March 1862, ORN, 7:11–12; A. Murray to S. C. Rowan, 8 February 1862, ORN, 6:557; R. Sheldon McCook to S. C. Rowan, 19 March 1862, ORN, 7:113–14; M. Woodhull to Gideon Welles, 1 August 1862, ORN, 7:607–8.

149. Log Entry, 9 September 1864, in Kent Packard, ed., "Jottings by the Way: A Sailor's Log—1862 to 1864," Part 2, *Pennsylvania Magazine of History and Biography* 71 (July 1947): 271.

150. William Van Cleaf to Mother, 27 March 1862, Van Cleaf Papers.

151. S. Phillips Lee to David G. Farragut, 28 June 1862, ORN, 18:612; LaRue P. Adams to L. A. Kimberly, 6 August 1864, ORN, 21:431; William Radford to David D. Porter, 16 January 1865, ORN, 11:465; James W. Shirk to David D. Porter, 22 May 1863, ORN, 25:27–28; David D. Porter to Gideon Welles, 23 May 1863, ORN, 25:22; A. W. Weaver to David D. Porter,

17 January 1865, ORN, 11:466–67; Percival Drayton to D. G. Farragut, 6 August 1864, ORN, 21:425–28.

152. Musicant, *Divided Waters*, 151.

153. Ibid., 150.

154. Ibid., 151.

155. Stephens, "Combat between the Merrimac and the Monitor," 11; Edward A. Pierson to Mother, 12 March 1862, Edward Pierson Papers, Manuscripts, New Jersey Historical Society, Newark, N.J.; Ringle, *Life in Mr. Lincoln's Navy*, 132.

156. Herman Melville, "The Cumberland," in *Battle-Pieces and Aspects of the War*, 53–54. Other poems that commemorated the fate of the crew include Robert Traill Spence Lowell's "The Men of the Cumberland," George Henry Boker's "On Board the Cumberland," and Henry Wadsworth Longfellow's "The Cumberland."

157. McDonald, "How I Saw the Monitor-Merrimac Fight," 650.

158. Log Entry, 19 August 1863, Poole Log; Diary Entry, 30 July 1862, Yost Diary; E. W. Goble to Joseph B. Boyd, 19 April 1863, Boyd Papers; Journal Entry, 29 May 1864, Hayden Journal.

159. Webster, "An August Morning with Farragut at Mobile Bay," 86; David G. Farragut to Gideon Welles, 12 August 1864, ORN, 21:415.

160. Journal Entry, 24 December 1864, Joseph Canning Journal, Joseph Canning Papers, Manuscripts and Archives, New York Public Library.

161. Isaac Bradbury to W. B. Smith, 11 February 1864, Isaac Bradbury Papers, Manuscripts, New-York Historical Society.

162. Journal Entry, 2 July 1863, Henneberry Journal.

163. John Swift to Rosie Whiteside,

2 July 1864, in Swift, "Letters from a Sailor on a Tinclad," 59.

164. Journal Entry, 17 January 1865, Canning Journal.

165. Cornelius Schoonmaker to Barnard Schoonmaker, 30 May 1865, Schoonmaker Papers.

166. Journal Entry, 13 August 1861, George Bright Journals, Bright Collection.

167. John Eliot Parkman to Mother, 20 March 1863, John Eliot Parkman Papers, Massachusetts Historical Society.

168. Sayres O. Nichols to Eliza Dunn Nichols, 19 April 1864, in Nichols, "Fighting in North Carolina Waters," 79.

169. Journal Entry, 6 February 1862, Henneberry Journal; Diggins, "Recollections of the War Cruise of the U.S. Flag Ship Hartford," 282, 286.

170. Abbot, *Blue Jackets of '61*, 133.

171. Diggins, "Recollections of the War Cruise of the U.S. Flag Ship Hartford," 286.

172. Abbot, *Blue Jackets of '61*, 133; Diggins, "Recollections of the War Cruise of the U.S. Flag Ship Hartford," 282; Diary Entry, 2 June 1864, Bellows Diary; Campbell, "The Mississippi Squadron," 60.

173. Log Entry, 19 June 1864, Poole Log.

174. Journal Entry, 24 December 1864, Canning Journal; Edward A. Pierson to Mother, 12 March 1862, Pierson Papers.

175. E. W. Goble to Joseph B. Boyd, 19 April 1863, Boyd Papers; Journal Entry, 15 March 1863, Henneberry Journal.

176. E. W. Goble to Joseph B. Boyd, 19 April 1863, Boyd Papers.

177. Journal Entries, 7, 29 February

1862, Henneberry Journal; William J. Clark to Mother, 14, 25 July 1863, Clark Papers; Diary Entry, 2 June 1864, Bellows Diary; Diary Entry, 24 April 1862, Simpson Diary; Log Entry, 15 March 1863, Lacy Log; A. H. Foote to Gideon Welles, 7 February 1862, ORN, 22:538; Egbert Thompson to A. H. Foote, 17 February 1862, ORN, 22:592; Theodorus Bailey to J. L. Davis, 20 April 1862, ORN, 18:137; John G. Walker to David D. Porter, 23 May 1863, ORN, 25:6–9; James A. Greer to David D. Porter, 24 May 1863, ORN, 25:26–27; R. S. McCook to George E. Belknap, 16 January 1865, ORN, 11:465.

178. William Van Cleaf to Brother, 23 May 1862, Van Cleaf Papers; E. W. Goble to Joseph B. Boyd, 19 April 1863, Boyd Papers.

179. Log Entry, 10 July 1863, in Packard, "Jottings by the Way," Part 1, 131; John H. Taylor to Wife and Children, 5 January 1862, in Alice P. Mortensen and Edwin H. Mortensen, eds., *The Family of John Henry Taylor, Jr.: Featuring Family Letters Written during and after the Civil War* (Baltimore: Gateway Press, 1995), 3–4.

180. Diary Entries, 6 June 1862, 15 July 1862, Morrison Diary; Diggins, "Recollections of the War Cruise of the U.S. Flag Ship Hartford," 90; Ringle, *Life in Mr. Lincoln's Navy*, 73.

181. Log Entry, 16 June 1864, in Packard, "Jottings by the Way," Part 2, 268; Journal Entries, 22, 27 July 1862, Harry A. Simmons Journal, "Journal of the Cruise in the U.S. Schooner Sophronia Attached to the Bomb Flotilla," 30 December 1861–31 July 1862, James S. Schoff Civil War Collection, William L. Clements Library, University of Michigan.

182. Journal Entry, 29 May 1864,

Hayden Journal; Diary Entry, 30 July 1862, Yost Diary.

183. Log Entries, 31 July, 19 September 1863, in Packard, "Jottings by the Way," Part 1, 137, 146.

184. Symmes Browne to Fannie Bassett, 12 April 1864, in Milligan, *From the Fresh-Water Navy*, 259; Journal Entry, 13 July 1863, Henneberry Journal; William P. Mack and Royal W. Connell, *Naval Ceremonies, Customs, and Traditions*, 5th ed. (Annapolis: Naval Institute Press, 1980), 174–84.

185. Hunter, *A Year on a Monitor and the Destruction of Fort Sumter*, 20; Daly, *Aboard the USS Monitor*, 216; George Clark, *Seven Years of a Sailor's Life* (Boston: Adams, 1867), 215–16; Log Entry, 11 August 1863, Lacy Log.

EPILOGUE

1. Diary Entry, 26 March 1865, Diary of Edwin R. Benedict, 1864–65, Special Collections, Woodruff Library, Emory University, Atlanta, Ga.; Journal Entry, 24 September 1864, Journal Aboard U.S. Gunboat Essex, 23 September 1861 to 2 June 1863, James E. Henneberry Papers, Research Collections, Chicago Historical Society, Chicago, Ill.; Diary Entry, 2 January 1862, Diary of John B. Wirts, Cruise of the Lancaster in the North and South Pacific from May 12, 1859, to October 15, 1861, Special Collections, University of California at Los Angeles, Los Angeles, Calif.

2. Cornelius Cronin, *Recollection of Service in the U.S. Navy: Being Reminiscences as They Have Occurred to My Mind from the Commencement and pending the Late War; while Serving on the U.S. Ships Sabine, Brooklyn, and Richmond* (n.p., 1894), 15; Autobiography Entry, 9 July 1862, "The Autobiography of Tim Finn,

1854–1896," Manuscripts, Center for American History, University of Texas, Austin, Tex.

3. Log Entries, 20 August, 26 September 1863, Milo Lacy Log, Manuscripts, Naval Historical Center Library, Washington Navy Yard, Washington, D.C.

4. Diary Entry, 24 January 1864, George R. Yost Diary, Illinois State Historical Library, Springfield, Ill.

5. Ann Preston to Fowler Preston, 30 April 1862, Preston Family Papers, Michigan Historical Collection, Bentley Historical Library, University of Michigan, Ann Arbor, Mich.

# Selected Bibliography

PRIMARY SOURCES, UNPUBLISHED

*Manuscripts*
Center for American History, University of Texas, Austin, Texas
    "The Autobiography of Tim Finn, 1854–1896"
Central Michigan University, Clarke Historical Library,
   Mount Pleasant, Michigan
      Ralzemond A. Parker Papers
Chicago Historical Society, Research Collections, Chicago, Illinois
      James E. Henneberry Papers
Cincinnati Historical Society, Manuscripts, Cincinnati, Ohio
      Joseph B. Boyd Papers
Columbia University, Butler Library, New York, New York
      Henry M. Bonney Journal
Connecticut State Library, History and Genealogy, Hartford, Connecticut
      Charles A. Hart Diary
Duke University, Books, Manuscripts, and Special Collections, Perkins Library,
   Durham, North Carolina
      U.S. Naval Papers
      Henry T. Rommel Papers
Emory University, Special Collections, Woodruff Library, Atlanta, Georgia
      Edwin R. Benedict Diary
      Frederick E. Davis Papers
Historical Society of Pennsylvania, Philadelphia, Pennsylvania
      William J. Clark Papers
      William E. Hinch Papers
      Log of John C. Huntly
      Frank S. Judd Diary
      Charles Alexander Schetky Papers
Huntington Library, San Marino, California
      Americana Collection, Americana Catalogue
        *The Boatswain's Whistle*
      Manuscripts
        George Adams Bright Collection
        Hugh Burns Memorandum Book
        Thomas A. Dornin Journal
        David G. Farragut Papers
        Gustavus Vasa Fox Papers
        James Glazier Collection

Charles L. Green Letterbook
David Low Huntington Papers
Calvin G. Hutchinson Papers
Official Correspondence, U.S. Navy
David D. Porter Papers
Richard Tyson Smith Journal
Smith-Spooner Collection
Gideon Welles Papers
Selim E. Woodworth Papers
Rare Books
Joseph Watson, "Life on Board a Blockader"
Illinois State Historical Library, Springfield, Illinois
William N. Bock Papers
Charles Hale Papers
Louis Kempff Papers
Alexander Mosley Pennock Papers
Samuel Pollock Papers
W. H. Price Papers
Joseph M. Willson Papers
George R. Yost Diary
Indiana Historical Society Library, Indianapolis, Indiana
Samuel C. Vance Papers
Library of Congress, Washington, D.C.
Manuscripts
Asa Beetham Papers
Osborne Family Papers
Hugh G. Thayer Papers
Naval Historical Foundation Collection
Joseph F. Green Papers
Thomas Lyons Journal
Cornelius Schoonmaker Papers
Francis L. Stickney Papers
Henry Clay Taylor Papers
Louisiana State University, Louisiana and Lower Mississippi Valley
Collections, Hill Memorial Library, Baton Rouge, Louisiana
Emily Caroline Douglas Papers
Freeman Foster Papers
Alexander R. Miller Memorandum Book
Robert A. Tyson Diary
Massachusetts Historical Society, Boston, Massachusetts
Barker-Edes-Noyes Papers
Joseph Lincoln Brigham Papers
Hibbard-Seaver Papers
Miscellaneous Manuscripts
John Eliot Parkman Papers

Missouri Historical Society, St. Louis, Missouri
  Amos Bellows Diary
  Bixby Collection
  Civil War Collection
  Warren D. Crandall Papers
  Edmund Curtis Ellis Papers
  Mississippi River Fleet
  Seth Ledyard Phelps Papers
  Thomas C. Wright Papers
Mystic Seaport Museum, G. W. Blunt White Library, Mystic, Connecticut
  Anonymous Journal aboard U.S.S. Ino
  Carsten DeWitt Journal
  Charles A. Poole Log
  William Wainwright Log
National Archives Building, Washington, D.C.
  Record Group 24, Records of the Bureau of Naval Personnel
    Entry 219, Weekly Enlistments from Rendezvous
  Record Group 45, Naval Records Collection of the Office of
      Naval Records and Library
    Entry 464, Subject File, United States Navy, 1775–1910
      Box 284, Naval Justice
      Box 286, Naval Justice
      Box 298, Living Conditions, Customs
      Box 356, Naval Recruiting
      Box 360, Naval Personnel, Miscellaneous Material
Naval Historical Center Library, Washington Navy Yard, Washington, D.C.
  Manuscripts
    Benedict Donohue Papers
    Elisha Hansen Letters, Naval War Correspondence
    Milo Lacy Log
Naval Historical Foundation Collection, Washington Navy Yard,
    Washington, D.C.
  John G. Morrison Diary
  Wallace Shugg Papers
New Jersey Historical Society, Newark, New Jersey
  Edward A. Pierson Papers
  P. H. W. Smith Collection, Chaplain Donald McLaren Papers
New-York Historical Society, New York, New York
  Manuscripts
    William Wesley Barry Papers
    Isaac Bradbury Papers
    Porter R. Chandler Papers
    Titus Munson Coan Papers
    James B. and Joseph T. Collins Papers
    Commander George Durand Papers

Gustavus Vasa Fox Papers
Joseph Fry Papers
R. M. Hodgson Log
Oscar C. Lewis Papers
Lyman Family Papers
McBean Collection
Frank H. Pierce Papers
Roll of Navy Enlisters at New York, 1861–1864
Edward Hallam Saltonstall Papers
Alban C. Stimers Papers
William F. Thoms Papers, Letters from Seamen in the Navy,
 New York Nautical School, 1853–1864
John Van Duzen Papers
Van Nest Papers
Naval Historical Society Collection
 Richard Worsam Meade II Collection
 Richard Worsam Meade III Collection
 Steam Room Log Book of USS Dictator
 Henry Augustus Wise Papers
New York Public Library, Manuscripts and Archives, New York City, New York
John J. Almy Letterbook
Joseph C. Canning Papers
Bartholomew Diggins Journal
John T. Hawkins Memorandum Book
Levi Hayden Papers
Thomas Turner Letterbook
Ohio Historical Society, Manuscripts, Columbus, Ohio
Symmes Browne Papers
John H. Dorman Papers
Otis F. Green Family Papers
Rutgers University, Special Collections and University Archives,
 New Brunswick, New Jersey
Charles Stuart Boggs Papers
Abraham Demarest Papers
Benjamin Heath Jr. Journal
Miles C. Smith Papers
William Van Cleaf Papers
Van Gieson Papers
Robert Wilkinson Papers
University of California at Los Angeles, Special Collections,
 Los Angeles, California
John B. Wirts Diary
University of Michigan, Ann Arbor, Michigan
Bentley Historical Library
 Michigan Historical Collection

Preston Family Papers
William L. Clements Library
    James S. Schoff Civil War Collection
        Cosam T. Bartlett Papers
        George M. Ransom Journal
        Henry A. Simmons Journal
        Joseph Titcomb Papers
University of Missouri, Western Historical Manuscript Collection,
    Ellis Library, Columbia, Missouri
        Fayette Clapp Diary
        Henry C. Fike Papers
        James C. Stephens Papers
University of North Carolina, Southern Historical Collection, Wilson Library,
    Chapel Hill, North Carolina
        Francis Gifford Papers
        George W. Harris Letters
        Frederic Sherman Letters
Western Reserve Historical Society, Manuscripts, Cleveland, Ohio
        William Pendleton Palmer Collection
            John P. Brogan Journal
            John Simpson Diary
Wisconsin Historical Society, Manuscripts, Madison, Wisconsin
        Harrison Family Papers
Yale University, Beinecke Library, New Haven, Connecticut
        Francis S. McKey Journal

PRIMARY SOURCES, PUBLISHED

*Government Documents*

*Annals of the Congress of the United States: The Debates and Proceedings in the
    Congress of the United States.* 12th Cong., 2d sess., November 2, 1812, to
    March 3, 1813. Washington: Gales and Seaton, 1853.

*The Congressional Globe: Containing the Debates and Proceedings of the
    Second Session of the Thirty-seventh Congress.* Edited by John C. Rives.
    Washington, D.C.: Government Printing Office, 1862.

*Official Records of the Union and Confederate Armies in the War of the
    Rebellion.* Ser. 1, 128 vols. Washington, D.C.: Government Printing Office,
    1880–1901.

*Official Records of the Union and Confederate Navies in the War of the
    Rebellion.* 31 vols. Washington, D.C.: Government Printing Office, 1894–1927.

*Public Laws of the United States of America.* Vol. 13. 38th Cong., 1st sess., 1863–
    1864. Edited by George P. Sanger. Boston: Little, Brown, 1864.

Secretary of the Interior. *Population of the United States in 1860: Eighth Census.*
    Washington, D.C.: Government Printing Office, 1864.

Secretary of the Navy. *Report of the Secretary of the Navy, with an Appendix*

*Containing Reports from Officers, December 1861.* Washington, D.C.: Government Printing Office, 1861.

———. *Report of the Secretary of the Navy, with an Appendix Containing Reports from Officers, December 1862.* Washington, D.C.: Government Printing Office, 1862.

———. *Report of the Secretary of the Navy, with an Appendix Containing Reports from Officers, December 1863.* Washington, D.C.: Government Printing Office, 1863.

———. *Report of the Secretary of the Navy, with an Appendix Containing Reports from Officers, December 1864.* Washington, D.C.: Government Printing Office, 1864.

———. *Report of the Secretary of the Navy, with an Appendix Containing Reports from Officers, December 1865.* Washington, D.C.: Government Printing Office, 1865.

———. *Report of the Secretary of the Navy, with an Appendix Containing Reports from Officers, December 1866.* Washington, D.C.: Government Printing Office, 1866.

*The Statutes at Large, Treaties, and Proclamations of the United States of America, from December 5, 1859, to March 3, 1863.* Vol. 12. Edited by George P. Sanger. Boston: Little, Brown, 1863.

U.S. Congress. *Report of the Joint Committee on the Conduct of the War at the Second Session, Thirty-eighth Congress.* Washington, D.C.: Government Printing Office, 1865.

———. House of Representatives. *Chaplains in Congress and in the Army and Navy.* House Report No. 124, 33d Cong., 1st sess., 27 March 1854 (ser. 743).

———. House of Representatives. *Colored Persons in the Navy of the United States.* Sec. of the Navy A. P. Upshur to Speaker of the House John White, 10 August 1842. House Document No. 282. 27th Cong., 2d sess. (ser. 405).

———. House of Representatives. *Report of the Secretary of the Navy Transmitting the Instructions Issued to the Officers of the Several Departments for the Enlistment of Seamen for the United States Navy.* House Executive Document No. 7, 37th Cong., 1st sess., 13 July 1861 (ser. 1114).

———. Senate. Letter of the Secretary of the Navy to Hannibal Hamlin, 30 March 1864. *Transfer of the Seamen from the Army.* Senate Executive Document No. 33, 38th Cong., 1st sess. (ser. 1176).

———. Senate. Senate Executive Document No. 56, 40th Congress, 2d sess., 7.

U.S. Navy. *Regulations for the Government of the United States Navy, 1865.* Washington, D.C.: Government Printing Office, 1865.

———. Department of the Mississippi. *Internal Rules and Regulations for Vessels of the Mississippi Fleet in the Mississippi River and Tributaries.* Cincinnati: Rickey and Carroll, 1862–63.

Books

*Annual Reports of the Protestant Episcopal Church Missionary Society for Seamen, 1851–1891.* New York: White and Ross, 1965.

Baker, La Fayette C. *History of the United States Secret Service.* Philadelphia: L. C. Baker, 1867.

Barnes, James A., and Elinor Barnes, eds. *Naval Surgeon Blockading the South, 1862–1866: The Diary of Samuel Pellman Boyer.* Bloomington: Indiana University Press, 1963.

Barrett, Edward. *Gunnery Instructions Simplified for the Volunteer Officers of the U.S. Navy.* New York: D. Van Nostrand, 1863.

Basler, Roy P., ed. *The Collected Works of Abraham Lincoln.* 9 vols. New Brunswick, N.J.: Rutgers University Press, 1952–55.

Beale, Howard K. *Diary of Gideon Welles: Secretary of the Navy under Lincoln and Johnson.* 2 vols. New York: W. W. Norton, 1960.

Blanding, Stephen F. *Recollections of a Sailor Boy; or, The Cruise of the Gunboat Louisiana.* Providence: E. A. Johnson, 1886.

Burton, Amos. *A Journal of the Cruise of the U.S. Ship Susquehanna.* New York: Edward O. Jenkins, 1863.

Clark, George E. *Seven Years of a Sailor's Life.* Boston: Adams, 1867.

Coffin, Charles C. *My Days and Nights on the Battlefield.* Boston: Estes and Lauriat, 1887.

Cronin, Cornelius. *Recollection of Service in the U.S. Navy: Being Reminiscences as They Have Occurred to My Mind from the Commencement and pending the Late War; while Serving on the U.S. Ships Sabine, Brooklyn, and Richmond.* N.p., 1894.

Daly, Robert W., ed. *Aboard the USS Florida, 1863–65: The Letters of Paymaster William Frederick Keeler, U.S. Navy, to His Wife, Anna.* Annapolis: Naval Institute Press, 1968.

———, ed. *Aboard the USS Monitor, 1862: The Letters of Acting Paymaster William Frederick Keeler, U.S. Navy, to His Wife, Anna.* Annapolis: Naval Institute Press, 1964.

Dana, Richard Henry, Jr. *Two Years before the Mast: A Personal Narrative of a Life at Sea.* 1840. Reprint, New York: World Publishing Company, 1980.

Defoe, Daniel. *Robinson Crusoe.* 1719. Reprint, New York: New American Library, 1960.

Gould, Benjamin A. *Sanitary Memoirs of the War of the Rebellion: Investigations in the Military and Anthropological Statistics of American Soldiers.* Cambridge, Mass.: Riverside Press, 1869.

Gould, William B. *Diary of a Contraband: The Civil War Passage of a Black Sailor.* Stanford: Stanford University Press, 2002.

Grattan, John W. *Under the Blue Pennant; or, Notes of a Naval Officer, 1863–1865.* Edited and with an introduction by Robert J. Schneller. New York: Wiley, 1999.

Hill, Frederic Stanhope. *Twenty Years at Sea; or, Leaves from My Old Log Books.* Boston: Houghton, Mifflin, 1893.

Hunter, Alvah F. *A Year on a Monitor and the Destruction of Fort Sumter.* Edited and with an introduction by Craig L. Symonds. Columbia: University of South Carolina Press, 1987.

Levy, U. P. *Manual of Internal Rules and Regulations for Men-of-War.* New York: D. Van Nostrand, 1862.

Marvel, William, ed. *The Monitor Chronicles: One Sailor's Account.* New York: Simon and Schuster, 2000.

Milligan, John D., ed. *From the Fresh-Water Navy: 1861–64; the Letters of Acting Master's Mate Henry R. Browne and Acting Ensign Symmes E. Browne.* Annapolis: Naval Institute Press, 1970.

Minton, Francis R., ed. *Journal of Patrick Meade, Jr.* Medford, Mass.: n.p., 1984.

Mortensen, Alice P., and Edwin H. Mortensen, eds. *The Family of John Henry Taylor, Jr.: Featuring Family Letters Written during and after the Civil War.* Baltimore: Gateway Press, 1995.

Moss, Lemuel. *Annals of the United States Christian Commission.* Philadelphia: J. B. Lippincott, 1868.

New York Bible Society. *Thirty-ninth Annual Report of the New York Bible Society: Auxiliary of the American Bible Society.* New York: New York Bible Society, 1863.

Olmsted, Frederick Law. *The Cotton Kingdom: A Traveller's Observations on Cotton and Slavery in the American Slave States.* 1860. Reprint, edited and with an introduction by Arthur M. Schlesinger. New York: Alfred A. Knopf, 1953.

———. *A Journey in the Back Country.* 1860. Reprint, Williamstown, Mass.: Corner House Publishers, 1972.

Paine, Albert Bigelow. *A Sailor of Fortune: Personal Memoirs of Captain B. S. Osbon.* New York: McClure, Phillips, 1906.

Rankins, Walter, ed. *Diary of a Union Soldier, 1864–1865.* Frankfort, Ky.: Roberts Printing Company, 1952.

Rockwell, Charles. *Sketches of Foreign Travel and Life at Sea.* 2 vols. Boston: Tappan and Dennet, 1842.

Roe, Francis Asbury. *Naval Duties and Discipline, with the Policy and Principles of Naval Organization.* New York: D. Van Nostrand, 1865.

Secret, Jeanette B. *Iverson Granderson: First Class "Colored" Boy, Union Navy (1863–1865).* Bowie, Md.: Heritage Books, 1998.

Selfridge, Thomas O., Jr. *Memoirs of Thomas O. Selfridge, Jr., Rear Admiral, U.S.N.* With an introduction by Captain Dudley W. Knox. New York: G. P. Putnam's Sons, 1924.

Smith, Edward P. *Incidents of the United States Christian Commission.* Philadelphia: J. B. Lippincott, 1871.

Stille, Charles J. *History of the United States Sanitary Commission: Being the General Report of Its Work during the War of Rebellion.* Philadelphia: J. B. Lippincott, 1866.

Symonds, Craig L., ed. *Charleston Blockade: The Journals of John B. Marchand, U.S. Navy, 1861–1862.* Newport, R.I.: Naval War College, 1976.

Thompson, Robert Means, and Richard Wainwright, eds. *Confidential Correspondence of Gustavus Vasa Fox, Assistant Secretary of the Navy, 1861–1865.* 2 vols. New York: De Vinne Press, 1918–19.

U.S. Christian Commission. *Hymn-Book for the Army and Navy*. Cincinnati: U.S. Christian Commission, n.d.

———. *Principles and Position of the United States Christian Commission*. San Francisco: Towne and Bacon, 1864.

———. *United States Christian Commission for the Army and Navy: Work and Incidents*. Philadelphia: U.S. Christian Commission, 1862–65.

Vail, I. E. *Three Years on the Blockade: A Naval Experience*. New York: Abbey Press, 1902.

Van Alstyne, Lawrence. *Diary of an Enlisted Man*. New Haven: Tuttle, Morehouse and Taylor, 1910.

Weaver, C. P., ed. *Thank God My Regiment an African One: The Civil War Diary of Nathan W. Daniels*. Baton Rouge: Louisiana State University Press, 1998.

Wills, Charles W. *Army Life of an Illinois Soldier: Including a Day-by-Day Record of Sherman's March to the Sea*. Compiled by Mary E. Kellogg; with a foreword by John Y. Simon. Carbondale: Southern Illinois University Press, 1996.

*Articles*

Anderson, William H. "Blockade Life." In *War Papers Read before the Commandery of the State of Maine, Military Order of the Loyal Legion of the United States*. 3 vols. Portland: Lefavor-Tower, 1898.

Anonymous. "The Age of Iron." *Harper's New Monthly Magazine* 27 (July 1863): 285–86.

———. "The Condition of the Sailor: Are Sailors Growing Worse and Worse?" *Sailor's Magazine* 34 (November 1861): 82–86.

———. "Life on a Blockader." *Continental Monthly* 6 (July 1864): 46–55.

———. "Only Three Chaplains in the Navy in Sea Going Vessels." *Sailor's Magazine* 35 (January 1863): 134–35.

———. "Naval Chaplains." *Sailor's Magazine* 35 (February 1863): 161–62.

———. "Religious Instruction in the Army." *Princeton Review* 35 (July 1863): 386–99.

Avery, William B. "Gun-Boat Service on the James River," 37–38. In *Personal Narratives of Events in the War of Rebellion, Being Papers Read before the Rhode Island Soldiers and Sailors Historical Society*. 3d ser., no. 3. Providence: N. B. Williams, 1884.

Basile, Leon, ed. "Harry Stanley's Mess Book: Offenses and Punishments aboard the Ethan Allen." *Civil War History* 23 (March 1977): 69–79.

Blakeman, A. Noel. "Some Personal Reminiscences of the Naval Service." In *Personal Recollections of the War of the Rebellion; Addresses before the Commandery of the State of New York, Military Order of the Loyal Legion of the United States*. 2d ser. Vol. 2. New York: Knickerbocker Press, 1897.

Butts, Francis B. "A Cruise along the Blockade." In *Personal Narratives of Events in the War of Rebellion, Being Papers Read before the Rhode Island Soldiers and Society*. No. 12, vol. 2. Providence: N. B. Williams, 1881.

———. "Reminiscences of Gunboat Service on the Nansemond." In *Personal*

*Narratives of Events in the War of Rebellion, Being Papers Read before the Rhode Island Soldiers and Sailors Historical Society.* 3d ser., no. 8. Providence: N. B. Williams, 1884.

Callender, Eliot. "What a Boy Saw on the Mississippi." In *Military Essays and Recollections: Papers Read before the Commandery of the State of Illinois, Military Order of the Loyal Legion of the United States.* Vol. 1. Chicago: A. C. McClurg, 1891.

Campbell, James Edwin. "Recent Addresses of James Edwin Campbell: The Mississippi Squadron." *Ohio Archaeological and Historical Quarterly* 34 (January 1925): 29–62.

Everson, Guy R., ed. "Service Afield and Afloat: A Reminiscence of the Civil War." *Indiana Magazine of History* 89 (March 1993): 35–56.

Gould, William B., IV. "Lincoln, Labor, and the Black Military: The Legacy Provided." Speech before the Military Order of the Loyal Legion of the United States in Honor of President Lincoln, Washington, D.C., 11 February 1995.

Heslin, James J., ed. "Two New Yorkers in the Union Navy: Narrative Based on Letters of the Collins Brothers." *New-York Historical Society Quarterly* 43 (April 1959): 161–91.

Holton, William C. "Cruise of the U.S. Flag-Ship Hartford, 1862–1863." Edited by B. S. Osbon. *Magazine of History with Notes and Queries* 22 (September–October 1922): 131–36.

Huch, Ronald K., ed. "The Civil War Letters of Herbert Saunders." *Register of the Kentucky Historical Society* 69 (March 1971): 17–29.

Hutchinson, William F. "Life on the Texan Blockade." In *Personal Narratives of Events in the War of Rebellion, Being Papers Read before the Rhode Island Soldiers and Sailors Historical Society.* 3d ser., no. 1. Providence: N. B. Williams, 1883.

Mahan, Alfred Thayer. "The Minor Trials of Blockade Duty." *Harper's Magazine,* October 26, 1907, 1556.

McDonald, Joseph. "How I Saw the Monitor-Merrimac Fight." *New England Magazine* 36 (July 1907): 548–53.

Melville, Herman. "A Utilitarian View of the *Monitor*'s Fight." In *Battle-Pieces and Aspects of the War.* 1866. Reprint, Gainesville, Fla.: Scholars' Facsimiles and Reprints, 1960.

Milligan, John D., ed. "Gunboat War at Vicksburg." *American Heritage* 29 (August–September 1978): 62–68.

———. "Navy Life on the Mississippi River." *Civil War Times Illustrated* 33 (May–June 1994): 16, 66–73.

Nichols, Roy F., ed. "Fighting in North Carolina Waters." *North Carolina Historical Review* 40 (Winter 1963): 75–84.

Nordhoff, Charles. "Two Weeks at Port Royal." *Harper's New Monthly Magazine* 27 (June 1863): 111–18.

Packard, Kent, ed. "Jottings by the Way: A Sailor's Log—1862 to 1864." Part 1. *Pennsylvania Magazine of History and Biography* 71 (April 1947): 121–51.

———. "Jottings by the Way: A Sailor's Log—1862 to 1864." Part 2. *Pennsylvania Magazine of History and Biography* 71 (July 1947): 251–81.

Patrick, Jeffery L., ed. "A Fighting Sailor on the Western Rivers: The Civil War Letters of 'Gunboat.'" *Journal of Mississippi History* 58 (September 1996): 255–83.

Post, Charles A. "A Diary on the Blockade in 1863." *United States Naval Institute Proceedings* 44 (March 1918): 2333–50, 2567–94.

Powell, Samuel W. "Blockading Memories of the Gulf Squadron." *Magazine of History with Notes and Queries* 8 (July 1908): 1–11.

Sands, Francis P. B. "Lest We Forget: Memories of Service Afloat from 1862 to 1866." In *Military Order of the Loyal Legion of the United States: Commandery of the District of Columbia*. War Papers 73. Washington, D.C.: Companion, 1908.

Schlesinger, Arthur M., Jr., ed. "A Blue Bluejacket's Letters Home, 1863–1864." *New England Quarterly* 1 (October 1928): 554–67.

Simms, L. Moody, Jr., ed. "A Union Volunteer with the Mississippi Ram Fleet." *Lincoln Herald* 70 (Winter 1968): 189–92.

Swift, Lester L., ed. "Letters from a Sailor on a Tinclad." *Civil War History* 10 (March 1961): 48–62.

True, Rowland Stafford. "Life aboard a Gunboat." *Civil War Times Illustrated* 9 (February 1971): 37–43.

Wait, Horatio L. "The Blockade of the Confederacy." *Century Magazine* 34 (May–October 1898): 914–28.

———. "The Blockading Service." In *Military Essays and Recollections: Papers Read before the Commandery of the State of Illinois, Military Order of the Loyal Legion of the United States*. Vol. 1. Chicago: A. C. McClurg, 1891–1912.

Weeks, Grenville M. "The Last Cruise of the Monitor." *Atlantic Monthly* 11 (March 1863): 366–72.

Wilkinson, William C. "The History of the Christian Commission." In *A Free Lance in the Field of Life and Letters*. New York: Albert Mason, 1874.

SECONDARY SOURCES

*Books*

Abbot, Willis J. *Blue Jackets of '61: A History of the Navy in the War of Secession*. New York: Dodd, Mead, 1890.

Abzug, Robert H. *Cosmos Crumbling: American Reform and the Religious Imagination*. New York: Oxford University Press, 1994.

Adams, Michael C. C. *Fighting for Defeat: Union Military Failure in the East, 1861–1865*. Lincoln: University of Nebraska Press, 1992.

Armstrong, Warren B. *For Courageous Fighting and Confident Dying: Union Chaplains in the Civil War*. Lawrence: University Press of Kansas, 1998.

Barker, Albert S. *Everyday Life in the Navy*. Boston: Gorham Press, 1928.

Barton, Michael. *Goodmen: The Character of Civil War Soldiers*. University Park: Pennsylvania State University Press, 1981.

Bauer, K. Jack. *Surfboats and Horse Marines: U.S. Naval Operations in the Mexican War, 1846–1848.* Annapolis: Naval Institute Press, 1969.

Bernstein, Iver. *The New York City Draft Riots: Their Significance for American Society and Politics in the Age of the Civil War.* New York: Oxford University Press, 1990.

Beyer, Walter F., and Oscar F. Keydel. *Acts of Bravery: Deeds of Extraordinary American Heroism, from the Personal Records and Reminiscences of Courageous Americans Who Risked Everything for Their Comrades and Country.* 1903. Reprint, Stamford, Conn.: Longmeadow Press, 1994.

Blight, David W., and Brooks D. Simpson, eds. *Union and Emancipation: Essays on Politics and Race in the Civil War Era.* Kent, Ohio: Kent State University Press, 1997.

Bolster, W. Jeffrey. *Black Jacks: African American Seamen in the Age of Sail.* Cambridge: Harvard University Press, 1997.

Booth, Alan, ed. *Human Crowding.* Blacksburg: Virginia Polytechnic Institute and State University, 1975.

Boynton, Charles B. *History of the Navy during the Rebellion.* 2 vols. New York: D. Appleton, 1869–70.

Browning, Robert M., Jr. *From Cape Charles to Cape Fear: The North Atlantic Blockading Squadron during the Civil War.* Tuscaloosa: University of Alabama Press, 1993.

———. *Success Is All That Was Demanded: The South Atlantic Blockading Squadron during the Civil War.* Washington, D.C.: Brassey's, 2002.

Buker, George E. *Blockaders, Refugees, and Contrabands: Civil War on Florida's Gulf Coast, 1861–1865.* Tuscaloosa: University of Alabama Press, 1993.

Burton, William L. *Melting Pot Soldiers: The Union's Ethnic Regiments.* New York: Fordham University Press, 1998.

Canney, Donald L. *Lincoln's Navy: The Ships, Men, and Organization, 1861–65.* Annapolis: Naval Institute Press, 1998.

Carr, Dawson. *Gray Phantoms of the Cape Fear: Running the Civil War Blockade.* Winston-Salem: John F. Blair, 1998.

Carrison, Daniel. *The Navy from Wood to Steel, 1860–1890.* New York: Franklin Watts, 1965.

Cecelski, David S. *The Waterman's Song: Slavery and Freedom in Maritime North Carolina.* Chapel Hill: University of North Carolina Press, 2001.

Christophe-Agnew, Jean. *Worlds Apart: The Market and Theater in Anglo-American Thought, 1550–1750.* Cambridge: Cambridge University Press, 1986.

Cott, Nancy F. *The Bonds of Womanhood: "Women's Sphere" in New England, 1780–1835.* New Haven: Yale University Press, 1977.

Creasey, George W. *The City of Newburyport in the Civil War, from 1861 to 1865.* Boston: Griffith-Stillings Press, 1903.

Creighton, Margaret S. *Rites and Passages: The Experience of American Whaling, 1830–1870.* Cambridge: Cambridge University Press, 1995.

Dening, Greg. *Mr. Bligh's Bad Language: Passion, Power, and Theatre on the Bounty.* Cambridge: Cambridge University Press, 1992.

Department of the Navy. Naval History Division. *Civil War Naval Chronology, 1861–1865.* 6 vols. Washington, D.C.: Government Printing Office, 1961–66.
———. *Riverine Warfare: The United States Navy's Operations on Inland Waters.* Washington, D.C.: Government Printing Office, 1967.
Drazin, Israel, and Cecil B. Currey. *For God and Country: The History of a Constitutional Challenge to the Army Chaplaincy.* New York: Ktav Publishing House, 1995.
Drury, Clifford M. *The History of the Chaplain Corps, United States Navy.* Vol. 1, *1789–1939.* Washington, D.C.: Government Printing Office, 1949.
Ernst, Robert. *Immigrant Life in New York City, 1825–1863.* New York: King's Crown Press, 1949.
Fellman, Michael. *Inside War: The Guerrilla Conflict in Missouri during the American Civil War.* New York: Oxford University Press, 1989.
Fingard, Judith. *Jack in Port: Sailortowns in Eastern Canada.* Toronto: University of Toronto Press, 1982.
Fite, Emerson D. *Social and Industrial Conditions in the North during the Civil War.* 1910. Reprint, New York: Frederick Ungar, 1963.
Forbes, Robert Bennet. *The Voyage of the Jamestown on Her Errand of Mercy.* Boston: Eastburn Press, 1847.
Fox, William F. *Regimental Losses in the American Civil War, 1861–1865.* Albany, N.Y.: Joseph McDonough, 1898.
Fredrickson, George M. *The Black Image in the White Mind: The Debate on Afro-American Character and Destiny, 1817–1914.* Hanover, N.H.: Wesleyan University Press, 1987.
———. *The Inner Civil War: Northern Intellectuals and the Crisis of Union.* New York: Harper and Row, 1965.
Fussell, Paul. *Wartime: Understanding and Behavior in the Second World War.* New York: Oxford University Press, 1989.
Gabriel, Richard A., and Karen S. Metz. *History of Military Medicine.* With a foreword by John Keegan. New York: Greenwood Press, 1992.
Garrison, Webb. *Mutiny in the Civil War.* Shippensburg, Pa.: White Mane Publishing, 2001.
Gerteis, Louis S. *From Contraband to Freedman: Federal Policy toward Southern Blacks, 1861–1865.* Westport, Conn.: Greenwood Press, 1973.
Gilmore, Michael T. *American Romanticism and the Marketplace.* Chicago: University of Chicago Press, 1985.
Glatthaar, Joseph T. *Forged in Battle: The Civil War Alliance of Black Soldiers and White Officers.* New York: Free Press, 1990.
Goffman, Erving. *Asylums.* New York: Doubleday, 1961.
Gosnell, H. Allen. *Guns on the Western Waters: The Story of the River Gunboats in the Civil War.* Baton Rouge: Louisiana State University Press, 1949.
Greenberg, Amy S. *Cause for Alarm: The Volunteer Fire Department in the Nineteenth-Century City.* Princeton: Princeton University Press, 1998.
Griffith, Paddy. *Battle Tactics of the Civil War.* New Haven: Yale University Press, 1987.

Grimsley, Mark. *The Hard Hand of War: Union Military Policy toward Civilians, 1861–1865*. Cambridge: Cambridge University Press, 1995.

Harrod, Frederick S. *Manning the New Navy: The Development of a Modern Naval Enlisted Force, 1899–1940*. Westport, Conn.: Greenwood Press, 1978.

Henningsen, Henning. *Crossing the Equator: Sailors' Baptism and Other Initiation Rites*. Copenhagen: Munksgaard, 1961.

Hess, Earl J. *Liberty, Virtue, and Progress: The Northerners and Their War for Union*. New York: New York University Press, 1988.

———. *The Union Soldier in Combat: Enduring the Ordeal of Combat*. Lawrence: University Press of Kansas, 1997.

Hill, Jim Dan. *The Civil War Sketchbook of Charles Ellery Stedman, Surgeon, United States Navy*. San Rafael, Calif.: Presidio Press, 1976.

Hohman, Elmo Paul. *History of American Merchant Seamen*. Hamden, Conn.: Shoe String Press, 1956.

———. *Seamen Ashore: A Study of the United States Seamen's Service and of Merchant Seamen in Port*. With a foreword by William S. Newell and E. S. Land. New Haven: Yale University Press, 1952.

Johnson, Ludwell H. *Red River Campaign: Politics and Cotton in the Civil War*. Baltimore: Johns Hopkins University Press, 1958.

Johnson, Paul E. *A Shopkeeper's Millennium: Society and Revivals in Rochester, New York, 1815–1837*. New York: Hill and Wang, 1978.

Jones, Virgil Carrington. *The Civil War at Sea*. 3 vols. New York: Holt, Rinehart, and Winston, 1961–63.

Kaestle, Carl F. *Pillars of the Republic: Common Schools and American Society, 1780–1860*. New York: Hill and Wang, 1983.

Karsten, Peter. *The Naval Aristocracy: The Golden Age of Annapolis and the Emergence of Modern American Navalism*. New York: Free Press, 1972.

Keegan, John. *The Face of Battle*. New York: Viking Press, 1976.

Knobel, Dale T. *Paddy and the Republic: Ethnicity and Nationality in Antebellum America*. Middletown, Conn.: Wesleyan University Press, 1986.

Laffin, John. *Jack Tar: The Story of the British Sailor*. London: Cassel, 1969.

Langley, Harold D. *Social Reform in the United States Navy, 1798–1862*. Urbana: University of Illinois Press, 1967.

Lemisch, Jesse. *Jack Tar vs. John Bull: The Role of New York's Seamen in Precipitating the Revolution*. New York: Garland Press, 1997.

Linderman, Gerald F. *Embattled Courage: The Experience of Combat in the American Civil War*. New York: Free Press, 1987.

Litwack, Leon. *North of Slavery: The Negro in the Free States, 1790–1860*. Chicago: University of Chicago Press, 1961.

Lonn, Ella. *Foreigners in the Union Army and Navy*. Baton Rouge: Louisiana State University Press, 1951.

Loomis, Reverend H. *Christian Work among Soldiers*. Yokohama, Japan: Fukuin, 1908.

Lott, Eric. *Love and Theft: Blackface Minstrelsy and the American Working Class*. New York: Oxford University Press, 1995.

Mack, William P., and Royal W. Connell. *Naval Ceremonies, Customs, and Traditions*. 5th ed. Annapolis: Naval Institute Press, 1980.

Marvel, William. *The Alabama and the Kearsarge: The Sailor's Civil War*. Chapel Hill: University of North Carolina Press, 1996.

May, Rollo. *The Meaning of Anxiety*. New York: W. W. Norton, 1977.

McColley, Robert. *Slavery and Jeffersonian Virginia*. Urbana: University of Illinois Press, 1964.

McLoughlin, William G. *Revivals, Awakenings, and Reform: An Essay on Religion and Social Change in America, 1607–1977*. Chicago: University of Chicago Press, 1978.

McNeill, William H. *The Pursuit of Power: Technology, Armed Force, and Society since A.D. 1000*. Chicago: University of Chicago Press, 1982.

McPherson, James M. *Battle Cry of Freedom: The Civil War Era*. New York: Oxford University Press, 1988.

——. *For Cause and Comrades: Why Men Fought in the Civil War*. New York: Oxford University Press, 1997.

——. *The Negro's Civil War: How American Negroes Felt and Acted during the War for the Union*. New York: Pantheon Books, 1965.

——. *Ordeal by Fire: The Civil War and Reconstruction*. New York: McGraw-Hill, 1992.

——. *What They Fought For, 1861–1865*. Baton Rouge: Louisiana State University Press, 1994.

Melville, Herman. *White-Jacket; or, The World in a Man-of-War*. 1850. Reprint, New York: Quality Paperback Book Club, 1996.

Merrill, James M. *The Rebel Shore: The Story of Union Sea Power in the Civil War*. Boston: Little, Brown, 1957.

Milligan, John D. *Gunboats down the Mississippi*. Annapolis: Naval Institute Press, 1965.

Mindell, David A. *War, Technology, and Experience aboard the USS Monitor*. Baltimore: Johns Hopkins University Press, 2000.

Mitchell, Reid. *Civil War Soldiers: Their Expectations and Their Experiences*. New York: Viking Press, 1988.

——. *The Vacant Chair: The Northern Soldier Leaves Home*. New York: Oxford University Press, 1993.

Moebs, Thomas Truxton, ed. *America's Naval Heritage: A Catalog of Early Imprints from the Navy Department Library*. Washington, D.C.: Department of the Navy, 2000.

Moorhead, James. *American Apocalypse: Yankee Protestants and the Civil War, 1860–1869*. New Haven: Yale University Press, 1978.

Moran, Lord. *The Anatomy of Courage*. Boston: Houghton, Mifflin, 1967.

Morris, Richard B. *Government and Labor in Early America*. New York: Columbia University Press, 1946.

Musicant, Ivan. *Divided Waters: The Naval History of the Civil War*. New York: HarperCollins, 1995.

Nash, Gary B. *The Urban Crucible: Social Change, Political Consciousness, and* the Origins of the American Revolution. Cambridge: Harvard University Press, 1979.

Owsley, Frank. King Cotton Diplomacy: Foreign Relations of the Confederate States of America. Chicago: University of Chicago Press, 1931.

Paludan, Phillip S. Victims: A True Story of the Civil War. Knoxville: University of Tennessee Press, 1980.

Paullin, Charles O. Paullin's History of Naval Administration, 1775–1911. Annapolis: Naval Institute Press, 1968.

Quarles, Benjamin. The Negro in the Civil War. Boston: Little, Brown, 1953.

Ramold, Steven J. Slaves, Sailors, Citizens: African Americans in the Union Navy. DeKalb: Northern Illinois University Press, 2002.

Rediker, Marcus. Between the Devil and the Deep Blue Sea: Merchant Seamen, Pirates, and the Anglo-American Maritime World, 1700–1750. Cambridge: Cambridge University Press, 1987.

Ringle, Dennis J. Life in Mr. Lincoln's Navy. Annapolis: Naval Institute Press, 1998.

Robinton, Madeline Russell. An Introduction to the Papers of the New York Prize Court, 1861–1865. New York: Columbia University Press, 1945.

Roediger, David R. The Wages of Whiteness: Race and the Making of the American Working Class. New York: Verso Press, 1991.

Rorabaugh, W. J. The Alcoholic Republic: An American Tradition. New York: Oxford University Press, 1979.

———. The Craft Apprentice: From Franklin to the Machine Age in America. New York: Oxford University Press, 1986.

Ross, Steven J. Workers on the Edge: Work, Leisure, and Politics in Industrializing Cincinnati, 1788–1890. New York: Columbia University Press, 1985.

Sellers, Charles G. The Market Revolution: Jacksonian America, 1815–1846. New York: Oxford University Press, 1991.

Shattuck, Gardiner H., Jr. A Shield and a Hiding Place: The Religious Life of the Civil War Armies. Macon, Ga.: Mercer University Press, 1987.

Soley, James Russell. The Navy in the Civil War: The Blockade and the Cruisers. New York: Charles Scribner's Sons, 1883.

Sperry, Willard L., ed. Religion in the Post-War World. Vol. 2, Religion of Soldier and Sailor. Cambridge: Harvard University Press, 1945.

Still, William N., Jr., ed., The Confederate Navy: The Ships, Men, and Organization, 1861–1865. Annapolis: Naval Institute Press, 1997.

Stivers, Reuben Elmore. Privateers and Volunteers: The Men and Women of Our Reserve Naval Forces, 1766 to 1866. Annapolis: Naval Institute Press, 1975.

Stott, Richard B. Workers in the Metropolis: Class, Ethnicity, and Youth in Antebellum New York City. Ithaca: Cornell University Press, 1990.

Stouffer, Samuel A., et al. The American Soldier: Combat and Its Aftermath. 2 vols. Princeton: Princeton University Press, 1949.

Taylor, William R. Cavalier and Yankee: The Old South and the American National Character. 1961. Reprint, Garden City, N.Y.: Doubleday, 1963.

Thernstrom, Stephan. *The Other Bostonians: Poverty and Progress in the American Metropolis, 1880–1970.* Cambridge: Harvard University Press, 1973.

U.S. Navy. *The Bluejackets' Manual.* Annapolis: Naval Institute Press, 1938.

Valle, James E. *Rocks and Shoals: Order and Discipline in the Old Navy, 1800–1861.* Annapolis: Naval Institute Press, 1980.

Valuska, David L. *The African American in the Union Navy, 1861–1865.* New York: Garland, 1993.

Villiers, Alan. *The Way of a Ship.* New York: Charles Scribner's Sons, 1953.

Voegeli, V. Jacques. *Free but Not Equal.* Chicago: University of Chicago Press, 1967.

Volo, Dorothy Denneen, and James M. Volo. *Daily Life in Civil War America.* Westport, Conn.: Greenwood Press, 1998.

Walkowitz, Daniel J. *Worker City, Company Town: Iron and Cotton-Worker Protest in Troy and Cohoes, New York, 1855–1884.* Urbana: University of Illinois Press, 1978.

West, Richard S., Jr. *Mr. Lincoln's Navy.* New York: Longmans, Green, 1957.

Wideman, John C. *The Sinking of the USS Cairo.* Jackson: University Press of Mississippi, 1993.

Wilentz, Sean. *Chants Democratic: New York City and the Rise of the American Working Class, 1788–1850.* New York: Oxford University Press, 1984.

Wiley, Bell I. *The Life of Billy Yank: The Common Soldier of the Union.* Baton Rouge: Louisiana State University Press, 1978.

Wise, Steven R. *Lifeline of the Confederacy: Blockade Running during the Civil War.* Columbia: University of South Carolina Press, 1988.

Woodworth, Stephen E. *While God Is Marching On: The Religious World of Civil War Soldiers.* Lawrence: University Press of Kansas, 2001.

Wyatt-Brown, Bertram. *Southern Honor: Ethics and Behavior in the Old South.* New York: Oxford University Press, 1982.

Zeydel, Edwin H. *Sebastian Brant.* New York: Twayne, 1967.

Zinni, Chester S., Jr. *A Concise History of the Book of Common Prayer, 1549 to 1979.* New York: Nomis Publications, 1981.

*Articles and Chapters in Books*

Aptheker, Herbert. "The Negro in the Union Navy." *Journal of Negro History* 32 (April 1947): 169–200.

Arnold, Allan A. "All Hands Drunk and Rioting: Disobedience in the Merchant Marine." In *Ships, Seafaring, and Society: Essays in Maritime History*, edited by Timothy J. Runyan. Detroit: Wayne State University Press, 1987.

Berkman, Paul L. "Life Aboard an Armed-Guard Ship." *American Journal of Sociology* 51 (November 1946): 380–87.

Bolster, W. Jeffrey. "To Feel Like a Man: Black Seamen in Northern States, 1800–1860." *Journal of American History* 76 (March 1990): 1173–99.

Bremner, Robert H. "The Impact of the Civil War on Philanthropy and Social Welfare." *Civil War History* 12 (December 1966): 293–303.

Brewer, Charles C. "African American Sailors and the Unvexing of the Mississippi River." *Prologue* 30 (Winter 1998): 279–86.

Buhl, Lawrence C. "Mariners and Machines: Resistance to Technological Change in the American Navy, 1865–1869." *Journal of American History* 61 (March 1974): 703–27.

Cain, Marvin R. "A Face of Battle Needed: An Assessment of Men and Motives in Civil War Historiography." *Civil War History* 28 (March 1982): 5–27.

Cornelius, George. "What Did Farragut See?" *Naval History* 8 (August 1994): 10–13.

Daly, Robert W. "Pay and Prize Money in the Old Navy, 1776–1899." *U.S. Naval Institute Proceedings* 74 (August 1948): 967–71.

Fredrickson, George M. "The Coming of the Lord: The Northern Protestant Clergy and the Civil War Crisis." In *Religion and the American Civil War*, edited by Randall M. Miller, Harry S. Stout, and Charles Reagan Wilson. New York: Oxford University Press, 1998.

Fromm-Reichmann, Frieda. "Psychiatric Aspects of Anxiety." In *Identity and Anxiety: Survival of the Person in Mass Society*, edited by Maurice R. Stein, Arthur J. Vidich, and David Manning White. Glencoe, Ill.: Free Press, 1960.

Gerteis, Louis S. "Blackface Minstrelsy and the Construction of Race in Nineteenth-Century America." In *Union and Emancipation: Essays on Politics and Race in the Civil War Era*, edited by David W. Blight and Brooks D. Simpson. Kent, Ohio: Kent State University Press, 1997.

Gilje, Paul A. "The Meaning of Freedom for Waterfront Workers." In *Devising Liberty: Preserving and Creating Freedom in the New American Republic*, edited by David Thomas Konig. Stanford: Stanford University Press, 1995.

Goetzmann, William H. "The Mountain Man as Jacksonian Man." *American Quarterly* 15 (Fall 1963): 402–15.

Goodrich, Carter, and Sol Davidson. "The Wage-Earner in the Western Movement." Part 1. *Political Science Quarterly* 50 (June 1935): 161–85.

———. "The Wage-Earner in the Western Movement." Part 2. *Political Science Quarterly* 50 (March 1936): 61–116.

Harris, Emily J. "Sons and Soldiers: Deerfield, Massachusetts, and the Civil War." *Civil War History* 30 (June 1984): 151–71.

Harrod, Frederick S. "Jim Crow in the Navy (1798–1941)." *Proceedings of the United States Naval Institute* 105 (September 1979): 46–53.

———. "Integration of the Navy (1941–1978)." *Proceedings of the United States Naval Institute* 105 (October 1979): 40–47.

Hess, Earl J. "The Northern Response to the Ironclad: A Prospect for the Study of Military Technology." *Civil War History* 31 (June 1985): 126–43.

———. "The 12th Missouri Infantry: A Socio-Military Profile of a Union Regiment." *Missouri Historical Review* 76 (October 1981): 53–77.

Hirsch, Charles B. "Gunboat Personnel on the Western Waters." *Mid-America* 34 (April 1952): 73–86.

Johnson, Robert Erwin. "Investment by Sea: The Civil War Blockade." *American Neptune* 32 (March 1972): 45–57.

Kane, Murray. "Some Considerations on the Safety Valve Doctrine." *Mississippi Valley Historical Review* 23 (September 1936): 169–88.

Laas, Virginia Jean. "Sleepless Sentinels: The North Atlantic Blockading Squadron, 1862–1864." *Civil War History* 31 (March 1985): 24–38.

Lathrop, Constance. "Grog: Its Origins in the United States Navy." *United States Naval Institute Proceedings* 61 (March 1935): 377–80.

Leland, C. G. "The Soldier and the Civilian." *Continental Monthly* 2 (July–December 1862): 281–84.

Lemisch, Jesse. "Jack Tar in the Streets: Merchant Seamen in the Politics of Revolutionary America." *William and Mary Quarterly* 25 (July 1968): 371–407.

Matthews, Donald G. "The Second Great Awakening as an Organizing Process, 1780–1830: An Hypothesis." *American Quarterly* 21 (Spring 1969): 23–43.

McKee, Christopher. "Fantasies of Mutiny and Murder: A Suggested Psycho-History of Seamen in the U.S. Navy, 1798–1815." *Armed Forces and Society* 4 (February 1978): 293–304.

Merrill, James M. "Cairo, Illinois: Strategic Civil War River Port." *Journal of Illinois History* 76 (Winter 1983): 242–56.

———. "Men, Monotony, and Mouldy Beans—Life on Board Civil War Blockaders." *American Neptune* 16 (January 1956): 49–59.

Mayers, Adam. "Stolen Soldiers." *Civil War Times Illustrated* 34 (June 1995): 56–59.

Price, Marcus W. "Ships That Tested the Blockade of Carolina Ports, 1861–1865." *American Neptune* 8 (July 1948): 24–39.

Quimby, Rollin. "The Chaplains' Predicament." *Civil War History* 8 (March 1962): 246–59.

Reidy, Joseph P. "Black Jack: African American Sailors in the Civil War Navy," 213–20. In *New Interpretations in Naval History: Selected Papers from the Twelfth Naval History Symposium*, edited by William B. Cogar. Annapolis: Naval Institute Press, 1997.

Riggs, David F. "Sailors of the U.S.S. Cairo: Anatomy of a Gunboat Crew." *Civil War History* 28 (September 1982): 266–73.

Rorabaugh, W. J. "Who Fought for the North in the Civil War?: Concord, Massachusetts, Enlistments." *Journal of American History* 73 (December 1986): 695–701.

Shannon, Fred. "A Post-mortem on the Safety-Valve Labor Theory." *Agricultural History* 19 (January 1945): 31–37.

Still, William N. "The Common Sailor: The Civil War's Uncommon Man; Part 1, Yankee Blue Jackets." *Civil War Times Illustrated* 23 (February 1985): 25–39.

———. "A Naval Sieve: The Union Blockade in the Civil War." *Naval War College Review* 36 (May–June 1983): 38–45.

Surdam, David G. "The Union Navy's Blockade Reconsidered." *Naval War College Review* 51 (Autumn 1998): 85–107.

Truesdale, John. "Bluecoats Afloat." In *The Bluecoats, and How They Lived, Fought and Died for the Union*. Philadelphia: Jones Brothers, 1867.

Vinovskis, Maris A. "Have Social Historians Lost the Civil War? Some

Preliminary Demographic Speculations." In *Toward a Social History of the American Civil War*, ed. Maris A. Vinovskis. Cambridge: Cambridge University Press, 1992.

Wiley, Bell I. "'Holy Joes' of the Sixties: A Study of Civil War Chaplains." *Huntington Library Quarterly* 16 (May 1953): 287–304.

———. "Johnny Reb and Billy Yank Compared." *American History Illustrated* 3 (April 1968): 4–9, 44–47.

Zurcher, Louis A., Jr. "The Sailor aboard Ship: A Study of Role Behavior in a Total Institution." *Social Forces* 43 (March 1965): 389–400.

*Masters Theses and Ph.D. Dissertations*

Buchanan, Thomas C. "The Slave Mississippi: African American Steamboat Workers, Networks of Resistance, and the Commercial World of the Western Rivers, 1811–1880." Ph.D. diss., Carnegie Mellon University, 1998.

Farr, James Barker. "Black Odyssey: The Seafaring Traditions of Afro-Americans." Ph.D. diss., University of California, Santa Barbara, 1975.

Glover, Robert. "The West Gulf Blockade, 1861–1865: An Evaluation." Ph.D. diss., North Texas State University, 1974.

Goodman, Michael Harris. "The Black Tar: Negro Seamen in the Union Navy." Ph.D. diss., University of Nottingham, 1975.

McDevitt, Theresa Rose. "Fighting for the Soul of America: A History of the United States Christian Commission." Ph.D. diss., Kent State University, 1997.

Merrifield, Edward F. "The Seaboard War: A History of the North Atlantic Blockading Squadron, 1861–1865." Ph.D. diss., Case Western Reserve University, 1975.

Nelson, Dennis Denmark. "The Integration of the Negro into the United States Navy, 1776–1947." M.A. thesis, Howard University, 1948.

Parker, Theodore R. "The Federal Gunboat Flotilla on the Western Rivers during Its Administration by the War Department to October 1, 1862." Ph.D. diss., University of Pittsburgh, 1939.

Polser, Aubrey Henry. "The Administration of the United States Navy, 1861–1865." Ph.D. diss., University of Nebraska, 1975.

Smith, Myron J., Jr. "The U.S. Gunboat *Carondolet*, 1861–1865." M.A. thesis, Shippensburg State University, 1969.

Steckel, Frances C. "Morale and Men: A Study of the American Soldier in World War II." Ph.D. diss., Temple University, 1990.

# Index

Able seamen, 34–35, 43

Accidents, 83–84

*Act for the Better Government of the Navy of the United States, An. See* Reform Act (1862)

Advances. *See* Wages

*African American in the Union Navy, The* (Valuska), 12

African Americans in the navy: compared with in army, 290 (n. 104), 294 (n. 171); emancipation, effect on, 173–74; and grog ration, 167; inclusion of in skilled work, 167–69, 289 (n. 93); in Mississippi Squadron, 81, 163–66; numbers during war, 12, 169; rating restriction, 158, 163–64, 170; reactions of white sailors to, 155, 158–64, 173–74, 282 (n. 2); recruiting of, 157–58, 165, 169–70, 283 (n. 9); and religion, 145, 278 (n. 141); segregation of, 164–67, 287 (n. 62), 289 (n. 93); wages for, 170. *See also* Contrabands; Former slaves; Racism of white Union sailors

Age of sailors, 5, 214–15 (n. 33)

Air below deck, 31–32

*Alabama*, 183, 200, 206

Alcohol, 143, 153; alcoholism, 106–8; deaths from, 80, 109; and depression, 74–75, 248–49 (n. 166); disrupting naval operations, 107–9; and enlistment, used during, 2–3, 106; grog ration, 2, 103–5, 125, 167, 260 (n. 23), 288 (n. 86); heavy drinking by sailors, x–xi, 5, 24, 99, 105–6, 108; post-combat use of, 105, 206–7; Reform Act ban on ships, 109–12, 118, 125, 148. *See also* Cultural lives of sailors; Qualities of sailors

Alger, William Rounesville, 22, 25, 129, 130

*Allegheny*, 24

American Bible Society, 148

American Seaman's Friend Society, 148

*American Soldier, The* (Stouffer), 126

*A. O. Tyler*, 53

Aptheker, Herbert, 12

*Arago*, 76

*Arkansas*, 192

Arnold, George E., 35, 53, 65, 75, 171, 173, 174

Articles of War, 93, 122, 138

Baker, La Fayette C., 2

Baptists, 135, 144, 150

*Baron DeKalb*, 95

Bartlett, Cosam T., 41, 45, 70, 73, 105, 119

Barton, Michael, 20

"Battle speed," 185

Battle stations drill. *See* General quarters

*Beauregard*, 95

Benedict, Edwin R., 69, 101, 106, 143

*Benton*, 78, 116, 122, 124, 187

Berth deck, 33, 150–51

Bibles, for Union sailors, 126, 130, 142, 149. *See also* Religion

*Bienville*, 110

Blackface minstrel shows/plays, 174–76, 292 (n. 143)

*Blackhawk*, 33

Blake, George S., 133

Blanding, Stephen, 72, 104–5, 111

Blockade squadrons, xii, 183; and blockade runners, 54, 57–59, 108; compared with traditional naval service, 54–55; effectiveness of, 59–

60, 240–41 (n. 41); effects on sailors of failure of, 60–62; looting, 64–65; mental strain of, 67–68, 72–76; peaceful uprisings on, 121; possible prize money altering strategy of, 62–64, 242 (n. 70), 243 (n. 78); and religion, 133, 146

Boatswains, 104, 105, 116, 122

Bock, William N., 93, 97, 120, 176, 183

Boiler explosions, 79, 109, 152–53, 191–93

Bolster, W. Jeffrey, 157

*Bombast Furioso*, 174–75

Book of Common Prayer, 136, 138, 276 (n. 90). *See also* Religion

Boston, 5, 21

Boy, as naval rating, 35; African Americans restricted as, 158, 163–64, 170. *See also* Hunter, Alvah; Mervine, Charles K.; Yost, George

Bradbury, Isaac, 55, 61, 64, 204

*Brazileira*, 69, 174, 176

Bright, George, 72, 101, 108, 112; and death, reactions toward, 204; and naval combat, 185; and safety of ironclads, 193

*Brooklyn*, x, 108, 110, 122

Browne, Harry, 42, 43, 105

Browne, Symmes, 31, 42, 193

Buffalo, N.Y., 3

Bureau of Medicine and Surgery, 106

Burton, William, 9

*Cairo*, 78, 193, 210

Cairo, Ill., ix, 24, 80, 82, 97, 109, 129, 133, 152–53

*Calypso*, 64

*Cambridge*, 61, 64

Canadian sailors, 3, 10–11

Canning, Joseph, 59, 61, 204, 206

Captains: encouraging men into battle, 187; role in funerals, 207; role in religious observances, 134–42. *See also* Officers

*Carondolet*, 78, 84, 87, 121, 159, 177

Casualties in naval combat, 182, 189–93, 294 (n. 3); boiler explosions, 79, 109, 152–53, 191–93; false sense of security about by sailors, 14–15, 184; fear of from torpedoes (mines), 184, 191, 193–94; from own equipment, 191–92

Catholics, 135, 142, 144, 145, 146

Charivari, 176, 292–93 (n. 148). *See also* Racism of white Union sailors

Checkerboard crews, 165

*Cimarron*, 199

*Cincinnati*, 78, 79, 93, 97, 121

Cincinnati, Ohio, 6

Civilians, killing of, 90–91, 92–93, 204–5

Clapp, Fayette, 91, 122, 124

*Clara Dolsen*, 113

Clark, George, 21, 24, 44, 101; and contrabands, 159, 162; and shipboard life, 32, 37, 42, 43

Cleaning the ship, ix, 45, 46–47, 205

Cleanliness, lack of in sailors, 31, 47, 53, 136–37

"Clearing the deck," 184–85. *See also* Naval combat

Coal heavers, 35, 83, 163–64, 170, 195. *See also* Arnold, George E.; Poole, Charles A.; Wainwright, William

Coan, T. M., 188, 190, 191

Cockroaches on board ship, 31

Coffin, Charles, 191

Cold Water River, 83

Collins, James B., 65, 190–91; and the blockade, 57–58, 61; and contrabands, 172, 174, 177; and shipboard life, 31, 37, 44, 55

*Commodore*, 128

*Commodore Morris*, 62, 161

*Conestoga*, 77, 109

Confederate navy, 14, 183, 184, 188–89

Confederate POWs in Union navy, 80, 250 (n. 19)

Conscription, 4, 15–17

Contrabands: barges housing, 159; enlistment in navy of, 12, 157–58, 165, 283 (n. 9); escape stories of, 161; naval regulations about, 162; welcome by white sailors, 158–59, 160–62, 163–64. *See also* African Americans in the navy; Former slaves; Racism of white Union sailors

Conversation, 70, 73–74. *See also* Cultural lives of sailors

Cotton, as plunder for sailors, 93–97; affecting naval operations, 63, 96–97

*Cotton Kingdom, The* (Olmsted), 156

Courage, 199–202

Cramped conditions on board ship, 32–34, 130; contributing to racial violence, 180; river gunboats, 82. *See also* Shipboard life

Cronin, Cornelius, ix–x, 188, 189

Cruisers, xiii

Cultural lives of sailors, 99–102, 125, 258–59 (nn. 3–5); dancing, 101–2, 177; fishing, 102; gambling, 101, 143; grumbling, 72–73, 112–14, 263 (n. 76); making sport/roughhousing, 23–24, 36–37, 38, 74–75, 162; music, 101, 103, 143, 152; relaxing, 150–51; skylarking, 116–18; swearing, 100, 112, 115–16, 131, 140; telling stories, 70, 73–74, 101; theater, 101, 174–76, 292 (n. 143); writing letters, xii, 101–2, 149–50, 151–52. *See also* Alcohol; Qualities of sailors; Religion; Shipboard life

*Cumberland*, sinking of by *Merrimac*, 201–2, 304 (n. 156)

Cumberland River, 77, 83

Dahlgren, John, 106

Dampness on board ship, 30, 31, 32

Dana, Richard Henry, Jr., 41, 156

Dancing, 101–2, 177

Davenport, H. K., 121

Davis, Frederic, 80, 82, 88, 89, 98, 129, 132

*Daylight*, 128, 145

Death: navy funerals, 145, 207; sailors' reactions to, 202–4; soldiers and, 204. *See also* Casualties in naval combat

Dechristianization, 130

*Dee*, 64

Deer Creek, Miss., expedition, 97

Depression, 33–34, 66–67, 72–76, 106–8, 148

Desertion, 102–3, 123; by contraband sailors, 169, 178

Diggins, Bartholomew, 41, 51, 68, 123, 173, 177–78; and naval combat, 185, 186, 187, 190, 196, 197, 198

Discipline in the navy, 100–101, 118–19; African Americans and, 169; alcohol disrupting, 107–9; difficulties of in river fleet, 80–81, 93–94; mutinies/uprisings, 121–25, 266 (n. 109); passive resistance of sailors, 112, 114–15; and Reform Act, 110–12; religion as part of, 136–37, 140

Disease on board ship, 30, 32, 228 (n. 23)

Divine service. *See* Sunday service

Double irons, 124, 170

Drills, 47–53, 195, 198. *See also* General quarters

Ducking, 118

Eads, James B., 77

Eastern Gulf Blockading Squadron, 33

*Eclipse*, 152–53

Eggo, James, 110, 171–72

Emancipation Proclamation, 172, 291 (n. 118)

Emancipation/slavery, sailors' reactions toward, 13, 160, 172

English sailors, 3, 10–11

Enlistment as sailors: African Ameri-

cans, 12, 157–58, 165, 169, 283 (n. 9);
vs. army enlistment, 1–5, 14–15, 212
(n. 2); average age of men, 5, 214–
15 (n. 33); Confederate prisoners
of war, 80, 250 (n. 19); and conscription, way to avoid, 15–17; and
economic necessity, x–xi, 7–8, 19,
215–16 (nn. 40–41), 216–17 (n. 49),
222 (n. 119); enlistment expiration,
11, 120, 121; general motivations for,
12–15; monetary incentives for, 3,
17–19, 54, 221 (n. 113); numbers from
Eastern cities, 5–6; occupations of
men, 6–7, 28, 215–16 (n. 41), 216–17
(n. 49), 227 (n. 4); physical examination, 29; for river fleet, 78, 79–81;
soldiers, 15, 41, 80–81, 124
Episcopalians, and the navy, 135–36.
*See also* Religion
Escapism, 101–2. *See also* Cultural
lives of sailors
*Essex*, 87, 142, 187, 193
*Ethiopeana*, 175–76
Ethnicity/class of men enlisting for
navy: vs. for army, 9–10; city dwellers, 1, 5–6; former slaves, 12–13, 157–
58, 165, 169, 219 (n. 73), 283 (n. 9);
recent immigrants, 8–9, 19, 135, 217
(n. 53), 218 (n. 65), 222 (n. 119), 275
(n. 75)
Everett, Edward, 31

*Fairplay*, 91
Farmers, 6, 7
Farragut, David G., 178, 193
*Fernandina*, 106, 123
Finn, Tim, 18–19, 25, 29, 42, 62, 65,
192
Firemen, 35, 83, 163–64, 170, 195. *See
also* Geer, George
Fishing, 102
Fitch, Le Roy, 86, 90
*Flag*, 56
Flogging, 148, 156, 170
*Florida*, 19, 22, 57, 108

Flying Squadron, 31
Foote, Andrew H., 19, 21, 80–81, 86,
165
*For Cause and Comrades: Why Men
Fought in the Civil War* (McPher-
son), 126
*Forest Rose*, 115
Former slaves: in army, 155, 219 (n. 75);
army campaign to recruit, 169–70;
enlistment in navy of, 12–13, 157–
58, 165, 219 (n. 73), 283 (n. 9). *See
also* African Americans in the navy;
Contrabands
Fort Caswell, 190
Fort Donelson, 81, 85
Fort Fisher, 182, 186, 204
Fort Henry, 80, 85, 187, 192
*Fort Hindman*, 51, 200
Foster, Freeman, 44, 83, 161
Fox, Gustavus Vasa, 17, 80, 133
"Fox and Geese," 117–18
Friendly fire, 57
Funerals, 145, 207

"Gaining one's sea legs," 38
*Galena*, 189
Galveston, Union shelling of, 204
Gambling, 101, 143
*Gazelle*, 88
Geer, George, 11, 15, 68, 119, 177; and
alcohol, 106, 110; and sailor qualities,
20, 25, 26, 113
General Order No. 4, 90–91
General quarters, 48–51, 57. *See also*
Drills; Naval combat
German sailors, 10–12, 135
"Getting clean," 13–14
*Glide*, 169
Goble, E. W., 53, 83, 115–16, 186, 206
Goldsborough, L. M., 121
*Goodmen: The Character of Civil War
Soldiers* (Barton), 20
Gould, Benjamin A., 10, 20
Grand Gulf, attack on, 187
Grant, Ulysses S., 41, 81

Grog ration. *See* Alcohol

Grumbling, 72–73, 112–14, 263 (n. 76)

Guardos, 28–29. *See also* Mustering

Guerrilla warfare along Western rivers, 77, 87–94, 98, 255 (n. 114)

Gulf Blockading Squadron, 52, 60

Gunboatmen, 77, 80

Gunboats, 77, 79–81; conditions on, 82–83; effect on Southerners of, 85–87; navigation of, 83–85; size of, 33; use of to quell mutinies, 124

Gunners, 33, 199–200. *See also* Cronin, Cornelius

Guns, 184, 187–88, 195–96; African Americans firing, 167–68; and alcohol, 108; drills with big guns, 50–51, 52, 172; drills with small arms, 48–49

Hammocks, ix, 36, 82

*Hartford*, 120, 123, 177, 186, 187, 197

Harty, John D., 3, 19

Henneberry, James E., 14, 26, 87, 159, 172; and death, reactions toward, 204; and naval combat, 184, 186, 187, 189, 192; and religion, 142, 146; and shipboard life, 101, 116, 120

Hog chains, 84, 252–53 (n. 60). *See also* Ironclads

Holystoning, ix, 45, 46–47, 205

Homesickness, 68–69, 149. *See also* Writing

*Hunchback*, 175

Hunter, Alvah, 32, 34, 36, 75, 207; and naval combat, 189, 191, 194

Hutchinson, Calvin G., 62, 161, 186, 194

Immigrants enlisting in navy, 8–11, 19, 135, 217 (n. 53), 218 (n. 65), 222 (n. 119), 275 (n. 75)

Impressment, 120–21

*Independence*, 135

Initiation rites, 36–37, 38, 162

*Ino*, 29–30

Insanity, 76

Inspection, 47, 136–37

Irish sailors, 8–11

Ironclads: hazards of, 184, 193–94; in Mississippi Squadron, 77–79, 84; sailors' faith in, 183–84, 206; and torpedoes (mines), 193–94

Island No. 10, 184, 191, 200–201

Isolation from society, 34, 54; effects of, 66, 248–49 (n. 166), 280–81 (n. 181); infrequency of mail, 68; loneliness, 143; and religion, 130, 154; and women, 34, 69, 130; writing letters, xii, 101–2, 149–50, 151–52

"Jack Ratlin's Lament" (Eggo), 110, 171–72

*Jamestown*, 41

*Jeff Thompson*, 95

*Kate*, 108

*Kearsarge*, 11, 26, 42, 50, 68, 200, 206

Keeler, William, 22, 106, 108, 111; and the blockade, 57, 62, 64, 68

Kemp, Daniel F., 33, 36, 113, 168; and naval combat, 186, 189, 191; and river fleet, 79, 83, 86, 88, 93, 97

Knot tying, 39

*Lackawanna*, 148, 177

Lacy, Milo, 21, 69, 74, 93, 107–8, 116, 141, 207, 209–10

*Lancaster*, 21, 25, 128, 192

Landsmen, 35–37, 41–43, 53. *See also* Bartlett, Cosam T.; Kemp, Daniel F.; Lacy, Milo; Post, Charles; True, Rowland Stafford

Langley, Harold, 156

Lee, Samuel P., 124

Leland, C. G., 15

Lemisch, Jesse, 157

Letter writing by sailors. *See* Writing

*Lexington*, 77

Lice, 31

Lincoln, Abraham: and chaplains in army, 144; Emancipation Proclamation, 172; and Sabbath observance, 147, 279 (n. 157); and United States Christian Commission, 281 (n. 185)

Lonn, Ella, 10

Looting, 64–65, 93, 109

*Louisville*, 78

"Mail buoy watch," 37

Making sport/roughhousing, 23–24, 36–37, 38, 74–75, 162. *See also* Cultural lives of sailors; Skylarking

*Manhattan*, 203

*Manitou*, ix

*Massachusetts*, 37

McNeil, Thomas, 116, 131, 132

McPherson, James M., 6, 7, 126

Meade, Patrick, 8, 74, 131, 191, 197

Meade, Richard Worsam, III, 42, 91

Meals on board ship, 29, 45–47

*Melting Pot Soldiers* (Burton), 9

Melville, Herman, 156, 202

*Merrimac*, x, 201–2, 304 (n. 156)

Mervine, Charles K., 45, 72, 76, 174; and alcohol, 105, 109; and naval combat, 199, 200, 206; and religion, 141–42, 143; and sailor qualities, 23, 25–26, 31

Messes, ix, 46–47, 69–70; racial segregation of, 164–66

*Metacomet*, 137

Methodists, 135, 144, 150

*Miami*, 178

*Michigan*, 3

Miller, William C., 68, 75, 116, 130, 131

Milligan, John D., 28

Mines. *See* Torpedoes (mines)

*Minnesota*, 40

Missionary Society for Seamen, 148

Mississippi River, 82, 83, 152–53

Mississippi Squadron, ix, xii, 93–94; African Americans in, 81, 163–66; and combat, 183; and contrabands, 159, 165, 176; and cotton as plunder, 93–97; enlistment for, 78, 79–81, 250 (n. 19); establishment of, 77–

78; and guerrilla warfare, 77, 87–94, 98, 255 (n. 114); penetrating Western Confederacy, 85–88; and racial segregation, 165–66; and religion, 133, 146, 151; river navigation, 83–84; types/size of boats in, 33, 77–79; uprisings on, 121, 124. *See also* River sailors

Mobile Bay, 182, 183, 188, 190, 203

Money, sailors' attitude toward, 24–25, 119

*Monitor*, x, 11, 78, 106, 111

Monotony on board ship, 65–68, 71–72

Morrison, John G., 82, 84, 93, 129, 142; and naval combat, 185, 188, 189, 207

Morse, De Witt C., 79, 87, 89, 90, 94, 97

*Mound City*, 78, 92, 109, 193

*Mount Vernon*, 161

Music, 101, 103, 143; hymns, 152

Mustering: into navy, 28–29; out of navy at end of war, 209–10

Mutinies, 123–24, 266 (n. 109)

*Nahant*, 34, 75

*Nansemond*, 171, 177, 179

National Sailors' Fair, Boston, 1864, 22, 31

"Nautical frame of reference," 39

Nautical language, 36–37, 44, 100

Naval Academy, 133

Naval combat: boiler explosions, 79, 109, 152–53, 191–93; casualties, 182, 184, 189–93, 196–97, 294 (n. 3); "clearing the deck," 184–85; courage shown during, 199–202; damage to ships, 184, 189–90; emotional effects on sailors, 182–83, 186, 191–98, 207–8; firing guns, 167–68, 187–88, 195–96; misconceptions of safety in by sailors, 14–15, 183–84, 193–94; nowhere to run, 198–99; post-battle atmosphere, 205–8; receiving fire, 188–90; sailors' reactions to death, 202–4; torpedoes (mines), 184, 191, 193–95; waiting, 186–87

*Naval Duties and Discipline*, 114

Naval ratings, 34–36; African Americans restricted in, 158, 163–64, 170

Naval recruiting stations. *See* Rendezvous

Navy chaplains, 133–36; attempt to abolish, 132; constitutionality of having, 147, 279–80 (n. 163); religious affiliations of, 135–36, 275 (nn. 73–74); shortage of, 126, 133, 136. *See also* Religion

Navy guns. *See* Guns

Navy physicians, xiii, 29, 106–7, 190

"Negro in the Union Navy, The" (Aptheker), 12

Netting, use of in naval combat, 185

*New National*, 109

New York City, 2, 3, 5, 21

New York Nautical School, 128

*Niagara*, 176

*Nigger in a Daguerreotype Saloon*, 175

Night watch, 55–58; inclusion of African Americans in, 168, 289 (n. 93)

North Atlantic Blockading Squadron, 110, 121, 124

*North Carolina*, 149

Occupations: of men enlisting in army, 6–7, 216 (n. 42); of men enlisting in navy, 6–7, 28, 215–16 (n. 41), 216–17 (n. 49), 227 (n. 4)

Officers, xiii; commissions for recruitment, 4; complaints by about sailors, 21, 41, 42–43, 81; and contraband sailors, 173–74, 179; lack of competency of, 44; quarters on board ship, 33; relations with sailors, 43–45, 113–17, 118–23, 124–25, 137; and training, 40–41; using religion to control sailors, 136–37, 140; violation of Reform Act, 120–21. *See also* Captains

*Official Records of the Union and Confederate Navies in the War of Rebellion, The*, 182, 199, 201

*Ohio*, 29

Ohio River, 8

Olmsted, Frederick Law, 156

Ordinary seamen, 34–35

Osborne, Joseph, 5, 24–25, 132, 147, 173; reasons for enlisting in navy, 14, 15, 17; and shipboard life, 33, 37, 67, 68, 69

*Osipee*, 64

*Ozark*, 79

Pacific Squadron, xiii, 70, 179

*Passaic*, 139

Patriotism/idealism, lack of in sailors, x, 13, 19, 114, 160

Paulding, H., 2

Paymasters, 119. *See also* Keeler, William

*Penobscot*, 176

*Peosta*, 85

*Petrel*, 96

*Pittsburg*, 78

*Pocahontas*, 113

Pook, Samuel, 77

Poole, Charles A., 143, 162, 171, 206; and death, reactions toward, 203; and isolation, 68, 69, 74; and shipboard life, 11, 14, 33, 38, 47, 52, 113, 118

Porter, David Dixon, 51, 96, 115–16; as commander of Mississippi Squadron, 21, 80, 81, 86, 90, 91, 93, 124; and cotton, 94, 95, 97; and enlistment, 3, 17; and racial segregation, 165, 167, 169, 289 (n. 93)

Post, Charles, 19, 40; and the blockade, 55, 59, 60, 61, 62–63, 67, 73

*Potomac*, 134

Powell, Samuel, 32, 43, 52, 60, 63, 73

*Powhatan*, 24, 76, 174, 199

Pranks, 36–38

Prayer Book Controversy, 135

Prayer meetings on board ship, 141, 145–46. *See also* Religion

Preston, Ann, 5, 210

Price, William H.: and contrabands, 160, 162, 168, 170–71, 172, 174; and safety of ironclads, 183

Prize money: allocations of, 65, 243–44 (n. 88); as enticement to enlist, 3, 17–19, 54, 221 (n. 113); as factor in blockade strategy, 62–64, 242 (n. 70), 243 (n. 78); lack of, 95, 209, 210

Prostitutes, 26, 131–32

Qualities of sailors: appearance/dress, ix, 19–20; courage, 199–202; gait, 30; generosity, 25–26, 160–61; lack of patriotism/idealism, x, 13, 19, 114, 160; roughness, xii, 20–24, 131–32; standing up for rights, 114, 122; stereotypes/myths, xiii, 5, 99–100, 128, 157, 283 (n. 11); values, x, 20, 22–23, 26–27. *See also* Alcohol; Cultural lives of sailors

Quarter deck, 33, 57

Race riots, 179, 293 (n. 152)

Racial segregation on ships, 164–66, 287 (n. 62), 289 (n. 93); failure of, 166–67

Racism of white Union sailors: compared with that of soldiers, 179–80; hostility, 155, 159–60, 162–63, 282 (n. 2); with integration of blacks, 169–77, 180–81; punished by officers, 179; and use of violence, 176–80, 293 (n. 152); "white man's war," 168, 289 (n. 90)

Rams, 184. *See also* Naval combat

Ratings. *See* Naval ratings

Rats on board ship, 30–31

*Rattler*, 97, 176

Recruiting for navy: African Americans, 12, 157–58, 165, 169–70, 283 (n. 9); broadsides, 2, 8, 9, 16, 17, 18; Confederate prisoners of war, 80, 250 (n. 19); fraudulent practices, 2–3; lack of recruits for river fleet, 78, 79–81; officers' commissions for

recruits, 4; rendezvous, xii, 2–3, 17, 19, 20, 28; soldiers, 15, 41, 80–81, 124. *See also* Enlistment as sailors

Red River, 87

Red River Campaign, 96, 97

Reform Act (1862): banning alcohol, 109–12, 118, 148; banning swearing, 112, 131; officers' violations of, 120–21; religious reforms of, 144

Refugees, 25–26

Reidy, Joseph, 12

*Reindeer*, 79

*Release*, 178

Religion: and African American sailors, 145, 278 (n. 141); Bibles for sailors, 126, 130, 142, 148, 149; on blockade squadron, 133, 146; denominations on board, 135–36, 144–45, 275 (n. 72); and discipline, as part of, 136–37, 140; Episcopalians and the navy, 135–36; lack of religiosity of sailors, 126–32, 142, 146–47, 154, 270 (n. 10), 271 (n. 17); navy's lack of provision for, 130–32, 142–44, 147–48, 154, 269 (n. 3); prayer meetings on board ship, 141, 145–46; regulated by captains, 134–35, 136–42; religious tracts/literature, 149, 150, 151, 153; on river fleet, 133, 146, 151; sailors' hymns, 152; and soldiers, 126–27, 154, 270 (n. 7); Sunday service, 132, 136–42, 147; United States Christian Commission work with sailors, 126, 148–54; women equated with, 138–40. *See also* Navy chaplains; Sunday service; Sunday work

Rendezvous, xii, 2–3, 17, 19, 20, 28. *See also* Recruiting for navy

Rendezvous Sample, 6–7, 9, 10–11

*Report of the Secretary of the Navy*, 182

*Richmond*, 192

River fleet. *See* Mississippi Squadron

River sailors: accessibility to land, 85;

and alcohol, 109; combat experience, 183; enlistment, 78, 79–81; looting/acts of brutality, 93–94, 109; roughness of, 21, 77, 79–80; training, 80, 83, 84–85; uprisings by, 121, 124. *See also* Mississippi Squadron

Roe, Francis A., 22, 24, 25

Round-the-clock duty. *See* Night watch

Runners, 2

*Sabine*, 108

Sails, 39

*St. Louis*, 78, 109, 191

St. Louis, Mo., 77, 78

*St. Mary's*, 179

Sand, use of in battle, 185

Scuttlebutt and yarns, 70, 73–74, 101. *See also* Cultural lives of sailors

Seasickness, 37–38, 62

*Sebago*, 194

Second Great Awakening, 126

Segregation. *See* Racial segregation on ships

Selfridge, Thomas O., 96, 97, 201

Shackles, as form of punishment, 124, 170

Shaw, George Bernard, 75

Shells, 184, 188–90. *See also* Naval combat

Sherman, Frederic, 47, 55, 67

Sherman, William T., ix

Shipboard life: cleaning, ix, 45, 46–47, 205; cramped conditions of, 32–34, 82, 130, 180; daily routine, ix, 45–53; dampness/air, 30, 31–32; disease/vermin, 30–32, 228 (n. 23); drills, 47–53, 195, 198; hammocks, ix, 36, 82; meals, 29, 45–47; monotony of, 65–68, 71–72; night watch, 55–58, 168, 289 (n. 93); prayer meetings, 141, 145–46; racial segregation, 164–67, 287 (n. 62), 289 (n. 93); seasickness, 37–38, 62; sleeping quarters, 32–33; social organization,

ix, 36–37, 38, 46–47, 69–70, 74–75, 140; training, 39–43, 80, 83, 84–85; weight gain from, 33. *See also* Alcohol; Cultural lives of sailors; Qualities of sailors; Religion

*Ship of Fools*, 72, 247 (n. 138)

Shipping articles, 29. *See also* Wages

Shore leave, 34, 66, 103, 107, 244 (n. 97)

*Silver Lake*, 14, 163

Simpson, John, 106, 110, 114, 122, 185

Situational slavery, 156

Skate-fish, 37

Skylarking, 116–18. *See also* Cultural lives of sailors; Making sport/roughhousing

Slavery: compared with sailors' situation, 156–57, 170–72, 282 (n. 4); perception of by poor whites, 155–56

Small arms drills, 48, 49

Social organization on board ship: breakdown of, 74–75; initiation rites, 36–37, 38, 162; messes, ix, 46–47, 69–70; and racial integration, 169–77, 180–81; and racial segregation, 164–67, 287 (n. 62), 289 (n. 93); religion as part of, 140

*Social Reform in the United States Navy* (Langley), 156

Sogering, 114–15. *See also* Discipline in the navy

Soldier transfers to navy, 15, 41, 80–81, 124

*South Carolina*, 38

Space, 32–34

"Splicing the main brace," 104. *See also* Alcohol: grog ration

Splinters, 190, 191. *See also* Naval combat

Sports, 101

Stealing, 25

Steam power, 79, 82–83; hazards of, 184

Stereotypes of sailors, xiii, 5, 99–100, 128, 157, 283 (n. 11)

Stille, Charles J., 127

Stockbridge, Joseph, 128, 134–35, 146, 147

Stouffer, Samuel A., 126–27

Stuart, George H., 150

Suicides, 76

Sunday service: absence of, 142–44; becoming voluntary, 126, 144–46; prayer meetings, 141, 145–46; provision of, 132, 136–42, 147; and United States Christian Commission, effect on, 153. *See also* Religion

Sunday work, 126, 134–35, 142–44; Lincoln's order to reduce, 147

Surgeons, 141, 191. *See also* Clapp, Fayette; Coan, T. M.

*Susquehanna*, 204

Sutlers, 69

Swearing, 100, 112, 115–16, 131, 140

Swift, John, 11, 15, 31, 188; and contrabands, 162, 173; and death, reactions toward, 204; and river fleet, 89, 92; and United States Christian Commission, 151, 153

Tar, use of for waterproofing, 30, 99–100

Tattoos, 20, 69, 129, 246 (n. 123), 271 (n. 22)

Technology, 182, 184, 194–95

*Tecumseh*, 203

Tennessee River, 77, 83

Theater, 101; blackface productions, 174–76, 292 (n. 143)

Thomas, Walter S., 17

Thoms, William F., 55, 75, 128

Tisdale, W. L., 151

Torpedoes (mines), 184, 191; sailors' anxiety about, 193–95

Toucey, Isaac, 144

Training/skills: on blockade squadron, 39–43; drills, 47–53, 195, 198; on river fleet, 80, 83, 84–85

True, Rowland Stafford, 14, 31, 47; and contrabands, 160, 163, 164, 166

*Two Years before the Mast* (Dana), 41, 156

*Tyler*, 77

Unemployment, as factor in enlistment, 7–8, 19, 215–16 (nn. 40–41), 222 (n. 119)

Union army: and African Americans in, 155, 169, 219 (n. 75), 290 (n. 104), 294 (n. 171); bounties for enlistment in, 3–4, 19; enlistment for vs. navy, 1–5; occupations of men enlisting in, 6–7, 216 (n. 42); perception of vs. Union navy, ix–xi, 4–5, 13–17; provision for religion in, 127, 144; qualities of men compared with navy, 20–21, 204–5; segregation in, 180

Union Jack, origin of term, 19, 222 (n. 123)

Union navy: enlistment for vs. army, 1–5; as institution, 100; numbers during Civil War, 1; occupations of men enlisting in, 6–7, 28, 215–16 (n. 41), 216–17 (n. 49), 227 (n. 4); perception of vs. Union army, ix–xi, 4–5, 13–17; qualities of men compared with army, 20–21, 204–5; racial segregation policies, 164–65; ratings system, 34–36, 158, 163–64, 170; and religion, lack of provision for in, 130–32, 142–44, 147–48, 154, 269 (n. 3). *See also* African Americans in the navy; Enlistment as sailors; Recruiting for navy

United States Christian Commission, 126, 128, 148–54, 281 (n. 185)

United States Congress: and regulation of navy, 109–10, 144; rejecting removal of chaplains from navy, 132

United States Navy. *See* Union navy

United States Sanitary Commission, 6–7, 20

Uprisings by sailors, 121–23, 125

Vail, Israel E., 21, 37, 66, 69, 102, 158
Valuska, David, 12
Van Cleaf, William, 8, 15, 25, 44, 82, 92, 173; and naval combat, 186, 191, 192, 198, 200–201, 206; and safety of ironclads, 183, 184
*Vandalia*, 5, 33
*Vanderbilt*, 132
Vicksburg, ix, 85, 182, 183, 187
*Virginia Mummy*, 176

Wages, 17, 29, 35; advances, 19, 221–22 (n. 116); for contraband sailors, 170; navy failing to pay, 119–20, 121, 209
Wainwright, William, 7, 17, 22, 52, 106, 113; and depression, 72, 74–75, 76; and religion, 138, 140, 141, 142, 146
War Department, and initial control of river fleet, 79–81
Welles, Gideon, 19, 76, 79, 81, 86, 124; and alcohol ban, 110; and blockade squadrons, 63; and contrabands in the navy, 158, 170; and sailor skills, 39; and torpedoes (mines), 193, 194; and United States Christian Commission, 150; and use of navy to avoid conscription, 16–17
Western Flotilla. *See* Mississippi Squadron

*Western World*, 121
West Gulf Blockading Squadron, 61
Whelan, William, 106–7
*White-Jacket* (Melville), 156
White River campaign, 109
Wiley, Bell I., 6, 7
Winslow, J. A., 4
Wirts, John, 21, 25, 38, 70, 209
Women: equated with religion, 138–40; isolation from, 34, 69, 130
Working-class origins of sailors, xi, 6–7; and alcohol, 105–6; and dissenting from "gentlemanly society," 13, 20, 21, 23, 100–101, 222–23 (nn. 129–30); and slavery/emancipation, 155–56, 171, 174, 180–81; and technology, 194–95, 296 (n. 13); and work stoppages, 121–22, 124–25
Writing, xii, 101–2, 152; and writing supplies from United States Christian Commission, 149–50, 151–52
Wyckoff, J. D., 151, 152

Yazoo River, 83, 207
Yost, George, 83, 89, 91, 193, 210
Young Men's Christian Association (YMCA), 148